MASSACRE AT SAND CREEK

HOW METHODISTS WERE INVOLVED IN AN AMERICAN TRAGEDY

GARY L. ROBERTS

Abingdon Press
Nashville

MASSACRE AT SAND CREEK
How Methodists Were Involved in an American Tragedy

Paperback: ISBN 978-1-5018-1976-6

Hardcover: ISBN 978-1-5018-2724-2

ePub: ISBN 978-1-5018-2586-6

Library of Congress Cataloging-in-Publication Data

Names: Roberts, Gary L., author.
Title: Massacre at Sand Creek : how Methodists were involved in an American tragedy / Gary L. Roberts.
Description: First edition. | Nashville : Abingdon Press, [2016]
Identifiers: LCCN 2016009698 | ISBN 9781501819766 (pbk.)
Subjects: LCSH: Sand Creek Massacre, Colo., 1864. | Chivington, John M. (John Milton), 1821-1894. | Evans, John, 1812-1861. | Cheyenne Indians--Wars, 1864. | Arapaho Indians—Wars. | Methodists—United States--Biography. | Church and social problems—Methodist Church. | Whites—Relations with Indians. | Indians, Treatment of—United States—History--19th century. | Indians of North America—Government relations—1789-1869.
Classification: LCC E83.863 .R595 2016 | DDC 978.8/02—dc23 LC record available at http://lccn.loc.gov/2016009698

16 17 18 19 20 21 22 23 24 25—10 9 8 7 6 5 4 3 2 1

MANUFACTURED IN THE UNITED STATES OF AMERICA

CONTENTS

Opening Words vii

Acknowledgments ix

Maps. xiii

Introduction. xv

Chapter 1   WHICH WAY? WHOSE WAY?. 1

Chapter 2   THE ROAD TO DOMINION 19

Chapter 3   THE BITTER CONUNDRUM. 33

Chapter 4   METHODISTS AND THE AMERICAN INDIAN 43

Chapter 5   JOHN MILTON CHIVINGTON:
             THE FIGHTING PARSON. 61

Chapter 6   JOHN EVANS, M.D.: ENTREPRENEUR AND
             PHILANTHROPIST 79

Chapter 7   COLORADO'S "INDIAN PROBLEM". 95

Chapter 8   THE PATH TO SAND CREEK 119

Chapter 9   PROTEST AND RECRIMINATION. 141

Chapter 10   METHODISTS, SAND CREEK, AND THE
             "INDIAN QUESTION". 159

Chapter 11:   CHIVINGTON AND EVANS: THE LATER YEARS...... 189

Chapter 12:   THE BALANCE SHEET................................ 217

Notes 249

About the cover: The killing ground of the Sand Creek Massacre site lies quiet and brown under a dark bank of clouds. In the clouds are two figures, Cheyenne chiefs by their dress, wearing scalp shirts that signify their bravery as warriors. The man on the left is War Bonnet, a seventy-year-old Council Chief of the Ovimana (Scabby Band).* He holds a pipe and a pipe bag and wears a single large eagle feather in his hair pointing to the right, as emblems of his office as a member of the Council of Forty-Four. The man on the right is Standing-in-the-Water, War Bonnet's fifty-year-old cousin, a member of the Wotapiu (those who eat with the Sioux) and a Soldier Chief of the Himoweyukis (Elk Horn Scrapers or Crooked Lances) soldier society. Both men were killed early in the slaughter at Sand Creek on the morning of November 29, 1864, and symbolize the betrayal Sand Creek represented. War Bonnet and Standing-in-the-Water, along with Lean Bear, one of the leading voices for peace and a Council Chief of the Hiseometaneo (Ridge Men), had been the Cheyenne members of a delegation of Southern Plains chiefs and head men who visited Washington, D. C., and met with President Abraham Lincoln in April 1863. On March 13, 1863, they were photographed at the studio of Noell and Addis in Leavenworth, Kansas. The images on the cover are from one of those photographs. Lean Bear spoke passionately on behalf of his people to President Lincoln, and the three Cheyennes returned to their people as advocates of peace. In May 1864, Lean Bear was shot down as he approached a unit of the First Colorado Volunteer Cavalry under the command of Lieutenant George S. Eayre, in an incident that helped to precipitate the summer conflict remembered as "The Indian War of 1864." With the deaths of War Bonnet and Standing-in-the-Water at the Sand Creek Massacre, all three of the Cheyenne emissaries to Washington the previous year had been murdered, while still clinging to their peaceful intentions.

*This identification is based upon exhaustive research and consultation, but some believe that the man on the left is Lean Bear and that the third Cheyenne in the original photograph is actually War Bonnet. See p. 102.

OPENING WORDS

Opening Words

AT DAWN ON THE MORNING of November 29, 1864, the United States Colorado Volunteers attacked peaceful Cheyenne and Arapaho people encamped along Sand Creek in the Colorado Territory. Two hundred and thirty people—mostly women, children, and elderly—were killed. Two congressional investigations and an Army hearing declared it a "massacre."

The two men most responsible were powerful, respected leaders in the Methodist Episcopal Church: Territorial Governor John Evans and Colonel John Chivington. The Church never condemned the massacre and never held these two men responsible. Most United Methodists today do not know this history.

In 2012, The United Methodist Church called for a study to "provide full disclosure of the involvement and influence in the Sand Creek Massacre of John M. Chivington, Territorial Governor John Evans, the Methodist Church as an institution, and other prominent social, political and religious leaders of the time."[1]

The Council of Bishops of The United Methodist Church appointed a Joint Advisory Committee, made up of Cheyenne and Arapaho descendants of survivors of the massacre and United Methodist leaders. We met to remember and honor those whose lives were taken, to discover the truth, and to find good ways to work together for healing and peace. We all came to this work with the question, Why? Why did this happen? How could any Methodist or anyone have such utter disrespect for other human beings?

Dr. Gary L. Roberts, a respected historian of the American West and the Sand Creek Massacre, researched and wrote the report. Gary worked from a lifetime

---

1. "1864 Sand Creek Massacre" petition adopted by the United Methodist General Conference in 2012.

commitment to learn and tell the truth about Sand Creek and a heartfelt need to ask the question, Why? We are deeply grateful to Dr. Roberts for producing such a thorough and careful report.

Nothing can restore the lives of the ancestors who were struck down at Sand Creek. As the committee gathered to pray, share meals, and have difficult conversations, we hope we have begun relationships that can help heal historic wounds. We are grateful for the time we have spent together and the hope that comes from respectful relationships. Read in the bitter account of this massacre an invitation to join the long, slow, healing work.

The committee offers the results of Dr. Roberts's work to the Cheyenne and Arapaho people, to The United Methodist Church, and to the community of all people who seek to live in a good way.

Joint Advisory Committee

Otto Braided Hair, Jr.	**Committee Co-chair and Northern Cheyenne Descendants' Representative**
Elaine J.W. Stanovsky	**Committee Co-chair and Bishop of the Mountain Sky Area**
Joe Big Medicine	Southern Cheyenne Descendants' Representative
Gail J. Ridgely	Northern Arapaho Descendants' Representative
Henry Little Bird	Southern Arapaho Descendants' Representative
Sally Dyck	Bishop of the Chicago Area
Alfred T. Day III	General Secretary, United Methodist General Commission on Archives and History
Steve Sidorak	United Methodist Office on Christian Unity and Inter-religious Relationships

Observers—Consultants

David Halaas	Historian and Author
JuDee Anderson	First United Methodist Church, Sheridan, Wyoming
Robert Williams	Former General Secretary, General Commission on Archives and History
Mike McKee	Bishop of the Dallas Area; Chair of the Justice and Reconciliation Leadership Team of the Council of Bishops

ACKNOWLEDGMENTS

A REPORT SUCH AS this is peculiarly dependent upon the cooperation of many people. While it takes the form of history, its focus has been determined by the purpose of the study as set forth in Petition 20760, Sand Creek Massacre (20767-IC-Non-Dis), passed at the 2012 General Conference of The United Methodist Church in Tampa, Florida. Conclusions were not predetermined, however. The sole intent has been to seek a balanced understanding of the responsibilities of John M. Chivington, John Evans, the Methodist Episcopal Church, and other agencies and persons in the Sand Creek tragedy. After fifty years of research on the Sand Creek Massacre, I cannot pretend that I began this project without opinions about what happened and why, but my previous understanding has been seasoned both by inquiry into new areas of research and by consideration of perspectives different from my own.

Preparing this report stretched my experience and *required* that I look to other sources, different ways of seeing (a term much used herein), and the confluence of ethics and actions, cause and effect, intent and result. I was not unmindful of the moral issues involved in the Sand Creek story. I've wrestled with them for a long time, but during the course of this project I found myself in unfamiliar territory at times, attempting to grasp—clumsily, I suspect—views and understandings beyond my former frame of reference. I have been humbled by the process of preparing this report, and I am keenly aware of questions not yet answered to my satisfaction. The issues are so basic and yet so profound that they have at times challenged all of my assumptions and called into question deeply held beliefs. Confronting them was painful at times, yet essential to the task.

That is why the insights of others have proven so important to this effort. I have been able to pursue the topic freely without pressure so that the report could be truly an independent evaluation, but I have needed and received advice from a wide range of people. Most importantly, the Joint Committee created by the Council of Bishops and co-chaired by Bishop Elaine J. W. Stanovsky, of the Mountain Sky Episcopal Area, and Otto Braided Hair, Northern Cheyenne Sand Creek Descendants representative, has assured the independence of the evaluation, while providing guidance and advice that have proven invaluable. The advice, given both by the committee in extended sessions, and by individual members of the committee in private communications, has directed me to considerations I might otherwise have missed and provided me with insights that have strengthened the report in those areas where my knowledge and expertise have been weakest. I have been the beneficiary of the committee's counsel, criticism, and affirmation, for which I am extremely grateful.

I cannot exaggerate the importance of Laird and Colleen Cometsevah to my research on Sand Creek. I met them first in 1978. While sitting in the kitchen of their home in Clinton, Oklahoma, I listened and learned as they talked quietly about Sand Creek along with Walter Roe Hamilton, Ruby Bushyhead, and Terry Wilson of the Southern Cheyennes. Later in the 1990s, I met the late Steve Brady of the Northern Cheyennes, who became a mentor and friend. Since then, I had the privilege of knowing Lee Lone Bear, Northern Cheyenne; Eugene Ridgely, Northern Arapaho; and other Cheyenne and Arapaho people, who are now deceased. All of them contributed to my understanding of Sand Creek long before this project began. In addition to the official tribal representatives of the Cheyenne and Arapaho Tribes of Oklahoma, Joe Big Medicine, Cheyenne; and Henry Little Bird, Arapaho; Gail Ridgely of the Northern Arapahos from the Wind River Reservation in Wyoming; and Otto Braided Hair of the Northern Cheyenne Tribe in Montana (previously acknowledged), who provided insight and advice throughout the development of this project, I am grateful for the contributions to this report of Anthony A. "Al" Addison, Willard Gould, Ben Ridgely, Crawford L. White, Sr., Nelson P. White, Jacqueline White, Northern Arapahos; Vanessa Braided Hair, Steve Brady, Jr., Norma Gourneau, Kaden Jeray (Walks Nice), Reginald Killsnight, Sr., Richard Littlebear, Mildred Red Cherries, Holda Roundstone, William Tall Bull, and Phillip White Man, Northern Cheyennes; Max Bear, Eugene Black Bear, and Karen Little Coyote, Southern Cheyennes; and Dale Hamilton, Southern Arapaho.

During the course of the preparation of this report, I have also had the generous advice of fellow historians, including David F. Halaas, former Colorado State Historian, consultant to the Northern Cheyenne Tribe, and friend of many years; Tom Meier, historian, consultant to the Northern Arapahos, and always thoughtful advisor; Ari Kelman, author of *A Misplaced Massacre: Struggling Over the Memory of Sand Creek*, whose award-winning book enlarged my perspective; Elliott West, author of *The Contested Plains*, whose original thought pushed me to consider new ideas; Henrietta Mann, Southern Cheyenne historian and educator, whose quiet insight demands respect and reflection; Jeff C. Campbell, meticulous investigator of Sand Creek, author of a number of publications for the Sand Creek Massacre National Historic Site, and friend; Craig Moore, Sand Creek National Historic Site Ranger and dedicated student of Southern Cheyennne and Arapaho genealogy; Gordon S. Chappell, Pacific Great Basin Support Office, National Park Service, who shared his important Joseph A. Cramer Letters with me; and Darius Salter, author of a forthcoming biography of Bishop Matthew Simpson. I am also grateful to the members of the John Evans Study Committee, Northwestern University, and of the John Evans Study Committee, University of Denver, whose reports provided critical insights and helped prepare the way for this work.

Similarly, the staff of the Mountain Sky Episcopal Area and the Rocky Mountain Conference, under the leadership of Bishop Stanovsky, was indefatigable in its support at every stage of the process. Nancy Cox, Executive Administrative Assistant to Bishop Stanovsky, and Youngsook Charlene Kang, Director of Mission and Ministry of the Rocky Mountain Conference, were generous and helpful. Other United Methodist leaders who provided support and advice included Stephen J. Sidorak, Jr., Ecumenical Staff Officer, Office of Christian Unity and Interreligious Relationships of the Council of Bishops; Mary Ann Swenson, United Methodist Bishop, Ecumenical Officer, Council of Bishops; Mike McKee, United Methodist Bishop, Justice and Reconciliation Leadership Team; and Sally Dyck, United Methodist Bishop.

A special acknowledgment must be made to JuDee Anderson and the United Methodist Church Native American Ministry at Sheridan, Wyoming, who in consultation with Steve Brady and Otto Braided Hair of the Northern Cheyenne Tribe, initiated Petition 20760, *1864 Sand Creek Massacre* (20760-IC-Non-Dis), which was passed on April 20, 2012, at General Conference in Tampa, Florida.

This report owes a huge debt to the General Commission on Archives and History of The United Methodist Church at Drew University, Madison, New Jersey. The project began during the tenure of Robert J. Williams, as General Secretary of the GCAH, and continued under his successor, Alfred T. Day III. Both have been tireless in their support and efforts on behalf of the committee's assignment. L. Dale Patterson, Archivist and Records Administrator, and Christopher J. Anderson, Head of Special Collections and Archives of the GCAH, and their staff, helped acquaint me with Methodist resources and collections.

Appreciation is also expressed to the staffs of the Methodist Archives, Iliff School of Theology, Denver, Colorado; Kansas Area United Methodist Archives; Baker University, Baldwin City, Kansas; Sand Creek Massacre National Historic Site, Eads, Colorado; History Colorado, Denver, Colorado; Western History Collections, Denver Public Library, Denver, Colorado; Manuscript Division, Kansas State Historical Society, Topeka, Kansas; Huntington Library, San Marino, California; Bancroft Library, University of California, Berkeley, California; Oklahoma Historical Society, Oklahoma City, Oklahoma; Yale Collection of Western Americana, Beinecke Library, Yale University, New Haven, Connecticut; Manuscript Division, the Library of Congress, Washington, D.C.; and the National Archives and Records Administration, Washington, D.C.

Although they played no direct role in the preparation of this report, I would be remiss if I did not acknowledge the part played in my understanding of Sand Creek by Raymond G. Carey, late professor of history at the University of Denver, and Michael Straight, deceased author of *A Very Small Remnant*, a novel about Sand Creek, who together taught me many years ago about the importance of balance in history by their own extended and tempered correspondence on the subject, which they generously shared with me. Similarly, Robert M. Utley, Howard Roberts Lamar, the late Richard Maxwell Brown, the late Arrell M. Gibson, and the late Francis Paul Prucha, both in their published works and in their patient advice on a more personal level, provided inspiration and examples while teaching me to revere the study of history as a special mission to understand the human condition in a spirit of humility.

I can only hope that I have honored the trust of all of those who contributed to this effort, as well as the Council of Bishops, while acknowledging my own responsibility, as primary author, for any mistakes and failures that may be found herein.

—Gary L. Roberts

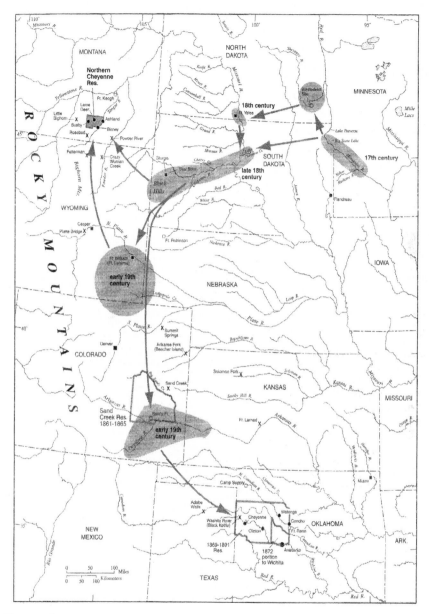

This map shows the territories, migrations, and reservations of the Cheyennes, as well as 19th-century battle sites and 21st-century towns. From *Handbook of North American Indians*, 13/2, ed. Raymond J. DeMallie (Washington, D.C.: Smithsonian, 2001), fig. 1, p. 864. Used by permission.

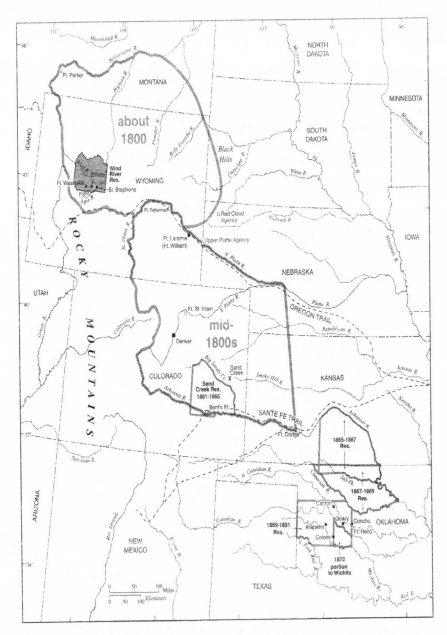

This map shows the location of Arapaho territory about 1800, Cheyenne and Arapaho territory in the mid-1800s, and reservations. From *Handbook of North American Indians*, 13/2, ed. Raymond J. DeMallie (Washington, D.C.: Smithsonian, 2001), fig. 1, p. 841. Used by permission.

INTRODUCTION

AT THE TIME, THE SAND Creek Massacre was a small affair, hardly more than a skirmish when compared to the great campaigns in Georgia, Tennessee, and Virginia that were moving toward climax that bleak November of 1864. Fewer than 250 souls perished at Sand Creek, a meager tally in light of the carnage of Chickamauga and Petersburg. By any reasonable measure, Sand Creek was hardly more than a footnote in the Civil War. And yet, for all of that the Sand Creek affair seized public attention in the winter of 1864-1865 and generated a controversy that still excites heated debate, more than 150 years later. The issues underscored by that day's bloody work were no less important than the momentous questions roused in the public mind by Sherman's "March to the Sea."

The Sand Creek Massacre touched questions more elemental than burned-out plantation houses and homeless civilians. If "war is hell" as Sherman proclaimed, at Sand Creek demoniac forces seemed unloosed so completely that humanity itself was the casualty. That was the charge that drew public attention to the Colorado frontier in 1865. That was the claim that spawned two congressional hearings and a military commission. Westerners vociferously and passionately denied the accusations. Reformers seized the charges as evidence of the failure of American Indian policy. Sand Creek launched a war that was not truly over for fifteen years. In the first year alone, it cost the United States government $50,000,000.

An American tragedy occurred there that remains a symbol of a conflict between what Americans believe themselves to be and the reality of what happened to Native peoples in the creation of the nation. Methodists have a special stake in this particular story. The governor whose policies led the Cheyennes and Arapahos to Sand Creek was a prominent Methodist layman. The commanding officer who ordered the attack on the Sand Creek village was a Methodist minister. Perhaps those were merely coincidences, but the question also remains of how the Church itself responded to what happened at Sand Creek. Was it also somehow culpable in what happened?

Since 1992, The United Methodist Church has attempted to address these questions in response to initiatives by Indian peoples and concerned Methodists. By apology and acts of repentance, the Church has sought to respond, culminating at the 2012 General Conference with a major "Service of Repentance for the Healing of Relationships with Indigenous Peoples" and a call for conferences and churches to build relationships with indigenous peoples. This was, and has been since, a major initiative for many churches and conferences. But there was yet a concern voiced by Cheyenne and Arapaho people that the Church had still not addressed questions of responsibility that matter to them. In response to these concerns, on April 20, 2012, at General Conference in Tampa, Florida, Petition 20760, *1864 Sand Creek Massacre* (20767-IC-Non-Dis) was passed by final vote as follows:

> The 2012 General Conference of The United Methodist Church hereby fully recognizes the Northern Cheyenne Tribe of Montana, and the Cheyenne and Arapaho Tribes of Oklahoma, and the Northern Arapaho Tribe of Wyoming as the Federally recognized Tribes as stated in the Treaty of the Little Arkansas with U.S. Government, as the official representatives concerning the Sand Creek Massacre.
>
> The 2012 General Conference of The United Methodist Church through the Council of Bishops and the appropriate boards and agencies shall consult on and support efforts pertaining to preservation, repatriations, healing, awareness, research, education and reparations with the Northern Cheyenne Tribe of Montana, the Cheyenne and Arapaho Tribes of Oklahoma, and the Northern Arapaho Tribe of Wyoming and their official Tribal Representatives for the November 29, 1864, Sand Creek Massacre.
>
> The 2012 General Conference of The United Methodist Church through the Council of Bishops and The General Commission on Archives and History shall authorize research by a joint team including an independent body and provide full disclosure of the involvement and influence in the Sand Creek Massacre of John M. Chivington, Territorial Governor John Evans, the Methodist Church as an institution, and

other prominent social, political and religious leaders of the time, and shall report back to the 2016 General Conference.

The United Methodist Church shall support and participate in the return to the "Tribes" of any Native artifacts or remains related to the Sand Creek Massacre.

Pursuant to paragraph three of this petition, a Joint Committee was organized consisting of ministers, laymen, historians, and tribal representatives of the Cheyenne and Arapaho Tribes of Oklahoma, the Northern Arapaho Tribe in Wyoming, and the Northern Cheyenne Tribe in Montana. In order to insure that the study was truly "independent," the committee chose a historian to write the report investigating the involvement of John M. Chivington, John Evans, the Methodist Church, and other prominent social, political, and religious leaders in the Sand Creek Massacre. The committee worked in consultation with the author in defining the scope of the report, concerns, and questions to be considered.

In crafting this report, it has been necessary not only to review the lives of Colonel Chivington and John Evans and the role played by the Methodist Episcopal Church, but also to consider a range of related and critical topics including the historical roots of the Sand Creek Massacre, the approach of the Church to American Indians over time, the differences in the ways of seeing in Euro-American culture and Native cultures, the forces at work in what has been called the "westward expansion" of Anglo-Americans in North America, the changing conditions of the nineteenth century, federal policy and law relating to Native Americans, and the responses of both white society and Cheyenne and Arapaho people to Sand Creek.

The basic method has been historical, but care has been taken to consider other ways of approaching the past since history is by definition a Western concept. Every effort was made to make the report balanced and fair in the belief that the results would be more accurate and convincing without the corroding influences of presentism (using the values of the present to judge the past) and legalism (making a predetermined case). There have been some surprises in the process that any other approach might well have missed, and the broad context within which the report was written has proven to be critical to the conclusions drawn.

It should be pointed out that language itself can be a problem. Certain terms are pejorative almost by definition. The use of terms such as "squaw," "buck," "papoose," "red skins," and "savage" are confined to quoted materials, primarily from recollections and historical documents. Such terms are demeaning and convey contempt and/or disrespect that the committee wished to avoid. Other expressions, such as "Indian fighter," "friendlies," and "hostiles" have also been used with care and are usually used with quotation marks. A few terms such as "raiders" or "raiding" can also be problematic, although within a military context, the word "raid" refers to a legitimate and specific form of military tactic. The committee has sought to avoid all evidence of pejorative language, except where it appears in historical documents and recollections and/or when it is used to convey the attitudes and values of the people and times under study.

A more difficult area of concern has been usage relating to proper identifications for the original inhabitants of the Western Hemisphere. This has generated debate even among the modern descendants of the original inhabitants. The term "Indian" has been used since the days of Columbus, deriving from the term "los Indios," but there have been arguments whether the term derived from a mistaken belief that the inhabitants Columbus encountered were from the Asia subcontinent or from a reference by Columbus that identified the inhabitants as "En Dios," in God, or "una gente in Dios," the people in God. The debate is largely a twentieth-century debate about the most respectful and appropriate term. For a time "Indian" fell from favor because it was a generalized term that groups many different peoples together within a single identifying category. It also was linked to Anglo-American usage that treated all Indians the same by means of a single narrowly defined image.

The term "Native American" was first used by the United States government as a category referring to the original inhabitants of the United States. Other terms such as "indigenous peoples" and "first Americans" were used by historians and anthropologists. In the 1960s with the growth of Native protests, the American Indian Movement (A. I. M.) took one position. With the advent of academic programs on traditional cultures, the term "Native American Studies" became more commonplace. The issue was largely an internal one. On the other hand, some leaders, like Russell Means, plainly declared, "I am an American Indian!" A few terms, like "Amerind," found little traction outside limited academic circles.

The methodology followed here uses a combination of these expressions, all intended to be respectful. Whenever possible, specific tribal names are used. Within discussions surrounding particular tribes, after initial identification, the term "tribes" is used to avoid pedantic language. "Indigenous peoples," "American Indians," and "Indians" are used to describe collective groups involving multiple tribes or generalized policies. "The Indian" is also used to refer to the collective image that characterized white policy and popular image. "Indians" in the plural is the form most commonly used by North American tribal people themselves.

"Native," always capitalized here, is used both as a noun and as an adjective, consistent with common usage in a large selection of recent works by both white and American Indian authors. The term "native American," without the capital "N," rarely used, would refer to any person born in the Western Hemisphere, or more particularly in the United States. "Indigenous people" refers to the original inhabitants of lands colonized by European nations. In preparing this report, care was taken to follow patterns of common usage from the most reliable sources rather than to take sides in any of the particular controversies over usage, which appears to have lost some of their former passion.

Another area that requires a special note at the outset is terminology relating to the Methodist Episcopal Church. First of all, there were many Methodist newspapers published in the nineteenth century. Most of them included as part of their title the words *Christian Advocate*. Examples would include the *New York Christian Advocate*, the *Central Christian Advocate*, the *Northwestern Christian Advocate*, the *Western Christian Advocate*, the *Pacific Christian Advocate*, and many more. The journal of each General Conference was labeled the *Daily Christian Advocate*. Wherever the term is used herein, the reference is to a Methodist Episcopal Church newspaper. It was said that most Methodists regarded their *Christian Advocate* as "the fifth gospel."

Preachers included exhorters, who were often laymen, deacons, who were ordained, and elders, who were ordained for pastoral service. The Church was divided into conferences and districts. Each district had a "presiding elder," the equivalent to today's "district superintendent." "Connection" was a formal recognition of a minister's relationship with a particular district. "Itinerancy," a vital concept in the early church, referred to the practice of moving from one church to another either as a "circuit rider" or as a "pastor." A "traveling connection" referred to a person who was enabled by a district to follow an itinerant ministry without being assigned to a particular church. If a minister left the ministry, either temporarily or permanently, the conference would declare him to be "located." "Location" could be at a minister's own request or by decision of the conference. All of these terms are used in describing the activities of John M. Chivington and the Church at large.

The Sand Creek Massacre was tragedy in the truest sense, raw, visceral, brutal, but with hints of heroism and even nobility in its blood-red story. It is also shockingly common, proving how unexceptional—and hence more terrifying—those events and the men who lived them were. Paradoxically, though, it did have profound effects not associated with other similar events. It became an emblem of the failure of Indian policy and a fulcrum of debate for decades. Even now, coming to grips with the Sand Creek Massacre involves hard questions and unsatisfactory answers not only about what happened but also about why. It stirs ancient questions about the best and worst in every person, questions older than history, questions as relevant as today's headlines.

CHAPTER 1

WHICH WAY? WHOSE WAY?

FOR THE VAST MAJORITY of Methodists, and of all who share the Euro-American tradition, the Sand Creek Massacre is a historical tragedy from the distant past, an unfortunate reminder of a dark side of American history best forgotten or acknowledged as an embarrassing example of past error in dealing with Native Americans. Even those who recognize its significance and its injustice see it in historical terms, perhaps important, but like Andersonville or the Homestead Strike or the Haymarket Riots or Ludlow or Selma, something to learn from and move on in the pursuit of the Great Values that are supposed to define the United States as a nation. The important thing is to acknowledge past error in the hope that it may inform the future and prevent such things from happening again.

Historians are concerned with what happened, why it happened, who was responsible, what can be learned from its study, and what it tells us about the past and about ways of looking at the past. Over time, Sand Creek has been justified and condemned with legalistic precision, based upon the written records that survived from that time, supplemented by archaeological findings and oral recollections. Historians explore conditions, chronology, motives, character, political and economic interests, and values. The need for historians, especially the best of them, is to learn and to explain, not caring what the truth is, but "concerned only with finding it," as Father Francis Paul Prucha expressed it. Significantly, Prucha did not claim truth is easy to find or that new tools and perspectives will not throw new light on it. "Finding it," after all, is a quest subject to fresh insights and new evidence. The Sand Creek Massacre is a "historical problem" to be solved and learned from.[1]

Living the Story

For Cheyennes and Arapahos, on the other hand, the Sand Creek Massacre is an enduring trauma, not history, not even past, certainly not something that can be forgotten with an embarrassed apology. To the Cheyennes and Arapahos in Oklahoma, Wyoming, and Montana, Sand Creek is profoundly personal. It is not an event they read about in books. They know the names of those who died there and of those who survived because they are family members. They grew up hearing the stories of what happened at Sand Creek from elders and relatives and pass them on after the manner in which they were told to them.

Sand Creek is also linked to enduring grievances, to promises made but never kept, to apologies offered that proved hollow and gratuitous. For Cheyennes and Arapahos, the site of the Sand Creek Massacre is a holy place, made holy by the blood of their ancestors. The betrayal that occurred there is different. It was there that trust was finally broken. In every negotiation between the Cheyennes and Arapahos and the federal government since 1864, the Sand Creek Massacre has been an ongoing presence, always there as an obstacle to trust even on issues seemingly distant—to whites, at least—from that long ago moment in time.[2]

The Cheyenne and Arapaho search for meaning is pursued in other ways. They listen to the old ones, remembering the stories in the ways they first heard them. They walk the ground at Sand Creek. They believe that the souls of the dead often remained in the places where they died. They hear the cries of women and children, the thunder of horses, the din of battle. They pray that they will be led to the places and to remnants that may survive of what happened there. They look for sacred signs. They take these things and use them in their quest to understand what happened. In these ways and others they gain insights.

Traditional Historical Method

Many historians have difficulty with this approach because it does not conform to the norms of traditional historical method. William T. Hagan wrote in his review of Father Peter John Powell's *People of the Sacred Mountain: A History of the Northern Cheyenne Chiefs and Warrior Societies, 1830-1879*, that Powell's narrative "presents without question a succession of miracles and other evidences of divine intervention as determining the course of Cheyenne history" that academic historians would discount or view with suspicion.[3] While raising questions about Powell's methodology, John Moore, an anthropologist who studied the Cheyennes extensively, wrote of Powell's book in yet another review, "One looks in vain . . . for a more common-sense evaluation of military tactics."[4] In other words, though not "academically sound," the Cheyennes and Arapahos contribute a vital perspective on what happened.

2

The problem is that many of those trained as historians, anthropologists, and archaeologists find that Indian explanations of what happened are often based upon supernatural causes and oral traditions that are unacceptable as explanations within the rational formats of Western thought. The most common response has been to dismiss Native understandings entirely. They appear to the Western mind to be superstition or myth, and, thus, not entitled to consideration as history. At the very least, such accounts are viewed as "unreliable" or "ahistorical." In 1865, the Minneconjou Sioux chief, Lone Horn, who warned U.S. government treaty commissioners of the dangers of building a road into Sioux country, told them: "if you white people go through our country, I fear as to those young men among us who have no father and mother to restrain them; I fear they will have trouble with your white people back here, who have no ears."[5] In the recorded exchanges between whites and Plains Indians, the reference to whites "having no ears" is a theme repeated over and over again. At the simplest level, this expression conveyed the idea that whites would not listen. Quick to judge and certain of superior understanding of what happened, settlers, soldiers, policy makers, missionaries, and historians have routinely discounted Indian accounts as having little or no value.[6]

But this poses a problem. Robert F. Berkhofer, Jr. argues that the task of the historian is not to judge according to one's own understanding of what is right and wrong or by one's own conclusions about past mistakes. He says, rather, that anyone who wishes to learn what happened must seek "to understand the past in terms of the actors' conceptions of their situations."[7] In other words, to leave out any side's view of what happened is certain to distort or corrupt conclusions. Differing value systems and ways of seeing must be taken into account. This is a challenging proposition because it requires becoming comfortable with mind-sets different from one's own. It is not an invitation to be uncritical but, rather, to expand the critical search into areas or points of view that may have been neglected or misunderstood. John C. Ewers insisted that it was not the purpose of the historian of Indian-white relations to be "kind to either party in this historic confrontation." Rather, he said, "I do think he should study this very complex theme in both breadth and depth, consulting and weighing all the sources he can find, so that he can be fair to both sides."[8]

Sand Creek: Massacre or Not?

In practice, most authors and readers prefer simple answers. Much of the literature on Sand Creek focuses on whether Sand Creek was a massacre or not. Far too many accounts amount to briefs for one side or the other. Authors set out to prove that Sand Creek was a massacre or that it was not. Unfortunately, either can be done simply by excluding the testimony that does not support the point of view being offered. Another approach, used most often by activists and reformers, complicates the "good guys"/"bad guys" approach through the use of presentism.[9] Presentism involves making judgments about past events based upon present-day standards, in effect blaming those in the past for not anticipating all of the moral and political changes since the time of the event. Frequently, presentism serves a political agenda, although in some cases it merely involves naïve assumptions that values are constant.[10]

For a long time historians took what might be called an "end justifies the means" approach that argued that the conquest of Native America was not only inevitable but beneficial. The advancing American frontier opened the way for civilization and for the American values of democracy, economic opportunity, and human rights. Even before Frederick Jackson Turner drafted the model of this view, it was expressed in many works of history and in commentaries by government officials and religious leaders.[11] A more complex, yet often misleading development began in the twentieth century, with what has been called by some the "victim ideology." This view depicts the relationship between European colonizers and indigenous populations as "one long undifferentiated tragedy inflicted on innocent—and passive—victims."[12]

Debates over the latter view have spawned "Native American studies," "American genocide studies," and "settler colonialism studies," all of which have added new perspectives and have value as much in the questions they raise as in the conclusions they reach.[13] They have served well to raise awareness of the mistreatment of American Indians over the centuries, but some of them have ill-served Indians by portraying them as helpless victims. Such a view demeans the power of various Native cultures by distorting their adaptability, their capacity to resist, their values, their diplomatic and military skills, and the genius of many of their leaders. A case can be made that Anglo-Americans were unable to defeat Native Americans without adopting their tactics because their own tactics were "inadequate to the task." It is true that Indians were frequently shocked by the ferocity of white warfare, but many tribes were able to hold the invaders at bay for far longer than the chroniclers of one massacre after another allow.[14]

As Jared Diamond notes, "The reason not to mistreat indigenous people . . . is that it is unjust to mistreat them." It is not necessary to build a false narrative to make the case. "The rights of indigenous people should be asserted on moral grounds,"

Diamond adds, "not by making untrue claims susceptible to refutation."[15] To argue that Native tribes effectively resisted white intrusion into the trans-Appalachian region for more than half a century through a remarkable combination of adjustments, adaptations, negotiations, intertribal alliances, and open warfare, does not justify the slaughter of the Conestogas or the Massacre at Gnadenhutten or Bad Axe. Nor, for that matter, does acknowledging intertribal warfare, the use of torture, or practices like scalping and mutilation of the dead by some tribes justify or ameliorate the mistreatment of Native Americans. It is hardly fair to warrior peoples, whose descendants still take pride in their military traditions, to portray them as passive.

What is most notable, in spite of the invasion of America, the subjugation of Indian peoples, and the abuse that accompanied and followed the conquest, was the survival of Native peoples in all of their diversity. Indigenous tribes were, indeed victims of forces beyond their control including Eurocentric ideas, attitudes, cultural forms, and technologies that influenced policy and conflict in ways that eventually overwhelmed them, but they were neither helpless nor guiltless in response. Some of the cultural changes were unintentional, but not all of them were unwelcome. Indians accepted, even welcomed, white technology, learned from white ways and ideas, and some, at least, saw the Europeans as benefactors and allies.

In the long run, what made the difference was not strategy and tactics, technology, will, or race. To think otherwise is to underestimate Native intelligence and Native capacity to adapt. Ultimately, the real issue was power. White America was able to work its will over time by sheer numbers and literally steam-driven organization that overwhelmed the independence and rate of response of traditional societies. Land, attitude, world view, and technology were all less important than population growth and political and economic organization. It was not the superiority of "civilization" over "savagery" nor racism over inclusion that ultimately determined the outcome, but the power to conquer over the power to resist.[16]

Made in One Image

Something more must be understood. The misunderstanding and disrespect that lay at the heart of the process was more than a simple division into good and evil. Something more complicated, and yet simpler, was involved, something central to the shared humanity of victims and victimizers. Herman Melville wrote in a review of Francis Parkman's *The California and Oregon Trail*, "We are all of us—Anglo-Saxons, Dyaks, and Indians—sprung from one head, and made in one image. And if we regret this brotherhood now, we shall be forced to join hands hereafter. A misfortune is not a fault; and good luck is not meritorious. The savage is born a savage; and the civilized being but inherits his civilization, nothing more."[17]

A common core of beliefs and values, a shared humanity, things which all people regardless of culture hold dear are part of the human condition as well as cultural differences. What, then, kept good men, white and red, from opening these resources? The easy answers are words like greed and prejudice and hatred, but beyond those flaws, something more subtle was always at work, fostering misunderstanding and abuse, suspicion and distrust, something that is fundamental to understanding tragedies like the Sand Creek Massacre. *Not every culture sees the world in the same way.*

Every people in the human family have thought itself special. The Egyptians, the Persians, the Greeks, the Romans, the Mongols, the Spanish, the British, the French, the Maya, the Aztecs, and all of the builders of empires across the centuries on every continent have proclaimed it so. The indigenous peoples of Africa, Asia, the Americas, and the islands of the Pacific were no less certain of it. The etymology of Native American tribal names reveals a remarkable consistency of using terms such as "the People," "Human Beings," "Called Out People," "the Chosen Ones," and similar expressions to identify particular groups as special and set apart from others. Cheyennes and Arapahos were not exceptions to the general premise.[18]

This should not be surprising. Human beings judge themselves and others by what they know. They view their own ways as the standard against which outsiders are measured. They assume a superiority of their groups based upon a collection of habits, customs, and beliefs and on their relationships with nature and with God. All manner of things may change around them from the way they live their lives to the places where they live, but most cling to a belief that theirs is the better way. This has been true of conquerors and conquered, of rulers and slaves, of nation states and tribes.

The myths and histories of the human experience are also replete with prophecies and admonitions that each people should remain separate and honor the ways of their fathers. Warnings abound of the consequences of forgetting the past. The near universality of such traditional stories is more than a historical relic. Over time these views have been changed and modified in response to contact with different parts of the human family, new experiences, and different ways of relating to others. Historical events, environmental changes, spiritual understandings, and cultural myths have altered group perceptions and led, at least in theory, to notions of mutual respect and universal human rights. But such understandings, when they have come, have been the result of slow, and often painful, processes, in which misunderstand-ings and lack of mutual respect have sustained conflict and lingering distrust, even after the desire for harmony has been accepted in principle.

This process has been complicated by differing ways of seeing on the part of dif-ferent groups. What has been determinative in the relationship of groups, however, has not been the superiority of one way of seeing over another, of a right way over a wrong way, but rather by the simple rule of power, of the capacity of one group to impose its will upon others. What is less well understood is that even the most op-pressive forms of power rarely, if ever, eradicate other ways of seeing.

One way of seeing may eventually overwhelm others, intellectually, economical-ly, politically, militarily, even religiously; but the way of seeing, including its tradi-tional values and world view, usually survives even in the face of change. Four hun-dred years and more of conflict between the European powers (and their offspring in American nation states) and the indigenous peoples of the Western hemisphere changed the face of what was called "the New World," but it did not change the es-sentials of Native ways of seeing. It changed much, to be sure, and it would be fool-hardy to claim that American Indians or their Euro-American conquerors have not changed their cultural mind-sets over time. The ability to adapt is strong, but it rarely takes the form of capitulation. Different ways of seeing remain and continue to affect relationships between diverse groups.[19]

The Linear View

The way of seeing of the Euro-American world—what is usually called "Western Civilization"—rests upon a linear view of life. Time moves chronologically along a line inexorably from beginning to end. This view implies an irreversibility of events and leads to the central concept of progress, with all of its rational, empirical, scien-tific, technological, and historical assumptions. Progress, like time, is linear, moving along a line through phases, passages from primitive to civilized. This view of life is analytic in nature, based on accumulating knowledge, understanding parts, dividing culture, and assigning value to discrete elements. Refining, inventing, plotting new strategies, seeking proofs are the methods of reason.

Westerners assumed an evolutionary world view long before the theory of evo-lution was ever advanced as a key to biological change. Civilized status is measured according to where human groups fit upon a series of scales, from hunter-gatherers to complex modern economies, from stone tools to the use of metals to modern science using many forms of energy and technology, from families to bands to tribes to kingdoms to nation states. The position of various human groups seems self-evident by this model. Science, philosophy, art, medicine, history, economics, ethics are similarly measured, then separated and dissected independently, boxed apart from each other into "disciplines."

Within each box, the linear measure moves from simple to complex with the complex usually being the more sophisticated form, meaning the "superior" form. It is an eminently practical system that allows a reasoned establishment of order. It assumes the "Great Chain of Being" that was embraced by the ancient Greeks and reaffirmed in the seventeenth and eighteenth centuries—a hierarchical view of the universe based upon science, progress, improvement, and order, from the most basic elements upward to God. Its analytic character has created skepticism, suspicion of the metaphysical and the spiritual, and an air of superiority that makes it dismissive of other ways of seeing. Ironically, even religious forms are frequently empty of spirituality and wonder, given over instead to rules, dogmas, and rituals that flush away the core principles of faith.[20]

In the Western way of seeing, reality is man-centered and time-centered; reality is explored—historically, scientifically, and religiously—in terms of the human experience over time. History is essential to this process. This way of seeing is concerned not merely with what happens to man or what man does, but also with what the human experience means. It is not enough to know that something happened. Humans must understand how it happened and why. Western religion and Western science have adopted the historical model as a basis of belief and of order. Christianity rests on a linear movement through time from Creation to the End of Time. It follows a chronological model, with lengthy genealogies, important events, and prophecies based upon the movement of time. Reason and analysis, even when couched in grand departures, are framed in the human-centered view of existence. Nature is something to be used by humans. Land, animals, plants, and every other form are to be subdued, overcome, and dominated. Uncontrolled land is wilderness, beautiful perhaps, but also foreboding, threatening, dangerous, somehow wasted in its natural state, something that must be "tamed."[21]

The Cyclic View

By contrast, the American Indian way of seeing is cyclic rather than linear. Its model is not a line, but a circle, not the Great Chain of Being, but the Great Harmony, encompassing life in a transcendent cycle, not an irreversible line. Its forms are metaphysical and focused upon where and how humans fit within the circle. Both the past and the future are but aspects of the present, and every creature within Creation has place and spirit, even including the animals that provide meat, the land that sustains them, the rocks, and the rivers. Nature sustains humanity, and humanity repays nature in a celebration of life. Thus, reality is nature-centered. It is Creation (the earth and the universe beyond and all of the creatures, great and small, animal and plant, stone and sand and loam, rivers and lakes, and oceans, mountains and plains, sun, moon, and stars) that is central. Humans are merely a part of the grand design; all things are equally important. There is an essential interrelatedness of all Creation. Faith, morality, and ethics are about understanding the right ways of maintaining the unity of all things because that unity is the Great Good intended by the All-Father.[22]

The Southern Cheyenne historian Henrietta Mann explains that "Cheyenne history is a continuum of sacred experiences rooted into the American landscape. . . . Their continuity as a people requires that they maintain their way of life. Specifically, they must maintain their traditions, beliefs, spiritual life, and through their ceremonies, maintain their sacred mission to keep the earth alive."[23] "*To keep the earth alive.*" That is an important concept, a purpose quite different from progress. The purpose is to stay alive and vital within the natural order, not to improve. Life is sacred, with features that transmit the central meaning of existence. Circumstances may change, but essential patterns do not. In the Native way of seeing, the behavior, the form, the spiritual power that were real at the Creation are renewed and time itself is repudiated and annulled in a cycle like that of the seasons. Seasons may change but the order of things remains within the Great Circle.

Reality is defined by space and place. Understanding this may help explain the profound attachment to the land so central to white-Indian conflict both in the past and the present. Space is about the wholeness of things, the four directions, sky and earth, the Great Harmony, the Medicine Wheel, and Indian ceremonies are about restoring the wholeness of what has become chaotic or corrupted in order to assure a renewal of the true way and to correct imbalances and brokenness in the circle. Place involves both sacred landmarks, such as Bear Butte in the Black Hills of South Dakota for the Cheyennes, and environments where particular peoples are supposed to be. The latter does not imply a single fixed spot, but rather that place where the people can thrive. Place is not a possession. It was here in the past and will be here in the future. Like animals and plants, people may move from one location to another, as the migrations of the various tribes clearly show, but finding place is essential to the unity. Being out of place destroys the unity and life of the people in the same way that moving grass from the plains to the desert would kill the grass.

Joseph Epes Brown wrote, "Events or processes transmitted through oral traditions tend to be recounted neither in terms of time past or time future in a lineal sense. Indeed most languages have no such tenses to express this. They speak rather of a perennial reality of the now."[24] What matters is the experience. There is no need to explain or question because experience has its own voice. History is not remembered as chronology. It is recounted in stories that recall important ideas and places, traumatic events like the loss of the Sacred Arrows to the Pawnees or the Sand Creek Massacre for the Cheyennes, great men and women, and moments that define who the Cheyennes and Arapahos are (as one example). In the telling of these stories, dates are not given beyond expressions like "a long time ago," "when my great-grandfather was a boy," or "in the time before the white soldiers came." This form of historical consciousness is concerned with the place the events described have among the people and the role the accounts still play in their lives.[25]

Of course, as Vine DeLoria, Jr., pointed out, over time, under the pressures of life changes brought about by contact with whites and the experience of the reservation system, government schools, and efforts to understand what was happening to them, Indian people absorbed some of the thinking of Western civilization. De Loria wrote, "We face the future immediately, and while we can be aware of the sound basis for primitive beliefs and customs, we can never return to them or take them up, expecting them to save us." What he hoped for was that the Native way of seeing could be understood, its essence preserved, and incorporated into "a more comprehensive and intelligent view of the world."[26] In fact, contact with the Western way of seeing has certainly modified some thinking and led to adaptations as a matter of survival, but the Native way of seeing remains vital in the decisions and mind-sets of today's Indian people.

The Native way was never static or obtuse. In fact, it has always been characterized by sensitivity and awareness. Vigilance and responsibility are what keep the world alive. Refining, inventing, and plotting new strategies may be facts of life, but when circumstances intrude with new wonders and challenges, they must be dealt with within the ancient, primal context. In this system there is little place for dominion. In order for it to function there is little place for the Western strategy of dividing culture or assigning value to discrete elements. Rather, the Native Way unifies the various aspects of culture and experience into a single whole.

Oglala writer Ed McGaa explains that in the Great Circle of Life, each person is driven by "a living circle of energy," built upon character, background, knowledge, and experience.[27] It is the natural way. American Indian historian Donald L. Fixico, of Shawnee, Sac and Fox, Muscogee Creek, and Seminole ancestry, explains:

> Nothing is transfixed. Nothing is secure or stable or permanent, and Indian people have accepted this situation. We want to believe that nothing has changed, but the reality is that all things change, even the story that we remember being told, but as long as the fabric of the truths of a story are retained, then we can accept it.[28]

Some entities are more powerful than others according to their strengths, and some are unknown; but Native people respect all entities because of their power to influence people. Balance is the object of life, Fixico argues, including balance within one's self, within the family, within the community, with external communities, including other tribes and the spiritual world, and with the environment and universe. He cites Mary Roberts's view that "implicitly contrasting Indians with whites, the Indian mind is not literal, specific, scientific—it is philosophical, vague, and poetic."[29]

Westerners may think, then, that the Indian way of seeing is naïve. Historians, government agents, and religious leaders have frequently thought so and dismissed the Indian way as "childish" or "primitive." Native scholars argue, by contrast, that the Indian way of seeing is grounded in the balance that Fixico describes and, in this way, attuned to the world in ways that the Western way of seeing left behind long ago on its linear scale.

Calvin Martin, who decades ago, pointed out the dangers of the Western view of history, with its essential ethnocentrism, argued that historians must cultivate the "metaphysics of the Native American lifeway" and underscored the importance of including the "cosmological perspective" of the Native way of seeing. That means, practically, that it is important to give Native Americans their own "historic voice." The cyclic view of life does not run along a scale of time in the way that Western thought does. It focuses rather on perpetual renewal, a constant reaffirmation of Creation. This view is "eternal, cyclical, endlessly repetitive, powered by Nature and cosmogonic."[30]

History for Native peoples is "sacred history," constantly linked to "the primordial unity from which it issued." In this view there is no need for "progress" in the way that the Euro-American view insists upon. The Cheyennes see themselves directly involved in Creation, "not just for their own sake, their own welfare, but for the welfare of creation in whose uterus they thrive."[31] For them, the land was life—not property or a place of residence. It is the connection to all things that matter. The indigenous way was fully capable of adaptation, but not for the sake of change. The biological and cosmological core remained. Much that whites did, including the introduction of Western ideas and beliefs, broke the links with Nature or separated the people from its forces.

The point of this discourse is not to argue for the superiority of one way of seeing over the other but merely to underscore that there are different ways of seeing. Understanding this means that people must learn to communicate effectively across cultural lines. The different ways of seeing must be understood and valued before words like "peace" and "reconciliation" can have meaning, purpose, or hope of reality. Other distinctions are important. A way of seeing reflects a centralized perspective on the nature of life developed and sustained over time. The linear approach of Western civilization is the product of thought and values and experience. It shaped the thinking of most of Europe and of the colonizing societies of the Western hemisphere and of other Eurocentric expansion. The cyclic way of seeing among Native Americans shaped their response to the invaders in terms of their thought and values and experience.

Culture may also vary within a particular way of seeing. Cheyennes, Arapahos, Navajos, Apaches, Creeks, Cherokees, Crows, Shoshonis, Lakotas, Ojibwa, Iroquois, Pequots, Delawares, and many other groups share the circular view of life; but they differ too. Culture differentiates. It provides the sources of identity. It is combative and defensive when challenged by others with other cultural values. Similarly, although they share a linear way of seeing, Spanish, French, Italian, English, German, and other Europeans represent different cultural perspectives that vary in emphasis, language, and experience. Indeed, cultures may vary within a single linguistic or national group. This means, practically, that within both the linear and cyclic ways of seeing, many different cultures emerged, approaching life within a particular way of seeing in essentially the same way, but experiencing life differently and having different traditions, spiritual forms, and languages as a result.

Historical Mind-set

Often overlooked is yet another critical consideration, which may best be defined as mind-set. Although the essential way of seeing remains consistent, mind-set changes based upon thought and experience. The mind-set of the Renaissance differed from the mind-set of the Age of Revolution and from that of the Age of Industrialization or of the Post-Industrial Age. Moreover, within any historical period, the mind-set may vary by nation or even within nations. The same must be said for changes of mind-set between and among North American Indian tribes. It must not be assumed that the Native mind-set was the same from the settlement of the English colonies through the allotment of tribal lands following the Dawes Act to the present. Even within particular tribes mind-sets may vary although the culture and the way of seeing are shared.

This may seem esoteric, which is evidence within itself of the difficulty of understanding and resolving cross-cultural differences, whether historical in nature or concerned with current policies and interaction. This is more complicated than the simple "clash of cultures" model that has been posited as an explanation of Indian-white relations in American history. Neither is it a matter of embracing multiculturalism. At the simplest level it is recognizing that there are different ways of seeing, different cultures, and different mind-sets. It involves not merely trying to understand the "other" way of seeing but of realizing that there are multiple ways of seeing cultures and mind-sets, not only at the time that events occur but also at the times they are studied. What has generally been called "white-Indian" relations was never a simple, bifurcated conflict with only two points of view; it was a dynamic and changing process dependent upon a variety of factors, affected by time, place, and perspective. There have been consistent patterns of behavior and thought, but to simplify the conflict to a generalized "them" and "us" conflict distorts what happened.

Father Francis Paul Prucha, perhaps the leading authority on American Indian policy, reminded those approaching the field that they not only face the challenge of understanding differing ways of seeing, but also of realizing that mind-sets change over time as well. "It is customary," he writes, "to insist that we grasp something of the world view of the Indian cultures (because we instinctively know they are different from our own), and we try not to judge one culture by the norms of another. What is often forgotten is that we must also understand past white societies and not assume that the 1830s [for example] can be understood by the norms and values of the 1970s [or of the 2010s]."[32] Confronting the past ought, at the very least, to generate new sensitivities and responses to the ideas and problems that the past left previous generations, rather than the application of present understanding alone.

13

In 1866, General Samuel Ryan Curtis, who commanded the Department of Kansas at the time of the Sand Creek Massacre, witnessed a sun dance. He wrote, "The scene closed leaving on my memory a picture of terrible superstition and sanguinary barbarity such as I hope never to witness." He described "this scandalous devotion" to the *Northwestern Christian Advocate*, adding that it "seems a reproach against the mission efforts of our age and people."[33] By way of contrast, Native observers were not so much shocked by the principles of Christianity or the teachings of Christ, as they were by the squabbling of missionary groups among themselves and the failure of Christians to live up to the principles they taught. The inconsistency was incomprehensible to them. James West, a contemporary Cheyenne, goes so far as to suggest that theology is a "non-Indian concept" standing in sharp contrast to "a spiritual way of life" as practiced by Native peoples.[34]

From the beginning, Anglo-Americans assumed a superior attitude toward the indigenous people they encountered. At times, they accommodated Indians in order to survive or simply from curiosity, but they also measured themselves against the Indians, and, given their technological superiority at arms and industry, and their "true faith," they quickly began to see themselves as a new breed of men, as free of Europe as they were privy to the bounty of the New World. They were "new," whether living in commonwealths of faith or building farms and plantations and towns. They had opportunities they had scarcely imagined before. Richard Slotkin points to Melville's Captain Ahab in *Moby Dick* as "an allegorical representation of the American world quest: he is obsessed, compelling, unstoppable, completely wrapped up in his own rhetorical justification and his sense of cosmic symbolism." This "new American" came at the expense of indigenous people not only through the bloody wars that "regenerated" the American vision but also through the arrogant assumption of the superiority of white ways.[35]

In 1899, George Bird Grinnell, an early student of Cheyenne culture and history, wrote of the reformers of the past who tried to help but instead furthered the damage to Indian people:

> The sincerity and earnestness of a majority of such philanthropists cannot be doubted, but in all their reasoning about Indians there has been one point of weakness: They had no personal knowledge of the inner life of the people they were trying to help. Their theories appear to have assumed that Indians are precisely like white men, except that their minds are blank and plastic, ready to receive any impression that may be

14

inscribed on them. These friends of the Indian had little acquaintance with Indian character; they did not appreciate the human nature of the people. They did not know that their minds were already occupied by a multitude of notions and beliefs that were firmly fixed there, rooted and grounded by an inheritance of a thousand years. Still less did they comprehend the Indian's intense conservatism, the tenacity with which he clings to the beliefs which have been handed down to him by uncounted generations."[36]

The reason was the inbred cultural arrogance of the linear way of seeing, the conviction that the only salvation for American Indians lay in recognizing and accepting the superiority of the "white man's way." Some white Americans openly wondered about it. Walt Whitman, in *Leaves of Grass*, pondered, "The friendly and flowing savage. . . . Who is he? Is he waiting for civilization or past it and mastering it?"[37] And Henry David Thoreau believed that white men and red were complements, that "the Indian remembered what the white man had forgotten, spoke what the white man could no longer comprehend," as Edwin S. Fussell puts it. Thoreau mused, "One revelation has been made to the Indian, another to the white man. I have much to learn of the Indian, nothing of the missionary. I am not sure but all that would tempt me to teach the Indian my religion would be his promise to teach me his."[38]

Such reflections were thought to be romantic pap by the majority of white Americans for most of American history. They were more likely to agree with the esteemed Bishop James Andrew of the Methodist Episcopal Church, South, who proclaimed in 1854: "our grand aim is to lead the young [Indians] into an entire abandonment of the language, and whatever is distinctively Indian; for after all the sentimentalism of poets and tourists, there is very little which belongs to the original savage character that is worth retaining."[39] So it was that many of those whites with the tenderest of hearts and the best of intentions were incapable of seeing beyond their own ancient way or of comprehending what Whitman and Thoreau sensed—questions that were closer to understanding than even the poets themselves realized. Indeed, in the end they would set aside their insights uneasily in favor of their ingrained understanding of progress and civilization.[40]

In 1919, A. McG. Beede, an Episcopal missionary on the Standing Rock Reservation in North Dakota, reported that the Sioux and Chippewa had little problem understanding "the modern scientific attitude" or grasping, even enjoying, the ideas and processes of chemistry and physics. He tested his ideas among the Chippewa and Cree for eight months. He wrote: "But Rising Sun [one of his students], speaking the conclusion of all, pronounced 'the scientific view' inadequate. Not bad or untrue, but inadequate to explain, among many other things, how man is to find and know a road along which he wishes and chooses to make this said progress unless the Great Manitoo by his spirit guides the mind of man, keeping human beings just and generous and hospitable."[41]

The irony seems to be that for all of its accomplishments and "progress" the Western way of seeing is less open to alternative points of view than the cyclic way. Native Americans learned more of the Western way than Europeans learned of the Native way. The reason seems to be that the linear way of seeing, for all of its talk about science and reason, is more rigid and dogmatic. Vine DeLoria, Jr., suggested that "in the Indian world, experience is not limited by mental considerations and assumptions regarding the universe. For the non-Indian the teachings of a lifetime come thundering down. Such things do not occur in time and space. Reality is basically physical. . . . Reality in a certain sense is what you allow your mind to accept, not what you experience. And a host of other beliefs rush in to cover up, confuse, and eventually eliminate the experience itself."[42]

"Domination and inequities of power and wealth are perennial facts of human society," writes Edward W. Said, whose broad exploration of the interaction of cultures worldwide, provides insights both into different ways of seeing and into ways that cultures are able to come together. He sought in comparative studies of imperialism and Native responses keys to understanding and arresting the continuing conflicts around the world between the architects of colonialism and their descendants and indigenous peoples and their descendants. He pointed out an almost universal tendency to blame the victims of colonialism for their treatment and subsequent woes, which, he suggested, is usually a guilt-driven response to perceptions inconsistent with what nations want to believe about themselves. But he also warned that "blaming the Europeans sweepingly for the misfortunes of the present is not much of an alternative. What we need to do is to look at these matters as a network of interdependent histories that it would be inaccurate and senseless to repress, useful and interesting to understand."[43]

Said argued something that should be obvious. Dominant cultures telling their Native "wards" that their societies are backward or savage or primitive or trying to convince them of the "good" that conquest and civilization have done for them, will not convince indigenous groups that it is true. "Even if you prevail over them, they are not going to concede to you your essential superiority or your right to rule them despite your evident wealth and power." Even without the big, empty spaces, expanding frontiers, or new settlements that marked colonial expansion in the United States during the nineteenth century, social relationships remain "a dimly perceived, basically uninterpreted and uncomprehended fabric." Selfish and narrow interests—patriotism, chauvinism, ethnic, religious, and racial hatreds—remain remorselessly present and prevent the cultural gaps from being crossed or even understood.

The need, he argued, is not so much for "learning about other cultures," which he finds vague and inane as a goal, but rather for studying "the map of interactions" between cultures. In order to have an informed, explicit understanding of the relationships "it is a useful preparation to look at what still remains" of colonialism's impact.[44] The residue of history in the present will provide insights into the issues that limit our understanding of the past. Said suggested that understanding present divisions may help illuminate the complex histories of conquerors and conquered created by the phenomena of "discovery" and "conquest." He advocated exploring present cultural interactions as a tool for better understanding the past by means of an appreciation of current cultural differences and ways of seeing. This is about opening the mind to a wider range of ideas, concepts, values, and beliefs, as a foundation that may provide keys to a clearer understanding of past relationships, conflicts, and particular events like the Sand Creek Massacre.[45]

If different cultures can identify present obstacles and understand them through dialogue that opens doors and breaks down ingrained prejudices and grievances, the past will be easier to understand at several levels including the reality that present mind-sets and past mind-sets are almost certainly different. Said concluded:

> No one can deny the persisting continuities of long traditions, sustained habitations, national languages, and cultural geographies, but there seems no reason except fear and prejudice to keep insisting on their separation and distinctiveness, as if that was all human life was about. Survival in fact is about the connections between things; in Eliot's phrase, reality cannot be deprived of the "other echoes [that] inhabit the garden." It is more rewarding—and more difficult—to think concretely and sympathetically, contrapuntally, about others than only about "us." But this also means not trying to rule others, not trying to classify them or put them in hierarchies, above all, not constantly reiterating how "our" culture or country is number one (or not number one, for that matter).

17

What is required, then, in order to understand a particular event like the Sand Creek Massacre is to explore the larger context of what happened in terms of all of the parties involved and the differences in their ways of seeing to learn why it happened and the levels of responsibility of the individuals involved and of the impact it had upon cultures and history. Only then can Sand Creek be understood and its moral consequences appreciated across the gaps that continue to exist and the mistakes that continue to be made.

CHAPTER 2

THE ROAD TO DOMINION

"Christian View of Earth"

WESTERN CIVILIZATION DREW ITS way of seeing from a variety of cultures ranging west from the Fertile Crescent along the north rim of the Mediterranean basin. What brought them together into a European world view was the emergence of a new religious faith during the first century A.D. The sect known as "Christians" found its identity in the teachings of Jesus of Nazareth, a first-century Judean prophet, who appeared during the reign of the Roman emperor Tiberius. It began simply enough, as a body of believers, inspired by an evangelical zeal to spread the teachings of Christ to others. This zealous effort led to the creation of the Christian church and the formalization of faith into an institution of religion. As the church spread west, its message was influenced by Greco-Roman ideas, philosophy, science, art, and government. The existence of the Roman Empire, its roads, its economy, its centralized power, and its military might, extended Christian influence until Christianity became the state religion of the Roman Empire itself.[1]

From the Old Testament, Christianity drew three powerful ideas. The first was God's commission to "subdue" the earth: "Be fruitful, and multiply, and replenish the earth, and subdue it: and have dominion over the fish of the sea, and over the fowl of the air, and over every living thing that moveth upon the earth" (Genesis 1:28 KJV). Second, Christians believed that they inherited the Israelites' claim to a "promised land": "Now the LORD had said unto Abram, Get thee out of thy country, and from thy kindred, and from thy father's house, unto a land that I will shew thee: And I will make of thee a great nation" (Genesis 12:1-2a KJV). Third, Christians believed they were God's "chosen people": "For thou art an holy people unto the LORD thy God: the LORD thy God has chosen thee to be a special people unto himself, above all people that are upon the face of the earth" (Deuteronomy 7:6 KJV).

Christians also embraced the evangelical command of Jesus to convert "all nations" to the Christian faith: "Go ye therefore, and teach all nations, baptizing them
in the name of the Father, and of the Son, and of the Holy Ghost: teaching them to
observe all things whatsoever I have commanded you: and, lo, I am with you always,
even unto the end of the world. Amen" (Matthew 28:19-20 KJV).

This combination of doctrines—the command to subdue the earth, belief in the
promised land, Christian status as a chosen people, and the admonition to convert
"all nations"—empowered the church, and as Christians grew from a persecuted few
to purveyors of a universal gospel, the link with the political and military strength
of the Roman Empire and its successor kingdoms made the church the most potent
force in Europe for a thousand years. The church's institutionalization and the rise
of the papacy resulted in a mass of new rules and doctrines, many of which had their
roots in the Greek and Roman past as well as in biblical texts. Greek and Roman
philosophy, science, and law shaped the linear view, and it, in turn, was embraced by
the church. Over time, the church gained a virtual supremacy in Europe, sustained
by a system of order it imposed.[2]

One other factor figured into the European system—a continuing series of wars.
The history of the Fertile Crescent and of the movement west through Greece and
Rome and eventually into the rest of Europe over the centuries involved ongoing
conflict. Some of the troubles were wars between empires or for the control of empires. But also, from the time of the Greeks, there was always a brutal "other" to be
overcome. Whether Persians, Gauls, Huns, Mongols, Tartars, Moors, Picts, Saxons,
Saracens, Vikings, Celts, or others from the fringes of "civilization," these peoples
were regarded as "savages" by the Greeks and Romans and by the successor Christian kingdoms even into the modern era. The "savage other" was always there with
cultures to be rooted out and land to be taken. Race came late to the rationale of
conquest. Savagery was the obstacle to be overcome.[3]

Conquest of the "Savage"

The conflicts of the Roman Empire led to the exclusion of savages from the conventions of war. The label of "savage" identified outsiders deemed so bloodthirsty and
dangerous that any tactic could be justified against them. They were, quite simply,
"beyond the protection of any humane convention." During the Principate (27 B.C.
to A.D. 284) and the later Roman Empire as well, these "others" were regarded as
extranei and subject to conquest as a right of self-defense and as an extension of civi-

lization.[4] The concept of the savage was sustained and extended with the blessings of the papacy in the centuries that followed. During the Middle Ages, the fragile Christian kingdoms were threatened by successions of attacks from the north and the east. These warrior invasions were noted for their ruthless style of warfare. They also represented nomadic and raiding cultures beyond the pale of Christianity and with little regard for its precepts. The conflict with the invaders was viewed as nothing less than a struggle between civilization and barbarism, between Christianity and heathenism.

Significantly, this led to an elaborate legal rationale justifying the conquest of non-Christian enemies, created largely by the church. The Church Universal was the great unifying force in Europe, in the face of confused, unstable, conflicted, and troubled political kingdoms. It spoke with one voice for all Christians. As more and more of the western tribes of Europe were converted, as the Norman invasion of Britain was consolidated, and as Europeans stalled the Saracen invasion from North Africa, the idea of a "frontierless jurisdiction" over the Christian body politic made more sense to rulers of the still fragile European kingdoms.[5]

By the time of Pope Urban II, a legal frame was in place to justify the jurisdiction of the church over all Christians and the extension of the boundaries of Christian control. This provided the foundation for the concept of "holy war" and the justification for Pope Urban II's call for a crusade to "liberate" Jerusalem from the Saracens, "an alien people, a race completely foreign to God, 'a generation of false aims, of a spirit that broke faith with God,' [which] has invaded Christian territory and has devastated this territory with pillage, fire, and the sword."[6]

Here was yet another manifestation of the "savage other," and during the years between Urban II's call for crusade in 1095 through the crusades that followed and into the papacy of Innocent IV (1243-1254), the legal rights of pagan peoples were debated at length both in traditional hierocratic and in humanistic terms. Pope Innocent would provide the complex legal synthesis and extend it beyond holy war. Innocent argued that all humans, Christian and infidel, were subject to the Pope's duty to "protect their spiritual well-being." He held that there was "only one right way of life" and concluded that the irrational behaviors of heathens required that armies join missionaries in the work of conversion. Here was the justification of the "right of conquest" by Christian nations. The Christian Europeans' view of reason and truth was binding on all people, everywhere.[7]

This was, in the words of Robert A. Williams, Jr., "the perfect instrument of empire."[8] It would not end arguments over the "rights of infidels," but it would provide a legal framework for conquest of lands beyond the Euro-Christian world. There were practical, nonreligious reasons that made its embrace more attractive. The evolution of Europe's nation states in the fifteenth and sixteenth centuries coincided with an increased crisis of resources. Europe was consuming itself. While its population was growing, many important resources were dwindling, including land, timber, food, and fisheries, as well as gold, silver, and other commodities needed for defense and power. Urbanization, pollution, and deforestation were also becoming serious problems. Columbus's "accidental discovery" of a "New World," seemed to be the answer for men armed with "the right of conquest," the admonition "to subdue the earth," the duty to convert nonbelievers into Christians, and the conviction that their ways were superior to the "others" they confronted in the new lands.[9]

During the papacy of Eugenius IV, in response to legal questions raised by Portugal, the *Romanus Pontiflex* was drafted. It created the first "juristic synthesis" of "colonizing discourse" since Innocent IV. The 1453-1454 version of *Romanus Pontiflex*, issued by Pope Nicholas V, was the most precise version, amounting to a "license of conquest" for Portugal in Africa. In 1493, Pope Alexander VI issued two papal bulls. The first granted to the crowns of Castille and Aragon in Spain all lands discovered west of the Azores excluding lands previously occupied by other "Christian nations." The second, issued in response to concerns raised by Portugal, clarified the division of lands between Spain and Portugal and confirmed the rule of law that the people of "discovered" lands were subject to the guardianship of the discoverers.[10]

While not acknowledged specifically in the papal bulls, other European nations pushed their own rights of conquest in the "New World" using the general principles laid out in the papal discourse. There would be conflicts over claims, but European nations almost universally disregarded the rights of indigenous peoples and came over time to modify the primary descriptor of the right of conquest by European nations to the right of conquest by Christian nations. As a leading nineteenth-century authority concluded: "It thus became a maxim of policy and law that the right of the native Indians was subordinate to that of the first Christian discoverer, whose paramount claim excluded that of every other civilized nation, and gradually extinguished that of the natives."[11] Thus the "Doctrine of Discovery" was accepted as the unquestioned right of Christian nations by European powers in the sixteenth century.

Doctrine of Discovery

The Doctrine of Discovery would be used to justify the conquest of the "New World" by the European powers and became the central tenet of secular law as well.

By the time that the United States of America was formed in 1776, it was a fundamental premise of every European legal system and survived into the new legal structure of the American system as well. Countries might vary in the way the doctrine was applied—the English insisting on treaties of cession, for example—but all regarded it as a "right" of Christian powers and superior in weight to any Native claims to the land. It would prove particularly important to the "settler colonialism" of the new United States as a foundational principle of westward expansion.

But the English had added something else by the time of the English Civil War—a deeply embedded sense of Anglo-Saxon superiority. The English were, as one historian writes, "awestruck by their own achievements" and committed to "alleged group virtues" that included notions of law and liberty that set them apart even within Europe. They came to see their world as "normative." England had dealt with the "savage others" of its own domain—the highlanders of northern Scotland, the Irish, and the Welsh—at times brutally and in ways that fixed patterns for dealing with the "others" they would confront in North America.[12]

The English systematically sought to root out cultural differences—the elimination of traditional Gaelic languages, outlawing everything from kilts to bagpipes, from painted faces to Catholicism. Scottish highlanders were considered savages, and Irishmen were even herded onto reservations (called plantations), and in their wars of conquest, the English slaughtered them with impunity. In the 1641 campaign in Ireland, Sir Charles Coote, an English general, was celebrated "When he (by good advise)/ Didd kill the Nitts, that they may not grow lice." The slogan was commonplace in the Irish conflict and would resonate over time in English and Anglo-American wars against American Indians, to gain prominence again during the Sand Creek controversy. Oliver Cromwell justified the butchery of 3,500 men, women, and children at Drogheda in 1649 as "merely righteous execution on barbaric and treacherous savages."[13]

As late as the 1730s, when General James Edward Oglethorpe amassed a military expedition to face the Spanish in Florida, he described a force composed of "White people[,] Indians and highlanders," indicating an ongoing view of highland Scots as savages.[14] The highlanders and Scots-Irish, who had little use for the English to begin with, usually pushed past the coastal settlements and cleared fields into the forests and the American highlands of the Appalachians. There many of them developed a kinship with Native peoples. Both were treated as tribal peoples. Both were regarded as barbarians. Both had been driven out of their home country. By the time of the Seven Years War, Scottish names were prominent in the leadership of the Creeks and Cherokees, and Scots played a prominent role in trade between Indians and the English.[15]

After the Glorious Revolution, England emerged as a country with constitutional government, economic prosperity, scientific and technological leadership that prepared them for a dominant place in the new world order. They also touted "the rights of Englishmen" as their great achievement. Their naval control of the Atlantic Ocean protected the establishment of colonies significantly different from those of other European nations. "Settler colonialism" was perhaps the key component of English success.[16] Empire involves the control of other people by conquest; settlement involves the reproduction of one society in a new place through long-range migration. Settlers created a largely uncontrolled dynamic once the coastal colonies were established and the indigenous peoples along the coast killed or driven into the interior. With no effective control by England or within the colonies themselves, the new settlers moved west in increasing numbers.[17]

Land, Land, Land

What drew them was the land—all that land, empty by any standard that made sense to white settlers who wanted a piece of their own more than anything else. Land stood at the center of their value system. It defined free men, set them apart from servants, peasants, and vagabonds, and enabled them to participate in government. Even in the nineteenth century, most landless Americans were not that far from European roots. Their ancestors had been drawn to America, not so much for gold or even faith, as for land. Land was freedom. It gave settlers place, identity, independence, and liberty, all things they would never have known had they stayed in England or Scotland or Ireland. Their children and grandchildren embraced those values and viewed them as rights.

Of course, the settlers knew that people occupied the land already, but individually each of them felt that of all those millions of acres, he could claim a few and do no harm. It was not a Doctrine of Discovery that drove the settlers, but, ironically, the same forces that fed their understanding of liberty and of rights, those rudimentary drives to be free of restraint and able to make their own way. The indigenous people they met were simply one more "natural barrier" between them and their dreams of owning land and being free. While governments, both in London and in the colonial capitals, were concerned about laws based on the Doctrine of Discovery to control and justify the usurpation of Native lands, settlers followed a consistent pattern of preemption even when it put them at odds with their own governments.[18]

Richard Slotkin, in his trilogy of books on the myth of the frontier, particularly his first, *Regeneration Through Violence,* argues that the defining experience of American history was the ongoing conflict between settlers and Natives. The Indian wars, he says, created a view of Americans as "a new race of people, independent of the sin-darkened heritage of man, seeking a totally new and original relationship to pure nature as hunters, explorers, pioneers and seekers." This rhetorical self-justification imagined an ongoing regeneration of the American character with the "winning" of each successive frontier.[19] This would seem to be sustained by Frederick Jackson Turner's classic essay, "The Frontier in American History." Although assailed by historians and social scientists in recent decades as a misleading explanation of what happened, Turner's essay and Slotkin's explanation do provide insight into how Euro-Americans perceived themselves as creators of a new and better society, as chosen people in a promised land.[20]

From the time of the Enlightenment, European philosophers, religious leaders, and politicians felt a need to justify their treatment of indigenous peoples and even to be "fair." From Voltaire to Jefferson, humanists embraced the humanity of American Indians and the possibility of their "improvement."[21] But even the most sympathetic Euro-Americans were limited by their linear way of seeing, which placed the "savages" on the linear scale between barbarism and civilization. The redemption of indigenous peoples lay in transition from their native state to the "superior" ways of white culture. In this process Christianity and civilization were linked inextricably so that one seemed impossible without the other. Linked to this conclusion was the assumption that whites would expand and Natives would give way.[22]

The process was never neat, not merely because whites were divided on how best to treat Indians, but also because Indians were divided on how best to respond. What never existed was a single approach on either side, since both the linear and cyclic ways of seeing allowed for multiple visions of what should happen and how. White attitudes and actions were more predictable, Native responses more complex and varied. Resistance, war, alliances, accommodation, trade, and acculturation marked Native reaction to white intrusion. American Indians were far more resilient and innovative than most interpretations allow—and certainly more so than whites.[23]

Indeed the "Indians as victims" approach seriously underestimates the vitality and power of Native responses. It ignores the cultural changes triggered by the presence of Europeans and Euro-Americans even before direct contact, many of which

were embraced, even welcomed, by the tribes. It implies a Native passivity that totally distorts the capacity to resist as well as the more basic role of war in pre-contact
times. During the wars between England and Spain, and more clearly, in the colonial
wars between England and France, Indians demonstrated military, diplomatic, and
economic skills far too often overlooked, so potent in fact, that they slowed the process of dispossession considerably. The conflict was never simply a matter of "them"
and "us." Rather than some static and helpless presence, Natives artfully adapted
their relations with Euro-Americans, fought among themselves for advantage, as
well as survival, and forged multitribal alliances.[24]

It is beyond the scope of this report to recount all of the conflicts of the English
colonies in America, all of the varied responses of Native peoples, or the debate over
the treatment of Indians by contemporaries. Suffice it to say, that the image of indigenous people as savages and white perceptions of their rights to the land were
reinforced by the colonial experience. It is important to add that original inhabitants
of the land responded to the invasion of their country in varied ways and that tribes
that never saw a white man during the colonial period were changed by events they
could not yet imagine. In Europe and America, a debate occurred over what was
moral and right in dealing with indigenous people, often growing in intensity and
fervor the closer to the conflict the dialogue occurred. There were men like Benjamin Church, an experienced "Indian fighter," who tried to stop the slaughter of Indian women and children at the Great Swamp Fight of 1676, only to be overridden
by Puritan divines who assured the colonists that they were acting within the will of
God and others who threatened to kill Church if he did not cease his efforts. Many
on that occasion "were much in doubt and afterwards inquired whether burning
their enemies alive would be consistent with humanity and the benevolent principles of the gospel."[25]

War and More War

The eighteenth century witnessed a broader conflict as a consequence of increased emigration into Indian country and of wars between the English, on the
one hand, and the French and Spanish on the other. From the western reaches of
New York, south along the backbone of the Appalachians through Pennsylvania and
Kentucky, to the frontier reaches of Georgia and Florida, Native Americans were
drawn into the international struggle for hegemony over North America. During
this process, Indian tribes often acted as the spearhead of European offensives on the

frontier. Other groups avoided the conflicts as they were able, but still fell victim to white violence. In effect, tribes made their choices according to what seemed to be in their own best interests. This included new pan-Indian ideologies and identity.[26]

At the onset of the Seven Years War in 1754, when Indians allied with the French launched assaults on the Middle Colonies, the fear and prejudices of the settlers deepened and the idea of coexistence, which had existed in some quarters, virtually vanished. Popular accounts that emphasized indiscriminate slaughter of men, women, and children, scalping, torture, and mutilation as the "savage" norm of Indian warfare gained general acceptance and provided justification for "war in kind" by whites.

Episodes like the slaughter of the peaceful Conestogas by the Paxton Boys proved unmistakably that American colonists were quite as capable of savagery as any other group of humans on the continent. It proved to be the case, however, that not all whites were ready for this inhumanity. Quakers uncharacteristically armed themselves and moved into Philadelphia when word spread that the Paxton Boys were planning to kill Indians there, although the Quakers, thinking them to be the Paxton Boys, almost fired upon German settlers who were marching to help protect the Indians as well. Benjamin Franklin, who was never a great advocate of Indian rights, felt compelled to write a pamphlet condemning the Conestoga affair.[27]

With the end of the British, French, and Indian War in 1763, the British, realizing the potential for chaos in the lands to the west, made a futile attempt to control the preemption of lands by passing the Proclamation of 1763. It intended to bar settlers from Indian lands west of the Appalachians until and unless lands were ceded by treaty. It failed, and instead became the first step on the road to the American Revolution.[28] No Parliament across the ocean, nor any colonial government, could stanch the settler invasion, and so the "war in the dooryard" continued. In 1776, when he drafted the Declaration of Independence, Thomas Jefferson would list as one of the colonies' grievances against the king that "He has excited domestic insurrections amongst us, and has endeavoured to bring on the inhabitants of our frontiers, the merciless Indian Savages, whose known rule of warfare, is an undistinguished destruction of all ages, sexes and conditions."

The American Revolution

The American Revolution proved bloody in the West as the British encouraged and supported tribal alliances against American settlements, which, in turn, deepened white Americans belief that all Indians were ruthless savages. Lieutenant-Colonel Henry Hamilton, the British commander at Detroit, offered bounties for the scalps of colonials. At one council, when Hamilton urged Native allies to kill Americans and threatened to withhold supplies if they did not, Half King, a Delaware chief, questioned him about the charge: "Father, only men in arms—not women and children?" Hamilton replied, "All, all! Kill all! Nits make lice!"[29]

George Rogers Clark, Hamilton's chief adversary, openly admitted his hatred for all Indians. In 1779, General John Sullivan moved against the Iroquois after making the toast, "Civilization or death to all American savages!"[30] Even after the war, the deepness of the animosity toward Indians was underscored when, in March 1782, militiamen tomahawked to death ninety-six unresisting Indian Christians at Gnadenhutten, Pennsylvania. It was a depraved action that finally drew criticism from many white Pennsylvanians.[31] Nonetheless, even humanitarians began to question whether Indians could be civilized. The most brutal imagery of Indian savagery was more widely accepted than ever.

So, the end of the American Revolution did not bring peace on the frontier, but rather created greater doubt that there was a way to resolve the great cultural gulf between whites and Native inhabitants. Reformers like David Schuyler Bogart argued that prejudice was key to the troubles with Indians, but suggested that "to exterminate Prejudice from the mind appears to be next to an impossibility."[32] Unfortunately, he proved to be right. And the literary genre most influential in shaping white attitudes embraced the view of implacable and unchangeable savagery as the "nature" of Indians. The Western linear way of seeing limited the capacity of even the most favorably disposed white observers to imagine that the gulf between Native and whites could be bridged. Lost entirely was the evidence of Native adaptability culturally, economically, and politically. Also lost were the tribal differences in culture and response, in favor of a collective "Indian." Regardless of tribe or disposition, all Native peoples were personified as "Indians," which was synonymous with carnage, brutality, and evil.[33]

During the years under the Articles of Confederation, neither the central government (if it could be called that) nor the state governments were able to control the push of settlers into "the Middle Ground" beyond the Appalachians or to suppress Native resistance. In fact, the most dramatic feature of those years was the continuing variety, vitality, and compromise of Indian resistance and accommodation. At the very moment that many reformers were dismissing the possibility of change, Indian adaptation, collaboration, and acculturation were growing. The possibility of compromise—that middle ground—was even stronger. But, tribes and alliances refused to acknowledge defeat, while white obstinacy and the continuing flow of settlers insured ongoing conflict.[34]

The situation was exacerbated by a flood of settlers into the trans-Appalachian West in a great arc from Kentucky into the Ohio country, west to the Mississippi, and north to Canada. This vast region became the "dark and bloody ground" that consolidated what Peter Silver has called the "anti-Indian sublime," a rhetoric of conquest expressed in a vast popular literature that defined Native character, behavior, and warfare as savage in the worst possible extremes. Silver argues that the anti-Indian fervor reflected

> . . . the priorities of the increasing numbers of people who lived on the receding border of Indian country. Anti-Indianism's rise was the result not of a realistic calculation of the national interest but of a vacuum of policies and power at the federal level. Amid popular demands that vacuum came to be filled by dreams of Indian treachery and American suffering—dreams that always returned to the prospect of new lands, and even new republics in the Ohio country.[35]

The chaos of the 1780s combined with the impotence of government at every level to control events persuaded a growing number of government leaders that the management of Indian affairs had to be centrally located at the national level and that a more humane and rational approach had to be found. In 1787, Henry Knox, Secretary of War under both the Articles of Confederation and during Washington's presidency under the new Constitution, warned the country that unless something was done, the treatment of American Indians would "fix a stain on the national reputation of America."[36]

Continental Congress and the Northwest Ordinance

One of the goals of the Continental Congress was to provide a model for the distribution of land in the Ohio country. Reports and laws related to this process also revealed a change of tone. The Northwest Ordinance of 1787 promised that "The utmost good faith shall always be observed towards the Indians, their lands and property shall never be taken from them without their consent; and in their property, rights and liberty, they never shall be invaded or disturbed, unless in just and lawful wars authorised by Congress, but laws founded in justice and humanity shall from time to time be made, for preventing wrongs being done to them, and for preserving peace and friendship with them."[37]

In July 1788, Secretary Knox railed against "the white inhabitants who have so flagitiously stained the American name." Knox came to the conclusion that "agreements based on the right of conquest did not work and that adherence to such a policy would continually endanger the peace of the frontier."[38] He sought a fair treaty system, and argued in 1789, "The Indians being the prior occupants possess the right of the soil. It cannot be taken from them unless by their free consent, or by the right of conquest in case of a just war. To dispossess them on any other principle, would be a gross violation of the fundamental laws of nature, and of that distributive justice which is the glory of a nation."[39] He advocated a return to the British approach of purchasing "the right of the soil" from the Indians.

President Washington embraced Knox's approach, and in the Trade and Intercourse Act of 1790 sought to prevent preemption of Indian lands. Knox and Washington were doubtlessly sincere in their desire both to treat Indians fairly and to prevent white preemption of Indian land, but their language within the laws emphasized the Indians' "right of occupancy" rather than ownership. Despite the concerns of Knox, however, the assumption of the Doctrine of Discovery adhered in their texts as well and would be reflected in the policies of Thomas Jefferson, himself an outspoken advocate of means to preserve Indian rights and American integrity.[40] There was throughout a sense of inevitability in the minds of authorities whose plans focused more on making dispossession less painful—and more legally sound—than on ending it altogether.

Men like Knox, Washington, and Jefferson were disturbed by the unrestrained preemption of western lands that seemed impossible to control. Washington described the settlers invading Indian lands as "a parcel of banditti whose actions are a disgrace to human nature." They were called "savages . . . our own white Indians," "semi-savages," and "the most abandoned, malicious, deceitful, plundering, horse-thieving rascals on the continent . . . the most vile and abandoned criminals." The West had become "a grand reservoir for the scum of the Atlantic states."[41]

Two problems complicated the task of dealing with the settler migration. The first was that it was impossible to control. Whatever the designs of the government for an ordered and "legal" process, the numbers swelled so that by 1800, whites outnumbered Indians in the Ohio country eight to one.[42] The invasion simply could not be stopped. The other problem was the plain fact that, while government officials and policy makers deplored the preemption, their ultimate goal was secure title to

Indian lands. The means of securing the land was deplorable, but the end was something they really desired.[43]

Remarkably, though, despite the settler migrations into the Northwest Territory, Indians sustained their resistance with remarkable success, holding their ground by a variety of strategies until the end of the War of 1812. The efforts of Tenkswatawa and Tecumseh, the charismatic Shawnee brothers who sought to forge a multitribal alliance, again brought the possibility of a genuine pan-Indian resistance. But Tenkswatawa, the Shawnee prophet, lost credibility after the Battle of Tippecanoe. Tecumseh tried to rebuild the alliance, but his death at the Battle of Thames in 1813 was more the result of British incompetence than of Native failure. His dream died with him. Resistance did not end there, however. Not until after the Massacre at Bad Axe in 1832 in the Black Hawk War, did all resistance collapse.[44] Only then could the process of removal west be completed. That meant that the tribes of the Northwest had resisted American expansion for close to seventy years. With removal largely accomplished by 1840, it had taken two hundred forty years for the Anglo-American conquest of North America to reach the Mississippi River.[45]

Policy of Removal

The transition to a policy of removal began during Thomas Jefferson's administration. The idea was simple enough. Indians should be relocated on lands beyond the press of white settlement. It was given a great boost in 1823 with the Supreme Court decision in *Johnson v. McIntosh*. In this landmark decision, the Doctrine of Discovery was affirmed as the cornerstone of American law insofar as Native rights were concerned. Chief Justice John Marshall held that the European nation "discovering" land in the New World had exclusive rights to claim Indian lands. Indigenous people had no superior, natural law-based claims to American soil. The acceptance of the Doctrine of Discovery was a crucial factor in American law for dealing with indigenous peoples.[46]

Marshall attempted to back away from some of his conclusions in *Johnson v. McIntosh* in the later cases of the *Cherokee Nation v. Georgia* and *Worcester v. Georgia* where he sought to limit the powers of removal. In *Worcester*, Marshall backed away from the Doctrine of Discovery, arguing that the "right given by discovery" was not absolute. He said that "It gave exclusive right to purchase, but did not found that right on a denial of the right of the possessor to sell." Viewed in this manner, the rights of individuals and states were limited but not the rights of Native tribes. Andrew

Jackson ignored this ruling, specifically declaring *Worcester* to be wrong, and in the cases of *Mitchel v. United States* (1835) and *United States v. Fernandez* (1836), the original formulation in *McIntosh* was reaffirmed.[47] As a result the controlling legal perspective in American Indian law remains the view fostered in *Johnson v. McIntosh*. It remains to this day the basis of American law with respect to Indian peoples. Native Americans had no unqualified sovereignty over their lands or status as independent nations. The tribes were "domestic dependent nations." In other words, American Indians were proclaimed by the court to be the wards of the United States government.

The treaty system would continue, in spite of Andrew Jackson's opposition to it, but what were negotiated were rights of occupancy, not sovereignty. Thus, the Western way of seeing came to control everything in American law. Alexis de Toqueville, the wise French observer of American life, remarked that the conduct of the United States toward its indigenous people "was inspired by the most chaste affection for legal formalities." What was missing, he noted, was "good faith." As a result, "It is impossible to destroy men with more respect to the laws of humanity."[48]

CHAPTER 3

THE BITTER CONUNDRUM

AT HEART, THE VIOLENT process between white men and red that unfolded in the United States was less about race, or even savagery, than it was about land. Savagery was an image generated by the need to rationalize the taking of the land. Legal forms that justified "the Right of Conquest" provided the means that supported the American claim that taking the land was a "right." John Quincy Adams presented a surprisingly consistent view of white attitudes in 1820, when he wrote, "But what is the right of a huntsman of the forest of a thousand miles, over which he has accidentally ranged in quest of prey?" This sentence alone contained many assumptions about the differences between Anglo-Americans and Indians and their relative values. But he drove home the point by asking, "Shall the exuberant bosom of the common mother, amply adequate to the nourishment of millions, be claimed exclusively by a few hundreds of her offspring?"[1]

This would be a consistent view, reiterated over and over again in the nineteenth century. Land not "used" for agriculture or other development of natural resources, land not "settled" and opened for "development" and the growth of towns and roads and civilization could rightly be taken for such "higher" purposes. Progress could not and should not be held back to maintain reserves for "savages" and their backward ways. John Marshall insisted that despite his own views of the natural rights of Indians based upon the "abstract principles of justice," the Doctrine of Discovery was the law of the land. He wrote, "However extravagant the pretension of converting the discovery of an inhabited country into conquest may appear; if the principle has been asserted in the first instance, and afterwards sustained; if a country has been acquired and held under it; if the property of the great mass of the community originates in it, it becomes the law of the land, and cannot be rejected by Courts of Justice."[2]

Forced Inculturation of Indians

The acquisition of the Louisiana Purchase by treaty between France and the United States in 1803, without the participation of any of the tribes who actually occupied the lands, underscored the legal presumptions of whites—the right to cede by France and the right to acquire by the United States without the consent of Native inhabitants was unquestioned. With that vast new mass of land claimed by international treaty, the United States looked beyond the Mississippi River and found a basis for a policy of removal of tribes east of the river to new "homes" in the West. At the beginning, this seemed to be a workable alternative to the only choices given to Indians—resist and die or assimilate and disappear.[3]

Even that was a chimera of wishful thinking. Alexis de Toqueville saw through it even before the policy makers had completed the task of removal:

> From whatever angle one regards the destinies of the North American natives, one sees nothing but irremediable ills; if they remain savages, they are driven along before the march of progress; if they try to become civilized, contact with more-civilized people delivers them over to oppression and misery. If they go on wandering in the wilderness, they perish; if they attempt to settle, they perish just the same. They cannot gain enlightenment except with European help, and the approach of the Europeans corrupts them and drives them back toward barbarism. So long as they are left in their solitudes, they refuse to change their mores, and there is no time left to do this, when at last they are constrained to desire it.[4]

Even Toqueville's rhetoric, though sympathetic to the Indians, was choked with the assumptions of the linear way of seeing and the judgments about indigenous people that came with it. The entire debate was infused by an ethnocentric world view already more than a thousand years old, embedded in Western thought and government like DNA. To have found anyone within Western society who did not accept the assumptions of the higher claim of the United States to the land would have been virtually impossible, even among the most sincere and dedicated reformers, including those who deplored the "forcible civilization schemes" of the government and the civilization plans of the reformers. In fairness, policy makers consistently sought ways to make the process easier. They sought an "alternative to extinction."[5] But they could find no way that did not involve the forced enculturation of Indians. The challenge was to do so fairly. Their linear way of seeing limited them to their own notions of progress.

They could not escape their conviction that the Indians' only hope was to embrace the principles of civilization. This meant changing their ways of life consistent with white views of work, language, values, and religion. Federal policy took shape in the hands of men schooled in the principles of the Enlightenment. They believed in the common origin of all men, in a certain natural equality, and in the perfectability of men. They did not argue an innate racial inferiority. They believed, rather, that human beings passed naturally through stages from savagism to barbarism to civilization. They rejected the notion that Indians were locked into a permanent savage state. They believed that as the environment changes, cultures change, until at last, civilization would be the logical inheritance of all men. And they saw themselves as agents of that process.

What mattered, then, was where particular societies fit on the linear scale of civilization. The goal of policy had to be to promote the civilization of the tribes. Trade, the introduction of agriculture, the promotion of private property ownership, education, and Christianization would be the instruments of change because the yeoman freeholder was the foundation of civilization as they understood it. Not only did the ideals of the Enlightenment and of Protestant Christianity support this position, but the emergence of "scientific racism" in the nineteenth century reinforced it and strengthened its rationale.[6]

By then, other alternatives were impossible. Even if policy makers could have closed the West to all settlement and avoided all trade and social interchange with the Indians, creating a vast enclave where the natives could live without contact, too much had already happened for such a plan to work. First, it would have been inconsistent with white Americans' vision of progress. Civilizing Indians was, for them, a positive goal. Moreover, although some of the tribes were only then encountering whites in person, changes had already taken place within their societies as the result of white presence in North America that could not be undone. The only way to have insured a different outcome was for the Europeans to have stayed in Europe. So the well-intended, well-meaning plans to protect Indian rights and lives were doomed to failure by a mind-set that could not escape its assumptions.[7]

The good intentions of policy makers were consistent over time in their commitment to the transition of Indians to a new way of life based upon the "Great Values." The policy makers and reformers underestimated the task, but they gave little thought to whether or not it was right. Their Eurocentric world view and their ethnocentric view of indigenous people blinded them to the reasons policies failed and to the arrogance of their belief that Native cultures were the great impediments to a satisfactory solution to the "Indian question."

Salvation and Civilization

Anglo-Americans seemed incapable of recognizing the value of cultures and beliefs other than their own. In the language of Protestant Christianity, Indians had to be "born again" as civilized men, not through some instantaneous conversion but through a guided transition to a new way of life. The intent of reformers was benevolent; they did not see themselves as the agents of extermination but of salvation. Their ability to confront the issues was trapped by their world view. Indeed, from their point of view, they were offering Indians their most precious gifts—salvation and civilization.[8]

Even if, by some miracle, an alternative could have been found by policy makers and reformers, its prospects for success would have been almost nil. The federal government never proposed extermination as official policy. Policy makers could not have comprehended the implications of the modern concept of "ethnic cleansing" given their nineteenth-century mind-set.[9] They passed Trade and Intercourse Acts to manage relationships. They passed laws against the preemption of Indian lands. They stationed troops along overland routes to act as a barrier between emigrants and Indians. The primary reasons these efforts to control the process failed had little to do with policy.

The first reason was that whatever differences existed between those who sought a fair Indian policy and those who demanded swift military conquest, the vast majority of Americans shared a view of Indians as backward, uncivilized, and heathen. The differences between them related to how "backward Natives" should be treated. Some thought they were redeemable; some thought they were beyond redemption. Some thought they could be saved through education and Christianity; some thought they were hopelessly savage and should be treated like wild animals. Some thought they could be helped; some thought they were beyond help. Some placed their faith in forced assimilation; some favored extinction as the only sure solution. But, at base, white Americans saw Indians as less than themselves by almost any measure they used.

Most Americans' views of American Indians were not based upon a consciously developed ideology. They did not need scientific proofs of racial inferiority, although they might use "scientific racism" or rely on popular beliefs as means of justifying their prejudices. They simply assumed that they knew what Indians were like, a priori. Indians were far behind on the scale of progress. They wore skins, not waistcoats and gowns. They did not have written languages. They had superstitions, not religion. They painted their faces, tortured, murdered, plundered, and killed innocent women and children. These characterizations provided the justification for extermination. Reformers did not so much debunk the assumptions as see them as things to be changed. But the core view of both rested on the same mythical foundations. Condescension, paternalism, and racial superiority were the common responses, however sincere the desire to help might be or maniacal the blood lust became.[10]

Another more practical obstacle stood in the way. Territorial expansion was a tenet of national policy. Although the laws and treaties were filled with assurances that Indian rights would be protected, the greater goal was the continued growth of the country. The whole debate over Indian policy was about the best way to deal with Indians on the path to national development. No one assumed a static state or a permanent "Indian country." This became more evident as decades passed and political conditions changed. The populist shift toward Andrew Jackson's common man gave new influence to the westering settlers. "The doctrines of agrarian democracy ... held that the social cement of the republic must be the self-interest of its citizens," Richard Slotkin suggests. "In economic terms, this meant that each citizen must be possessed of sufficient property to guarantee the subsistence of himself and his family, or must at least have a credible prospect of attaining that level of economic independence through his labor."[11] The myth of the frontiersman thus shifted from the troublemakers of which Washington lamented and emerged as the archetype of the New American. With this view came a fear that the closing of the frontier would pose a serious threat to American democracy itself.

"Manifest Destiny"

America was changing in other ways as well. With the growth of eastern cities, the settlement of the cis-Mississippi territories so recently the scene of wars with eastern tribes, the development of a new manufacturing economy, and continuing population growth, the conviction that expansion must continue was reinforced. Railroads and new forms of industry also loomed on the horizon. "Manifest Destiny" was already embraced in practice even before John O'Sullivan proclaimed "the right of our manifest destiny to overspread and possess the whole of the continent that Providence has given us for the development of the great experiment of liberty and federated self-government entrusted to us."[12]

While the ideological assumptions and political purposes of Manifest Destiny were questioned by many, the notion of an America that stretched from sea to sea was assumed by people of many persuasions. Indeed, the growing sectionalism that eventually led to a Civil War focused less on slavery in the beginning than on opening lands west of the Mississippi to settlement. In the beginning, the debate over slavery focused on white issues and their effect on white men. "Popular Sovereignty," "Free Soil," and "the dignity of labor," were all code phrases in the debate over national expansion as certainly as they were expressions of positions on slavery.

The primary reason for the failure of policy in its efforts to respect and protect Indian rights over and over again was not so much ideological, philosophical, or mythological. It lay, instead, in the sheer numbers of American settlers. Whatever the methods devised, policy makers could not deliver on Jefferson's promise that Indian lands would never be "invaded or disturbed" without the consent of the tribes. While lawmakers and bureaucrats debated, settlers moved west. Once settlers decided that a place was worth having, there was no stopping them. And when land was overrun and baptized with blood, the army moved in and new treaties were made, as unenforceable as the ones before them until, at last, settlers understood that Indian policy was impotent, however well-intentioned it was. What happened seemed inexorable, inevitable, as certain as the seasons.

The United States was developing a "collective identity" for the first time that carried with it an ideology of "an existing territorial state" and "a missionary sense of cultural superiority." The social order was rigid and divided at the same time. Both in its new populism and new oligarchy, the new order was presented not as political theory but as experiential reality. Making this possible required a system of order for all of the national territory. The Northwest Ordinance provided the model. Jurgen Osterhammel argues that the new system "translated sovereignty claims into property issues, territorial interests into economic interests, and in doing so bound together public and private interests in the acquisition of land."[13] Then, ironically, the "democratization" of the United States led to more aggressive policies toward indigenous people.

The result was a mind-set, amounting to a national consensus concerning who the Indian was. The choice of the singular term "Indian" was deliberate. It indicated the box that Native Americans of all tribes, predilections, and cultures had been

38

dumped into. It was easier to deal with one image than face the reality of diversity among indigenous peoples. White Americans might disagree on the questions of how the Indian should be treated, of whether he could be "saved," or which policies ought to be followed. Some were generous and hopeful and mindful of dearly held values. Some were ready to exterminate the "encircling foe." Some simply expected the Indian to vanish over time. Some embraced such things as the "New American School," phrenology, craniology, and the Bible, in finding justifications for their views.[14] But almost without exception, Americans saw the "Indian" as a "problem," innately inferior, that stood in the way of progress and destiny and had only two choices—change or die. The "savage other" remained intact. Few lessons had been learned; many prejudices had been reinforced. And the national self-awareness guaranteed that little would change.

Sweet Medicine and the Cheyenne Nation

Half a continent away tribes like the Cheyennes and Arapahos were not aware of—or prepared to understand—the implications of these changes for them. So far, they had been spared the direct pressure that other people had experienced. Their lives had already been altered by the presence of Europeans as the result of pressures on them from other tribes closer to whites. From their homes near the Great Lakes, they dispersed westward for more than a century before they reached the area of the Black Hills. They had been masters of evasion, adaptation, diplomacy, and change. By the time they acquired horses and abandoned their horticultural past, the Cheyennes were more properly a nation rather than a tribe. They had been brought together and given unity by social organization, a political system of remarkable design and foresight, common moral principles, and spiritual institutions.[15]

This achievement was largely the work of the prophet Sweet Medicine, the great culture-hero of the *Tsistsistas*. Some say that the prophet lived among them four lifetimes, teaching them what they must do and how they must live, but he was a real person and a political genius.[16] At *Noaha-vose,* or Bear Butte (near present-day Sturgis, South Dakota), Sweet Medicine received *Mahuts,* the Four Sacred Arrows, and with them the means of unifying the nation. Noaha-vose was the Cheyennes' Sinai, Sweet Medicine their Moses. Sweet Medicine saw the potential dangers of the new horse culture insofar as social and political unity was concerned. The various *manhao* (residence bands) would be scattered for much of the year, which would increase the possibility of division and weakness. To prevent this, he created the

Council of Forty-Four, including the chiefs of the various manhao and four Old Man Chiefs who would make decisions for the nation. These chiefs were often called "peace chiefs," and their emblems of office were pipes, pipe bags, and a single eagle feather, pointing right, in their hair.[17]

Sweet Medicine also created the military societies as a means of binding the manhao together. Membership in the societies came from all of the different residence groups. These soldier societies maintained discipline at tribal gatherings, ceremonies, and hunts, watched over the people, and provided the fighting forces. By recognizing the authority of soldier chiefs in matters of war, the tribal—or national unity—was strengthened. No soldier chief could be a member of the Council of Forty-Four, so that a division of authority existed, designed to maintain unity.[18] This structure was also held together by the four Sacred Arrows, two of which were "man arrows" to kill their enemies and two of which were "buffalo arrows" to provide the resources to sustain the people, and by the Sun Dance.

At some point in their movements the Tsistsistas encountered a related group, the Suthaio. The Suthaio brought with them the Sacred Buffalo Hat, given to them by the holy man, Erect Horn. It had powers for the Suthaio, similar to those of the Sacred Arrows for the Tsistsistas. In time the two groups were consolidated to form the Cheyennes, the Suthaio were admitted to the council as one of the manhao, and the sacred objects and rites of both were absorbed by all. In this way, the Cheyennes followed a new life consistent with the ways of Maheo, the All-Father.[19]

The nineteenth century found the Cheyennes closely allied with the Arapahos who preceded them into the area and who were skilled traders who knew the lands and tribes to the south. What attracted both were the great grasslands of the high plains. They also renewed their association with the Lakota, even then extending themselves on the Northern Plains.[20] Together, the Lakota, Cheyennes, and Arapahos forged a powerful alliance, securing a region from the Missouri River to the headwaters of the Smoky Hill and Republican Rivers. This coalition also established economic and military dominance over common foes—the Crows, the Utes, and the Pawnees.[21]

The Cheyennes and Arapahos extended the influence south. The Arapahos crossed the North Platte early in the new century, and soon most of the Cheyennes were located between the North Platte and the South Platte, although some remained more closely aligned with the Lakota in the north. In 1820, good hunting between the South Platte and the Arkansas, and new sources of white trade goods on the Arkansas, drew the Cheyennes further south.[22] Their presence was strong

40

enough that the Kiowas retreated below the Arkansas under pressure. The arrival of the Bent brothers (William and Charles) and Ceran St. Vrain on the Arkansas in the 1820s strengthened the Cheyenne and Arapaho hold on trade, and victories over the Kiowa and Comanche led eventually to a grand council in 1840 in which a peace was made that was never broken. That meant that the plains from West Texas to the Canadian line were dominated by a single coalition.[23]

Consequences of the Discovery of Gold

Then, with the Cheyennes and Arapahos at the pinnacle of their power, everything changed. The 1840s saw increased migration on the overland routes west, accelerated at the end of the decade by the land cessions of the Treaty of Guadalupe Hidalgo, followed almost at once by the discovery of gold in California. Suddenly, the Santa Fe Trail and the Overland Trail were filled with tens of thousands of settlers. In a matter of ten years, the essentials of the horse culture were seriously threatened. In the 1830s, travelers wrote about the tree-lined creeks and rivers; in the 1850s, travelers complained that there was not enough wood to build fires. Without the watershed provided by trees, water dried up. Grass was overgrazed and dry so that forage for horse herds and wild game became scarce. The overland routes were not roads or trails, but swaths of land sometimes miles wide that changed the lay of the land and interrupted the migration of the buffalo. In a remarkably short time, three hundred thousand settlers took up residence in California. Oregon was filling up. Few of the settlers were stopping on the Great Plains, but many were advancing west in Kansas. Just "passing through" devastated the environment.[24]

In 1851, the United States government called a great treaty council at Fort Laramie. Some of the tribes were intimidated by the Lakota-Cheyenne-Arapaho combine and did not attend. A few others left. But the great problem lay in the treaty itself. It was not a traditional treaty of cession. Its primary purpose was to define the ranges of the various tribes, so that the government would be able to treat in the future with particular tribes for particular lands. Since the plains culture was not based upon land ownership, but upon control of lands that shifted with herd movements and military pressures, this was an almost impossible thing for the tribes to understand. To make matters worse, the tribes were asked to select single leaders to speak for them. This too was outside the tribes' experience.

Nevertheless, the treaty makers got what they wanted with mountains of "gifts" and promises of lasting peace. The government created a paper demarcation of power on the plains. For example, the lands between the North Platte and the Arkansas were recognized as the domain of the Cheyennes and Arapahos, in spite of the continuing presence of other tribes, from Lakota on shared lands below the Platte to Kiowas who still hunted along the Arkansas in the South. Utes, Shoshoni, Pawnees, and Crows also ventured onto these lands from east and west in search of horses and buffalo. Nor did the treaty take into account the Cheyennes who ranged as far north as the Powder River country.[25]

Perhaps inevitably the settler migrations led to conflicts with the tribes, particularly the Lakota and Cheyennes. The Cheyennes managed to stay clear of the troubles until 1856-1857, when a series of incidents led to a military expedition against them commanded by Colonel Edwin V. Sumner. At Solomon's Fork, the army routed the Cheyennes.[26] Badly shaken, those from the northern manhao fell back to the secluded reaches in the north, while the southern manhao, more directly in the path of settlement, moved closer to the Arkansas and sought accommodation. An internal schism was developing within the nation, still largely unrecognized.

Then, gold was discovered in Colorado. Within a year, 100,000 settlers poured onto the central plains, along the Platte River route and even through the center of Cheyenne lands along what would become known as the Smoky Hill Trail. These settlers were not passing through. They saw their fortunes on the Front Range of the Rockies, in the very heart of Cheyenne and Arapaho land. Weakly, the government pointed out that the lands being preempted were on unceded Indian land. And still the settlers came.[27]

CHAPTER 4

METHODISTS AND THE AMERICAN INDIAN

Early Methodists in America

AMERICAN METHODISM AND THE United States of America grew up together, nor was it just a matter of chronological parallels. Their common roots were in England, but both colonial Methodists and Anglo-colonial government were transformed by experience in ways that maintained vital connections to the past, yet took surprising directions in both beliefs and forms that eventually led to important separations in thought and action.

John Wesley was the inspiration and theologian for Methodism both in England, where he lived all but two years of his life, and in America; but his personal experience in America, while profoundly important in his own spiritual development, was not what he expected. He and his brother Charles sailed for Georgia, in 1735, at the invitation of the colony's founder, James Edward Oglethorpe, who wished him to serve as minister to the colonists and as missionary to the Indians. "My chief motive for going is the hope of saving my own soul," Wesley wrote. "I hope to learn the true sense of the gospel of Christ by preaching it to the heathen."[1] The journey to Georgia proved to be a personal test of faith for Wesley. He met but never preached a single sermon to the "Georgian Indians." From the reports of others, he described them as "being none of them able to give any rational account of themselves." He wrote:

> They are inured to hardship of all kinds, and surprisingly patient of pain. But as they have no letters, so they have no religion, no laws, no civil government. Nor have they any kings or princes, properly speaking, their "micos" or headmen having no power either to command or punish, no man obeying them any farther than he pleases. So that everyone doth what is right in his own eyes; and if it appears wrong to his neighbor the person aggrieved usually steals on the other unawares, and

43

shoots him, scalps him, or cuts off his ears; having only two short rules of proceeding—to do what he will, and what he can.

They are likewise all, except (perhaps) the Choctaws, gluttons, drunkards, thieves, dissemblers, liars. They are implacable, unmerciful; murderers of fathers, murderers of mothers, murderers of their own children. . . .

Wesley described several different tribes and their various "qualities." Of the Creeks, he noted, "They are more exquisite dissemblers than the rest of their countrymen. They know not what friendship or gratitude means. They show no inclination to learn anything, but least of all Christianity, being full as opiniated [*sic*] of their own parts and wisdom as either modern Chinese or ancient Roman."[2] He made these judgments and more not by observation but by conversation with others who "knew" the various tribes. His mission "to preach to the heathen" was stillborn, and his personal life was so tortured that he returned to England in 1737, more uncertain of his faith than when he left. "I went to convert the Indians," he would write, "but, O! who shall convert me!"[3]

A romanticized view of John Wesley preaching to the Indians of Georgia during his brief mission to the colony. Note that by the time this romanticized image was prepared, his supposed congregation had become the universal "Indian" in the mold of the Plains tribes. (General Commission on Archives and History of The United Methodist Church, Drew University, Madison, New Jersey)

The experience proved transformative for him and for the church. George White-field, a friend of the Wesleys, who arrived in Georgia simultaneously with their departure, was much kinder to him, than John Wesley was to himself. Whitefield proclaimed Wesley's contribution to America "inexpressible."[4] He returned to England briefly himself, where he led revivals and drew the wrath of many Anglicans, with his simple admonition, "Ye must be born again." He returned to the colonies in 1739 to begin a year-long crusade, beginning the "Great Awakening" that changed the religious culture of much of Colonial North America.[5] In the meantime, Wesley worked to refine his own understanding of the gospel and to establish within the Anglican Church, his Methodist societies.

Despite the growth of Methodism in both England and the colonies, its message was designed for white men, both churched and unchurched, and the eighteenth century passed with no direct Methodist mission to American Indians. The Church did struggle over the increasing conflict between homeland and colonies. In spite of his disagreements with the Church of England, Wesley insisted that kings ruled by divine right and that Christians should be loyal to the king as well as to the church. After the Seven Years War, as resistance mounted against English rule in the colonies, Wesley insisted that Methodists should remain loyal to their king. Life, liberty, and the pursuit of happiness, that Thomas Jefferson would claim to be "unalienable rights," were to Wesley the gifts of God.[6]

For a time, Methodism faltered in some areas because of the tension between loyalty to governing authority as preached by Wesley and other English Methodists, including the elders sent from England to minister to American churches, and the revolutionary attitudes of many of their congregations. Wesley himself was conflicted initially about what should be done. He argued with English leaders that the colonists had a just cause while insisting that "Those who fear God, honour the King." He feared that the republicanism taking shape in America would "unhinge all government . . . and plunge every nation into anarchy." He spoke of American "sin" and English "righteousness" in the American Revolution.[7]

The tension between the Enlightenment thought of John Locke and Adam Smith that influenced John Wesley and the enthusiasm of the revivalism more common in America, contributed to internal divisions. Thomas Rankin, Wesley's chief assistant in America, and Francis Asbury, the leading spokesman for Methodism in America, both had British sympathies. Asbury understood the American cause, but he saw politics as a distraction from the mission of the church.[8] Neutrality became a trademark for Methodism, and some members were persecuted by their neighbors because of it. With the end of the Revolution, American Methodists took bold new steps. In 1784, they formed the Methodist Episcopal Church, separate from John Wesley and the British Methodists.[9]

"New" American Methodists

The new American Methodists adopted a system of circuits for ministry and created annual conferences to pass the rules by which the Church would be governed. One of Francis Asbury's remarkable achievements as the leader of American Methodism was to maintain its commitment to organization and leadership—and to method—while also embracing enthusiasm and the direct intervention of the Spirit.[10] This mixture of elitism and populism ironically created a tension that proved to be the key to Methodist success. The Church combined personal piety and practicality that thrived through camp meetings and circuit riders and sustained itself by close organization and control. One mechanism was "the class meeting." Class meetings were small group meetings that met regularly, not for Bible study but "to watch over one another in love." Through this process, particularly in areas without regular pastors, the class meetings raised funds and monitored the members' spiritual growth and conduct.[11] It became another powerful tool in the growth of the Church. This admixture of revivalism, class meetings, and organization would prove critical as the Methodist Episcopal Church moved west with the nation.[12]

In 1787, John Wesley confessed to Francis Asbury his continuing "concern" for "the progeny of Shem" (Wesley's reference to American Indians) who seemed "quite forgotten." He wrote, "Does it not seem as if God had designated all the Indian nations not for reformation, but destruction? How many millions of them have already died in their sins! Will neither God nor man have compassion upon these outcasts of men?" He lamented that it was impossible for mere men to help the Indians, but he asked, "Is it too hard for God?" He urged Asbury to "Pray ye likewise [to] the Lord of the harvest, and he will send out more labourers into His harvest."[13] But the attitude of American Methodists remained one largely of indifference.

At the end of the Revolution, more than 100,000 white settlers lived west of the Appalachians in that great arc of territory still the heart of the contest between the new nation and the Native tribes resisting its advance. There, in that great mass of settlers, was the future of Methodism and the settlers' hope of salvation. The settlers gave little thought to Native rights, nor the Methodists to Native souls. Methodist ministers shared the experiences of the settlers and often expressed the same views about the dangers and character of American Indians. Methodists embraced the idea that westward migration was inevitable and right. They believed that Anglo-Americans would develop the new lands and, eventually, civilize its indigenous inhabitants. And they saw great hope for the social development of the West in the Christian tradition.[14]

Spreading Scriptural Holiness

When the American Methodist movement was organized as a church at the Christmas Conference at Baltimore in 1784, a question was raised about Section I of the first *Discipline:* "What may we reasonably believe to be God's Design in raising up the Preachers called Methodists?" The answer was, "To reform the Continent, and to spread scriptural holiness over these Lands."[15] The brash egalitarianism of Methodist circuit riders saw all persons, of every class, under the condemnation of God without redemption. That included American Indians. The circuit riders who formed the majority of the Methodist preachers focused on salvation rather than ethics or principles, and even those who were more conversant in the underlying theological principles did not challenge the basic institutions of the times.[16]

Methodism was a systematic, disciplined faith, based on Bible reading, attention to the inner life as well as moral behavior; but in the beginning Methodists' individualistic beliefs held that if men's souls were saved, social change would follow. The object, then, was to change individuals. Specific social reforms were not emphasized. Questions of public morality were matters of individual moral regeneration, not political action.[17] "The Methodists preached a message of the common man and used the common man to preach it."[18] Most were, as one author puts it, both "untutored" and "uncultured."[19] While this had advantages in gaining the acceptance of their congregations at revivals and meeting houses, it also meant, practically, that Methodist circuit riders shared both the experiences and at least some of the prejudices of the settlers. They were itinerants, which meant that they did not put down roots, but they did relate to the hardships and the viewpoints of settlers. And that included their views of the Indians.[20]

Thomas Hinde, an influential Methodist preacher in the Ohio country, praised western Methodists for their role in the "violent contest" with the Indians. At the same time, he condemned white settlers responsible for atrocities against the Indians. He saw a great link between civilization and conversion, "even among our American Indians." He wrote, "Dost thou not know the order of grace and of providence? The 'best wine is kept to the last.' Here are displays of heaven's favours. And when the glad tidings of 'great joy' which shall be sounded through all the earth shall have passed this great theater, it will return in swelling waves of glory from the west to the east."[21] As Jeffrey Williams notes, the nation was critical to God's plan: "Christianity followed the spread of the pioneers to create a new empire bathed in vital religion."[22]

There was, though, a great fear that grew over time and helped to spark the Second Great Awakening. It was the danger of primitivism—a fear that westering settlers might sink into barbarism, that the wilderness would drag them down into the savagery they despised in the Indians. The belief was based on a simple premise. Once whites left the more settled areas and entered into "unorganized" country, they also left behind the social, political, economic, and moral institutions that provided order. Effectively returned to a state of nature, settlers tended to depend upon themselves. Violence, disorder, and moral decline were consequences.[23]

This view was broadly shared by a number of denominations, and it remained a central concern well into the nineteenth century. As a result, the chief concern of missions on the moving frontier was for white settlers. Horace Bushnell, prominent minister and educator, summarized the view as late as 1847. He argued, forthrightly, citing the example of Micah from the Old Testament that "emigration, or a new settlement of the social state, involves a tendency to social decline." He described a "wild race of nomads roaming over the vast western territories of our land—a race without education, law, manners, or religion," but he was not speaking of Native Americans. A society, he said could not take its roots with it. The old roots of "local love" and "historic feeling" were left behind. Education faltered. As their tastes grew wild, "their resentments will grow violent and their enjoyments coarse. The salutary restraints of society being to a great extent, removed . . . they are likely even to look upon the indulgence of low vices and brutal pleasures, as the necessary garnish of their life of adventure."

He continued:

> Still we are rolling on from east to west, plunging into the wilderness, scouring across the great inland deserts and mountains to plant our habitations on the western ocean. Here again the natural tendencies of emigration toward barbarism, or social decline, are displayed, in signs that cannot be mistaken. The struggle through which we have passed, is continually repeating itself, under new modifications. We see the same experiment involving similar jeopardies; and we draw out of our own

48

experiences warnings to make us anxious, and encouragements to make us hopeful for our country—a double argument of fear and hope, to make us doubly faithful in our Christian efforts for its welfare.[24]

Bushnell singled out Methodists as having "a ministry admirably adapted, as regards their mode of action, to the new west—a kind of light artillery that God has organized, to pursue and overtake the fugitives that flee into the wilderness from his presence."[25] He not only praised their evangelism, but noted, as well, their enthusiasm for building colleges to sustain knowledge and learning. This mission against barbarism, he predicted, would lead to a time when "knowledge, virtue and religion, blending their dignity and their healthful power, have filled our great country with a manly and happy race of people, and the bands of a complete Christian commonwealth are seen to span the continent."[26] This report, published by the American Home Missionary Society, did not mention indigenous peoples, but it does provide insight into the priorities of evangelical Christians, priorities that were plainly political as well as religious.

On March 3, 1819, the Congress of the United States passed the "Civilization Bill" designed to prevent "the further decline and final extinction of the Indian tribes" and to introduce among the tribes "habits and arts of civilization." The law included an appropriation of $10,000 for the creation of schools.[27] On April 5, 1819, the Missionary Society of the Methodist Episcopal Church was organized, and the Society applied for funds to support schools. In 1820, the Methodist General Conference authorized the "establishment of Indian schools" pursuant to the recommendation of the Missionary Society.[28] The effort met with limited success. The more centrally organized Baptists and Presbyterians had an advantage over the Methodists' diverse organization. Consistently, the annual reports of various conferences revealed that conference missionary societies either failed to report to the Missionary Society or to the conferences.[29]

Several initiatives did take place in the 1820s, the most successful being among the Wyandots in the Ohio country, and those among the Cherokees, Choctaws, Chickasaws, and Creeks in the Southeast. Efforts were also made among the Shawnees, Delawares, Potawatomis, Mohawks, Oneidas, and a few other tribes. Methodists took pride in their efforts among "the terror of our day" as they classed Native people.[30] The approach was clearly assimilationist in design. The strategy included teaching piety and hard work, teaching "useful arts," redefining the roles of the sexes, teaching reading and writing, modifying culture by cutting men's hair, requiring them to wear Western clothing, changing their names, teaching the value of property directed ultimately to private ownership of land. No effort was made to understand Native ways, values, or beliefs; and Methodists had an added burden since their Indian ministries relied upon the same itinerant system as other congregations. This meant that ministers rarely remained with any group long enough to develop real empathy with them had they been so inclined.[31]

John Stewart and the Mission among the Wyandots

Interestingly, the mission among the Wyandots had been started on the Upper Sandusky in 1814-1815, by a man of mixed African and Indian ancestry named John Stewart. His biggest supporter among the Wyandots was William Walker, Sr., a white man who had been kidnapped by Delawares in Virginia at the age of eleven. He had married the daughter of a French trader and a Wyandot woman. Stewart struggled for a time, but in February 1817, he preached a sermon on the Last Judgment so eloquently that the Wyandots reacted like settlers at a camp meeting. Several chiefs and numerous others were converted on the spot.[32] Stewart was not licensed to preach as a Methodist until 1818, when the Ohio Conference officially approved a mission to the Wyandots. Bishop William McKendree was so impressed with Stewart's efforts that he collected funds to purchase a farm near the Wyandots for Stewart and his family.[33] He was soon joined by Moses Heckle as the result of Wyandot entreaties. In 1819, James Montgomery was appointed the first official missionary to the Indians.[34]

In 1821, James B. Finley followed and provided strong leadership. Most importantly, he had the support of many of the Wyandot leaders who believed Christianity and education offered them the best way to survive in the midst of white settlement. Finley eventually became a sub-agent to the Wyandots as well as a missionary. In 1825, the War Department promised the Wyandots, "Brother, your Great Father will never use force to drive you from your lands," but pressure for removal was already strong. Finley fought for his charges, but he came to see that his efforts would fail. Later, he would write, "Who can stop the march of the white population? Neither mountains, deserts, seas, rivers, nor poles. To talk, therefore of giving the Indian a country where he will be delivered from the advances and impositions of the lowest and worst class of our citizens, is chimerical."[35]

Finley did face opposition from traditionalists, but it was less prominent than in the days of John Stewart when the chief John Hicks had told Stewart:

I, for one, feel myself called upon to rise in the defense of the religion of my fathers. . . . No, my friend, your disclaiming so violently against the modes of worshipping the Great Spirit, is in my opinion, not calculated to benefit us as a nation; we are willing to receive good advice from you, but we are not willing to have the customs and institutions which have been kept sacred by our fathers, thus assailed and abused.[36]

The Wyandot experience proved to be a model that Methodists cited to prove their success. T. Scott Miyakawa has suggested that "the sympathy such frontier Methodists as McKendree and Finley had for the Indians stands out in sharp relief against the widespread western prejudice. The denomination as a whole pioneered in its concern for the Indians, and this interest was another influence on its growing social awareness."[37] His claim for the denomination seems generous in light of what happened. Men like Stewart, McKendree, and Finley proved exceptional, although there were other serious efforts, the most successful being missions in the Southeast, among tribes with significant groups that had chosen the way of acculturation already.[38]

Jason Lee and the Mission to Oregon

Perhaps the most ambitious missionary initiative by the Methodist Church came in 1832 when the General Conference charged the bishops "to extend, with all practicable dispatch, the aboriginal missions on our western and northwestern frontiers."[39] The specific region in question was the Oregon country, and the initiative was reported to be in response to four Flathead Indians, visiting "St. Louis, in search of the white man's God."[40] In July 1833, Jason Lee was appointed missionary to the Flatheads, although it soon became apparent that the mission field had far more tribes to contend with than the Flatheads alone. Lee was also disillusioned that the Indians did not seem to have the enthusiasm of the small party that visited St. Louis, but, rather, that both Indians and white traders in the region opposed the efforts. Only a remnant of the Flatheads remained, as the result of conflict with the Blackfoot. Lee was persistent, however. He established a mission at Willamette north of present-day Salem, Oregon, and proposed a patient plan to choose two men without families to "throw themselves into the nation," live among them, learn their language, and preach the gospel until the way opened to introduce schools, agriculture, and "the arts of civilized life."[41]

By 1838, the mission had been enlarged and its scope widened. Other missionaries had arrived as well, including Presbyterians Marcus Whitman and Henry H.

Spalding who worked among the Cayuse and Nez Perce.[42] They were determined in their labors, although Lee noted that both "Mr. W & Mr. S use highhanded measures with their people, and when they deserve it let them feel the lash."[43] Lee even felt that perhaps he had been too lax in his methods. Lee's requests for more assistance led some to criticize the mission as a cover for a plan of colonization. The church insisted that its only mission was the salvation of souls; but a party of fifty-one persons departed for Oregon in September 1839, the largest single missionary group from the United States up to that time.[44]

The Oregon mission's work was further complicated by the arrival of a French Canadian Catholic mission from Quebec and an increasing number of white settlers. What finally caused the greatest challenge to Lee's mission was financial. Lee was replaced in 1843. Two years later the *Christian Advocate* announced the liquidation of the secular work of the Oregon Mission.[45] Lee's work would continue to be criticized as more colonial in nature than evangelical. He himself wrote, "That the Indians are a scattered, periled, and deserted race, I am more and more convinced; for it does seem that unless the God of heaven undertake their cause, they must perish from off the face of the Earth, and their name be blotted out from under heaven. God grant that a remnant may be saved, as trophies of the Gospel of Christ, and a seed to serve him."[46]

In 1847, Marcus Whitman and his wife, Narcissa, who had never won the confidence of the people they were sent to serve because of their high-handed and paternalistic ways, were killed along with twelve others by Cayuse, who also carried off five men, eight women, and thirty-four children as captives.[47] This would be the beginning of a dark time in Oregon. Although the chiefs responsible turned themselves in and were subsequently hanged, the missionary bubble had burst, and many white settlers in the region openly demanded extermination.[48]

Indian Missionary Conference

Mission strategy was already changing by then for Methodists. The Removal Act had accomplished its purpose. In 1844, the General Conference established the Indian Mission Conference, the first conference designed specifically for Indians and allowing for Native preachers.[49] Three districts were created: the Cherokee, the Choctaw, and the "Kansas River." The bulk of the conference was located in the newly created Indian Territory, prepared for the removal of the "Civilized Tribes" of the Southeast and for other smaller groups.[50]

The exception was the Kansas River District, which crammed an amalgamation of tribes into a small space—Shawnee, Delaware, Peoria, Kickapoo, Potawatomie, and, eventually Wyandot—located in an area marked by the forks of the Missouri and Kansas Rivers in the northeast corner of what would become Kansas Territory. Here was evidence not only of the church's assimilationist policies but of the federal government's goals as well. Far from being "removed" from contact with whites, these tribes were at the jumping-off point for white expansion beyond the Mississippi. The Delawares had signed forty-five treaties with the federal government (averaging one every two years) by the time they assumed their pittance of land in Kansas. Both the government and Methodists saw what to them seemed the best of situations—the total dismantling of the tribes and their reservations in favor of allotment of lands to individuals.[51]

This appeared to be possible because these eastern tribes had been changing dramatically. Among the Wyandots, for example, people were still divided over religion and traditional ways. The Methodists had the strongest hand, but the Jesuits still had a following and a few traditionalists fought to hold on to the old ways. Some compromise was made by the development of new tribal institutions alongside the continuation of dances, ceremonies, and other traditions. Over time, even before the ascendancy of the Methodists among them, their system evolved from their former culture in which women played a larger role, to one based loosely on the American system. By the time the Wyandots were well settled, the number of tribal members of mixed ancestry had greatly increased, and the majority of people had acculturated to the point where they dressed, lived, and even spoke like whites.[52]

The Split in the Methodist Episcopal Church

In 1844, the same year that the General Conference established the Indian Mission Conference, the Methodist Episcopal Church split over slavery. Although there was no formal secession, the Methodist Episcopal Church, South, had a decided advantage among the tribes of the Indian Territory and gradually dominated the Cherokee and Choctaw Districts. With strong connections in Arkansas, and especially in Missouri, they also maintained an interest in the Kansas River District. This meant that missionaries from the Methodist Episcopal Church, South, and the Methodist Episcopal Church competed for followers in the Kansas River District. Their disputes reflected the troubled conflict on the Missouri-Kansas line. Several of the tribes, including Wyandots, had members who owned slaves, and by the 1850s there were two separate meeting houses on Wyandot lands.[53]

By 1853, the Wyandots, most of whom were also strong Unionists, had considered allowing whites to lease land on their reserve and holding an election for a delegate to the United States Congress. On July 26, 1853, a gathering of Wyandots, government employees, and white traders chose William Walker, Jr., the dominant figure in Wyandot leadership, as the provisional governor for the Territory of Nebraska.[54] In 1855, six Wyandot chiefs signed a treaty that dissolved the Wyandot tribal organization and provided for allotment of their lands. Five of the six chiefs had promoted the organization of the Territory of Kansas. Not all of the Wyandots accepted this arrangement. Some left Kansas and traveled to Canada closer to their traditional homeland; others moved to the Indian Territory and the embrace of the Methodist Episcopal Church, South. Those who remained in Kansas and accepted allotment became American citizens, effectively accomplishing the goals of both the federal government and of Methodists.[55]

John Beeson and the Quarterly Meeting

In the Oregon country, matters continued to deteriorate following the murders of the Whitmans. The Rogue River War, as it came to be called, was a particularly vicious affair that by 1855 was marked largely by citizen militias bent on extermination and plunder of Indian lands.[56] General John E. Wool, the commander of the U.S. Army's Department of the Pacific, denounced both the governors of Washington and Oregon for their ruthless war against the Oregon tribes. The conflict escalated until General Wool reported, "It has become a contest of extermination by both whites and Indians."[57] During this bloodbath, the most consistent voice in defense of the Indians was an Englishman named John Beeson. Beeson converted to Methodism at the age of fourteen, although his connection to the Methodist Episcopal Church, if any, is unclear. He immigrated to the United States in 1832 and settled in Illinois. He took up the abolitionist cause, and his farm soon became a station on the Underground Railroad. Eventually, though, he moved to Oregon in 1853 and into the middle of a particularly virulent struggle between settlers and Indians.

On October 7, 1855, in response to rebuffs from the military officers who blamed whites for most of the problems, a gathering of settlers collected in Jacksonville, Oregon, to plan the extermination of the Indians in the Rogue valley. The gathering occurred at the Quarterly Meeting of the Methodist Church. After a lengthy discourse on settler grievances and justifications for extermination, the presiding officer asked if anyone wished to speak on a religious subject. Beeson quietly stood and asked all of those present to reject the idea of extermination. As Christians, he told them, they must be the servants of justice and humanity, not vengeance. His appeal met with a cold response. Not one person supported him, and the next day the killing began. Beeson said later that he believed that had the ministers, especially the presiding elder, spoken up, the outcome might have been different. He also recalled that one man told him afterward that he was led into the killings "by the preachers."[58]

Beeson became such a vocal defender of the tribes that Oregon's newspapers refused to print his letters (including the Methodist papers, the *Pacific Christian Advocate* and the *California Christian Advocate*, both of which thought his views too controversial). His correspondence to other territories and states was intercepted and destroyed, and his life was threatened. His home was burned, and he left Oregon with a military escort to prevent his murder.[59]

A month after he left, the *Oregon City Argus* finally published an article in which Beeson admonished Oregon's settlers to treat Indians fairly, to "do good, love truth, be just and fair to all, exalt the RIGHT, though every ism fail."[60] In 1857, he published *A Plea for the Indians*. In it, he quoted from the report of the Missions Committee at General Conference of the Methodist Episcopal Church in 1856:

> So far as the moral condition of the Indians is concerned, it will answer our present purpose to say, that they are wretched heathen, in the lowest depths of moral degradation.

> But it is also true that there remains to be seen among them but slight traces of the moral benefit which, it was hoped, these astonishing sacrifices and labors [of the missionaries] would confer. They are almost, if not quite, as degraded and destitute of every thing embraced in morality, civilization, and religion, as they were when the first Missionary to this land found them in their nakedness, their ignorance, and their pollution.[61]

Beeson was plain: "And this is a Report of that Civilization that has depraved them [the Indians] with its vices, and maddened them with its crimes—of that Religion that has invaded their dominions, robbed them of their lands, made them outlaws in their own country, hunted them in their own woods, murdered them on their own hearth-stones, violated their homes, and thrust the plow into their sepulchers, until its very corn becomes a vampire, and sucks up the sacred ashes of their Fathers' Graves."[62] He chided the churches for insulting the tribes' self-respect and religion.

He blasted them for sanctioning outrages, violating justice, and failing to understand the gospel they claimed to preach. He wrote:

> There must then be some radical error in their treatment; and this becomes the more certain when we consider that simple moral means, combined with the arts and graces of a true Christian life, under ordinary circumstances, never fail to develop and refine them. Taking all these circumstances into consideration, I would respectfully suggest a thorough reorganization, and entire change of forces. Let them, at least, have a religion that will not insult their common sense, by presenting itself with Whisky and Creeds in one hand, and Bibles and Bowie-knives in the other.[63]

Beeson made his point plain in the introduction of his second edition:

> I have not objected to Christianity, but CREEDS; for I believe that if the pure and holy principles taught by Jesus Christ were presented to the Indians, not in forms and theories only, but in deed and spirit—in the combined power of truth and life—they would grow up into Christianity by the natural determination of a strong veneration, and a fine sense of the Beautiful and True. But, on the other hand, is it not unreasonable to expect that they should renounce the Faith of their Fathers, which they cherish with the utmost tenacity, for unintelligible doctrines, about which Christians themselves are not agreed? The reflective mind of the Indian associates the faults and the faith of the White Man with the wrongs perpetrated upon himself. He sees Drunkenness, Debauchery, and wasting diseases follow in his path, and Tribes that were before comparatively pure, healthy, and happy, perishing from the face of the Earth; and he inevitably casts the blame on Christianity itself; for with him Religion is the strongest motive-power of nations and of men.[64]

He asked his readers "how we ourselves should feel if a more powerful people should take possession of our country, spread themselves in overwhelming numbers over our cities and villages, devouring our substance and treating us with contempt, and at the same time requiring us to forsake our religion, demolish our churches, tear down our school-houses, and adopt a faith which we could not comprehend, and ceremonies and habits we could not approve?"[65] Doubtlessly, modern critics could, by present-minded analysis, point to errors or prejudice in Beeson's own presumptions; but he was neither sanctimonious nor condescending in his tone. He singled out Methodists in his criticism both because of his own Methodist roots and because he thought them the most active in missions in the Oregon country that he knew. What he failed to understand, however, was the mind-set of the Church.

Civic Theology

By the 1850s, Methodists had lost the simple innocence of the gospel and even of the doctrines of grace and sanctification. Wesley had linked obedience to God to loyalty to the king, so it was not a giant leap. But Methodism's great surge had come during the move westward among the people who accepted the anti-Indian sublime. Methodists, like other Americans, acted toward them on the basis of this image of the savage and never attempted to know indigenous people or to learn what they thought, knew, believed, valued, or felt. The country's growth blended with biblical notions of "chosen people" and "the promised land," to make the "savage other" even more alien to the principles of the Church. What emerged was a "civic theology" that linked Anglo civilization and Christian evangelization. Unlike the Methodists of the Revolutionary era, Methodists were now moving into the political arena. Loyalty to the Union was a religious duty, and Christianization was essential to civilization.[66]

As one recent writer notes, "These changes allowed Methodists to become major players in defining the national interest and to announce their willingness to violently defend those interests as part of God's battle against evil."[67] Ministers might debate whether Indians had to be converted in order to be civilized or civilized in order to be converted, but they were linked in the conviction that both were essential to the salvation of the Indian.[68] And so the worst images of the Indian as savage were accepted by ministers as naturally as by scalp-taking frontiersmen. From Francis Asbury to James Finley to dozens and more of ministers and *Christian Advocate* writers, Methodists celebrated the settlers' use of violence against American Indians as necessary and heroic.

There is no doubt that some within the church were tempered by compassion, but even they were tainted by the assumption that Native cultures had to be eradicated by one way or the other. They might prefer assimilation, but they accepted violence as a possible alternative. The language that made this view clear appeared as frequently in Methodist publications as in popular magazines.[69] There were dissenters like Samuel Doughty and Stephen Olin, who argued that God had given America to the Indians, only to have it taken away by war and "the contaminating vices of civ-ilized life, unaccompanied by a single safeguard or one redeeming principle, which education and religion have invented to counteract their destructive influences."[70]

William H. Goode

Ironically, William H. Goode, the indefatigable agent of Methodist missions to Indians and to white settlers in the West for nearly twenty years, was uniquely opti-mistic. During his lifetime, he worked to create new districts and conferences from the Mississippi River to the Rocky Mountains, served Indian missions from the In-dian Territory and Kansas, along the Arkansas and the Platte Rivers, and oversaw the organization of the Rocky Mountain District of the Kansas-Nebraska Conference in 1859 and 1860. In 1860, following his visits to the Colorado Territory, he wrote, "The work of Indian missions is a great and glorious work. Actual results establish this, despite all the hindrances that have intervened."[71]

Goode saw with clarity that the problem was not an "Indian problem" but a moral problem. It appeared, he wrote, that the Indian was "fading away," but he believed that the cause was the white man's "oppression, his cruelty, his contaminating vices." He wrote flatly, "It is vain to plead Anglo-Saxon destiny; it is impious, thus inci-dentally to claim Divine sanction to violence and wrong." More than most of his contemporaries, Reverend Goode saw the dilemma. The tribes had been uprooted again and again and moved to "new" homes:

> But scarcely are they settled in their new homes, till the avarice and cupidity of our people are directed to the new lands assigned them. The treaties have conveyed the right to the soil in perpetuity. Terms have been used to express to their minds, in the strongest manner possible, the completeness of their title, and the assurance that they should never again be disturbed. They are told that in their new home they shall have "all the land, and all the trees, and all the stone, and all the buffaloes, and all the elks, and all the deer, as long as the sun shines, and leaves grow on the trees, and water runs down hill." But in a little time they are forced or persuaded into new treaties, and another removal, and subjected anew to the same hardships and exposure.[72]

His diagnosis was at once penetrating and caring, but his solutions were already shopworn. He favored allotment in severalty, abandonment of the annuity system in favor of funds "applied to useful public objects within the tribes," education, strict enforcement of treaty provisions, high standards for agents, and "when a sufficient number of tribes is prepared for the measure," the creation of a separate, independent state within the Union. Some of these ideas were new, but they remained within the essential framework of policy that assumed acculturation was the only answer. It could hardly have been otherwise.

He was, after all, an evangelical Christian who had spent his ministry spreading the gospel as the great hope of humankind. His caring was rooted in his belief that the answer for Indians and for whites lay in the same solution—"Patient continuance in well doing." As he contemplated conditions on the overland routes and in the Rocky Mountain settlements he had recently visited, he knew that his dream would not be possible without continuing attention to the white settlements in new territories. He saw more clearly than most the problems faced by white settlers and believed that they had to have the mentoring of the Church. The gospel was the grand solution for him because he trusted it beyond all else as a corrective to men's treatment of one another. For him it was the greatest gift, the common denominator that could fill the "mighty chasm" between the races.[73]

Like John Beeson, there was no arrogance in Goode's message. Nor could he be called naïve; he had served too long over too wide a ground. No one was more experienced than he. Had there been more men like William Goode, the way might have been opened to a broader understanding and more creative solutions to ameliorate if not to alter the mind-set of the times. It was too much to be hoped for because the forces against them were too great. But Goode was an exception. The truth was that "It cannot be fairly claimed that the Church had an Indian mission program. Although the Missionary Society nominally sponsored the missions, it exercised no real supervision over them."[74]

Despite Goode's confident hope, missions to the Indians ceased to have the priority they once did, except in the Indian Territory, oddly enough. The Church at large was pessimistic and despondent of any success in serving the Indians. It was moving away from the traditional view of itinerancy that Goode saw as a key to success. More important, Methodists were struggling on a larger stage, or so they believed, in a contest that would again link their faith and their patriotism. The Civil War loomed. In the 1850s, Methodists were redefining themselves according to middle class values that emphasized a character of "restraint, sobriety, and self-control." Piety, domesticity, manners, dignity, temperance, education, public service, and generosity were now more important in defining the Christian way than they had been even a few years before.[75] This amounted to a step away from the enthusiasm of the camp meeting and charismatic expression. The Civil War helped to redefine the connection between patriotism and faith, as concern for Native peoples slipped further from view.

As the Church became more political, its social concerns were essentially focused on the white community and constrained by the ideology of the United States as the promised land and Americans as a chosen people. Even the slavery question was a white issue concerned with white society's view of itself. Slaves and blacks at large existed within the context of whites' views of themselves and linked to questions of morality and economic growth. By contrast, Indians were not only a people outside of white culture—still the "savage other"—but also an obstacle to America's Manifest Destiny.

CHAPTER 5

JOHN MILTON CHIVINGTON: THE FIGHTING PARSON

JOHN MILTON CHIVINGTON WAS a son of the settler invasion into the trans-Appalachian west from Virginia through Kentucky and into the Ohio country. His parents were Irish and Scottish, part of the Gaelic backbone of migration into the great arc of Middle Ground at the center of Indian resistance to American expansion. His father, Isaac Chivington, was born on August 15, 1790, some say in Virginia, others in Kentucky or Galliopolis, Ohio.[1] He continued to move west over time as a typical frontiersman.

Among the earliest settlers of Warren County, Ohio, was William Runyon, a Scot, who emigrated from New Jersey to Harrison County, Virginia, where he started a family. Runyon lost everything to Indians "who attacked and burned his dwelling in Virginia." Runyon moved on through Kentucky to Ohio, where he settled in Harlan Township in 1805, the year Ohio became a state.[2] John Chivington's mother, Jane Runyon, was Runyon's daughter, born in Virginia between 1791 and 1795. Her father acquired land northeast of Cincinnati, and became a leading citizen. Isaac Chivington and Jane Runyon were married in Ohio on April 18, 1810, and purchased two sections of timbered land in Warren County, northeast of Cincinnati. They had their first son, Lewis, in 1811.[3]

Isaac was a big man, six feet, six inches tall, who cleared timber for sale, but his struggle for the land involved more than lumber. Tenkswatawa and Tecumseh, the Shawnee brothers who dreamed of a pan-Indian coalition to reclaim Native lands and independence, posed a threat to white expansion in the Ohio country. In 1811, a force under General William Henry Harrison struck Prophetstown at Tippecanoe, while Tecumseh was in the south seeking allies. Afterward, Tenkswatawa, the Shawnee Prophet, was largely discredited among the tribes, and Tecumseh struggled to rebuild his alliances. Reluctantly, he joined the British in the War of 1812, where he proved himself to be a skilled leader. He was largely responsible for the capture of Detroit on August 16, 1812, but his fainthearted British allies proved undependable.[4]

In the year that followed, General William Henry Harrison began to build a second Northwestern Army. Tecumseh again proved his mettle against the Americans at Fort Meigs, but his British counterpart timidly withdrew, providing Harrison more time to build his army. Isaac Chivington was one of the volunteers who joined; another was William Runyon.[5] On October 5, 1813, Harrison attacked the combined force of British and Indian troops. Quickly abandoned by the British, Tecumseh desperately drew Harrison's men into a swamp and forced the Americans into hand-to-hand conflict. It was a wise tactical maneuver, but Harrison's troops seriously outnumbered the Indian coalition. Tecumseh was killed, and his followers were scattered.[6]

The Battle of Thames broke the back of Native resistance in the Northwest, and Isaac soon returned home to his wife and son. A daughter, named Sarah, was born a year or so later. John Milton Chivington was born on January 27, 1821, and Isaac Watts Chivington followed on August 18, 1824.[7] When he was thirteen, Lewis joined his father cutting timber, but he had little time to learn the family business. Isaac Chivington died on December 18, 1825, leaving his wife and family dependent on the fourteen-year-old Lewis.[8]

Little is known of John Chivington's youth. His mother, of stern Presbyterian stock, was, by all accounts, a formidable woman. She held the family together after her husband's death. She had some education, naming her two younger sons after English poet John Milton, and Isaac Watts, the "Father of English Hymnody" and religious nonconformist. She saw to her children's religious instruction with access to both Presbyterian and Methodist churches in nearby Lebanon.[9] John and Isaac worked with their older brother cutting and rafting timber for a time, but John left the family fold before he reached eighteen. He worked as an apprentice carpenter and supplemented his income as a prize fighter in the river towns. He ventured into Indiana in the 1830s, and while he was there, living in Milton, he met and married Martha Rowlison on July 24, 1839.[10]

Conversion of John Chivington and His Path to Preaching

In 1842, or perhaps during the winter of 1843-44 when "a most remarkable revival" took place at Zoar Church, the oldest Methodist Church in Hamilton Township, Ohio, John Chivington was converted. The revival preachers were named Fife and Smith, and their powers as revivalists were "unrivaled." More than two hundred souls were converted, marking the beginning of Zoar Church's greatest growth.[11] According to family tradition, Chivington began to study under the tutelage of a Methodist bishop at Cincinnati shortly thereafter until Chivington satisfied himself that he could "give a reason for every particle of faith that is in me."[12] Bishop Joshua Soule had moved to Lebanon in 1825, it is true, but Chivington's connection to a bishop has not yet been confirmed.[13]

His mentor was more likely the Reverend Michael Marley, a well-known and respected minister. "Michael Marley was a well-made, hardy man of good size," a contemporary wrote of him. He remembered:

> I think I have never known the man who could go into the depths of theology equal to Michael Marley, and he was a student until the end of his life. He would remind one of a man stationed at divergent roads in the wilderness, all unsafe but one, and a departure would hazard life, and it was his business to set them in the safe way. He was able to resolve apparent conflicting passages of Scripture . . . thus clearly bringing out and presenting truth; and, when in his strength, he had great ability to force and apply his logical conclusions.[14]

It is easy to see Marley's style in Chivington's later sermons, explaining the righteous way, then pointing out the dangers of other ways, sending out "in a thrilling, warning voice, showing the dreadful results, reaching out through countless ages, so as to alarm the fears of the guilty."[15]

According to at least one source, Michael Marley, the presiding elder, licensed Chivington to preach at Zoar Church in September 1844. The source adds, "Three years later the same Quarterly Conference recommended him to the Annual Conference, 1847." The record remains obscure, but Chivington began his work there as a lay preacher or "exhorter" at the very least.[16] In 1846, he took another important step in his life. Members of his mother's family, the Runyons, were Masons, and he was a founding member of Butlerville Lodge No. 135, F. & A. M. in 1846.[17] He was successful enough in his church work that in 1847, he was recommended to the annual conference on probation. In 1848, Chivington was admitted to the Illinois Conference, Quincy District, at Payson, on a trial basis. The following year, still on trial, he transferred to the Missouri Conference and LaGrange Mission. In 1850, he was admitted to full connection, elected a deacon, but not ordained, and moved to Shelbyville Mission. In 1851, he was ordained a deacon at the St. Joseph Mission in the Missouri Conference.[18] In 1852, he was ordained an elder in the Missouri and Arkansas Conference, serving the Savannah and St. Joseph Mission in the Platte Mission District. In 1853, he was assigned to the more demanding Wyandotte, Delaware, and Shawnee Indian Mission at present-day Kansas City.[19]

Chivington and the Wyandots

He arrived in the fall of 1853, during an increasingly troubled time. Wyandot politics by then was enmeshed with national politics, territorial expansion, and slavery. The Wyandots were themselves divided. There were even two Methodist churches in the jurisdiction. William Walker was himself a slaveowner, and in May 1854, the Methodist Episcopal Church, South, would authorize its own Kansas Mission Conference.[20] On September 6, 1853, George W. Manypenny, the Commissioner of Indian Affairs, visited the Wyandots to discuss the possibilities of the allotment of Wyandot lands, and, on September 14, Colonel John Charles Fremont, preparing for yet another exploratory mission in the West, camped at the Methodist mission while he outfitted the expedition and hired Delaware scouts.[21] Chivington likely did not arrive until Manypenny and Fremont had left, but on September 27, Reverend Daniel Dofflemeyer, representing the Methodist Episcopal Church, South, returned as a missionary to the Wyandots. Chivington tried to cultivate the support of the governing elite, led by William Walker, Jr., but the situation was still troubled. Curiously, Chivington's name is scarcely mentioned in the historical record during his tenure. His name does not appear once in Walker's Journals.[22]

With the passage of the Kansas-Nebraska Act on January 4, 1854, the situation changed yet again, and the Methodist Church recognized a need to move into the new territories quickly. William H. Goode, a venerated and experienced minister, was selected to visit the country and determine the need for missionaries in the region. Early in July 1854, Goode reached the Mission in Kansas. He was intrigued by the Wyandots because of their apparent acculturation, but left them on July 7, in company with Reverend Chivington, to explore the area further. On July 9, Goode preached the first sermon to white settlers in the region at a log cabin at Hickory Point on the Santa Fe Road with Chivington and Reverend Still in attendance. He would return to the Wyandot lands later for a brief visit.[23]

Not long after Goode's departure, Chivington organized the Wyandot Lodge of Masons under the dispensation of the Grand Lodge of Missouri, on August 11, 1854, at the home of Matthew Walker, the brother of William Walker, Jr. With eight members in attendance, most of them Wyandots, Chivington was named Worshipful Master.[24] This action confirmed where he stood in the tribal disputes, and subsequent actions made it clear that one of the keys to Goode's interest was the movement of the tribe toward full assimilation.

In September, Goode would report in a letter to the *Western Christian Advocate*, "Our Wyandotte Mission is prospering under the fearless and faithful labours of Rev. J. M. Chivington. I should think it would take several United States agents to drive him from the field." This acknowledgment is the only real notice of Chivington's work among the Wyandots.[25] By then, Chivington was secretary of the Missouri Conference and had been assigned to Hedding Chapel and City Mission at St. Louis, in the St. Louis Mission District.[26] Goode apparently thought Chivington was ready for a regular church appointment because he recommended that Chivington "be given work on one of the regular fields under his [Goode's] care." Accordingly, Chivington was named the presiding elder of the Platte Mission District of the Missouri Conference.[27]

Missouri was deeply divided over the slavery question, and northern Methodists, by their zeal against slavery and for the free soil verdict advanced by the Kansas-Nebraska Act, were openly blamed as provocateurs because of their open partisanship. As a result, pro-slavers increasingly singled out Methodists as targets. The Church in Missouri and Kansas was seen as a weapon of the antislavery movement. In addition to the "Border Ruffians," who routinely crossed into Kansas, voted in elections, but did not settle there, Missouri pro-slavers organized secret societies called "Blue Lodges" or "Self-Defensives." As "Bleeding Kansas" earned its name, the Methodist Episcopal Church in Missouri became a target. Beatings, shootings, tar-and-feathering, and the destruction of the property of ministers became commonplace. Reverend L. B. Dennis had property, including horses, stolen and destroyed by Southern partisans. The *Central Christian Advocate* blamed the Methodist Episcopal Church, South and other Southern churches for creating the climate that precipitated the violence.[28]

Chivington and the Platte River District

Platte County, Missouri, Chivington's new home, was a hotbed of controversy over the slavery question, and he faced his first major test as a minister because of it. In the summer of 1854, B. F. Stringfellow organized the Platte County Self-Defensive Association. Like other similar groups, they wore "a wisp of hemp" on

The Reverend John Milton Chivington. John Chivington was already an imposing figure in this 1850s image of him. (Mazzulla Collection, Amon G. Carter Museum of Western Art, Fort Worth, Texas)

their coat lapels as an identifying mark and used the "sound of the goose" as their password.[29] Their first goal was to protect slavery in Missouri, and they regarded any antislavery sentiment as abolitionism. On April 15, 1855, a mob gathered in Parkville to threaten Methodist ministers promoting abolition. *The Parkville Industrial Luminary*, whose editor, G. S. Park, had spoken out against the Association, was burned and the press dumped into the river. Park, who was out of town at the time, was given three weeks to settle his affairs. Three Methodist ministers were singled out by name. Two of them, Christian Morris, pastor at Hillboro, and a Reverend Allen, left the state. Who the third person was is not clear.[30] A report in the *New York Times* noted that "It was decided by the meeting that no Methodist preacher should preach in the County on pain of being tarred and feathered for the first offense and hanged for the second."

In July 1854, at the quarterly meeting of the Platte Mission District, a mob of eighty men appeared, "carrying tar and feathers and hemp along with them." The *Times* reported, "The excitement is great. These humble and pious ministers of religion will be driven out, and utter lawlessness prevail."[31] Chivington's outspoken efforts "to organize the Methodist Church for the Republican Party" made him a target. Now, confronted by the "Self-Defensives," Chivington challenged the mob. One account says that he took off his coat and threatened to whip anyone who wanted to fight after he had finished his sermon, while a more popular view held that when he took the pulpit, he drew two pistols from his coat, laid them on the pulpit alongside his Bible, and announced that "by the grace of God and these two revolvers, I am going to preach here today."[32] Jesse Haire said the effect was clear: "Thay [sic] allways [sic] afterwards let him alone."[33]

Perhaps. Or perhaps the Church transferred him to the position of pastor of the Omaha Methodist Episcopal Church of the new Kansas-Nebraska Conference in 1856 because of threats against his life and concerns of friends, including a congressman, that he would be killed. In any case, it was hardly a major promotion.[34] When he arrived in Omaha, his church had six members. Nevertheless, he carried with him a fresh confidence. He was imposing both in physical form and in ministerial voice. He dominated other men by sheer personality and charisma. In his first Thanksgiving service to his new congregation, he told them "that he could not see what, in the least, any of those present had to be thankful for."[35]

Moving into the mainstream of the Church, he took his tasks seriously and pushed for a stronger position within the Church as well as being outspoken for a free Nebraska and the Republican Party. He was named presiding elder of the

Omaha district.[36] He worked to improve schools, reduce crime, and, on September 20, 1857, he was involved with the formation of the Masonic Grand Lodge of Nebraska, serving as Grand Chaplain.[37] He was named to the Board of Stewards of the Conference, but "by vote of conference, was excused from serving," possibly because of his duties as presiding elder.[38] He was plainly active in a number of ways, but, a contemporary recalled, "Mr. Chivington was not as steady in his demeanor as becomes a man called of God to the work of the ministry, giving his ministerial friends regret and even trouble in their efforts to sustain his reputation."[39]

Chivington Moves to Nebraska

In 1858, he was transferred to the Nebraska City Conference as presiding elder. At the time Kearny City and Nebraska City were locked in a fight to control the county, and Nebraska City itself was scarcely settled. Family sources say that when he arrived he found the local church taken over by a saloon. Chivington reportedly smashed liquor barrels and reclaimed the church.[40] He continued his crusade, assisted by his brother Isaac Chivington, who was also a Methodist minister.[41] At the first quarterly meeting at Table Rock in Pawnee County, John Chivington prayed "that the Lord would send the people here and make them so poor that they could not get away."[42]

In March 1858, the presiding elder attended a quarterly meeting at Bellevue City, and preached a sermon while there. Something of a theme was emerging. He said forthrightly, "Some one [sic] has informed me, that there has been a minister here, who did not preach hell fire and damnation, and I think he gained and [sic] unenviable reputation. Such a minister as that, who will stand up and preach a *mutilated* gospel, is a greater sinner than any one [sic] in this audience."[43] He also reportedly denounced the minister to the conference ministers after the preacher in question, the Reverend Mr. Goss, left for the east, "but *coward* like, he [Chivington] did not dare to 'face the music,' and make the charges openly to Mr. G. but like a *valiant* man, when that gentleman is absent from Nebraska, and it is not possible for him to defend himself, Mr. Chivington marches up with the boldness of a lion, and plies the blow."[44] The *Bellevue Gazette* defended Goss, saying that "instead of trying to impress his hearers with merely how they could *escape hell*, he labored to teach them that they should do right from an instrinsic [sic] love of right, and that a future reward would be a legitimate result." The editor noted, "Such a gospel as Mr. Chivington proposes to preach, may suit the *tastes and feelings of the hog and hominy eaters* of Missouri, but we hardly think it will go down with the intelligent people in Nebraska."[45]

The attack on Chivington prompted a defense in a letter to the editor by "A FRIEND," who argued that it was Chivington's right as presiding elder to warn his congregations against "erroneous sentiments." The editor responded that Chivington could have and should have spoken to Goss in private rather than publicly announcing that "he preaches infidelity."[46] This prompted another editorial defending Chivington in the *Omaha Nebraskian*.[47] Chivington was off to an auspicious beginning in the Nebraska City district. By the time he left Nebraska for Colorado, he was regarded by many as "a public speaker and sound theologian." The *Nebraska Advertiser* proclaimed, "We cannot but regard him as a man of extraordinary natural abilities, destined to make his mark in the religious world."[48]

In 1859, at the annual conference, he chaired the Committee on Slavery. Its report declared "that as God has made of one blood all nations of men, we recognize in every human being the offspring of the common Father and admit the universal brotherhood of man."[49] He was by then a leader in the conference, even if still controversial. He had a growing family and a reputation as a preacher in the style of Peter Cartwright.[50]

At the annual conference of 1860, held in Leavenworth, Kansas, John M. Chivington was appointed presiding elder of the new Rocky Mountain District of the Kansas-Nebraska Conference.[51] He and his family left for Denver on April 23, 1860. The *Nebraska City People's Press* bid them farewell with this observation: "Mr. C. is particularly fitted by his energetic and persevering character, and his experience among border men, for the post which has been assigned to him by the Conference. He carries with him the best wishes of a large portion of the people of this Territory ... who have learned to respect and esteem him for his manly character in society, and his zeal and activity in his spiritual calling."[52]

Methodism in the Mining Camps

The discovery of gold in the Rocky Mountains in 1858 sent a flood of 100,000 settlers into unceded Indian lands in little more than a year, every one of them hoping to strike it rich. Armed with fresh ideas of squatter sovereignty so recently affirmed in Kansas and Nebraska, they set about quickly trying to establish government in the mountains. Legally a part of Kansas, the mining camps on the Front Range all violated existing law. Some of the settlers even attempted to establish "The Territory of

Jefferson." Not until February 4, 1861 was Colorado Territory formally established, but in the interim, the mining camps managed to avoid some of the worst displays of boom town life in their demand for law and order. They even managed to coexist in relative quiet with the Arapahos who lived in the area of Denver and other camps. Their laws paid little attention to the Indians, however.[53]

The first Methodist service in the camps was apparently conducted by George W. Fisher, a lay pastor, on November 21, 1858, in a log cabin owned by two gamblers. Fisher conducted other services in Denver and Central City that winter.[54] At the Kansas-Nebraska Annual Conference in 1859, Bishop Levi Scott selected two ministers as missionaries to the camps. The first was William H. Goode, who had been the point man for the development of churches in Kansas and Nebraska. He was joined in the mission by the Reverend Jacob Adriance, a young minister who had known Chivington in Nebraska.[55] Adriance was truly the "Father of Colorado Methodism." They reached Denver on June 28, 1859, and conducted a series of meetings in Denver, Central City, Golden, Auraria, and Boulder. Adriance's diaries attest to his commitment and provide a guide to his work during 1859, and Goode wrote regular letters about the progress of the ministry to papers in Kansas. Chivington departed for the camps from Nebraska City on April 23, 1860. Adriance was in Nebraska at the time and hoped to travel west with him, but he arrived too late, on May 8, the same day that Chivington reached Denver.[56]

Chivington made a strong impression on the citizenry. He preached his first sermon, on the Sunday after he arrived, at the Masonic Hall in Denver.[57] Adriance reached Denver on June 16 and camped near the Chivingtons, spending most of the day visiting with his new presiding elder. The following day, he attended Chivington's service in the morning and Joseph T. Canon's in the evening.[58] Adriance was assigned to Boulder and Golden City, and Canon to Mountain City. Chivington secured the services of Reverend A. P. Allen as a "supply" at Denver. Together, they set about their work. At the first quarterly meeting at Mountain City, described by Chivington as "one of the most extraordinary ever held in this, or any other country," he claimed that more than a thousand people took the Lord's Supper.[59]

Chivington's style appealed not only to the miners, but to the rowdies and sports as well. Miners dropped their picks and shovels, and gamblers put down their cards and dice to hear him preach. Jesse Haire wrote, "Hundreds on the Mountain side stand listening to his eloquence, who have not listened to a sermon in their natural lives except when they were boys."[60] Chivington and his colleagues visited the various camps, preaching with fervor everywhere they went and dealt with every kind of citizen. In November, he rented a building on the south side of McGaa Street, and the *Rocky Mountain News* announced that he was canvassing for subscriptions to build a brick church.[61]

He made a strong impression at the annual meeting of the Kansas Conference in March 1861, looming over everyone in sight, wearing a wolf-skin cloak decorated with wolf tails from his shoulders to the hem of his "Rocky Mountain mantle." "His intellect is strong and well trained for his work," a correspondent wrote. "He could readily take two ordinary men, one in each hand, and knock their heads together, were he assaulted or disposed to engage in such achievement."[62] The six-foot, four-and-one-half inch tall Chivington was "just the man for this country," Haire observed.[63]

Efforts to Organize Colorado

On April 12, 1861, Confederate forces fired on Fort Sumter in South Carolina. En route back to Denver from annual conference, Chivington was injured in a stagecoach accident.[64] He reached Denver on April 27, the day after a Union rally, to find the city divided much as Missouri had been in his days there. On the following Sunday, Chivington preached. He recalled that in his sermon, he quoted Stephen Douglas, "There be but two parties—patriots and traitors," which he claimed caused a "decided sensation in the audience." He could later claim that 1861 was the "busiest year" of his life, and it may well have been.[65]

In addition to preaching the gospel and the Union cause, he was also promoting freemasonry, organizing new lodges, and becoming the first Grand Master of Colorado.[66] Moreover, even before William Gilpin, the first governor of Colorado Territory, arrived in May, efforts were being made to organize troops, a movement that Chivington supported. Rebuffed by Secretary of War Simon Cameron, Governor Gilpin took it upon himself to organize a regiment on his own authority. He cited Colorado's defenseless condition, the withdrawal of regular army troops on the overland routes, and the substantial number of Confederate sympathizers in the Territory as reasons. He went so far as to claim that sixty-four thousand Indians were gathering on the Arkansas River in league with the Georgia miners and other Confederate supporters. He was also worried by the declining economy and the exodus of settlers returning east.[67]

During the summer and fall of 1861, recruitment for the First Colorado Volunteer Regiment proceeded. John Potts Slough, a lawyer and temperamental partisan who hailed from the same part of Ohio as Chivington, and Samuel F. Tappan, a Massachusetts abolitionist who had been active in Kansas politics, led the effort and won respectively the rank of colonel and lieutenant colonel for their efforts.[68] Chivington was also active in recruitment, which brought him to a critical juncture in his life. Gilpin offered him the position of regimental chaplain, but Chivington refused the position. "I feel compelled to strike a blow in person for the destruction of human slavery," he told the governor, "and to help in some measure to make this a truly free country. Therefore, I must respectfully decline an appointment as a non-combatant officer, and at the same time urgently request a fighting commission instead."[69]

Colonel John M. Chivington. This photograph, taken in 1862 or 1863, shows the "fighting parson" in full military dress. (History Colorado, Denver, Colorado)

By his own account, Chivington spent much of 1861 preaching on Saturdays and Sundays and drilling troops as the regimental major during the rest of the week. He "soon became the regiment's most influential officer," according to Irving Howbert, whose father was a Methodist minister.[70] Susan Ashley described "a parson in military clothes who preached a rousing patriotic sermon" in her recollections.[71] Chivington preached the funeral of a soldier, and he told the congregation that he was "an American citizen before I became a minister, and that if the Church had required me to renounce any of my rights of manhood or American citizenship before I could become her minister, I should have very respectfully declined."[72]

Bound in Union blue with brass buttons, Chivington was impossible to ignore. In August 1861, the *Denver Colorado Republican and Rocky Mountain Herald*, reported that Chivington was in the mountains recruiting, adding, "We are glad to record Elder Chivington as Major in the army—we expect he will make as good a soldier in the field as in the pulpit and hard to beat—Roll up, all ye soldiers of the cross, and join the army under Major Chivington to defend the Union."[73] On February 19, 1862, the *Rocky Mountain News* reported, "Major Chivington has been treating himself to a most rich and elegant new uniform, hat, sword, etc, in the newest and nicest regulation style. He has also purchased a superb mounted saddle for his mammoth horse, 'Bucephalus,' which saddle is the most richly gotten up institution of its kind we have ever seen in this country."

He was also a storm center. When the local sutler had a flag made for the First Colorado regiment, he gave it "to our big preacher for him to present it to the regiment when on perade [sic]. So he waved it in the are [air] and it was a large one."[74] Already he was behaving as if he were the regimental commander. Colonel Slough favored guerilla tactics, while Chivington insisted on close order drill. This dispute divided the officers. Slough's lack of control and Chivington's insubordination naturally caused problems in the ranks. During the sustained inactivity of 1861, the divisions threatened the regiment. Two companies refused to be mustered as infantry and left camp supported by their officers. Most returned, but Slough incarcerated many of them and cashiered the officers. By December, 1861, idle troops were causing problems with local civilians. Chivington was the chief beneficiary of the situation.[75]

Trouble within the First Colorado Regiment

In January 1862, word reached Denver that a Confederate army under General Henry H. Sibley was mobilizing in New Mexico with the prospect of invading

Colorado. When Colorado authorities did not send troops at once, members of the First and many citizens blamed the inactivity on Acting Governor Lewis Ledyard Weld and Colonel Slough. An officer (or officers) wrote an inflammatory letter to the *Rocky Mountain News* signed "Union" that accused Slough of preferring to "be a living coward to a dead hero" and urged that the soldiers "demand to be led into battle." The author closed by suggesting that they "Let the Major [Chivington] lead you on and success is certain." Slough was infuriated and threatened to arrest William N. Byers, the editor of the *News*, if he did not reveal the author's name. Byers gave Slough the letter, and even though the identity of the person responsible for the letter could not be determined, Slough ordered Captain Jacob Downing, a brash young attorney close to Chivington, confined to his quarters.[76]

By the time the First Colorado Regiment prepared to move out of Denver for New Mexico on February 22, 1862, in freezing weather, the regiment was more seriously divided than ever. Downing's company refused to comply with marching orders until forced out by two other companies on Slough's order. At that point, Downing, who was still under house arrest, was ordered to report to Slough. Slough confronted him directly, asking him if he had written the letter to the *News*. Downing denied it, and Slough ordered him to take command of his company. Within minutes the column moved out.[77] The troubles did not end there.

On February 28, Company I refused to move out when ordered because it had only two wagons, while other companies had three. The hotheaded Slough got into an argument with the company commander, Lieutenant Charles Kerber. When Kerber defied him, Slough called upon Captain Edward W. Wynkoop and Company A to disarm Company I. Kerber then ordered his company to load their weapons. At that point, Slough ordered Major Scott J. Anthony and Company E to assist Wynkoop and pointed his own revolver at Kerber. When a soldier in Kerber's company threatened to kill Slough, violence seemed certain. Then, the colonel abruptly wheeled about and ordered Chivington to move the troops west. Chivington smoothed the matter over by simply pointing out that the regiment was short a wagon and that the situation would be remedied as quickly as possible. Again, Chivington emerged the winner.[78]

Later Slough and Chivington got into an argument over drilling the troops. When Chivington appealed directly to the troops, Slough screamed that Chivington could "take 'em and go to hell with 'em."[79] From that moment, the regiment was virtually two separate units. It was a disorganized rabble that arrived at Fort Union, where more shenanigans followed. An officer was shot by a well-liked sergeant, who was later tried and executed.[80] When Colonel Slough decided to defy his orders to remain at Fort Union and advance against the approaching Texans, the First was "scattered from Dan to Beersheba, burying plunder, drinking, fighting, and carousing with Mexican women at the Lome, a small *Sodom* five or six miles from Union. There were dozens of us too drunk to know friends from foe, consequently most provokingly troublesome."[81]

Faced with a fight, however, the Coloradans showed surprising sand. On March 26, in defiance of his own orders not to engage the enemy, Major Chivington brashly attacked the Confederate advance guard at Apache Canyon. Chivington was praised for his performance that day (Downing was lavish in his accolades), but others expressed the view that the regiment seemed to have "no head; no one to go ahead and give orders" and gave the glory to Captain Samuel Cook for the charge that won the day.[82] When Chivington did not return on March 26, Slough wrote that half his regiment had "gone off to hell with a crazy preacher who thinks he is Napoleon Bonaparte."[83]

When he learned of Chivington's success at Apache Canyon, however, Slough moved to take advantage of the edge the fight had given his command. He split the regiment into two units. Slough would face the rebel advance at Pigeon's Ranch, while Chivington would move west in hopes of striking the Confederate rear. Slough had a hard fight and had to fall back. Chivington's forces stumbled onto Sibley's supply train in Johnson's Canyon, a thousand feet below his troops. After extended discussions with his officers, Chivington ordered an attack down the precipice and took the supply train by surprise. The destruction of the Confederate supply train at Johnson's Ranch forced the withdrawal of Sibley's forces and ended the New Mexico invasion.[84]

Chivington Granted Location to Become Military Commander

In the wake of victory, Slough resigned his commission as commander, ostensibly to protest an order from General Canby to fall back to Fort Union. His men complained about his decision to return to Fort Union, and Downing again used the opportunity to call him a coward. Slough scarcely had time to express indignation, before a petition of officers secured "Old Chiv" a promotion over the head of Lieutenant Colonel Tappan.[85] Chivington saw his first action as regimental commander at Peralta and took command of the Military District of Southern New Mexico at Fort Craig, where his regiment continued to enjoy a bad reputation for its conduct and lack of discipline.[86] Chivington's mind was elsewhere. On April 30, 1862, he wrote to the new governor, John Evans, urging him to use his influence to have the First Regiment returned to Colorado. If something were not done, he wrote, at least two companies of Colorado Volunteers would be attached to a New Mexico regiment and "have the deep mortification of belonging to and having to associate with a set of Blanked thieves, Greasers and Base Cowards." He yearned for an enemy "worthy of our steel."[87]

Chivington had already made some changes. He had requested "location" from the Kansas Conference of the Methodist Church. Not everyone had been pleased with his dual role as presiding elder and military commander. When the annual conference opened in Wyandotte that spring, the Reverend W. A. Kenney, presented the request, and the conference acted: "Bro. Chivington [was] granted a location at his own request. The certificate of location was placed in the hand of a com[mittee],—consisting of the P. E. of the R. M. Dist, and Preachers in charge of Denver & Central City—Who are required to examine his acts—including his Book Debt, and if satisfactory pass over to him his certificate of location."[88]

Reverend Kenny died before he could return to Denver. On May 2, 1862, the Reverend Hugh D. Fisher of Leavenworth wrote a letter to a local paper, praising Chivington for his "heroic conduct" in New Mexico. He also announced that his brother, William H. Fisher had accompanied Baxter C. Dennis, Colorado's new presiding elder, to continue the work of the Church in Colorado. He finished his letter with this: "We believe the Cross of Christ should be elevated on the tops of the mountains; and just beneath it, only a little lower, should flaunt in the breezes of Heaven, the glorious Stars and Stripes."[89] At the same time, the *Atchison Union* offered praise for Chivington:

> We happen to know that same Chivington; he is one of the Peter Cartwright school of Methodist preachers. All our old friends in Northeast Missouri will remember Chivington, of Shelbyville in earlier days. It will be gratifying to them to know that the man who so fearlessly fought the devil out in the brush, is now fighting him on the Plains, in the mountain gorges of Colorado, and New Mexico. He was brave in peace while carrying the cross of Christ, and now the stars and stripes. "Honor to whom honor is due."[90]

Such stories had their effect on Chivington. He now saw his road to glory in the army. On June 25, he wrote to Reverend Hugh Fisher asking him to use his influence with Senators Lane and Pomeroy of Kansas to help him secure a brigadier's star. "Having gone into this war," he confided to his friend, "I want to make the most of it." He added, "If I can get this appointment now, after the war I can go to Congress or [the] U.S. Senate easy."[91] It was a telling letter. Virtually everyone in Colorado expected Chivington to be awarded the commission.

Governor John Evans Champions Chivington

When the regiment was finally ordered to return to Colorado, Chivington hurried back to Denver ahead of the regiment and without escort, as Colorado's hero. On August 7, 1862, Chivington departed for Washington, to plead his case for promotion, carrying with him letters of endorsement from Governor Evans and Hiram Pitt Bennet, Colorado's delegate to Congress, as well as a resolution from the Colorado legislature.[92] The *Rocky Mountain News* said that he hoped to have his regiment transferred to General John Pope's division, and expressed the hope that he would return with a brigadier general's commission.[93]

According to Chivington's recollections, he met with Secretary of War Edwin Mc-Masters Stanton, who offered him an appointment to train troops in the District of Columbia. He said that he responded, "I would rather command the First Cavalry of Colorado than to command the best brigade in the Army of the Potomac."[94] Perhaps, but he was still pushing the issue of a brigadier's commission. On October 31, writing from Chicago, Governor Evans again urged the appointment, this time directly to Abraham Lincoln: "I have known the Colonel well for years, first as a leading Methodist preacher, and since as a thoroughly loyal, bold, brave and judicious commander."[95]

Chivington did secure permission to mount the First Colorado Regiment as cavalry, and he told Lieutenant Colonel Tappan that he expected to be promoted and given command of the Military District of Colorado.[96] Tappan thought his chances were good. On November 8, the *Atchison Weekly Champion and Advocate* reported that Chivington had departed Atchison the previous night "to take charge of the troops in Colorado, which, according to the division made by Gen Curtis, commander of the department, comprises the 11th district. The number of troops in Colorado is now nearly 3,000, and should there be a general Indian war, which is yet feared by men on the border, his position will be one of great importance and weighty responsibility." The paper added that if any more brigadier generals were needed, Colonel Chivington should be one of the first appointed. He arrived by stage in Denver on November 19, 1862.[97]

On December 24, 1862, John Evans again pushed for the appointment in a letter to Lincoln, arguing that Colorado "is entitled to this."[98] In January 1863, President Lincoln presented a list of nominations for military promotions to the United States Senate. On the list of promotions to brigadier general was "J. M. Chivington." Unfortunately, the nominations arrived "too late for confirmation by the Senate."[99] The only brigadier approved from Colorado was John P. Slough, which infuriated Chivington and displeased many Coloradans.[100] Slough was by then the military governor at Alexandria, Virginia, and a favorite of Secretary of War Stanton. Chivington did not give up, however.

As late as December 1863, he was still pleading with Bishop Matthew Simpson to press his promotion. "If I could get this promotion it would very materally [sic] help our plans out here of which I have no doubt Gov Evans has informed you. We Work in harmony. Can you get it?"[101] Even *Frank Leslie's Illustrated Newspaper* in New York pled his case, writing that he was entitled to a star by virtue of "his rank and services, tried courage and ability." The article closed with this portrait: "[A]s a fighting preacher, he will ornament and dignify the position. Tall, powerfully athletic, a giant in size, [he is] the very embodiment of physical energy and mental vigor. His flashing eye and voice of unusual depth and power are striking characteristics of the man. These qualities, combined with his being a strict disciplinarian, make him unusually fitted for high command."[102]

But Chivington did not get his star. One important reason was a letter written by General Slough to Secretary of War Stanton in September 1863. Slough reminded Stanton that he had recommended Chivington for promotion months before, but wished "to place myself right by withdrawing my recommendation." He then told Stanton that the former chief justice of Colorado had informed him that Chivington and others had conspired to have him assassinated en route to New Mexico. This, together with newspaper accounts from New Mexico claiming that Chivington had taken undue credit for the destruction of the Confederate supply train at Johnson's Ranch, and a series of quarrels between Chivington and several officers in the First Colorado Cavalry, doomed his hopes for a general's shoulder straps.[103]

CHAPTER 6

JOHN EVANS, M. D.:
ENTREPRENEUR AND PHILANTHROPIST

JOHN EVANS, LIKE JOHN Chivington, was born in Ohio. In fact, both of them were born in Warren County, scarcely ten miles apart, although no evidence suggests that they ever knew each other there. Evans was born on March 9, 1814, in a log cabin near Waynesville, to David and Rachel Evans, a Quaker couple, as the first of eleven children.[1] His father, like most of his neighbors, was a farmer, but he was dissatisfied with the meager income he received for it, so he went to work for his father as a tool-maker in his augur shop. Later, he opened a general store in Waynesville, although he continued to make tools and farm on the side. David Evans prospered as his family grew.[2]

Young John was educated in Quaker schools and did well. He was a member of the Franklin Society (later the Waynesville Literary Club) as a follower of the traveling speaker, C. P. Bronson, who offered his own system of elocution that young Evans found liberating.[3] Unlike the young John Chivington, he did not have to work. He said later that he was "lazy" as a boy.[4] In August 1834, he entered the Hicksite academy in Richmond, Indiana. He responded well to his studies there, but after a single term, his father insisted that he return home to the farm. David Evans and his son battled for months over John's determination to continue his education. His father was especially opposed to John's interest in medicine, but he finally agreed to allow him to attend the Gwynedd Boarding School in Montgomery County, Pennsylvania.[5]

Gwynedd was disappointing to him. The curriculum was far from challenging and, while he enjoyed learning, John needed something more. He still wanted to be a doctor, which led to more arguments with his father, who finally agreed that he could study medicine but at his own expense. The experience of visiting cities like Baltimore and Philadelphia, along with the disappointment at Gwynedd also led him to doubts about his faith. "I am almost no Quaker," he wrote to his cousin and friend, Benjamin Evans.[6] On January 1, 1836, John enrolled in Clermont Academy on the outskirts of Philadelphia, where he entered into the life of a student, both as a dedicated scholar and as a young man exploring the worldly wonders that Philadelphia had to offer. He also had growing interests in both investment and politics, and his choice of the Whigs as a party in the latter reflected his views of the former.[7]

He entered Cincinnati College's medical school in the fall of 1836. In 1837, Evans began courting Hannah Canby, the daughter of a Warren County physician named Joseph Canby.[8] They were soon engaged. He graduated on March 3, 1838.[9] Times were hard for a while, as he sought a place to practice and satisfy his fiancée's desire to remain close to her family. Eventually, he was married to Hannah Canby, in December 1838, and began a practice in Attica, Indiana, in July 1839.[10] Evans continued to struggle financially, and his disenchantment with his Quaker faith continued to deepen.

It was during this time that he first heard Bishop Matthew Simpson preach. Simpson was the president of Asbury University (later DePauw) in Indiana at the time. "Bishop Simpson was an eloquent preacher then," Evans recalled. "He is the first man that ever made my head swim in talking. He carried his eloquence up to a climax and I had to look around to see where I was."[11] Evans attended another Simpson meeting the next night. Soon afterward, he was invited to attend the Love Feast of the quarterly meeting. "[I]t made such an impression on my mind that I joined the church and have been a Methodist ever since." It was the beginning of a lifelong friendship between Evans and Simpson.[12] They also had a common interest in education. Simpson was an early advocate of the establishment of colleges to educate Methodists in order to preserve Methodism itself. This was a step away from the previous generation's reliance upon God's grace rather than "book learning."[13]

Jacksonian Democracy and "Christian Republicanism"

Indeed, Evans and Simpson epitomized the changes that were overtaking the Methodist Church at the time. In the days of Francis Asbury, Methodists had been essentially apolitical. They saw themselves as "citizens of Zion" and harbored an antipathy toward Calvinist ideas that merged state and church after the manner of the Puritans. Many Methodists saw politics as the author of social and religious discord.[14] By the 1820s, Methodist ideology (as opposed to theology) was changing. At its center was the conjunction of the Second Great Awakening and the Second

Party system. The emergence of Jacksonian Democracy, with its emphasis on the rise of the common man, universal white male suffrage, equality of opportunity, and individual enterprise, fit well with the frontier populism and revivalism of the Second Great Awakening.[15] Both also fed the ideas of Americans as a chosen people, a covenant between God and the United States in a new promised land, and a belief that religion was essential to national prosperity. What emerged was a growing view among Methodists and other evangelical denominations that one historian has called "Christian republicanism."[16]

This new ideology seemed liberating and consistent with core beliefs. It also provided context for public issues like Westward expansion, Indian removal, slavery, and sectionalism. Initially, the new Democratic Party profited most, especially among the settlers who made up the congregations and mission fields of Methodist itinerants. In fact, revivalism contributed a model for political campaigns in both form and language. A consequence of these developments was that "moral suasion proved demonstrably insufficient" in dealing with the social challenges of the "new America."[17] This led both churchmen and laymen to a reexamination of the role of government in the management of social issues like Sabbath breaking, dueling, drinking, care for the sick and needy, and family abuse, along with questions like Roman Catholic immigration, land policy, and Indian removal. Methodist women also grew more vocal in the new political environment, pushing petitions to criminalize seduction, regulate asylums and prisons, change property laws, oppose Indian removal, restrict slavery, and prohibit alcohol sales. They were not yet pushing for suffrage, but they assumed a much larger role in promoting social justice.[18]

Methodism had thrived among the poor and was looked down upon by Congregationalists, Presbyterians, Episcopalians, and other denominations as the refuge of backward laymen and ignorant and ill-prepared ministers. Indeed, some Methodists saw in their common roots a unique virtue that they continue to extol. They even criticized some denominations—Quakers, for example—for becoming too "respectable." But the perception itself gradually changed, largely as the result of two developments. The first derived from the Methodist emphasis on order and a leadership that valued education. The other was a growing number of successful Methodist laymen, many of whom could point to and take pride in their common origins, who were anxious to contribute to the Church. One indication of the change was the growing number of Methodists who joined the Whig Party. The Whigs appealed to upwardly mobile Methodist laymen with the party's emphasis on self-control, self-discipline, economic improvement, and respectability.

The "New" Businessmen and Methodism

John Evans was the perfect example of the economically successful Methodist layman with an interest in success and community. Evans, like Chivington, joined the Masons, receiving the degree of Master Mason at Attica Lodge No. 18, on July 16, 1844. When he moved to Indianapolis, he became the Indianapolis Lodge's first

John Evans. Physician, philanthropist, prominent Methodist layman who helped found Northwestern University and the University of Denver, railroad entrepreneur, Republican, and governor of Colorado, Evans was removed as governor for his part in the Sand Creek Massacre. (History Colorado, Denver, Colorado)

Worshipful Master. He would also join the Knights Templar in May 1848.[19] At that point, the North Indiana Conference of the Methodist Episcopal Church still discouraged such affiliations, especially for ministers.[20] But Evans's persona by then was already clear. He was a public man, well-liked by those who knew him, a joiner, a successful businessman who enjoyed "speculative investments." He was the model of the "new" businessman emerging in the United States during the 1840s.[21]

His philanthropic impulses also became clear in Indiana. While at Attica, Evans began to write articles on the importance of public institutions for the insane. He and his partner, Isaac Fisher, drafted a memorial in late 1841, asking that a hospital for the insane be established by the state legislature.[22] The issue floundered for several years, in part because of the dilatory tactics of Governor Samuel Bigger. In 1842, Bigger handed his opposition a very large cudgel, when the Presbyterian governor announced that there was "not a Methodist in America with sufficient learning to fill a professor's chair."[23] This thinly veiled attack on Asbury University united Methodists against him and, led by President Simpson, they beat Bigger in the 1843 election, even though many of them had to leave the Whig Party (at least for that election) to do it. Simpson launched his own attack against the governor, campaigning as eloquetly as he preached. Bigger had threatened that if Methodists abandoned him, the Whigs would "blow their college and church to Hell."[24]

That did not happen. Instead, Methodists became a powerful force in Indiana. Because of this, in December 1843, Evans presented a plan for financing construction of his hospital. On January 15, 1844, Evans's proposal was voted into law. In 1846, John Evans was named the first superintendent of the Indiana Hospital for the Insane to supervise its construction and develop its policies. He was also teaching at Chicago's Rush Medical College. He did not intend for his position as superintendent to be permanent, and in 1848, he resigned, although he continued to serve on its board. The long fight did, however, gain for him a wide reputation as a leader in the treatment of the insane.[25] More important, as his biographer, Harry Kelsey points out, it gave him a taste for the challenge of such contests, which seemed more important than their successful completion. Once successful, he needed a new cause.[26]

Simpson also learned much from his experience in Indiana. First, he had learned that his causes could be advanced in the political arena. Thereafter, he built political connections, courted influential politicians, and garnered support for his causes. He was a power to be reckoned with in Indiana. Second, he realized that there were influential laymen who were willing to share their wealth with the church and with its ministers, men such as him. They offered their hospitality, endowments, lecture fees, and financial advice. He saw this as a logical progression. God was blessing men for their diligence, and they, in turn, were sharing their success with the Church.[27]

Simpson made full use of this series of blessings. He grew increasingly anti-slavery in his views and was soon embroiled in the conflict within the Methodist Episcopal Church on the subject, especially after the 1844 General Conference, which saw the Church split over the question. He rose quickly in influence, and in 1848 was chosen as editor of the *Western Christian Advocate* at Cincinnati. This gave him a forum for his views, and, although he avoided most of the controversy that characterized other *Advocates*, he was able to extend his vision. But when the Fugitive Slave Law was passed in 1850, his strong stand against it drew a vitriolic reaction over his meddling in political matters. Within the church, he was praised for "the nerve to dare to do right."[28]

In 1852, he was elected bishop at General Conference and moved to Pittsburgh. The appointment enlarged his influence still more. He traveled widely and was criticized for his "liberal" views on church structures and the introduction of pews in them. In 1855, he persuaded wealthy laymen in Pittsburgh to build Christ Church, which was the first edifice of its kind and size for any Methodist congregation in the United States. Not only was it an imposing structure, but also it led to the introduction of pews and changes in worship form and style. In return, wealthy laymen gained more influence within the congregation. In 1856, Simpson clearly believed that the Church had to change and that it had to move toward an educated ministry. He was opposed by men like Peter Cartwright, who complained about "these velvet-mouthed and downy D. D.'s" and believed that the new trends insulted the itinerant circuit riders who had built Methodism in the first place.[29]

Evans was also looking for new opportunities. His work in Chicago was still linked to the field of medicine. He wrote articles for medical journals, developed a reputation as a good professor, invented a medical device called an "obstetrical extractor," using silk bands, which he claimed was superior to metal forceps, and edited a medical journal. He was one of the founders of the Chicago Medical Society. He was involved in the creation of female wards at the Illinois General Hospital. After a major cholera outbreak in 1849, he argued in a medical paper that contagion caused the spread of epidemics.[30] It was an impressive resumé. Then, he suffered a personal tragedy. His wife, Hannah, died on October 9, 1850. She was buried in Attica, Indiana, alongside three of her children.[31] Evans was devastated. For months, he seemed inconsolable, but by 1852, he had recovered sufficiently to renew his medical and business endeavors.

Evans: Real Estate, Railroads, and the Republican Party

Evans had been an early investor in Chicago real estate, and he soon gave up the medical profession to pursue his business interests. He invested in a bank, served on Chicago's city council, and realized Chicago's potential as a trading center.[32] Increasingly, though, he was drawn to railroads. In 1852, he was one of the key organizers of the Fort Wayne and Chicago Railroad, which would eventually become a part of the Pennsylvania Railroad system. As a member of the Chicago city council, he was able to allow the Fort Wayne and Chicago Railroad to enter the city and to secure right-of-way to the Indiana line. He sold stock for mortgages along the right of way, secured bonds with the mortgages, and sold them on the New York market.[33] He was learning the system fast. On August 18, 1853, he also married again, this time to Margaret Gray, the daughter of a prominent Maine lawyer, shipowner, and shipbuilder, who was also an ardent Methodist.[34]

Another part of Evans's ongoing education was his connection to the Methodist Episcopal Church. His friend, Bishop Simpson, who saw education as a critical part of ethical development, was supportive of Evans's activities..[35] As early as 1850, Evans and Orrington Lunt, with the encouragement of Bishop Simpson, began to make plans for a university in the Chicago area. It took them five years to see results, but in 1855, Northwestern University was realized "under the patronage of the M. E. Church and the endorsement of Simpson." Evans chose a site outside the city, which became Evanston, Illinois. He was also a major investor in the town's real estate. The university was soon joined by the Garrett Biblical Institute. Evans built a fine home adjacent to the campus and added another important accomplishment to his record.[36]

Evans continued his labors on behalf of Northwestern University and his philanthropic enterprises, but he had grander plans. He saw the railroad as the great key to American development, and looked for opportunities. In 1857, he became involved in a scheme to build a new town in Nebraska at the juncture of the Platte River and the Missouri River. This was the point that the Burlington Railroad, a land grant company formed before the Civil War, intended to cross the Missouri and to extend westward. Evans's group secured two sections of land for his future city. The new town, named Oreapolis, would be modeled after Evanston but on a grander scale. He wanted an edge over other towns that hoped to be doorways to the West. Oreapolis would be a cultural center, as well as the point of origin for the transcontinental railroad, already being much discussed by businessmen and congressmen.[37]

He envisioned a university, a seminary, and a Bible institute as part of the plan, and, as had become his pattern, he enlisted the support of the Methodist Church. One of the people who represented the Kansas-Nebraska Conference in the planning was the Reverend John M. Chivington.[38]

In 1858, when gold was discovered in the Rocky Mountains, Evans revealed his dream to his second wife, in a way that provided insight not only into his design but also into his reason for being interested in Colorado. He told her that he would build a road "that will be a great thoroughfare to the gold regions" and the Pacific Ocean beyond. Oreapolis would be a great city without doubt.[39] But time was not on his side. The Civil War seemed inevitable, and while Evans persisted in pushing the Oreapolis plan as a key to accessing the gold fields, the project simply did not have the backing it needed to succeed. He made a vain attempt to secure support from the Chicago Board of Trade for a "Chicago to Pikes Peak Express," to connect Chicago with "the Mines" of the Rockies, hoping that the Express would be a precursor for a later railroad.[40] Later, he lent his efforts to a project to complete a railroad from Cedar Rapids to the Missouri River. This plan also failed, but on March 20, 1860, when the legislature in the State of Maine incorporated "The People's Pacific Railroad Company," John Evans of Illinois was named "commissioner."[41]

The Oreapolis dream died, but Evans continued to consider ways to build a railway west from Plattsmouth or Omaha on a central route through the heart of the plains, as the most direct route for a transcontinental railroad. On a practical level, these experiences introduced Evans to a number of important Nebraskans, including a young man named Samuel Elbert, who would later become his close associate, his son-in-law, and lifelong friend. More important, Evans was drawn into the larger plans for a transcontinental railroad. One of his connections was Samuel Ryan Curtis, an Iowa congressman, who had worked earlier with the Lyons and Iowa Central Railroad, which had been taken over by the Chicago and Northwestern Railroad. In 1859, Curtis was serving on the House Select Committee on the Pacific Railway. Curtis was a capable and practical man who would play a large role in John Evans's life.[42] In March 1860, Theodore Judah, representing a group of railroad enthusiasts from as far away as California, approached Curtis, who drafted a bill for a transcontinental railroad, leaving open the question of routes and surveys for later decision. The bill failed, but the issue was very much alive.[43] And Evans was in on the ground floor.

One recent scholar observed that "John Evans's career exhibits an almost miraculous convergence of religious obligation and capital accumulation."[44] A third pillar

86

was added to Evans's structure by the Republican Party. Like Simpson, Evans had shifted his political connection to the new party. His friendship with Bishop Simpson deepened in 1859, when Evans persuaded him to settle in Evanston. Simpson had been extremely ill in the winter of 1857-1858, and Evans sought to move him closer than the bishop's Pittsburgh home, which he felt delayed his recovery. Later that year, Simpson accepted the position as president of Garrett Biblical Institute in Evanston.[45] Evans now had direct access to Simpson as "neighbor, counsellor, and leader."[46] The move was fortuitous for Evans, not merely for his wisdom and faith, but for his political and economic connections.

Simpson, Evans, and Antislavery

In the first place, Simpson's theology was simple and appealing to a practical man like John Evans. He was solid on the key precepts of Methodist principles, among which he emphasized, first, active and positive social engagement, and, second, self-discipline as a proper form of religious practice.[47] Furthermore, Simpson had become the master lobbyist for the Methodist Church. He moved through the halls of Congress and the offices of business leaders and politicians with a smooth and forceful style that made him welcome.[48] He and Evans had embraced the Republican Party, with its commitments to free soil, free men, and business expansion. Evans was an early opponent of slavery and worked very hard during his years in Chicago to build the Illinois Republican Party. He supported Lincoln, but he does not appear to have had close connections with him prior to Lincoln's election as president in 1860.[49] Simpson, however, was in the thick of it, with access to Lincoln's ear. He was determined to make Lincoln aware of the power and the presence of Methodists as his supporters and to have their voice heard.[50]

John Evans was not chosen as a delegate for the Republican National Convention in 1860, but his friend and fellow Methodist, Samuel Elbert, was a member of the Nebraska delegation. Elbert and several members of the Nebraska legislature initiated an effort to secure the governorship of Nebraska for Evans. Bishop Simpson then intervened through Senator Henry S. Lane of Indiana and Senator James Harlan of Iowa to urge Evans's appointment. Simpson also wrote Lincoln directly. In March, the New York *Herald* even announced that Evans had been chosen for the post; but at the end of the month they were disappointed to learn that Dr. William Jayne had received the appointment. At a later date, Lincoln claimed that he had never received the request of the Nebraska legislature.[51]

Simpson complained bitterly to Lincoln. In October 1861, Lincoln offered Evans the governorship of Washington, but he turned it down. Washington was too far away from Evans's businesses and, more important, from his designs for a railroad through the central plains and the development of the mining region.[52] In November, Evans used another route to inch himself a little closer to success when he boldly challenged a proslavery letter to the *Chicago Journal*. In what one historian has called "one of the most significant developments in the emancipation struggle," Evans declared that in all matters the federal government should favor freedom over slavery. This drew him into a public argument with Democrat Walter B. Scates, an eminent Illinois judge. In his newspaper exchange, Evans argued that

Bishop Matthew Simpson. Prominent bishop of the Methodist Episcopal Church, outspoken Methodist lobbyist, and friend of Abraham Lincoln, Simpson helped to reshape the Church by a more prominent role in politics. Although he was a close friend of Governor John Evans and worked to prevent Evans's removal as governor of Colorado in 1865, Simpson himself never publicly expressed himself on the subject of the Sand Creek Massacre. (General Commission on Archives and History of The United Methodist Church, Drew University, Madison, New Jersey)

in fighting the war, all means should be used, including the confiscation of slave property.[53]

Fresh from this bold exchange, Evans went to Washington, D.C. seeking support for a federal armory in Chicago. While he was there, he learned that Governor William Gilpin would likely be removed as governor of Colorado Territory. He approached Senator Harlan about the matter. Harlan, Lyman Trumbull, and others urged Lincoln to name Evans to replace Gilpin. Lincoln nominated Evans for the post. He was approved by the Senate, and Lincoln signed the commission on March 26, 1862. John Evans soon headed west.[54]

Quite apart from the war enveloping the country, the United States was changing by 1862. It was the kind of change that divided as well as united. While committed to an ideology of unity, the country was rediscovering a class system that they had only recently set aside for Jacksonian Democracy. Most likely, it was inevitable. As men looked at cities like Chicago and St. Louis and Cincinnati in the West, and watched the growth of industry and commerce, it was hard to hold on to the idea of the West in the same way. A middle-class society was evolving with emphasis on sobriety, self-control, individual initiative, refinement, manners, and success.[55] The times also witnessed the spread of social clubs and values that foretold the Victorian era. Ohio and Illinois and Indiana were no longer the West of settlers and conflict. They were the home of farms and towns and order. And through the fields, railroads were changing the landscape and the way that men made a living. Commerce and industry drove the economy.

Manifest Destiny Justified

That did something to men, even to their ideas about their "Manifest Destiny." It became more than a theory. It took on the character of fact. It generated pride. It seemed obvious to them that there was an Anglo superiority proven by the cities that sprang up, the fields that spread over the land that once had been forested, the schools that grew, and the economy that boomed. They sought to explain it with science, affirm it with ideology and myth, and justify it with religion. Americans were the chosen ones, the mountains and plains of America, the promised land. Even before the war ended, it was a confident America that looked to the future, although the war itself obscured the changes for a time.

It had all been told by Methodist exhorters who saw in the gospel that the "wilderness shall bloom like a rose," but by the eve of the Civil War the old divisions within the church seemed sharper somehow. Thomas Hinde had presented the vision of the West that many of the common folk still embraced, so different from the threat of barbarism:

> Here the slanderous tongue does not reach him. The watchings against the devices of a subtle enemy are past. Here all have sufficient employ in attention to their own concerns. . . . Here in tranquility he reviews his life; reflects on the fleeting moments of infancy, childhood, and youth, gathers up the fragments of past experience, and solemnly lays the whole to heart. In humble devotion with his companion and children, he falls to his knees, morning and evening before the Almighty Being that created him, and adores his God. . . . He in fact begins to live anew.[56]

Such views still resonated among common men who saw themselves as "conquering the world for Christ." In fact the new middle-class values of much of the Methodist Episcopal Church seemed threatening to many. Men like Peter Cartwright called the church to reliance on the simplicity that resulted from personal experience with God. The pursuit of refinement and education was dangerous, he claimed, declaring, "I do firmly believe that if the ministers of the present day had more of the unction or baptismal fire of the Holy Ghost promoting their ministerial efforts, we should succeed much better than we do, and be more successful in winning souls to Christ than we do."[57] The new middle-class values were changing from the revivalist, camp meeting enthusiasm of the past to a more staid expression without emotional or bodily intensity.

In some respects, this debate was not new. Methodism had from the beginning struggled with its populist determination to reach the untutored masses in contrast to its organizational forms and elite leadership. It fought through battles over everything from education to pews, from meeting houses and arbors to stained glass churches, from the necessity of the physical experiences associated with camp meetings and revivals to conversion through the "still small voice" or other, more passive expressions of conversions, for some as easy as a simple act of repentance. It is perhaps dangerous to generalize, but in general, as far as church members were concerned, the differences between the Peter Cartwrights and the Matthew Simpsons of the denomination were matters of social class.

Christianity and Civilization

John Evans represented the rising middle class of Methodism, linked arm in arm with the promise of worldly success through economic opportunities in business.

As the recent *Report of the John Evans Study Committee* at Northwestern University has pointed out, Evans's "unfailing dedication to the Methodist Church over the decades consisted mainly of dutiful activity rather than profound reflection. His conversion did not so much change his behavior as convince him that working hard and fostering beneficial social institutions affirmed a person's spiritual development and gave worldly evidence of grace."[58] Practically, that meant that ends were more important than means, works more important than ethics.

The good that men do will live after them was a concept that Evans embraced, but the evidence of "good" lay in the things built—churches, colleges, universities, and hospitals. Railroads were a part of that list, too, because railroads would hasten the growth of civilization and the transformation of the wilderness into a garden. For him, as for many white Americans, the connection between Christianity and civilization was inseparable. One could not exist without the other. Building railroads was a way to spread both and to bring a peace upon the land that would justify whatever it took to make it happen. The transformation already achieved by the westward movement carried with it a sense of entitlement to the lands still "unsettled."

Indeed, "By 1860 Methodists had adopted a 'Calvinist' understanding of political responsibilities, viewing the state as a moral being and believing Christians as active citizens had to take responsibility for ensuring the highest standards of virtue flourished in civic life."[59] This was a far cry from Francis Asbury's insistence that "Our Kingdom is not of this world." Moreover, "Of all Methodists, it was the triumphalist Republicans—nourished by a postmillennialist creed that celebrated conscience, obedience to a higher law, and a strong sense of social responsibility—who had traveled furthest from the outlook of their church's first, apolitical generation to identifying the arrival of the kingdom of God with the success of a particular political party."[60]

The "higher" claims of civilization and Christianity therefore justified extreme measures to enable them to overcome all resistance. Methodism, especially after the Civil War began, increasingly linked Christianity and patriotism—the cross and the flag, in that order. Bishop Simpson began in 1860 to deliver a series of sermons in which he called upon the faithful to embrace the cause of Union at arms.[61] On April 21, 1861, the *Christian Advocate and Journal* declared, "Hath not he who placed Moses in Mount Sinai to utter law over the wilderness, placed us on this continent to shout the Gospel over two oceans? Will he suffer the mission to be confounded? Hath not he who bound us in one language, laws, and religion, also riveted our states together by the mountains and cemented them by the streams?"[62]

Right of Conquest and the Pacific Railway Act

Here were all of the components of the ancient Right of Conquest—a chosen people in the promised land, fighting a just war. Once Simpson proclaimed, "I would say it with all reverence, God cannot do without America."[63] Ironically, in addition to linking patriotism and faith, Simpson achieved a new respectability for Methodists, under the aegis and principles of the rising middle class with all of the attendant values it proclaimed. In 1854, Bishop Simpson had written for the *Annual Report of the Methodist Episcopal Church Missionary Society*, "Providence has clearly designed this country as a land of Protestants; and God has prepared us to receive the nations of the world by the vigour and purity of our civil and religious institutions and by *the successive and vast extensions of our territory*" [italics added].[64] This was a view that John Evans could embrace with enthusiasm and the reason why "John Evans's career exhibits an almost miraculous convergence of religious obligation and capital accumulation."[65]

When John Evans stood on the balcony of the Tremont House in Denver, Colorado Territory, on May 16, 1862, and spoke to the crowd that had come to welcome him as their new governor, he blamed all of their economic woes on the lack of a railroad and spoke to them about Colorado's opportunities and future prospects. He spoke of the territory's potential as a mining center and the future for farming in the Platte River valley. He had reason to be optimistic. He knew that the Homestead Act would be passed in a matter of days on May 20, 1862, and the Pacific Railway Act would soon become law (July 1, 1862). His speech also revealed something else.[66]

John Evans had not come to Colorado as the result of political ambition. His vision was much larger than governing a territory with the small population Colorado had in 1862. The "go-backs" were numerous with the prospects of more if economic conditions did not change. Evans was there to fulfill the dream he had nourished since before Oreapolis. He was there to secure a Colorado route for the transcontinental railroad, to make Denver into a great city and Colorado into a prosperous territory, decidedly Republican and worthy of statehood. These goals were worthy, and he gave little serious weight to such "impediments" as Native rights to the land. His goals were not merely economic; they were, by the reasoning of the time, divinely justified.

The Pacific Railway Act provided that the government would extinguish Indian land rights in order to create a right-of-way two hundred feet wide through new territories including Colorado. For each mile of track laid, the government promised

6,400 acres of land (10 square miles) adjacent to the track. An estimated 20,000,000 acres of public land and $60,000,000 in loans were at stake along the various proposed routes. The primary author of the act was Samuel Ryan Curtis, who had resigned his seat in Congress to join the Union Army. In 1862, he was commanding troops in Kansas and Missouri.[67]

What Evans found when he arrived in the territory was hardly encouraging, but he was determined to secure the transcontinental route for Colorado. He went right to work, determined to make Berthoud Pass the doorway to the Pacific. It was, he said, "designed by the Great Master Mechanic."[68] The Surveyor General, F. M. Case, took a decidedly different view, arguing that the grade was far too steep and that a three-and-a-half-mile-long tunnel would have to be built.[69] But Evans did not give up. He had been named as one of the 158 commissioners of the Union Pacific Railroad (as had General Curtis), and he soon left, on August 18, 1862, to attend the meeting of the Board of Incorporators in Chicago, where he argued for the Colorado route through Berthoud Pass. He returned to Colorado without the endorsement he had hoped for but still determined. His reason for being in Colorado was abundantly clear, and for him and for most of his fellows, supported by conscience, social responsibility, and a higher law.[70]

CHAPTER 7

COLORADO'S "INDIAN PROBLEM"

"Everything Will Be Changed Forever"

IN THE 1840s, THE mounted warriors of the Cheyennes and Arapahos had few memories of earthen lodges or the constraints and benefits they provided. All but the oldest of them were free from even the memory of such things. What they possessed was a vision of life that muted history and even the warnings of Maheo and Sweet Medicine. What they knew and what they claimed seemed to be what had always been. What was in their present was the only view that mattered. Tradition itself was reshaped yet thought ancient by all save the keepers of wisdom. It could hardly have been otherwise. The grass stretched south in great waves for hundreds of miles. The rivers and creeks were lush with timber. Ponds and seeps were abundant in the grasslands. Bison herds stretched in tens of thousands. Mule deer, elk, antelopes, and bears shared the heart of their world. To the south, the great need to make this life work—horses—beckoned to them. William Bent's Fort on the Arkansas River offered trade goods, and the Cheyennes and their Arapaho allies were masters of trade to the north. The few soldiers who traveled the overland routes posed no threat.

At that moment the warnings of Sweet Medicine from that long ago time at Bear Butte were all but forgotten. "Think before you decide," he had told them. "Everything will be changed forever." When the young Lewis Garrard visited the Cheyennes, he understood the lure of their way despite his ingrained prejudices:

> I thought, with envy, of the free and happy life they were leading on the untamed plains, with fat buffalo for food, with fine horses to ride, living and dying in a state of blissful ignorance. To them, with no other joys than those of the untaught savage, such a life must be the acme of happiness; for what more invigorating, enlivening pleasure is there

than traversing the grand prairies, admiring the beauties of unkempt, wild, and lovely nature, and chasing the fleet-footed buffalo—to send the death-abiding arrows, with the musical twang of the bowstring—then partaking of the choice parts, cooked by themselves, by their own fires; and afterward, lying down to enjoy such sweet sleep as is within the comprehension of those only who have traveled and hunted on the lordly parks of the Far West.[1]

But by the time of the Colorado gold rush, all of that was disappearing. The buffalo and other wild game were growing scarcer, the horse herds were dwindling, the grass was disappearing, the trees along the rivers and creeks were mostly gone, the seeps and ponds were drying up, and trade was more difficult.[2] The settlers came to stay in the mountains for the first time, without invitation, and without regard for Cheyenne and Arapaho ways. They built their towns in the wintering grounds of the tribes.[3] Left Hand and Little Raven, the Arapaho chiefs, tried to coexist with them at the camps near Denver. Horace Greeley, the editor of the *New York Tribune*, interviewed Left Hand there and came away impressed only by his "savagery," although even his interview revealed Left Hand to be the wiser man. When miners plundered one of the Arapaho villages, raped women and girls, and stole horses, Left Hand controlled his people and prevented trouble. But by the time William Bent met with the chiefs in the fall of 1859, he warned the Office of Indian Affairs in Washington, "A desperate war of starvation and extinction is . . . imminent and inevitable, unless prompt measures shall prevent [it]."[4]

Treaty of Fort Wise

In fact, Kiowas and Comanches attacked emigrants on the Arkansas route, and some Cheyennes and Arapahos joined them. The result was an initiative originated by William Bent, Left Hand, and Little Raven to negotiate an agreement between the Southern Arapahos and Cheyennes and the U.S. government to protect tribal interests. This led to the misguided and imperfect Treaty of Fort Wise in 1861, signed by a handful of chiefs, including Cheyenne chiefs Black Kettle, White Antelope, Lean Bear, Old Little Wolf, Tall Bear, and Lone Bear, and Arapaho chiefs Little Raven, Storm, Shave Head, and Big Mouth, by which they accepted a small reserve extending north from the Arkansas River to Sand Creek and west to a point just east of Booneville.

The rub was that only three Cheyenne manhao participated in the negotiations, and they insisted that the treaty's provisions would be binding on them alone because they had no authority to speak for the rest of the tribe. Similarly, the important voices of Left Hand and Friday were missing from the agreement. The language of the treaty made it clear that it applied only to "the Arapahos and Cheyennes of the Upper Arkansas." It also plainly stated that the treaty did not include any cession of lands north of the South Platte. That meant that Cheyenne and Arapaho land rights north of the South Platte—where most of the settlements were located—were still intact. As written, the treaty was bound to cause trouble.[5]

Evans's Approach to Indian Affairs

Almost certainly, John Evans had given the matter of Indian affairs little thought when he arrived in Denver in May 1862. Even though his job involved ex officio responsibilities as Superintendent of Indian Affairs for Colorado, policy was set in Washington and agents had the responsibility for carrying it out. His role would be supervisory and hardly a matter of great concern. He carried with him thoughtless images and assumptions about "Indians." The ideas he held were about a vague "them." He gave little thought to Cheyennes or Arapahos or Utes as people or as major factors in his mission as governor. He assumed, as a matter of course, that the "higher purposes" of settlement and development would control outcomes. That meant practically that he saw his role as managing the dispossession of the tribes in order to open lands for settlement.

Evans's essential paternalism was evident in his first contacts with the Cheyennes and Arapahos. Two days after his arrival in Colorado, he witnessed a victory dance of a party of Arapahos, Cheyennes, and a few Lakota returning from an attack on the Utes with six scalps. What he saw confirmed his belief in their essential barbarism, and he lectured them like children on the senselessness of their ongoing conflict with the Utes. The Arapahos and Cheyennes interpreted his words as support for the Utes in a fight that had nothing to do with whites. The day after, he received a delegation of Utes and parleyed with them. A fight was narrowly averted between the tribes, and the Utes told Evans that "the best thing that could be done with an Arapaho or a Cheyenne was to kill him."[6]

Even then, Evans was more dismissive than concerned. He had a railroad to build, a metropolis to construct at Denver, economic growth to promote, a state to create, and political and personal ambitions to realize. John Evans's attentions were simply directed at other matters he deemed more important during his first year in office as governor. For one thing, he was disappointed in both Colorado's economy and its laws. He spent some of his time traveling to see the territory, and he had hoped to postpone the legislature's meeting until February 23, 1863. He was not allowed to do this, but when the legislature convened in July 1862, Evans had handed them a busy agenda, consolidating counties, redrawing legislative districts, revising mining laws, revising the territory's militia law, offering a new law that could secure a claim on every newly discovered lode for the use of schools, seeking passage of a corporation act, appointing a committee to draft a "full code of Statute Law," and proposing measures relating to taxation, probate law, a territorial prison, with federal subsidy, and new treaties with the Utes, Apaches, Kiowas, and Comanches within the territory. At that point, he still assumed that matters with the Cheyennes and Arapahos had been settled. The legislature responded enthusiastically.[7]

During the session, Evans received word that his daughter, Margaret Gray Evans, only five years old, had died of scarlet fever in Evanston.[8] He made plans to return to Chicago in August. He busied himself in the meantime exploring the route for the transcontinental railroad. On August 18, 1862, he departed to make his case for a Colorado route in Chicago and to prepare to move his family to Denver. In October, 1862, Evans went to Washington to ask for more troops in the wake of the Minnesota Uprising. He visited with Commissioner Dole and talked with him at length about the troubles between the Utes and the Cheyennes and Arapahos. In November, he left with his family for Denver. Initially, they moved into the Tremont House until he could build a home. In April 1863, the family moved into their new home at the corner of Fourteenth and Arapahoe Streets. In June, his wife gave birth to another child. During this time, he was already exploring investment opportunities, and, in fact, brought several individuals to Colorado, including Bishop Matthew Simpson, to discuss investments.[9]

Evans also continued his strong support of the Methodist Church. He found Colorado's churches still receiving support from the national Missionary Society, and he immediately set to work improving the situation. He was instrumental in bringing the Reverend Oliver A. Willard to Denver to preach. Willard was another product of Evanston, Illinois, and the brother of Frances E. Willard, the founder of the Women's Christian Temperance Union. Chivington described him as a young man "of very frail physique, but of giant intellect and most remarkable gifts." He said, "Willard could preach equal to any young man I ever heard."[10] Mrs. John Evans shared this assessment. Willard and his young wife, whose father was a minister and professor at Garrett Biblical Institute, traveled with the Evans family to Denver in the fall of 1862.[11]

On July 10, 1863, the Rocky Mountain Conference was formed. On July 21, Bishop Edward R. Ames, who presided over the organization of the conference, urged that a new brick church be constructed in Denver. John Evans contributed $1,000 to the project that day. On July 22, 1863, Willard's church (still meeting in its temporary quarters) was incorporated as the First Methodist Episcopal Church in Denver. The papers were drawn up in the governor's office, and Evans was one of the incorporators. Evans was already planning to build a university as well. The first planning sessions were held in the fall of 1862. Evans donated the land for the university across the street from his home, and a contract for its construction was let in June 1863.

The one thing that was incompatible with his goals, as he understood them, was his responsibility to manage and protect the interests of the Indians. At first, he appeared to believe that reconciling the two would pose no large problem, but Indian affairs not only proved to be more complicated than he suspected, but also they directly threatened his economic and political plans. Rumors of Indian raids along the Platte created unease in the settlements, so much so, that in July 1862, the *Denver Daily Rocky Mountain News* proclaimed that "it is time the red skins learned to behave themselves, they are paving the way for extermination faster than nature requires, and need another General Harney to regulate them."[12]

Evans does not appear to have shared the sense of danger that the settlers did at that point. Instead he made proposals for extinguishing the land claims of the Utes, Comanches, Kiowas, and Apaches, and prepared a plan for settling the Cheyennes and Arapahos on the Sand Creek reserve. He proposed (a) holding a few chiefs responsible for the actions of all, (b) allotting land to Indian families, (c) encouraging farming and stock raising, and (d) educating children. He explained to Commissioner William Palmer Dole in August 1862, that civilization could come only "by suspending the wild influences of their aboriginal state and condition in their children."[13]

As he explained years later, he believed the Indians had to be taught the "proper doctrine" that "they had a right to hunt on the land, but that right must be subject to the higher occupation of the land for a larger population and for civilization."[14] Still, in October 1862, after he returned from his trip to his meeting of the board of directors of the Union Pacific Railroad, and another to Washington, he wrote Commissioner of Indian Affairs Dole that "we have but little danger to apprehend from Indian hostilities."[15] Two developments changed his mind.

The Minnesota Massacre

The first was the "Minnesota Massacre," which made national news in August 1862, only weeks after the passage of the Pacific Railway Act, when the Santee Sioux commenced a war in Minnesota. Evans later claimed that Colorado's Indian troubles were "the legitimate consequence of the teaching of Little Crow, the head of the Siouxs [sic] in Minnesota, and not from any local contest that we had with the Indians, because the settlers generally treated them pretty nicely, and did the best with them that they could."[16] Settler casualties in Minnesota were high. Five were killed on August 17, and by the end of the following day, four hundred settlers had been slain. The war ended quickly in Minnesota, with General Henry H. Sibley driving a divided resistance west. More than 2,000 Sioux were captured. Of those, 308 were condemned to death by a military commission. Lincoln personally reviewed the trial records and reduced the number to 38, who were hanged on December 26, 1862, in the largest mass execution in American history.[17]

Sioux survivors, driven permanently from Minnesota, fled west into Dakota Territory. The conflict created a sensation among both western settlers and people living in the East. Yet, when Colorado's troop strength was reduced further, Evans complained about its economic impact, but played down the prospect of Indian troubles. In this assessment, he was backed initially by the *Rocky Mountain News*. The *News* declared on January 15, 1863, "It is useless to think of retaining twelve hundred cavalry and still a greater number of infantry, lying here comparatively idle." Still, continuing reports of murdered settlers in Minnesota underscored Colorado settlers' sense of isolation and caused them to look at the Colorado tribes with greater apprehension.

On January 29, 1863, just two weeks later, the *News* reflected public concerns, writing, "Were the troops removed, we fear the Indians would take advantage of their absence to renew, in our midst, the horrors of the Minnesota massacre. And at any rate the fact that there were not troops here sufficient for our protection would greatly retard emigration and materially effect [sic] the prosperity of the Territory." In 1863, Charles S. Bryant and Abel B. Murch published a book entitled *A History of the Great Sioux Massacre by the Sioux Indians* that demonstrated that old ideas were alive and well. "It is a conflict of knowledge with ignorance, of right with wrong," they wrote. "The inferior race must recede before the superior, or sink into the common mass, and, like the rain-drop falling upon the bosom of the ocean, lose all traces of distinction."

They returned to ancient arguments:

> Again we come to the great law of right. The white race stood upon this undeveloped continent ready and willing to execute the Divine injunction, to replenish the earth and SUBDUE it. The savage races in possession of it either refused or imperfectly obeyed this first law of the Creator. On the one side stood the white race in the command of God, armed with his law. On the other, the savage, resisting the execution of that law. The result could not be evaded by any human device. God's law will ever triumph, even through the imperfect instrumentality of human agency. In the case before us, the Indian races were in the wrongful possession of a continent required by the superior right of the white man. This right, founded in the wisdom of God, eliminated by the ever-operative law of progress, will continue to assert its dominion, with varying success, contingent on the use of means employed, until all opposition is hushed in the perfect reign of the superior aggressive principle.[18]

Bryant and Murch built their account of what happened in Minnesota around this theme, wrapped in the idea that Christianity had the right to assert the principle by blood if necessary. Whether John Evans ever read the book, the ideas would be embraced by him. In the short term, however, the practical Evans proceeded with plans to move all of the Cheyennes and Arapahos onto the Sand Creek reserve. He expected them, he wrote Commissioner Dole, on February 26, 1863, to "quietly accept under the Treaty if the Department will aid in the matter."[19] At that point he was more concerned about dealing with other tribes—Comanches, Kiowas, Plains Apaches, and Utes. When delegations were sent to Washington that spring, the Cheyennes and Arapahos who went were added at the last minute as an afterthought. Left Hand, who hurried to join the delegation, found that it had already left when he arrived at Fort Lyon. He was angry over the perceived insult.[20]

Boundary Limits and Tribal Gatherings

The second development was a legal one—and the decisive one for Evans. In December 1862, Samuel Browne, the U.S. District Attorney for Colorado, complained to the Secretary of the Interior that the Treaty of Fort Wise failed to define the boundaries of ceded lands, which was creating problems in the courts. On February 22, 1863, Dole advised Browne that the lands ceded extended from the South Platte to the Arkansas. With this information in hand, Browne halted land surveys north of the South Platte and published the boundary limits in the territory's newspapers.[21] On April 10, 1863, Evans challenged this interpretation, warning Dole that if the interpretation was not changed, "we are liable to have an Indian war on our hands." Now, for the first time, he reported depredations and claimed that the Cheyennes and Arapahos were planning to drive the whites "off of what they claim to be their lands." He begged Dole to change the interpretation "to give us authority to avert this threatened repetition of the Minnesota war."[22] Other officials joined the chorus,

Cheyenne Delegation to Washington, 1863. This photograph was made in Leavenworth, Kansas, en route to Washington. Left to Right: Samuel G. Colley, Agent of the Upper Arkansas Indian Agency; Lean Bear (the most prominent and most photographed chief of the Cheyennes on the visit); War Bonnet (Council Chief); and Standing-in-the-Water (Soldier Chief). The council chiefs are identified by a single eagle feather in their hair, pointing to the right, and by the pipes and pipe bags they carry. Lean Bear was killed in the spring of 1864 while approaching Colorado troops to parley. Both War Bonnet and Standing-in-the-Water were killed in the Sand Creek Massacre. (William Blackmore Collection, Pl XXXVIII, Ethnography Department of the British Museum, London. © The Trustees of the British Museum. Used by permission.)

although there was little evidence to support the claims of Cheyenne or Arapaho hostility.[23] In May, Dole buckled under the pressure and instructed Evans "to adopt such a kind of policy as may be found expedient."[24]

Browne challenged Dole's decision and predicted that if the commissioner did not secure a new treaty "we may have trouble with these bands."[25] The normal spring and summer movements of the tribes fed the rumor mill as did reports of General Sibley and General Alfred Sully leading expeditions into Dakota Territory to mop up the Santee Sioux who had fled Minnesota and to overawe the Lakota.[26] Evans also became embroiled in a quarrel with a man named John W. Wright, who was sent to survey the Sand Creek reservation. Evans pressured the Indian agents to provide information concerning the mood of the Indians, and planned a conference with the Cheyennes and Arapahos for September 1, 1863.[27]

As early as June 24, 1863, he told Dole that while he had "little fear" of the Arapahos, he was certain that the Cheyennes were "meditating war."[28] It was a rough summer, and the tribes suffered from lack of water and grass and from the spread of diphtheria and whooping cough. It was true that the Cheyennes, in particular, were sullen and uncooperative. They understood what Evans wanted and found it unacceptable. Rumors fed Evans's worst fears, especially with reports that the Lakota were sending pipe bearers to the Cheyennes and Arapahos following Sully's fight with Santees and Yanktonais at Whitestone Hill in August 1863.[29]

Evans's planned conference never took place. He found only four lodges of Cheyenne at the conference site. Elbridge Gerry did find a large encampment on Beaver Creek. The Cheyennes expressed a willingness to meet with Evans, but said that sickness prevented them from moving. Even then, Black Kettle was too sick to leave his lodge. The chiefs were united in denouncing the Treaty of Fort Wise as a "swindle," and when Gerry told them that the governor wanted them to live like white men, Bull Bear of the Dog Soldiers told Gerry, "You tell white chief, Indian maybe not so low yet." The mood was so sullen in the camp that when Bull Bear agreed to talk to Evans, his fellow Dog Soldiers refused to allow him to go. Gerry reported to Evans his failure and his pessimism.[30]

The governor's handling of the arrangements was clumsy and inept, and he paid little attention to the reasons the tribes provided for not attending. Evans, and others in authority, never understood the ordinary seasonal movements of the tribes—or seriously tried to learn. This meant that any activities that brought Cheyennes or Arapahos closer to settlers were interpreted as threatening. Large tribal gatherings were seen as preparations for war. Small groups were regarded as war parties.

Ordinary trade, buffalo hunting, coming out of winter encampments in the spring or going into winter encampments in the fall all had sinister meanings to whites the Indians encountered. Evans saw anything out of the ordinary (from his point of view) as evidence that war was inevitable.

His planned conference in September was a clear case in point. It was scheduled at a time when the tribes were holding tribal ceremonies and preparing for the winter. Most important, after Gerry's report, Evans simply seemed to give up. He was in a position to say that he had tried, at the least. What is not clear is what he intended for the future at that moment.[31]

On September 22, 1863, Evans wrote a half dozen letters expressing his fears. Yet, in a letter to Dole, on October 14, he noted "a period of quiet among the Indians, and a general feeling of security from danger in the public mind."[32] He even suggested that the "wisest policy" was to encourage the tribes to be scattered into small groups. For those who understood tribal patterns the "period of quiet" was predictable. As late as November 2, 1863, Evans advised Agent Colley that he was "well satisfied that until we are ready for them on the Reservation they will do better to be out after game."[33]

Negotiations with the Utes

Governor Evans also placed a priority on negotiating a treaty with the Utes, and after his failed mission to the Cheyennes, he turned his attention to them. His impression of them seemed favorable from the beginning, and it did not escape notice that they were situated on lands more likely to have mineral resources and settlement potential than Cheyenne and Arapaho ranges. In fact, many of the Colorado settlements were on the lands held by the Tabegauche Utes. In their case, Evans's decision to send the Ute chiefs to Washington had paid off. Their chiefs, especially Ouray, returned to Colorado impressed by white power. Ouray was also paid a salary, earmarked for an interpreter. The treaty was important enough that John G. Nicolay, Lincoln's secretary, was sent to observe the negotiations, and Simeon Whiteley, a Lincoln loyalist who was also a newspaper editor, was named as agent. Whiteley would serve not only as Ute agent, but also as an operative of the Republican Party, as political leadership looked to the possibility of a statehood movement in 1864. Michael Steck, the Superintendent of Indian Affairs in New Mexico, was also present.

At Conejos, on October 7, 1863, with great fanfare provided by the Utes themselves, the chiefs signed a treaty giving up their claims to New Mexico, the Front

Range, and the San Luis Valley, in exchange for a reservation in the Gunnison Valley and $20,000 in trade goods and provisions for a period of ten years. Evans was elated, but some of the Utes who were not included, including those at the Middle Park Agency, were unhappy with the result and demonstrated their discontent dramatically enough that Agent Whiteley had abandoned his post well before the negotiations at Conejos. Lafayette Head was appointed as the new Ute agent. The governor had his prize, however, and, he hoped, security for most of the mountain towns and mining districts. Nicolay believed that Evans would be needed in Washington to complete the treaty. In a cryptic note to President Lincoln on October 12, Nicolay wrote, "Please delay any opinion as to Governor Evans until you hear from me."[34]

On November 7, after reports of horses stolen by Arapahos near Denver, Evans requested that Chivington try to recover the horses, but told him "to proceed in such careful and prudent manner as to avoid any collision with the Indians or causes of ill feeling that is consistent with the performance of the duty required."[35] That same day, Evans received a report from Robert North, an eccentric white man who had lived among the Arapahos, of a secret plan among the tribes to commence a war in the spring. North provided what Evans wanted or feared.[36] From that time forward, Evans was convinced that war was certain, although other reports were not as convinced of imminent danger.

Evans had other reasons to believe the worst. On September 5, 1863, while Evans waited for Gerry's report, the Union Pacific, Eastern Division, began to lay track at Wyandotte, Kansas. This gave Evans an added sense of urgency about the "land question." While in the East that December, he attended a meeting of the "Managers of the Pacific Railroad" in New York. He returned to Denver, believing that a Colorado route for the railroad was still possible.[37] This meant that the Indian question needed to be resolved quickly. On December 14, he wrote Secretary of War Stanton outlining a plan for Colorado's defense and justified it on the basis of "extensive depredations recently committed" which forced him "to apprehend serious difficulties early in the coming spring."[38] Yet, on December 20, he wrote an interesting letter to Commissioner Dole, telling him that the Cheyennes and Arapahos "utterly refuse" to accept the Fort Wise treaty and asking permission to negotiate with the tribes for another reservation site. Unfortunately, he never pursued this idea.[39]

Petty Quarrels and Rumors of War

While Evans grappled with territorial issues, Chivington wasted most of 1863 in petty quarrels with other military officers. Rumors had spread in 1862 from New Mexico that regular army officers Captain William H. Lewis and Captain Asa B. Carey were responsible for the seizure of the supply train at Johnson's Ranch during the Glorieta campaign. New Mexico sources claimed that Chivington wasted hours before deciding to make the attack, and that he was "strutting about in plumage stolen."[40] Other sources claimed that Captain Samuel Cook deserved the credit for the victory at Apache Canyon the day before. One thing that was certain was that Captain Cook was bitter over what had happened in New Mexico. Even the *Santa Fe Gazette* said flatly that "the charge made by Capt. Cook in Apache Canyon was as brilliant a feat as has been performed by any body of men of the same number since the war began, yet we see little or nothing said about it by our Denver neighbors."[41] The *Gazette* also pointed out that while the burning of the wagons at Johnson's Ranch was important, it was not "a regularly devised military plan." Chivington stumbled onto the supply train, the paper said, and left the actual plan—and Slough at Pigeon's Ranch—in jeopardy. "But for this General Chivington has been manufactured into a hero."[42] Before year's end there would be charges that Chivington and others had conspired against Colonel Slough and perhaps planned to kill him.

More troubling were Chivington's conflicts with other officers in his command, from Lieutenant Colonel Tappan down to Captain Cook and several junior officers. Initially, his most serious quarrel was with Colonel Jesse Henry Leavenworth, the commander of the Second Colorado Cavalry, who was stationed at Fort Larned. Leavenworth deplored the inactivity of the troops in Colorado and suggested that most of the troops were there for the profits of speculators. He claimed that four companies could defend Colorado and the overland routes. The rest, he said, were there "to protect new town lots, and eat corn at $5.60 a bushel."[43]

In the spring of 1863, Leavenworth saw a potential conflict building on the Arkansas between Fort Lyon and Fort Larned. Despite orders to cooperate, Chivington specifically ordered Tappan, who was commanding Fort Lyon, not to support Leavenworth. When Tappan defied his orders and marched to Leavenworth's aid at Larned, Chivington removed him from command at Fort Lyon and shipped him off to Fort Garland, a far less important post. During this quarrel, an incident occurred at Fort Larned, in which a sentry shot and killed Little Heart, a young Cheyenne, who tried to ride down the sentry. Leavenworth managed to prevent an incident, and the chiefs concluded that the shooting had been justified.[44] Leavenworth protested, ironically at a time in August 1863, when a group of officers in the First renewed efforts to secure Chivington's promotion. As a result, an officer was dispatched to inspect Colorado. He produced a devastating report on the state of Chivington's command. Military discipline had virtually collapsed. "The Commanding General is astonished, to learn that such a state of things exists and insists that the abuses be at once corrected."[45]

In spite of this sorry report, Chivington was able to save himself and to have Leavenworth removed from command based on irregularities in the organization of his regiment. Chivington also caused another ruckus by refusing to move to the assistance of General James B. Carleton in New Mexico when ordered to by head-quarters, but his main target remained Lieutenant Colonel Tappan. He made life miserable for Tappan during the rest of 1863, primarily involving the conduct of troops involved in the pursuit of the Espinosas, a family that was murdering citizens in the area. At the end of the year, Chivington requested that Tappan be mustered out "for the benefit of the service."[46] But Tappan had connections, too, and Samuel Robbins, the Chief of Cavalry of Colorado, gave Tappan a favorable report. Robbins was threatened, but held his ground.

Tappan would continue to be hounded by charges and accusations from his District Commander even after the Department of Kansas was created. Of course this led to a division among the officers and even within the ranks. Many saw Chivington as a grasping, vindictive man and chafed under the ongoing inactivity of the regiment. In New Mexico, General Carleton was moving on the Navajos; in Utah, General Patrick Edward Connor was launching an expedition against the Shoshoni, but the only real fighting in Colorado was within the First Regiment itself. In fact, Hiram Pitt Bennet, Colorado's congressional delegate, suggested, on September 5, 1863, that a Colorado regiment could be spared to support Connor.[47] As late as February, 1864, the rumor was circulating as far away as Fort Laramie that Chivington was being ordered to Washington "to answer the charge of incapability of holding office." A soldier wrote his sister, "It has been reported that his men are undisciplined [sic] that he can do nothing with them at all, that he allows them to go about the City dressed in citizens clothes and 'many other things prejudicial to good order and military discipline.'"[48] Chivington added no laurels to his record in 1863.

Spring 1864: The Peace Unravels

With first movements in the spring of 1864, most of the Cheyennes and Arapahos were east of the mining camps near the headwaters of the Smoky Hill and Republican Rivers and moving farther east. Of course, spring forays were launched as always to locate buffalo, grass, horses, and other necessities. These parties were small, well-mounted, and determined to assert dominance over essential resources as the horse culture always had, and included forays against the Utes. They posed little direct threat to whites, but their very presence raised fears among the settlers. On April 7, General Curtis was advised that cattle had been stolen from a government contractor in Denver. Curtis ordered Chivington, commanding the District of Colorado, to pursue the thieves. Curtis also sent messages to General Robert Mitchell and Colonel William Collins. Both Mitchell and Collins were skeptical of the reports, but Chivington immediately blamed the Cheyennes and put a force into the field commanded by Lieutenant George Eayre. No evidence existed to prove that a theft had actually taken place, but Chivington advised Curtis that Cheyennes were responsible.[49]

Troop movements prompted more rumors of more depredations. Major Jacob Downing, Chivington's bulldog district inspector with an intense hatred of Indians, struck a village near the Platte and burned the camp when the inhabitants fled without a fight. Later, a group of Cheyenne Dog Soldiers, planning to join a raid against the Crows, picked up four stray mules. When the owner met them, the Dog Soldiers demanded a reward for returning them. As a result, the owner went to the military, and a force under Lieutenant Clark Dunn, another of Chivington's more aggressive officers, took the field. Near Fremont's Orchard, Dunn got into a running fight with the Dog Soldiers. In neither case was there any evidence of intent on the part of the Cheyennes to move against whites.[50]

These episodes were enough to convince Evans that his predictions of a war "were too well founded to justify indifference."[51] The cautious Curtis issued orders on April 18, 1864, that troops "try to prevent irritations of Indian difficulties."[52] By then, Lieutenant Eayre, who had not been heard from, had skirmished with two separate camps and burned them when the Cheyennes fled. Eayre later reported to Chivington that the Cheyennes had stolen the contractor's cattle and "that they meditate hostilities against the whites."[53] Major Downing also advised Chivington, "Everything indicates the commencement of an Indian war."[54]

On the other hand, several officers reported that the Cheyennes were frightened and anxious to maintain good relations with whites. Elbridge Gerry reported on April 14, 1864, that the tribes were unaware of any sorties against whites, and John Prowers, an Arkansas valley rancher married to the daughter of One Eye, told Colley on April 19, that the Cheyennes had no intention of joining a war.[55] Captain David Hardy recovered fifty head of cattle that had been found by the Cheyennes, and he reported the Indians "very frightened." Captain Samuel Cook wrote Chivington's adjutant on April 22 that "the Indians are very much alarmed and appeared to be very anxious to keep on good terms with whites."[56] Other commanders could find no trace of Indian hostility. The evidence was far from convincing that a war was planned by the Cheyennes and Arapahos.

Evans, however, picking and choosing his sources, believed he had the evidence to make his case. Then, Curtis advised his commanders that he needed troops urgently. Already supporting Union operations along the Red River against Confederate troops, he now expected William Clarke Quantrill's guerillas to move into Kansas and trouble from the Kiowas below Fort Larned. On April 28, 1864, Curtis ordered Chivington to move all the forces he could spare to the "extreme South East of your district" because of the Confederate movements in Texas and the Indian Territory.[57] Chivington reacted by requesting permission to call out the militia and asking that he be allowed to launch a raid into northwestern Texas.

He wrote, "If there should be further Indian troubles, *which does not seem probable* [italics added], the militia are armed and can take care of them." This came only days after Evans had requested more troops and after Chivington received reports of the movements of Downing and Dunn on the Platte west of Julesburg. Chivington played down the threat. He suggested calling out the militia, adding, "Don't think they will be needed but the possibility they may."[58] Even the *Weekly Rocky Mountain News*, said, on May 4, "this Indian war was 'a heap of talk for a little cider.' White men have undoubtably been the aggressors."[59] Evans, by contrast, continued to urge support against an imminent Indian war.

Major Downing, ever the aggressor, was anxious to pursue the matter of Indian hostility, as well. While Chivington prepared to move into southeastern Colorado as Curtis commanded, Downing took the field. On May 1, 1864, he captured and tortured a Cheyenne, who agreed to lead the troops to a village at Cedar Bluffs. On May 3, Downing attacked. He killed several before the survivors escaped into a draw and managed to hold him off. Downing was very pleased with himself, and wrote Chivington, "I believe now it is but the commencement of war with this tribe, which must result in their extermination."[60] Evans agreed. Chivington ordered troops to the Arkansas, leaving one company at Fremont's Orchard on the advice of General Curtis to keep them there "till we know Indians will remain quiet."[61]

Lean Bear and Star Murdered

Lieutenant Eayre was still in the field, and reports from Captain J. W. Parmetar at Fort Larned and General Robert Mitchell expressed doubts about Indian hostilities.[62] Evans was now demanding that Colorado's troops be returned from Kansas to prevent the settlements from being wiped out.[63] At mid-May, Eayre materialized, reporting that he had been attacked by Cheyennes and had weathered a seven-and-a-half-hour battle.[64] What had happened was much more serious. On May 16, Eayre had killed two chiefs who rode out to parley with him, Lean Bear, one of the most prominent peace chiefs, and Star. Black Kettle eventually managed to stop the fight that followed, although Wolf Chief said that it was a long time "before the warriors would listen to him. We were all very mad."[65]

The murders of Lean Bear and Star resulted in a series of raids between Fort Riley and Fort Larned the following day, but at a gathering shortly afterward, most of the Cheyennes opposed war.[66] More important, only one man was killed on May 17, Samuel D. Walker, at John J. Prater's trading post on the stage road at Cow Creek near Salina, Kansas. The Cheyennes' vengeance consisted primarily of running off stock. On June 4, the *Junction City Smoky Hill and Republican Union* reported that apart from the death of Walker, "it has turned out that no settlers were massacred, no houses burned, [and] no villages sacked."[67] The Cheyennes took horses, mules, and cattle, but hurt no one in the other attacks along the route in Kansas and destroyed no property. Even with these restrained strikes, the only attack by Indians in Colorado was the incident on the Platte route in April.

On May 27, 1864, the *Black Hawk Daily Mining Journal* reported that the Indian war had blown over for the moment. "Col. Chivington says the Platte route was never more free from Indian insolence, than at present." Chivington said that most of the Indians were moving in the direction of Fort Larned and that the Sioux were "very friendly or afraid, which amounts to the same thing." The First Regiment, Chivington claimed, was "concentrating at Ft. Lyon, for a raid into Texas." The *Journal* noted, "We rejoice that the boys are to be relieved from their long and killing inactivity, though we confess to little faith in raids in general, and raids into Texas in particular.—The Colonel is evidently seeing visions and dreaming dreams of Secesh

[Confederate] stock and plunder including material for a regiment of disaffected Texans, and perhaps one of 'unbleached Americans.' In which case, it would be just to call these visions of the Colonel highly colored."

On June 7, 1864, Chivington finally left Denver for the Arkansas, more than a month after he was ordered south. When he arrived at Fort Lyon on June 11, he advised Curtis that while he believed that the Kiowas and Cheyennes intended to fight and "will have to be soundly thrashed before they will be quiet," he could keep the route between Larned and Lyon clear "of Indians and Robbers & if the Major General directs, I can make a campaign into Texas or after Indians on Smokey Hill & Republican."[68] Chivington obviously believed he had matters well in hand, this only days after Evans, on May 28, had begged Curtis not to leave Colorado defenseless. "Now we have but half the troops we then had and are at war with a powerful combination of Indian tribes who are pledged to sustain each other and to drive the white people from their country."[69] In June, a Cheyenne named Spotted Horse met with Evans to explain the Cheyenne side of the story, but Evans was still skeptical.[70] On June 10, the last company of the First Cavalry departed Camp Weld for the Arkansas.

At that point, then, the leaders were divided. Evans was promoting the idea of imminent danger, demanding "a severe chastisement," while assuring Dole that "All that can be done by prudence to keep others from joining in the fray should be done while the military bring the others to terms."[71] Curtis and other officers in the Department of Kansas were still convinced that matters, while tense, were under control. Chivington had moved his troops into southeastern Colorado. When pressed by William Bent to move quickly to assure peace, Chivington replied that if war did come "the citizens would have to protect themselves."[72]

The day after the last troops left Denver for the Arkansas, June 11, three riders charged into Denver to report Indian attacks near the city. The Hungate family—a man, his wife, and two small children—had been murdered and their bodies mutilated at the ranch of Isaac P. Van Wormer east of Denver. Evans was frantic. He wired Secretary Stanton that Indian hostilities had commenced. He reported "extensive Indian murders" had been "reliably reported" within twenty-five miles of Denver to Commissioner Dole. He demanded that Curtis return "the whole regiment" to defend the settlements.[73] Inexplicably, the mutilated bodies of the Hungates were displayed on the street in Denver, heightening the dread and anger. Denver already was on the verge of panic when on June 15 reports reached Denver of a large party of Indians moving on Denver.

Fear took command, with citizens rushing into the streets and taking refuge in the Denver Mint and the upper story of the Commissary building on Ferry Street. Men broke into the military warehouses and stole guns and ammunition. Through the night, chaos reigned.[74] It turned out that the Indian army was a herd of cattle being driven toward Denver by Mexican cowboys, but hysteria was the order of the day.[75] Evans was caught up in it himself. His dispatches to Stanton, Dole, and Curtis were frantic and exaggerated. Evans did pull himself together and produce in a matter of hours a plan of action. He demanded that the First Colorado be returned to Colorado. He proposed to organize the militia under federal authority. He introduced the idea of a one-hundred-day regiment for service against the Indians. He proposed a major offensive against the tribes. He proposed that friendly Indians be gathered at "places of safety." On June 15, he wrote Dole a lengthy report arguing that the Indians had been the aggressors in the spring raids, while acknowledging that some opposed the fighting.[76]

His plan had a certain logic. If the peaceful Indians came in and were treated well, those inclined to resist might follow suit and the war end. The responses he received from Dole and Curtis were tepid at best. Curtis was also receiving correspondence from other commanders that conciliation was the best course. Dole was receiving similar reports from the Indian agents. The best course, T. S. McKenny, Curtis's inspector general, advised was "to try and conciliate them, to guard our mails and trains well to prevent theft, and stop these scouting parties that are roaming over the country who do not know one tribe from another, and who will kill anything in the shape of an Indian. It will require but few murders on the part of our troops to unite all of these warlike tribes of the plains."[77]

Nathaniel Hill, a professor of chemistry from Brown University who would build a fortune in Colorado as the result of improved smelting techniques and serve one term as United States Senator from Colorado, had been in Colorado only a few days when he wrote, "Rumors are floating around every day of some Indian depredation; but when you resolve it all down to simple fact, it amounts to a few soldiers killed in April, one family murdered a few days ago . . . and numerous little thefts." Of Evans, Hill wrote, "The Governor is a very fine man, but very timid, and he is unfortunately smitten with the belief that they are to have an Indian war."[78] Curtis agreed with that assessment, which set Evans off. He demanded that Curtis show that he was wrong about the threat. Curtis shot back that "while prepared for the worst, we may not exert ourselves in pursuit of rumors. . . . [H]owever much we may have reason to apprehend a general Indian war we should not conclude them as such a thing in actual existence before doing all in our power to prevent such a disaster."[79] On June 20, Major Henry Wallen expressed the view that war could still "be prevented by prompt management."[80]

Evans, for his part, was frantic, regularly adding telegrams and letters to the files of Curtis, Stanton, Dole, and even General James H. Carleton in New Mexico. The settlers, already suffering from the effects of spring floods, lived on a steady diet of rumors and believed the worst. The only question was who to blame, and Evans was increasingly blamed by many. Additional urgency was added when Congress passed an enabling act for Colorado statehood, and a constitutional convention had been called for July—a critical matter within itself, but doubly so in the context of the "Indian problem." The Indian troubles also endangered his plans for a Colorado route of the transcontinental railroad. Colorado's economy was in trouble. He had to do something.[81]

Proclamation of Peace

On June 26, 1864, General Carleton wrote Evans to advise him that he was in the field against Apaches, but he urged Evans to avoid war with any tribe "altogether" if possible. When a war "is commenced it should be commenced because they have been the aggressors and are clearly in the wrong." He advised Evans on his views of fighting Indians, but he said, "I mention these matters to your excellency, so that all efforts for peace may be resorted to before war is resorted to."[82] On June 27, the next day and well before he had time to receive Carleton's letter, Evans issued his proclamation "To the Friendly Indians of the Plains," inviting Indians disposed to peace to come in to places of safety near military posts.[83] William Bent, when he learned of the proclamation, escorted a party of Cheyennes into Fort Larned to discuss the proclamation with Captain Parmetar, the dissolute commanding officer. At the least, they left optimistic about maintaining peace.[84]

The proclamation was bound to fail, however. All of the problems were east, concentrated either on the Arkansas near Larned in Kansas or on the Platte. Moreover, General Curtis had issued orders restricting Indians from congregating at military bases. Evans was clearly nervous. On July 2, 1864, Congress passed new legislation that raised the governor's hopes for a Colorado route for the transcontinental railroad when it authorized the Union Pacific Eastern Division to meet the Central Pacific "provided it reached the hundredth meridian before the Union Pacific line out of Omaha did," according to Evans's biographer.[85] This increased the urgency of resolving the Indian troubles in order to clear the way. Evans saw himself in a race, and his future was the prize.

At the same time, Chivington, who had done virtually nothing that he had been asked to do by Curtis, had returned to Denver late in June, ostensibly to help restore order there although there were no troubles to quell. He was now talking fight. He wrote Curtis on July 5, 1864, "My judgment is that the only way to conquer a peace is to follow them to their settlements & then chastise them."[86] On the other hand, the Cheyennes and Arapahos were convinced that "the Big War Chief in Denver had told his soldiers to kill all their squaws & pappooses."[87] Special Agent H. T. Ketcham wrote Evans on July 1, that he had heard these charges, adding, "But the killing of defenceless women, and innocent helpless children for the crimes of their fathers, is so barbarous, so contrary to the practice of civilized warfare, So revolting and so shocking to humanity, that I cannot believe that Col. Chivington whose courage, benevolence, piety & patriotism are unquestioned, ever issued such an order."[88] What was clear, however, was that the bands would be reluctant to come in because they were convinced that the whites wanted war. Only the most tractable would even consider presenting themselves at military posts or agencies in Colorado.

Crisis at Fort Larned

Curtis believed that Chivington was still at Fort Lyon. On July 7, he ordered Chivington to proceed from Fort Lyon to Fort Larned to deal with a building crisis there. Several days later Major Edward W. Wynkoop received orders from headquarters by courier to move to Larned with four companies. Rather than obeying the order, Wynkoop forwarded the message to Denver for approval from Chivington, who had instructed him not to leave the District of Colorado without his permission. Unfortunately, Chivington had left Denver by then to return to Lyon. He did not arrive until July 15.[89] On July 16, Evans wrote Curtis, "It is very important that Col. Chivington operate with his command on these infernal Indians."[90] Chivington finally left Lyon for Larned on July 17, the very day that the situation at Larned erupted into violence.

Captain James W. Parmetar, the commanding officer at Fort Larned, was a "confirmed drunkard" and generally incompetent. Because of this the post was a tinder box. In July, Kiowas ran off the post's horses, and Satanta, one of the Kiowa chiefs, shot and wounded a sentinel. Left Hand and a party of Arapahos approached the fort on July 17 and sent a message by a soldier to Parmetar promising to fight the Kiowas and help recover the stock. Parmetar responded by firing a howitzer at the party of Arapahos. Infuriated, some of the young Arapahos joined the Kiowas. By the time Chivington arrived by stagecoach on July 20, open resistance on the part of the tribes, including the Cheyennes, was very real. Within three days, a combined force of Cheyennes, Arapahos, and Kiowas killed twelve men, wounded three more, and ran off six hundred head of stock.[91]

The same day, July 20, an infuriated Curtis, advised a Kansas commander that he would go to Larned himself, blaming the crisis there primarily on Chivington. On July 27, 1864, Curtis issued Field Order No. 1, which included the following instructions: "Indians at war with us will be the object of our pursuit and destruction, but women and children must be spared."[92] Curtis marched from Fort Riley to Fort Larned with four hundred men. On July 29, he secured Fort Larned. Curtis was livid with Chivington, chastising him for disobeying orders and returning to Denver when he had been ordered to defend the Arkansas route. "I fear your attention is too much attracted by other matters than your command," he wrote on July 30.[93] Because the failure of policy had occurred on the Arkansas route between Larned and Lyon in Chivington's district, Curtis removed Fort Lyon from the District of Colorado and created a new district, the District of the Upper Arkansas, to be commanded by General James G. Blunt. The new district included the Arkansas route from Larned to Lyon.[94]

Chivington protested, but to no avail.[95] To make matters worse, while troops from Nebraska and Kansas were in the field looking for the tribes, Chivington was spending a significant portion of his time campaigning for Congress in the event statehood passed—and for congressional delegate if it didn't. The only Colorado troops actively engaged were those stationed at Fort Lyon and Fort Larned in the new District of the Upper Arkansas, and a few troops on the South Platte. Chivington even diverted some forces to chase Confederate guerillas reported to be in the area. Evans, who was also campaigning for statehood and a seat in the U.S. Senate, continued to plead for assistance, by now viewed by nearly everyone in authority as an alarmist.[96]

Renewing the Council of Forty-four

Significantly, between June 11 and July 17, there were no confirmed reports of Indian attacks within the Territory of Colorado. The incidents that did happen were the work of the Lakota on the Platte in Nebraska and the Kiowas on the Arkansas in Kansas. The reasons were simple enough. For the Cheyennes, all roads led to the Solomon Fork in north central Kansas that summer. The Sacred Arrows had been bloodied when a Cheyenne named Winnebago killed another Cheyenne man, and the Arrows had to be renewed in holy ceremonies by Stone Forehead, the Arrow Keeper, before war could be considered seriously.

Moreover, it was time for an important gathering that occurred only once every ten years. It was time to renew the Council of Forty-Four, to choose again the chiefs who would lead Maheo's people. This gathering was the reason for the great camps that were reported in some accounts, not a war council, but the renewal of leadership for all of the Cheyennes, north and south. The chiefs were chosen in the ancient way, four chiefs for each manhao and the four Old Man Chiefs. Black Kettle was formally seated on the Council for the first time, and Little Wolf became the Sweet Medicine chief. Since such a gathering had not occurred since 1854, few whites on the central plains were even aware of such a thing or its meaning.[97]

When the renewal was accomplished, and the great camp began to disperse, most of the northern manhao crossed the Platte and moved into the north country where they spent a peaceful summer. The southern manhao remained in the region of the Solomon, the Republican, and the Smoky Hill in western Kansas intending to hunt and keep away from whites. The Dog Soldiers and many young men, on the other hand, concluded that the whites who had killed Lean Bear had not left them alone and that it was time to exact a toll. They turned their ponies north toward the Platte. They struck first on July 17 (the same day that Captain Parmetar fired on the Arapahos at Fort Larned), at Fremont's Orchard, Junction Ranch, Junction Station, Murray's Station, Bijou Ranch, Beaver Creek Ranch, Godfrey's Ranch, and Washington's Ranch. The Lakota were also active between Deer Creek Station and Fort Laramie. General Robert B. Mitchell put troops into the field, mostly small parties that were extremely vulnerable, but they appeared to have the desired effect.[98] By July 29, 1864, the *Omaha Nebraskian* reported, "All quiet on the Platte. A dispatch from Julesburg this morning informs us that the aborigines have changed their base, and that the property taken by them from the emigrants and freighters has all been retaken." The report was premature.

Message from Black Kettle and other "chieves." This is one of two copies of the Cheyennes' written overture for peace in August, 1864. It was delivered to Fort Lyon by One Eye and Minimic on September 4, 1864, and led directly to the Camp Weld Conference. (The Colorado College Library Colorado Room, Colorado Springs, Colorado)

CHAPTER 8

THE PATH TO SAND CREEK

ON AUGUST 7, 1864, the Indian war exploded with full force along the Platte River and in western Kansas. Between August 7 and August 28, at least fifty whites were killed along the Platte route alone, and attacks increased along the Arkansas, mostly in Kansas. Curtis was inundated with requests for assistance from every district and territory in his command.[1] Chivington chimed in as well, noting that most of his troops were chasing Confederate guerillas and asking that the five companies of the First Colorado Cavalry at Fort Larned be returned to his district.[2] Evans added, "We are in a desperate condition on account of our communications being cut off by Indians."[3] The mail was cut off, the shipment of goods held up, and communication lines in danger. Without any doubt, Colorado's commerce was threatened and its population afraid. George Bent said that the camps on the Solomon Fork in central Kansas were "full of plunder." He remembered, "War parties were setting out every day, and other parties coming in loaded with plunder and driving captured herds of horses and mules."[4]

On the day that the Indian assault began on the Little Blue in Nebraska, Colorado businessman Joseph Kenyon wrote to his New York associate, Samuel Barlow, "We are at present fearfull [sic] of trouble with the Indians on the Plains as they have already driven away and killed many of the Settlers on the Platte & they are still suffered to commit these depredations while our Officials are stumping the Territory for State Organization & their promotion to Congress[,] Governorships &c."[5] Four days later, in another letter concerning the threat to Colorado, Kenyon wrote, "We are indebted to an imbicile [sic] Executive for this state of things as a little decision coupled with good sense would two months ago have avoided what must now cost many lives and I fear a general suspension of business for months to come."[6]

Campaign for Statehood

The statehood campaign had been launched in July, while Chivington was supposed to be on the Arkansas between Fort Lyon and Fort Larned. It was quickly linked to the "Denver crowd," a reference to "'Granny' Evans, Elder Chivington, and the rest of the 'Methodist ranters.'"[7] On July 27, the *Black Hawk Mining Journal* reported, "Old John [Evans] works the lead, Gen. Teller on the near wheel, Col. Chivington on the off wheel, Byers is the horse 'to let,' and Rev. [Charles] King the dog under the wagon."[8] The timing was not good. Given the tensions and uncertainties concerning the Indians, the campaign for statehood gave the enemies of Evans and Chivington, and of statehood itself, an opportunity. Despite Ned Byers's efforts in the *Rocky Mountain News* to make a case that Colorado would not have been ignored if it had been a state, the anti-state forces made their argument against Evans, Chivington, and their handling of affairs. The *Mining Journal* said, on August 13, "The Government does no injustice to us in throwing the work of defense into our hands, and if we attend to that work, we are competent to keep the route open between here and the States, and to protect our territorial settlements. But instead of attending to it, our military leaders are stumping the Territory for offices for themselves."

Even Chivington's soldiers were critical. On July 28, before the war began in August, the *Journal* published a letter from Fort Lyon which said, "This war is nothing but a political hobby, so plain a blind man can see it, and the instigators of it should suffer. Who but them ought to atone for the lives already lost by their infernal scheming." Another soldier was quoted on July 29, "we have as yet had no encounter with any foe but of the bedbug and mosquito tribes." Major Wynkoop was criticized for trying to obtain the proxies of the whole regiment and "cast them for Gov. Evans or Col. Chivington, just the reverse of what the boys wish."[9] The day after the attacks began in Nebraska, the *Journal* said, "Col. Chivington can make five times the personal capital for Congress by protecting the Platte Route, than he can buy in stumping the territory with the Rev. Dr. King for state organization."[10]

Still, Evans suffered most. He was criticized for being an alarmist and damned for failure to take action to protect Colorado from the "Indian threat." Under pressure, he continued his letter writing campaign. Once fighting renewed on the Platte and returned to the Arkansas, he was desperate. On August 10, Evans appealed to the public through the *Rocky Mountain News* to defend themselves from the "merciless savages." He warned citizens not to kill "friendly Indians" as that would "only involve us in greater difficulty." He also wired Stanton, requesting permission to raise a cavalry regiment for one hundred days.[11] Byers added his opinion that "a few months of active extermination against the red devils will bring quiet and nothing else."[12]

The next day, August 11, Evans issued a second proclamation, this one authorizing citizens "to go in pursuit of all hostile Indians on the plains, scrupulously avoiding those who have responded to my call to rendezvous at the points indicated; also to kill and destroy as enemies of the country . . . all such hostile Indians. "[13] He also telegraphed Curtis again that day, begging that both Colorado regiments be returned to Colorado and that an additional five thousand men be deployed along the Platte and Arkansas routes. He wrote Curtis that the Indian alliance "is not undoubted," and asked, "Would it not be well to defend the Overland Stage route at all hazards? This will give us the best protection for travel." George K. Otis, the superintendent of the Overland Stage Company, endorsed Evans's letter.[14] An exasperated Curtis responded to Evans, "I wish you would give me facts, so I may know of your disasters."[15] That generated more pleas from Evans, until Curtis lamented to his adjutant on August 20, "Everything from Colorado is censational [sic]."[16]

Third Colorado Calvary

Curtis could only suggest that Evans use militia. But Evans's pleas for permission to raise a one-hundred-day regiment, paid off. He received authority from Washington to raise the Third Colorado Cavalry for one-hundred-days service, and, on August 23, he issued his call for volunteers.[17] When the rumor reached Denver that a force of Cheyennes, Arapahos, Kiowas, Comanches, and Apaches were gathering to attack the settlements, Evans wired Washington of "unlimited information of contemplated attack by a large body of Indians in a few days along the entire line of our settlements."[18] In response to increasing criticism, the *Rocky Mountain News* mounted a full-scale defense of Governor Evans's actions, and on August 24, asked, "Shall we not go after them, their lodges, squaws, and all?"[19] On September 1, President Lincoln reported to Curtis that he had met with Otis concerning the security of the Platte route and urged the general to have a "full conference with him on the subject."[20]

At that point, Denver businessmen demanded that Chivington declare martial law in the city. Chivington issued the order, suspending civil authority, including the court system, as well as closing all businesses except for two hours a day. All men were ordered to enlist in some form of military service. Denver became an armed camp. The provost guard roamed the streets, and literally forced men to enlist in the new Third Regiment. Militia, as well as Thirdsters, drilled in the streets. Parties of men from outlying areas came and went as part of the enlistment process. The political opposition claimed that forced enlistment was used to influence the coming election and that the real reason for declaring martial law was to fill the Third Regiment and to deliver statehood on the votes of the enlistees.[21]

Chivington reveled in his newfound power. Sam Tappan later recorded in his diary two incidents involving Chivington's behavior during his "reign." In the first, he said that Surveyor Case went to Chivington to request permission to leave town. Chivington told him to sit down, then tossed his pen on the desk and leaning back in his chair, said, "I believe I could run an empire." The second incident occurred when Mr. Gove, a local locksmith asked permission to repair a lock for a customer who had come in from outside the city, assuring the commander that it would take only a few minutes. Chivington told him, "No, if you do a stitch of work I will put you in irons and stand you on the corner of the street as an example to this people."[22]

During this "craze," Reverend John L. Dyer, Colorado's "Snow-Shoe Itinerant," arrived with mail from the camps to find citizens constructing a fort on the edge of town. He remembered, "I laughed at Colonel Chivington, and said to him that a few old squaws would upset the fort. He replied: 'If you were not in the mail service, and made light of and discouraged our movements, you might find yourself in a calaboose.'"[23] Dyer passed the incident off as a joke, but the colonel's response was consistent with other stories of his high-handed manner.

Chivington also seized five members of the Reynolds gang (Confederate guerillas) being held by U.S. Marshal A. C. Hunt, and put them into military confinement. They were supposed to be transferred to Fort Lyon for trial before a military commission. Escorted by troops from the new Third Colorado Cavalry, four days out of Denver, the prisoners were shot "while attempting to escape." Chivington was accused of ordering the executions. He reportedly told bystanders later, "I told the guard when they left that if they did not kill those fellows, I would play thunder with them."[24]

These extreme measures shocked many. FitzJohn Porter, a Democrat and another business associate of Samuel Barlow, complained on August 27 to his friend, "We have been afflicted with imbecility in the management of civil affairs to such an extent that a tyro in military affairs, Col Chivington (the preacher and pretended soldier) aided by a few aspirants to political preference struck and suspended the functions of the Governor (Candidate for the Senatorial chair under the State organization) and of all civil process and law in Arrapaho [sic] county and threatened the same up here [Central City] if we, the people, did not furnish sufficient men for the one hundred day regiment in the U.S. Service in order to ensure his retention in service after the expiration of his enlisted term." Porter said that rumors were common that "Chivington and his friends kept up their reports of indians to throw the governor into contempt and become candidate for the Senate himself, if we became a state." He also said, "During all this time though Chivington had U.S. troops under him[,] he did not go himself or send a soldier to learn the truth of the reports. Most of the murdered and scalped have come into Denver surprised to hear that they and all in their vicinity had been wiped out."

Nor did Evans escape Porter's wrath. Porter said that during the excitement about the Indian assault on Denver, Evans was so frightened, he "took to a well and sent up in a bucket such official dispatches as 'Maj. General Teller, Central City, The Indians have combined and are upon us. Our city is threatened with destruction and we with massacre. For God's sake hurry down the noble mountain boys. We will defend our homes to the last drop of our blood. Hurry, hurry, we go to the intrenchments [sic].' It is also said he got afflicted with too much water that night, and was confined to his bed or room as long as an indian [sic] was reported about."[25] Porter was plainly an enemy of both Chivington and Evans and did report these things as rumors, but they are interesting to the extent that they suggest that Chivington and Evans were not acting in concert as most accounts have supposed.

Statehood Defeated

Near the end of the campaign for statehood, Chivington told a crowd at Denver that his policy toward the Indians was to "kill and scalp all, little and big; that nits made lice."[26] In an effort to defend himself against his enemies who accused him of doing too little, Evans began to publish his correspondence—months of it—in the *Rocky Mountain News* to prove that he had tried to get help for Colorado.[27] The declaration of martial law was an embarrassment for Governor Evans, and prospects were so grim for statehood that on September 2, Evans withdrew from the senatorial race, hoping that his withdrawal would save the measure. It did not. On September 13, 1864, statehood was soundly defeated, and Alan Bradford beat Chivington in the race for congressional delegate.[28] Both Chivington and Evans felt the sting. Chivington realized at that point that his positions as colonel and district commander were about to end, leaving him without any official position. Evans called the defeat "the greatest mortification of my life."[29] The only consolation prize for either was that on September 19, Evans was able to announce that the Third Regiment was filled.

Even that was bittersweet because a dead calm had settled on the plains. Throughout the Department of Kansas, officers reported quiet. The Indians were gone from the overland routes. The last reported incident in Colorado occurred near Fort Lupton, on August 25, when a white herder was shot near Hall's Ranch near Fort Lupton.[30] More important, the day before the Third was reported filled, Evans received a telegram from Major Wynkoop at Fort Lyon informing him that the Cheyennnes and Arapahos had made an overture of peace. He told the governor that he had conferred with the tribes on the Smoky Hill, secured the release of four prisoners, and was escorting the chiefs to Denver to meet with him.[31] Evans was mortified.

The next day, September 19, Chivington received a message from Wynkoop: "I start for Denver tomorrow with chiefs of Arapaho & Cheyenne Nations as well as four prisoners."[32] This was not good news for Chivington either. His term of enlistment was due to expire on September 23, although he would not leave command until he was officially relieved. His total troop strength had been reduced well below six hundred men, excepting the new one-hundred-day regiment, a frail reed to rely on for success. If he did not accomplish something in the uncertain time he had left, he would be left with nothing but the memory of Glorieta, poor comfort to an ambitious and egocentric man like Chivington.

His response to Wynkoop's news was noteworthy. He immediately telegraphed Curtis, asking that ordnance bound for New Mexico be diverted to him for a campaign against "Indian warriors congregated eighty miles from Fort Lyon, 3,000 strong."[33] Chivington used Wynkoop's letter for its intelligence on the location of the main camps. He then wrote Curtis, "Winter approaches. Third Regiment is full, and they [the Cheyennes and Arapahos] know they will be chastised for their outrages and now want peace. I hope the major-general will direct that they make full restitution and then go on their reserve and stay there."[34] Ned Byers played the matter down in his paper, saying, "If the Arapahoes and Cheyennes do not want to participate in the war, all they have to do is to withdraw to their reservation where they will be protected and not molested."[35]

Camp Weld Conference

On September 27, Wynkoop arrived in Denver ahead of his command and went directly to Evans as Superintendent of Indian Affairs. Evans waffled. He told Wynkoop matters were out of his hand, and that the Indians needed to be punished more to ensure peace. More than once he asked, "What will I do with the Third Regiment if I make peace?" He told Wynkoop, "The Third Regiment was raised to kill Indians, and kill Indians it must."[36] But he could not refuse to meet the chiefs. The following day the *News* reported that Byers had met with Wynkoop as well, concluding, "we believe it is the part of prudence to compromise with the tribes named upon the terms which they propose. They have unquestionably had great provocation for hostilities, and were not the first to violate friendly relations."[37] The Weld Conference was held that afternoon.

As the *Black Hawk Mining Journal* reported, "The INDIAN COUNCIL amounted to this. Governor Evans shifted the responsibility onto Col. Chivington, and he shifted it onto Major Wynkoop."[38] The *News* was much more upbeat. Byers wrote, ". . . the council broke up with the belief that these chiefs will use their utmost power to induce their tribes to lay down their arms, a consummation devoutly to be hoped for." He also reminded readers that there were still enough Kiowas, Comanches, and Sioux at war "to satisfy the most ambitious."[39] Evans advised Sam Colley, "the Upper Arkansas Indian Agent, this arrangement relieves the Indian bureau of their care until peace is declared with them."[40] Yet, he had told the chiefs at Camp Weld that the first proclamation was still open to them. And, in his annual report to Dole, on October 15, he expressed his belief that the chiefs "were in earnest in their desire for peace, and offered to lay down their arms or to join the whites in the war against the other tribes of the plains." He added, though, "A peace before conquest, in this case, would be the most cruel kindness and the most barbarous humanity."[41]

General Curtis, without really knowing any of the details of Wynkoop's expedition, advised Chivington on September 28, 1864, the day of the conference, "I want no peace till the Indians suffer more. . . . No peace must be made without my instructions."[42] Chivington showed this message to Wynkoop before the major departed for Lyon with the chiefs and his escort. Chivington saw it as the "waffle room" he needed; Wynkoop was more optimistic. When Wynkoop reached Lyon on October 8, he found two hundred Indians camped "fifteen miles from here."[43] On October 10, Captain Silas Soule, still confident that Chivington supported the peace initiative, wrote Chivington with the news that the tribes were coming into Fort Lyon, and Wynkoop wrote a lengthy report to Curtis asking for his instructions the day that he returned. "I think that if some terms are made with these Indians that I can arrange matters so, by bringing their villages under my direct control that I can answer for their fidelity."[44] He sent the message to Curtis by special dispatch with a carefully briefed officer. Curtis, still focused on other matters, did not respond favorably. For one thing, he was angry that Wynkoop left his post in the District of the Upper Arkansas and carried the chiefs to meet with Evans and Chivington in the District of Colorado. For another, his knowledge was still limited, and he was convinced that Wynkoop misjudged his control of the situation.

Incident at Smoky Hill

He based this on an incident that occurred on September 23. After the chiefs left the Smoky Hill villages, three bands, including the people of Black Kettle, War Bonnet, and White Antelope moved southeast toward Fort Larned hoping to winter near Pawnee Forks, separating themselves from the Smoky Hill villages to wait on the outcome of the conference. Unfortunately, en route they ran into an expedition commanded by General Blunt. An advance unit, commanded by Major Scott Anthony, skirmished with a few warriors. Anthony charged a small camp and chased a few Cheyennes for several miles, when other Cheyennes from the villages showed up and encircled Anthony's troops. He took refuge on a knoll near Ash Creek, besieged by several hundred warriors. In the meantime, a party of Cheyennes and Arapahos en route to Fort Larned met Blunt's main force. Standing-in-the-Water rode right up to General Blunt and shook his hand. This party and Blunt's troops rode along together until they stumbled onto Anthony under siege. At that point, the situation quickly escalated. The Cheyennes and Arapahos broke away at a gallop, and Blunt charged to Anthony's aid. Blunt then pursued the warriors in the direction of the villages. They held Blunt back long enough for the villages to be evacuated and fought a holding action while the women and children escaped over the back trail toward the Smoky Hill.[45]

The incident was unfortunate. Blunt was puzzled by the Indians' behavior even though he was unaware of Wynkoop's expedition. When he returned to headquarters, he found an order from Curtis waiting for him. "Pap" Price had crossed the Arkansas into Kansas. Blunt was ordered to meet this new challenge, as Curtis wheeled his army about to face the Confederates. This meant that Curtis had little time to think about Wynkoop's effort when he first learned of it, while Blunt's report convinced him that the Indians Blunt had confronted were the very bands Wynkoop claimed to control (which was true). The result was that Curtis told the frontier districts they would have to fend for themselves and decided that the Indians were asking for peace solely because winter was approaching. On the other hand, when the people who had fought Anthony and Blunt returned to the Smoky Hill encampment, the reports convinced many of the Cheyennes and Arapahos that the whites were not serious about wanting peace.[46]

Another troubling result was that the Price campaign gave Chivington another chance. He would not be replaced as commander of the District of Colorado, and Curtis would not be looking over his shoulder. On October 10, the Third Colorado took first blood near Valley Station on the South Platte. The troops found a small encampment led by Big Wolf, a Cheyenne chief. Private Morse Coffin placed the dead at ten: four men, four women, and two babies. Sergeant Henry Blake said in his diary that they captured all ten—five men, three women, and two children—and then shot them all. Coffin wrote, "I strong denounced this part of the work, using cuss words."[47] Chivington, however, was elated. He talked about moving against the Republican River camps, even requesting weapons from Wynkoop at Lyon on October 16.

The situation continued to erode the prospects for peace. The Price campaign led Curtis to replace General Blunt with Major B. S. Henning as commander of the District of the Upper Arkansas. Three days after Henning took command, he ordered Scott J. Anthony to assume command at Fort Lyon and send Wynkoop forward to Larned. Henning, anxious to prove himself, took a hard line against Wynkoop's conduct and reported a variety of infractions at Lyon. While Wynkoop proceeded to defend himself with letters in his possession from officers at Fort Lyon and ranchers in the area, Anthony moved to set the house in order. Yet Henning continued to refer to the "Arapaho Indian prisoners" at Lyon, in his reports.[48]

Overland Trail

When troubles flared on the Overland Trail in July and August of 1864, both Chivington and Evans were criticized by newspapers in Nebraska and Utah for not doing more on the Platte route in Colorado. In Utah, the *Union Vedette*, a newspaper edited by Captain Charles Hempstead, who served on General Patrick Edward Connor's staff, needled Chivington consistently through August. He suggested that if Chivington could not keep the Platte route open, General Connor, who had led the attack on the Shoshonis at Bear River the previous year, could. Hempstead was especially critical of the Camp Weld meeting, arguing that the overture of the Cheyennes and Arapahos should have been rejected out of hand. Despite the fact that he knew few details about the situation, he argued that the overture was a familiar game of suing for peace in the fall with plans to reopen hostilities in the spring.[49]

One of the individuals who were hit particularly hard by the summer war on the Platte was Ben Holladay. He had eventually closed the Overland Stage Company. On October 3, 1864, the *Alta California* reported that over 70,000 letters and 180 sacks of newspapers from the eastern United States had been sent east, shipped south to the Isthmus of Panama and transported across to the Pacific side and shipped north to San Francisco for delivery in Utah, Colorado, and Dakota. In mid-October, Holladay wired Secretary of War Stanton to urge a winter campaign under the command of General Connor, who had crushed the Shoshoni at Bear River in January 1863.[50] This resulted in a truly remarkable order from General Henry Halleck to Connor, ordering him to protect the overland route from Salt Lake City to Fort Kearney "without regard to departmental lines." Halleck told Connor that his order did not alter command structure and that in joint operations, the senior officer would command.[51] This led to a wire to Chivington on October 22, asking, "Can we get a fight out of the Indians this winter?" Connor also pointedly asked if Chivington would support the campaign, providing both troops and grain for his horses.[52]

Chivington immediately wired Curtis on October 26 to ask if departmental lines had been changed and if he was to allow Connor to give directions in his district.[53] At the time, Curtis was fighting Price's Confederates, so he made no immediate response. Chivington also began to move his troops further south, after Colonel Shoup reported that his scouts had found no sign in the direction of the Republican.[54] The Thirdsters were grumbling because of bad weather and inaction. On November 3, word reached Camp Elbert at Bijou Basin, southeast of Denver, to prepare for active duty. Bad weather slowed the process, but on November 14, five of the six companies at Camp Elbert crossed the divide and headed for the Arkansas.[55]

Chivington was already maneuvering. Connor had left for Denver with two companies of cavalry and Ben Holladay, immediately after wiring Chivington on October 22. On October 24, John Evans wired Connor, "[G]lad you are coming. . . . Bring all the force you can, then pursue, kill, and destroy them."[56] Evans could see the earlier support of Otis for a plan to keep the Platte route open paying off. The *Rocky Mountain News* was practically drooling over the prospect of Connor taking charge. Denver prepared for Connor's arrival like he was a savior. However, heavy snows forced him to leave his escort at Fort Bridger and proceed to Denver by stagecoach with Holladay.

Winter Campaign

Connor arrived in Denver on November 14, the same day that the Third Regiment troops at Camp Elbert moved south toward the Arkansas. He was greeted enthusiastically. The First Colorado Regiment's band serenaded him at the Planter's House with Chivington and "a large assemblage" of citizens in attendance. The following day, the *News* observed, "Colorado will appreciate [Connor's] mission. He comes here to take a look at the field and ascertain the feasibility of punishing the Indians on the Overland mail route." He was described as "a fighter and a gentleman and a soldier to boot." He was "a man who suits the genius of this West." It concluded, "We congratulate Colorado on the accession of so superior an officer to our section of the prairie west."[57]

Evans met with Connor on November 15. It was a cordial meeting, and the governor certainly encouraged a campaign. Connor's business, however, was with Chivington. Evans had requested permission to visit Washington on October 18, but when he did not receive a response from Secretary of State William H. Seward, he decided to make the trip anyway. The particulars of any campaign was a military matter. On November 16, Governor Evans departed by stage for the East. He wrote later, "I had no intimation of the direction in which the campaign against the hostile Indians was to move, or against what bands it was to be made, when I left the Territory last fall."[58]

As late as November 19, the *News* said, "Should a winter campaign be deemed at all feasible, the General will organize an expedition to that end and at the proper time return to Denver and command in person." This was what Chivington feared. Unlike Evans, he was brusque and uncooperative with the "hero" of Bear River. He told Connor that he had plans of his own and refused to commit to the campaign Connor was planning. The day after Evans left, November 17, Chivington turned down the general's request for support. On November 20, he and his staff left Denver with a battalion of the First Colorado Cavalry to join the Thirdsters already gathering on the Arkansas under their regimental commander, Colonel George L. Shoup.[59]

An angry Connor reported to Halleck from Denver on November 21, complaining of district commanders [he had only met one] who "appear to be of the opinion that they can spare no troops for a Winter Campaign." He said that he could not attempt an expedition without greater authority, adding, "Any expedition which would not probably result in their signal chastisement would be productive of harm rather than good." He expressed hope that "an effective blow can be struck in time to prevent the renewed outrages which may be anticipated during the coming summer."[60]

Connor was skeptical of Chivington's expedition, and his analysis of the situation in Colorado was perceptive. Captain Hempstead explained in the *Union Vedette:*

> In Denver there are no troops stationed, save a detachment for Provost Guard duty. The 1st Colorado is considerably scattered, but is being gathered in to be mustered out of service, the term of enlistment of most having expired. The 2nd Colorado is doing duty in Missouri & the 3[d] (the hundred day men) are camped in Bijou Basin and about to start on an Indian hunt. As their term of service will expire on the 20th of December, they have but little time to win glory or do much in the way of finishing the savages. Col. Chivington, the Dist. Commander started a day or two since to command the expedition.[61]

On November 23, Governor Evans wired General Curtis from Atchison, Kansas, asking if he could meet with him in Leavenworth. Curtis responded "at any hour." On November 24, they conferred and produced a remarkable body of paperwork. First, Curtis wrote a letter that urged Evans—in light of conditions and the possibility of "a winter campaign [Connor's] against the trespassers"—to press Washington for 2,000 cavalry (1,000 for the Platte and 1,000 for the Arkansas) with equipment and winter gear. He also urged Evans to make the argument that the overland routes were the "proper base lines" for operations. Both men were optimistic about success because of Lincoln's September letter to Curtis about the importance of the Platte route. Then, Evans wired Secretary of War Stanton about the importance of a winter campaign. Curtis also pressed Stanton to support "the vision expressed by Gov. Evans." These messages were endorsed, the first by William Palmer Dole, the Commissioner of Indian Affairs, and the second by John Palmer Usher, the Secretary of the Interior. Plainly, Evans and Curtis had designed a winter campaign of their own which could be coordinated with Connor's expected expedition.[62]

Chivington, by this time, was out of the loop. On November 24, he advised Curtis that "Indians attacked two trains below Fort Lyons. Killed 4 men, drove off 200 head of stock, will clear them out if possible in a few days."[63] No one else ever mentioned this incident, which suggests that it was a ploy to justify his location. Everyone else was talking winter campaigns against the tribes. Chivington was pursuing a rogue course of his own and justifying his decision to leave his own district using reports of attacks on the Arkansas. At this point, even Evans had given up on Chivington. He had expected Chivington to cooperate with Connor and support a major expedition. Anything less would not serve Evans's purposes. The plan that Evans and Curtis were proposing would take weeks, if not months, to mount. A major campaign utilizing troops from Kansas, Nebraska, and Colorado, in coordination with Connor's drive from the west, was a grand design to open the overland routes and clear them of Indian resistance. Neither Evans nor Curtis was aware of Chivington's plan, already put in motion. Evans never wavered in his hard line in support of a major campaign.

Notably, Evans advised Stanton that "a portion of the tribes of the Arapahoes & Cheyenne Indians want peace and have gone to Fort Lyon under an armistice or some arrangement of the kind with Maj Wynkoop."[64] Later, after leaving Leavenworth, Evans confided in the editor of the *Northwestern Christian Advocate* in Chicago that all of the Indians in Colorado were hostile except for about six hundred near Fort Lyon.[65]

Sand Creek "Prisoners"

The situation at Fort Lyon had changed less than might have been expected with the change of command there. Expedience directed Major Anthony's course. On November 16, well after Anthony told the chiefs to move to Sand Creek, he advised Curtis, "I am satisfied that all of the Arapahoes and Cheyennes who have visited this post desire peace." He said that he told them he could not make peace until authorized by Curtis. He added, "My intention is to let matters remain dormant until troops can be sent out to take the field against all the tribes."[66] On November 25, he told Major Henning that the Arapahos and Cheyennes were regularly inquiring about word from headquarters. He offered his opinion. "Yet if I had 1000 men here for the field I would after providing for a few Indians who have all the time been friendly . . . go out against the main band of Cheyennes & Sioux and try and recover the stolen stock and punish them for what they have done."[67] Nevertheless, officials, both military and civilian, from top to bottom consistently referred to the people at Sand Creek as prisoners. Even Evans, in his annual report of October 15, reported to Dole that the Arapahos had "surrendered."[68]

Anthony received little help. Henning waited for Curtis, but on November 20, he told Anthony, "The way you have arranged with the Arapahoes . . . calling them prisoners will undoubtably answer for them, but I would not have any more such prisoners and you must keep them all away from the Post." Henning said that he expected that no permanent peace would be made until the tribes were subdued, but

131

said that he did "not see that you could have done differently with them [the Arapahos]."[69] On December 2, after Sand Creek, but before he knew of it, Curtis finally told Henning that he was "entirely undecided and uncertain as to what can be done with such nominal Indian prisoners."[70]

On November 28, the day before Sand Creek, Curtis advised General Carleton of the situation, "They insist on peace or absolute sacrifice as I choose. Of course they will have to be received, but there remains some of these tribes and all of the Kiowas to attend to, and I have proposed a winter campaign for their benefit."[71] On December 5, 1864, Curtis even suggested that the Indians at Lyon "be located at some more convenient point for feeding them."[72] What is clear from all of this correspondence is that from the moment their chiefs left Denver, the Cheyennes and Arapahos at Fort Lyon, and later Sand Creek, were considered to be prisoners.

Chivington arrived at Boone's Ranch on November 23, 1864, and prepared to move east along the Arkansas toward Fort Lyon. Only a "Bear River" style victory could save his future now. He pinned his hopes on the Third Colorado Regiment whose one hundred days of service were rapidly being used up, and on the Cheyenne and Arapaho bands that he knew were in the vicinity of Fort Lyon in response to promises he had made to them at Camp Weld.

When Chivington took command of the Third Colorado at Boonesville, an officer reported that it gave "pretty general dissatisfaction."[73] Chivington proceeded east with the utmost secrecy in the direction of Fort Lyon, stopping all east-bound traffic that might warn the Cheyennes and Arapahos or Fort Lyon. On November 27, he dispatched detachments of troopers to the ranches of John Prowers and William Bent, both of whom had Cheyenne relatives, to prevent them from warning the Cheyennes.[74] At Spring Bottom that evening, a civilian overheard Chivington's officers discussing scalps, and he swore later that Chivington said to them, "Well, I long to be wading in gore."[75] The next day, Chivington's troops encountered a patrol from Fort Lyon commanded by Captain Soule. Soule's initial surprise at seeing his commander soon turned into trepidation as Chivington made inquiries about Indians in the vicinity. The temper of the conversation and the care Chivington took to keep Soule's patrol with his command convinced Soule that the Indians encamped at Sand Creek were his target.[76]

Confusion in the Camp

What surprised Chivington most was the resistance he found to the idea among the officers at Fort Lyon. Soule expressed his fears to other officers so forcefully that he was ordered to stay away from Chivington. However, several other officers protested so vehemently that Chivington threatened them with arrest, screaming, "Damn any man in sympathy with Indians!"[77] Also present at Fort Lyon were Samuel Colley, the Indian agent, who added his protests, and Lieutenant Colonel Tappan, Chivington's arch-enemy in the First Colorado Regiment, who was returning from a trip to Washington. He observed closely but kept silent.[78]

Nevertheless, when Chivington's column moved out on the evening of November 28, 1864, the Lyon Battalion was part of it.[79] Anthony told his officers that Chivington intended to strike at the heart of native resistance on the Smoky Hill. He told them that the object of moving against Sand Creek was to surround the camp, spare Black Kettle and the other "friendlies," recover stolen stock, and kill any "raiders" that might be found there.[80] Of course, that was not what happened. It was never the real plan.

Chivington's column of 675 men marched due north from Fort Lyon, then, turning northeast, continued through the cold, clear night until, near dawn, they struck the Great South Bend of Sand Creek. A supply train of 115 wagons pursued a different course, marching northeast from Fort Lyon to the junction of Rush Creek and Sand Creek well below the South Bend. It was a bone-cold night, starlit and clear. At first light, the troops were ordered forward at a gallop, causing some of them to yell at each other that this was a hell of a way to surprise an Indian camp. For nearly two miles they rode, closing up the ranks, then reined up sharply on command.[81]

Ahead of them, Colonel Chivington, unmistakable by his size, with his staff and scouts, scanned the flats beyond from a point where the bluffs slipped down to the level of the creek bed. In the distance, the lodges of the Cheyennes and Arapahos hugged the north bank of Sand Creek, white like splotches of snow in the half-light of dawn. The column strung out, still unable to see the camps because of the bluffs to the west. From their position, the advance troops could see that the camp was already awake. Smoke curled up from the first cooking fires.[82]

Women, their morning chores interrupted by the noise of the moving column and initially uncertain whether it was a buffalo herd or white soldiers, raised the alarm, and men, women, and children stumbled out of their lodges in confusion. There were no sentries. Horse herds above and below the camps had not been kept close to the village as they would have been had the people expected an attack. Kingfisher, a young Cheyenne up early to check on the horses, saw soldiers first driving off horses on the bluffs south of the camp. He encountered Little Bear, who was on the bluffs to drive his own horses closer to the village. Kingfisher told him what he had seen, and Little Bear could see the long line of troops positioned southeast of the village and sprinted back toward the camp to raise the warning.[83] Other young people scrambled to reach the horses at the first alarm, while the majority of the people were still in a state of confusion about what was happening. Standing-in-the-Water, White Antelope, War Bonnet, and Lone Bear moved toward the east end of the village and strained to see what was happening.

Black Kettle, the Cheyenne peacemaker, tried to calm his people. Still the believer, he called out to them not to be afraid, that the soldiers would not harm them. Many listened to him, gathering around him as the troops approached, watching as he raised an American flag over his lodge with a white flag beneath it hoping he was right. A few of the few men who were there were shouting to one another, gathering their weapons, and urging the women and children to move up the creek away from the soldiers' advance. But mostly, confused by the circumstances, the Cheyennes and Arapahos lingered too long in their uncertainty, held in place by promises plainly broken, until the soldiers opened fire.

The Massacre

After Chivington had given his initial instructions to battalion commanders about the attack, he addressed the troops, "I shall not tell you who to kill today, but remember our murdered women and children whose blood saturates the sands of the Platte!"[84] Now, it was clear to the officers of the Lyon battalion that Chivington had never intended to spare anyone. Then the two battalions of the First Regiment moved toward the village three-quarters of a mile away while elements of the Third advanced along the bluffs south of the creek to cut off the horse herds. As the First moved into the valley, Captain Luther Wilson's battalion crossed in front of Anthony's Lyon battalion and drove northwest at a gallop to cut off the village from yet more horses north of the village. Anthony's battalion cantered in good order toward the camps, disciplined and eerily quiet, even its commander, the dour Major Anthony swearing that he would not "open the ball."[85]

As the young ones clambered up the bluffs to reach the horses, they saw soldiers there too, a company of the Third Regiment racing along the bluffs to separate the horses from the village. As they turned back toward the village, the young people could see Wilson's troops slashing between the camp and the horses on the north side then swinging abruptly toward the lodges.[86] They were the first to open fire. Behind Major Anthony, the bulk of the Third regiment pressed forward, fearful of being left out of the fight. The companies of Soule and Cramer were soon under fire from the rear, and they bolted to the left and moved up the south bank between the creek and the bluffs to get out of the way of the Third. By then, some of the Thirdsters on the bluffs were turning toward the camp and creating a cross fire in the village.[87]

Chivington and his staff followed with the artillery batteries close behind Anthony's troops. Now the mountain howitzers of the First Colorado's battery fired shells that exploded high above the lodges (likely by design), followed by a second barrage from the Third's battery that screamed into the lower end of the village. Fragments of hot iron tore through the lodge skins, and the people began to run. Black Kettle stared in disbelief, then turned to follow his fleeing people through the village toward the creek bed. Beside him, his wife, Medicine Woman Later, fell from a soldier's bullet. Thinking her dead, he hurried on, shouting directions and encouraging the people. In the soft sand of the creek bed, it was hard to run.[88]

Old White Antelope, betrayed once too often, refused to flee even then. He ran toward the troops waving his hands and crying out in English, "Stop! Stop!" As rifle balls kicked up the dirt around him, he stopped and began to sing:

Nothing lives long.
Only the earth and mountains . . .

A rifle ball struck him as he stood there. And then another. He pitched backward into the dry creek bottom, dead.[89] Also killed in the early moments of the attack were Standing-in-the-Water and War Bonnet, who with Lean Bear had gone to Washington the year before, dead at the hands of the soldiers they thought would protect them. Lone Bear (One Eye) fell trying to stop the fighting. Three white men in the village trading—a trader, the agency interpreter, and a soldier from Fort Lyon—tried to stop the attack, but they were driven back under fire to War Bonnet's lodge.[90]

A day of slaughter had begun.

Although a few Cheyenne and Arapaho warriors fought fiercely, it was not a battle. The number of men of fighting age in the village was limited, and, cut off from their horses, were in no position to put up a substantial defense. Twenty to thirty men led by Big Head offered the only real organized resistance of the day, attempting first to reach the horse herds and then resisting deployment of troops on the left flank. Most of them were killed because of overwhelming numbers. Another small group of mounted warriors that included Howling Wolf skirmished with Thirdsters northwest of the camp, then withdrew to provide protection for the fleeing people.

For the most part, the fighting men struggled on foot to protect fleeing women, children, and the old as they hastily dug sand pits or tried to defend others on the open prairie beyond.[91] The heaviest fighting took place in the pits. The killing spread over miles before the day was over, but, except for the two battalions of the First Colorado Cavalry, most of the troops—the inexperienced Third Regiment—were more a mob than a military command. They had, one of them said, "burst on the camp like so many wild fellows."[92]

Little Bear recalled, "The people were all running up the creek; the soldiers sat on their horses, lined up on both banks and firing into the camps, but they soon saw that the lodges were now nearly empty, so they began to advance up the creek, firing on the fleeing people."[93] It was then that the people began to hide in the creek bed, digging in and creating pits. The killing was heavy, but the defense was strong enough that the Thirdsters did not make a concentrated attack. Later, the Third's howitzers were brought up and fired into the pits until they ran out of shells, and the troops assumed that the slaughter was complete. In fact, a surprising number of people survived the shelling.[94] By then, the majority of the Third Regiment was scattered, Irving Howbert recalling, "after that we fought in little groups wherever it seemed the most effective work could be done."[95]

Some of the women tried to surrender. As Robert Bent testified later, "I saw five squaws under a bank for shelter. When the troops came up to them they ran out and showed their persons to let the soldiers know they were squaws and begged for mercy, but the soldiers shot them all."[96] On another part of the field, a child barely old enough to walk toddled across the sand. Major Anthony said, "I saw one man get off his horse . . . and draw up his rifle and fire—he missed the child. Another man came up and said, 'Let me try the son of a bitch; I can hit him.' He got down off his horse, kneeled down and fired at the little child, but he missed him. A third man came up and made a similar remark, and fired, and the little fellow dropped."[97]

The killing continued into the afternoon. "I never saw more bravery displayed by any set of people on the face of the earth than by these Indians," one officer reported. "They charged on the whole company singly, determined to kill someone before being killed themselves. . . . We, of course, took no prisoners."[98] Eventually most of the soldiers lost interest or ran out of ammunition and turned their attention to robbing and mutilating the dead. When two members of the Third Regiment brought in a woman and a child, their commander told them, "Take no prisoners." The woman turned her back to the soldiers and she and the child were killed.[99] Another officer "shot and killed three women and five children, afterwards scalping the women."[100]

Scalping and more extensive mutilation of the dead continued. Soldiers cut off ears and fingers and the genitals of both men and women. One pregnant woman was slashed open and her unborn child cut from the womb. The body of White Antelope was extensively mutilated. He was scalped several times, his ears were taken, and his scrotum cut off to make a tobacco pouch. Men and women who feigned death or lay wounded tried to defend themselves when the scalpers came, but they could not. When night fell, some of the Cheyennes and Arapahos who had hidden in the sand or in other places slipped out and began to make their way north toward the Smoky Hill.[101]

The most remarkable thing of the day was that so many of the Cheyennes and Arapahos escaped; nearly two-thirds of the encampment managed to survive despite the assault and the flight into freezing weather, half-clothed and virtually unarmed.[102] A disciplined force could have taken a much heavier toll. Several soldiers were killed by friendly fire. Others were caught separated from their fellows and killed. That evening, however, Colonel Chivington wrote his first report claiming to have bested "from nine hundred to one thousand warriors."[103]

The next day, the atrocities continued. One officer, collecting trophies, found a baby still alive and blew out its brains.[104] Some of the worst atrocities occurred that next day. In the afternoon, the half-Cheyenne son of John Smith, the interpreter, was murdered by soldiers, who later dragged his body around on the killing ground.[105] Charles Bent's life had been spared only because Captain Silas Soule took him with Charlie when he was sent to the wagon train south of the command for more supplies.[106] The troops slept on the field again that night, and when the troops pulled out the following morning, a small group of women and children were left behind and killed by the rear guard.[107]

It was by then a seriously divided command. The companies of Silas Soule and Joseph Cramer had refused to participate in the fight. One of the men of the First Colorado's battery under Lieutenant Baldwin said later that his group was so angry that they were ready to take on the Thirdsters because of what happened. He even said that he was surprised Chivington survived the fight because of the animus against him.[108] Even some members of the Third were shocked by what had happened, one man, at least, simply refusing to participate further.[109] The only prisoners were the wives of white traders John Smith and Charlie Windsor at Fort Lyon, two young Cheyenne girls, and an Arapaho boy, who were later displayed as trophies in Denver. A few other children may have survived; later reminiscences said that small groups or individuals had taken children prisoner and refused to kill them. They were spirited away and not taken to Denver.[110]

Colonel Chivington had promised an extended campaign, but after Sand Creek, he turned southeast, away from the concentration of Cheyennes and Arapahos, ostensibly in pursuit of Little Raven's Arapahos down the Arkansas. This too angered the troops of the Lyon Battalion, including Major Anthony. Five days later without ever seeing an Arapaho, Chivington called an end to his expedition. Notably, Chivington hurried ahead of the column, as he had done in New Mexico, paused briefly at Fort Lyon where he boastfully compared himself to Harney and Connor and quickly departed by stage for Denver, leaving Colonel George Shoup to bring up the Third Regiment. The Third, weighed down with booty, followed.[111]

At Fort Lyon, the officers of the First were still infuriated over what had happened. And in the villages of the Cheyennes and Arapahos on the Smoky Hill the anger swelled as the survivors told their stories of what had happened at Sand Creek. They had lost about 230 people there, but between two-thirds and three-fourths of them were women and children. Thirteen council chiefs and four soldier chiefs of the Cheyennes were also among the dead. Left Hand, the great voice for peace among the Arapahos, was mortally wounded, and died later on the Smoky Hill. Bosse and Heap of Buffalos, who had attended the Camp Weld meeting, were killed. Close to two hundred men, women, and children were wounded.[112] Although a majority of the villagers escaped, it was a devastating blow. The camp was a chiefs' camp, a test case of the white man's intent. Now the tribes had their answer.

"Minnie Tappan." One of three children taken to Denver after Sand Creek and publicly displayed as trophies of the fight. Two of the children were Cheyenne and sisters, one of whom apparently died. The third child was an Arapaho boy. The older girl, pictured here, was baptized "Minnie Haha" at St. Paul's Episcopal Church in Central City, Colorado, on December 24, 1866. She was later taken east to Boston by Samuel F. Tappan, who had presided over the military commission that investigated the Sand Creek Massacre. Tappan was a member of the Peace Commission of 1867-68 and later a prominent Indian reformer and spiritualist. Minnie died of tuberculosis at the age of sixteen while a student at Howard University in Washington, D. C. (Tom Meier Collection)

CHAPTER 9

PROTEST AND RECRIMINATION

"Among the feats of arms in Indian warfare, the recent campaign of our Colorado Volunteers will stand in history with few rivals, and none to exceed it in final results," proclaimed the *Denver Rocky Mountain News* when the first reports of the Sand Creek campaign reached Denver early in December 1864.[1] The *Central City Miners' Register* added, "The good work is begun, and we hope no respite will be given to the savage till at least four thousand of them have been killed. The true policy is to give them no quarter, but to kill male and female, old and young, that none may be left to tell the tale."[2] And even the *Black Hawk Mining Journal,* which had been critical of both Chivington and Evans, declared, "It is impossible to exaggerate the value of this occurrence to Colorado. It is the dawn of a new era, indeed, the rising of a new sun for the Territory."[3]

This was the theme reflected in the reports of the expedition's commander, Colonel John Milton Chivington, and his subalterns, who plainly saw themselves as heroes. Chivington called the Sand Creek affair, "the most bloody and hard-fought Indian battle that has ever occurred on these plains."[4] In the spirit of the moment, Captain Theodore G. Cree, an officer of the Third Colorado Regiment, exulted that the men of the Third Colorado Volunteer Cavalry had "won for themselves a name that will be remembered for ages to come."[5] He could not have imagined the irony of his statement at the time. At the moment, he celebrated, and the citizens of Colorado—most of them—celebrated too.

Chivington had achieved his purpose, and now he meant to make the most of it. But his design was already in trouble. The first dispatches about Sand Creek reached Denver on December 7, the same day that Chivington ended his "expedition." Two days later, Stephen Selwyn Harding, the chief justice of Colorado, penned a letter to John W. Wright, a former agent of the Indian Office and friend of John Palmer Usher, the Secretary of the Interior, declaring that he had received evidence that would prove that the Sand Creek attack "on the defenseless savages was one of the most monstrous in history."[6] Clearly the official dispatches were not the only reports to reach Denver quickly.

Judge Harding had enjoyed a decent reputation in Colorado until August 1864, when the courts, forced to settle jurisdictional disputes in criminal cases, had reopened the question of Indian land title, by declaring all lands north and west of the South Platte to be legally Indian lands. The court's decisions made him a target of the statehood movement, which claimed that the decisions were politically motivated. The courts' rulings were even blamed for causing the summer war with the Indians.

The person who contacted Harding about Sand Creek was never identified, but the chain of correspondence suggests that it may have been one of the interested civilians at Fort Lyon. Harding knew Samuel Colley, the Indian agent for the Cheyennes and Arapahos, and Dexter Colley, the agent's son, who was in business with John Smith as traders at Fort Lyon. All of them had made it clear that they would do their best to bring Chivington down for what he had done.

Colley was close to the Commissioner of Indian Affairs, William Palmer Dole, and took steps to inform him about Sand Creek at once. He also wrote letters to John Palmer Usher, the Secretary of the Interior, and to Senator James Rood Doolittle, the chairman of the Senate Indian Affairs Committee. Harding's task was to reinforce these efforts where he had the most influence. John W. Wright was the conduit for this effort.

Opposing Views

Wright had close ties to Usher, as well as reasons to be interested in the controversy. Wright had been the government contractor who had surveyed the Sand Creek reserve in 1863. He had become a bitter critic of Governor Evans's management of Indian affairs and was closely aligned with the Colleys at Fort Lyon. By December 1864, Wright was in Washington pursuing other opportunities and well-placed to act as an agent against Chivington. Harding was the logical man to make the contact because both he and Wright were from Indiana and had moved in the same political circles. Moreover, Harding's son had accompanied Wright to Lyon when the surveys were made in 1863.[7]

Chivington reached Denver on December 13, 1864. Two days later, he requested permission to visit department headquarters to discuss Indian matters. On December 16, he wrote yet another report of the Sand Creek fight for General Curtis, in which he lobbied for another campaign. Mysteriously, though, just four days later, on December 20, he requested that Curtis relieve him of command.[8]

On December 16, the same day that Chivington wrote his detailed report, an unidentified officer wrote a letter about Sand Creek from Denver to General John P. Slough, Chivington's old enemy, who was then the military governor at Alexandria, Virginia, hoping "to counteract any good impression that may have been made in Washington by the report of Chiv's pretended fight with the Indians." He advised Slough that Chivington had "butchered about 200. 40 warriors the balance Squaws and papooses."[9]

The officer in question could not have been an officer of the Lyon Battalion. The officers at Fort Lyon were busy, however. On December 10, 1864, Lieutenant Colonel Tappan had expressed concern for the safety of William Bent and the Indians at his ranch. Accordingly, Major Anthony ordered Lieutenant Cramer to proceed to Bent's Ranch to protect the people there. When Cramer arrived, he relieved Captain Theodore Cree of the Third Regiment and told him in no uncertain terms that Chivington was looking for "a brigadier general's commission" and that Sand Creek was a massacre.[10]

On December 14, 1864, Captain Henry Booth, inspector of the District of the Upper Arkansas, reported that Indian hostilities had suddenly increased between Larned and Lyon. He noted further that "the Indians will no doubt be exasperated by the late action at Fort Lyon and we have reason to suppose will harass the travel on the Road more than ever." He advised headquarters that he would proceed to Fort Lyon to learn more.[11]

On that same day, Silas Soule wrote a detailed account of the Sand Creek affair to Edward W. Wynkoop, his former commander, who, like Soule, was thought to be one of Chivington's "pets." It was a graphic and sickening account. In the letter, Soule indicated that Lieutenant Cramer was also writing him and expressed hope that Chivington "will be dismissed when the facts are known in Washington."[12] Tappan was still at Lyon at that time, recovering from an injury. He recorded in his diary that when Chivington stopped at Lyon on his way to Denver, he had boasted that Sand Creek would give him "command of a brigade." Tappan wrote Slough and others, not the least of whom was Colonel Orville Babcock, General Grant's adjutant, who he had met while briefly attached to Grant's headquarters during his recent visit to Washington. His sentiments were clear: "the affair at Sand Creek is a proclamation to the Indians that we are determined not to keep our word with them, but to wage a war of extermination against them, to butcher and scalp their women and children, to assassinate all who fall into our hands as prisoners, to show no mercy, but excel them in savage cruelty."[13] These would be only the first letters Tappan sent to both military and civilian authorities. He departed for Denver on December 15.

On December 19, Lieutenant Cramer penned his own report to Major Wynkoop. He expressed his mortification over the affair and his hope that Chivington would be cashiered as a result. "If you are in Washington," he wrote, "for God's sake, Major, keep Chivington from being a Bri-g. Genl, which he expects." He also told Wynkoop that he was preparing a report for General Slough, assuring Wynkoop that he would "write him nothing but what can be proven."[14]

The Third Regiment reached Denver on December 22 and marched through the streets to the cheers of the crowds. But the references to scalps and other trophies that were gleefully described in the press and openly displayed in bars and theaters also motivated enemies of Chivington and Evans to question what had happened. They had no trouble finding Thirdsters who described the affair as "very murderous" and who "made no boast of it at all."[15] The celebration was about to come to an end.

On December 26, 1864, Harding's letter to Wright appeared anonymously in the *New York Herald.* It was picked up the next day by the *Washington Star,* and on December 31, the story broke in Denver, unleashing speculation about the identity of the "gentleman in high position." By then the *Auburn* (New York) *Advertiser* had identified Harding as the offending official. It would be a few weeks before these reports reached Denver, and in the interim, Sam Tappan's life was threatened as a possible suspect and both Harding and U.S. Attorney Browne had been accused of spreading "infamous lies" about Sand Creek. The man who revealed Harding's identity to the *Advertiser* was his predecessor as chief justice of Colorado, Benjamin F. Hall, who was close to William H. Seward and no friend of Chivington. Hall had learned about the situation directly from Harding, and he too was applying pressure where he could.[16]

Before Christmas 1864, the first reports of Chivington, Anthony, and others had reached General Curtis and Major Henning, commanding the District of the Upper Arkansas. When Major Wynkoop first saw the reports at Fort Riley, he went "wild with rage."[17] Shortly thereafter, he received Cramer's letter and hastily copied it and sent it, along with a letter of his own, to Hiram Pitt Bennet, Colorado's congressional delegate. By then, Bennet was en route to Washington with George K. Otis, Ben Holladay's superintendent of the Overland Stage Company, to press for a winter campaign against hostile Indians commanded by General Connor, as the result of an increase in raids already attributed to Sand Creek by military authorities.[18]

Investigation Ordered

On December 31, Wynkoop was ordered back to Fort Lyon to reclaim command of the post and to investigate Sand Creek. That same day, General Slough forwarded the letter he had received from the unnamed officer to Secretary of War Stanton. On New Year's Day, escorted by Soule, Captain Booth, the district inspector, visited the site of the massacre, counting sixty-nine dead bodies on the field, three fourths of them women and children. Shortly thereafter, Tappan received a letter from Colonel Babcock advising him that Grant and General John Rawlins concurred "in damning Sand Creek as infamous" and on January 12, General Curtis made it plain to Governor Evans that "I abominate the extermination of women and children."

Delegate Bennet had also received a frantic letter from Jerome B. Chaffee, a representative of Colorado's mining interests, that Chivington's attack had seriously inflamed the situation in Colorado at precisely the moment when the terms of service of the Third Regiment and most of the First were ending, leaving the territory unprotected. Bennet transmitted the letter to General James A. Hardie who forwarded it to General Henry Halleck, and on January 11, 1865, Halleck ordered General Curtis to investigate.[19]

Bennet visited Stanton who referred him to General Grant at City Point, as General of the Army. There Bennet proposed a winter campaign commanded by General Connor. When he had finished his presentation, Grant told him, "I have heard of Sand Creek, and I can but regard that as a massacre." He hesitated to order a winter campaign, however, and told Bennet he would consider the matter and respond through Stanton. Ironically, for the moment at least, the Sand Creek affair had already made Washington officials more cautious about authorizing major campaigns against tribes so obviously betrayed.[20]

Bennet returned to Washington, and on January 30, he wrote to Slough that he had learned by a copy of a letter to Major Wynkoop from Lieutenant Cramer, that Cramer had written a full report of Sand Creek for the general. He requested a copy of the report, declaring, "I propose to show Chivington in his true Colors to the country and place the great responsibility of that Massacre on him, and so far as I can relieve the common soldier and the citizen of the Territory of all blame in the transaction."[21] Jerome B. Chaffee, who was in Washington when the news broke, wrote his friend Dr. L. B. McLain on January 8. He expressed his concerns about Indian policy and the potential threat to Colorado if something were not done. "I hope Chivington will be sustained," he wrote, "unless he has done something that is worse than I anticipate. If his crime consists only in killing Indians, then his crime is our profit and every Coloradan ought to stand by him. In these times I care nothing for men only as they subserve the interests of the country."[22]

In the meantime, the pressure was mounting on Congress. On January 9, 1865, Senator Doolittle requested that the matter of Sand Creek be referred to the Indian Affairs Committee for further study.[23] On January 10, Godlove Orth, the congressman from Judge Harding's home district in Indiana, introduced a resolution that the Joint Committee on the Conduct of the War investigate the incident.[24] Charles Sumner called Sand Creek "an exceptional crime; one of the most atrocious in the history of our country."[25] Three days later, after a lengthy debate, Senate S. R. No. 93 passed, withholding the pay of the officers and men of the Third Colorado Regiment until the facts were determined about the affair.[26] Bennet hoped to present his evidence on the subject when the resolution was brought up in the House, but it was tabled without debate.[27]

Governor Evans Under Attack

Governor Evans was in Washington when the news broke in December. The timing could not have been worse. Lincoln was under strong pressure to reorganize his cabinet. John Palmer Usher, the Secretary of the Interior, was a cabinet member who was the target of several groups, at least in part because of his independence. Even a group from his home state was after his job. In fact Usher had discussed with William Palmer Dole, his Commissioner of Indian Affairs, the possibility of submitting resignations even before the November elections, although he hoped he would be retained. In December, Evans, along with other prominent Methodists, endorsed Senator Harlan to replace Usher.[28] Evans remained in the city hoping to secure the removal of Colorado appointees who had opposed statehood, and was blindsided by the reports of the Sand Creek Massacre. Caught off guard by what had happened, he initially did not know how to react beyond defending the territory and his management of Indian affairs. He complained strenuously that the reports threatened his efforts to secure arms for the Colorado militia. On January 13, during the debate on the joint resolution, Evans found himself under attack for complicity in the affair.

Senator James Harlan of Iowa and Senator Samuel C. Pomeroy of Kansas both defended Evans as a man of integrity, although they were on different sides on the issue of withholding the pay of the Third Regiment. In making a case against the measure, Senator Pomeroy defended Chivington as a man of character and a Methodist minister. When Harlan, who supported the measure, questioned Chivington's Methodist credentials, Pomeroy drew Evans into the equation: "Governor Evans, a man distinguished for his philanthropy and kindness and religion, not only strongly recommended Colonel Chivington, but has indorsed his act since it has been reported to have been committed; and I notice that the papers in that Territory speak in the highest terms of Colonel Chivington." Harlan, thinking that he was helping Evans, stated that the Indians were near Fort Lyon at the invitation of the governor when they were attacked: "Here the Governor of the Territory invites the peaceable Indians to separate themselves from the hostile Indians in order that they may be protected; and when they are fairly settled down in their camps in pursuance of this invitation the armed white men fall on them and massacre them."[29]

This exchange forced Evans to make a statement, and on January 18, Evans published a letter in the *Washington Chronicle* defending himself while declining "to express either approval or disapproval [of Sand Creek], until the facts shall be ascertained." This discussion prompted John W. Wright to write Senator Pomeroy. He challenged the senator's view of Evans in blistering terms and published his letter as a pamphlet before the end of the month. Evans was culpable, Wright declared, both for not allowing the Cheyennes and Arapahos time to respond to his first proclamation and for issuing the second proclamation, which became a permit for Chivington to do what he did. Wright said flatly, that "An Indian war is on the country. Every effort has been made for two years to produce it, and the Indian has suffered outrage and wrong by the hand of the white man."[30]

Evans, who could not return to Colorado because of the winter war on the Platte, lingered in Washington to build his defense, engaging supporters like Harlan, Doolittle, Bishop Simpson, and James M. Ashley. He had to neutralize a significant opposition from Colorado, including Delegate Bennet, Allen A. Bradford (Bennet's replacement), Jerome Chaffee (who found the "something worse" than he had anticipated in Chivington's act), George Otis, John P. Slough, and more. On March 6, 1865, Evans wrote seven letters to Lincoln concerning Colorado appointments, and on March 14, he wrote six letters to Ashley calling for the removal of Colorado officials and submitting names for replacements. Then, Evans and Ashley presented the governor's case to President Lincoln, arguing that the attacks on Evans were being made by "disloyal" federal appointees. Evans appeared to make his case, and Ashley followed up the meeting with a strong letter of support for Evans and a condemnation of other appointees in Colorado as "Copperheads."[31]

147

Also early in March, Secretary of the Interior Usher met with Lincoln, and on March 9, Usher sent Commissioner Dole to the White House with his resignation along with an understanding that he would remain in office until May 15, to give the Senate time to confirm the appointment of his successor. Lincoln had already decided on Harlan for the post, which was good news for Evans and Simpson; but Usher was surprised that Lincoln submitted Harlan's appointment on the same day he gave Lincoln his resignation. And Harlan was enraged that Usher would remain in office for two more months. He was anxious to begin his reforms in the Office of Indian Affairs at once.[32] Nevertheless, the appointment of Harlan gave Evans hope that Lincoln would sustain him as well.

Joint Committee on the Conduct of War

However, Evans was not free of the specter of Sand Creek yet. On March 13, 1865, the Joint Committee on the Conduct of the War began its investigation of Sand Creek.[33] On March 15, Evans appeared before the committee. Again, he refused to defend Chivington's attack outright, but the questioning was tough:

Question: With all the knowledge you have in relation to . . . depredations by the Indians, do you think they afford any justification for the attack made by Colonel Chivington on these friendly Indians. . . .?

Answer: As a matter of course, no one could justify an attack on Indians while under the protection of the flag. . . . I have heard, however . . . that these Indians had assumed a hostile attitude before he attacked them. . . . I suppose they were being treated as prisoners of war in some way or other.

Question: But . . . do you deem that Colonel Chivington had any justifications for that attack?

Answer: I would rather not give an opinion . . . until I have heard the other side of the question. . . .

Question: I do not ask for an opinion. Do you know of any circumstance which would justify that attack?

Answer: I do not know of any circumstances connected with it subsequent to the time those Indians left me.[34]

On May 4, 1865, the Joint Committee on the Conduct of the War recommended the removal of Governor Evans and the arrest and trial of Chivington and Anthony. Of Evans, the committee said, "His testimony . . . was characterized by such prevarication and shuffling as has been shown by no witness they have examined during the four years they have been engaged in their investigations."[35] Of Chivington, the committee wrote, "your committee can hardly find fitting terms to describe his conduct. Wearing the uniform of the United States which should be the emblem of justice and humanity . . . he deliberately planned and executed a foul and dastardly massacre which would have disgraced the veriest savages among those who were the victims of his cruelty."[36]

Practically, with Chivington and Anthony already out of the army and beyond its reach for court martial, the only real target was John Evans. John Palmer Usher, on the last day of his tenure as Secretary of the Interior, advised President Johnson, "The conclusion of the Committee is evidently just, and I join in asking that their recommendations be carried out."[37] Congressman Ashley immediately sprang to Evans's defense with a strongly worded appeal to Secretary of State William H. Seward, denouncing the report of the committee and recounting Evans's meeting with Lincoln in March. He advised Seward that "this whole matter was talked over and satisfactorally [sic], at least to Mr. Lincoln."[38]

Allen Bradford, Colorado's new representative, wrote a blistering letter about Evans on the same day, May 22, concluding, "In his management of the Indian affairs in the Territory, he has pursued a policy that has intensified the hostility of the Indians and provoked their attacks upon the citizens of the Territory and the routes of travel, thus preventing emigration and disturbing business and trade. He has given countenance and encouragement to the massacre of peaceable Indians and destroyed their faith and confidence in the sincerity and obligation of Government Treaties."[39] Bradford, Bennet, Chaffee, John Slough, and others kept up the pressure. By mid-June rumors reached Denver that Evans would be replaced by Slough, and Evans even wrote Slough requesting that the transition take place as quickly as possible.[40]

While these battles were being fought in Washington, Sand Creek was under scrutiny in Colorado as well. On January 14, 1865, Wynkoop arrived at Fort Lyon to resume command. He spent the next two days inquiring into Sand Creek. Both Soule and Cramer were gone, en route to Denver to muster out their companies. But there were other voices. Wynkoop dutifully recorded affidavits, and on January 16, wrote an emotional and damning report, describing Chivington as an "inhuman monster." It was hardly a dispassionate analysis, but it would appear in all of the official investigations of Sand Creek that followed.[41] A few days later, Major Anthony resigned his commission "on account of my connexion [sic] with the 'Sand Creek affair' which really disgraced every officer connected with it, unless he was compelled to go under orders."[42]

Military Commission Established to Investigate Sand Creek

Colonel Thomas Moonlight, who succeeded Chivington as commander of the District of Colorado had found an effective force of only two hundred men in the entire district when he arrived on January 4, and only forty troopers to patrol the line between Denver and Julesburg where the greatest concentration of renewed resistance was reported. Curtis returned Fort Lyon to the District of Colorado, and, on February 1, 1865, Moonlight ordered the establishment of a military commission to investigate Sand Creek. Ironically, as the senior officer in Colorado not present at the Sand Creek Massacre, Lieutenant Colonel Tappan was appointed to conduct the investigation.[43] On February 18, the new Methodist Church in Denver was dedicated, and Colonel Chivington presented a gold watch to Reverend Willard on behalf of himself and others.[44] The colonel was publicly calling the investigation a forum for his vindication.

The testimony of Silas S. Soule and Joseph A. Cramer provided the bedrock of the case against Sand Creek before the military commission, although in the weeks that followed a substantial body of evidence reinforced it. Soule was a rakish sort, reform minded and carefree, who had taken up causes before in his life and who might have been dismissed as an idealist without hard evidence of his actions, but Cramer was steady and practical, a plain, bluntly honest man who had risen through the ranks and was promoted to lieutenant based on his service. Together, they made a powerful and persuasive team.[45] As early as February 24, 1865, the *Black Hawk Mining Journal* reported, "we are informed that assassins have twice attempted the life of Capt. Soule within six weeks. Soule is a witness who expects to testify before the Court of Inquiry, and his testimony is evidently feared; hence he is shot at nights, in the suburbs of Denver."

In March, the military commission traveled to Fort Lyon to question witnesses there. On April 9, 1865, Wynkoop wrote his friend, Cramer, "I think that God Almighty will see that the guilty are punished eventually, and the virtuous receive their reward. Remember me kindly to Soule and all other friends."[46] On April 23, Soule, who was provost marshal of Denver, was murdered by an unassigned trooper, fulfilling Soule's prediction that he would be assassinated. Afterward, Chivington tried to blacken Soule's name before the commission, but managed only to convince many that he was responsible for Soule's death.[47] The commission did not complete its work until the end of May, after a spirited but unconvincing defense on Chivington's behalf.

Special Joint Committee on the Condition of the Indian Tribes

Only days after the Joint Committee on the Conduct of the War began deliberations, a Special Joint Committee on the Condition of the Indian Tribes was organized to investigate federal Indian policy on a broad scale, but one of its tasks was to report on Sand Creek. Eventually, Senator Doolittle, Senator F. S. Foster, and Congressman Lewis Ross traveled west, escorted by General Alexander McDowell McCook, to Fort Riley, Fort Lyon, and Denver. On the way, the committee members visited the Sand Creek site where congressmen picked up "the skulls of infants whose milk teeth had not been shed—perforated with pistol and rifle shots."[48] Cramer wrote Henry C. Leach, a Denver businessman and politician, about the visit on June 14, 1865, and Leach responded, "I was delighted that at last the truth begins to prevail. Baby skulls will be very ornamental in the white house, or on the arches of [the] Capitol [sic]." He brought Cramer up to date on the political efforts of his group, and ended confidently: "We shall win this fight, and the devil will get his wandering child—old Chiv."[49]

In June, Chivington published a "Synopsis" of the evidence presented before the military commission. Actually, it was a highly selective presentation of quotes from the defense testimony, interspersed with his own running commentary. In effect, he blamed the controversy on the Indian agent and traders who were profiting from the situation at Fort Lyon and on jealous army officers. He pandered to the settlers' fears and scolded everyone who doubted that he had saved the territory. His feelings came through loud and clear: "It is not surprising that the Indian believes himself to be the white man's superior. White men on the frontiers, do you desire to become the servile dogs of a brutal savage? If you do, this policy will suit you, though I thought differently and acted accordingly?"[50]

Colorado Methodists Support Chivington and Evans

Colorado Methodists rallied to the cause of Chivington and Evans. Oliver Willard testified to the Doolittle Committee that Chivington had told him that Evans did not know about the Sand Creek attack until after it was over. On April 5, six Colorado ministers including Willard, drafted a strongly worded letter of support for Chivington, describing him as "a model for large-hearted liberality and Christian energy." They then endorsed Sand Creek and declared, "We believe that our only hope for safety as a territory lies in the repetition of like battles with the same results. In the destruction of these Indians, the murdering and scalping of white men, women and children, was by such avenged. We are fully persuaded that the laws of war in this action were fully respected, and only fear that similar occurrences are likely to be too unfrequent [sic] for an immediate and complete subjugation of the treacherous, bloodthirsty red men."[51]

In June, Bishop Calvin Kingsley arrived to preside over the Colorado Annual Conference. He was quickly won over by the Coloradans. He telegraphed Bishop Simpson to use his influence to prevent the removal of Governor Evans. In a letter to Simpson, he decried the "sentimentalism" that "too often procedes [sic] in the utter absence of all knowledge of the Indian character." He used Chivington as authority that Evans was not in Colorado at the time of Sand Creek, "and the Col informs me, that neither the Gov or any other person knew any thing [sic] of his plans until after the battle was fought and the Indians routed. But the affair offered a good pretext to the political opponents of the Gov and they have availed themselves of it with strong hopes of success in Washington." He said that he had not met a man in Colorado "who does not justify Col. C. for the course he took in whipping the Indians."

He was lavish in his praise of Evans. He lauded his "good moral and religious influence," his honest administration, his support of mining interests, and his influence for the admission of Colorado as a state and a "speedy completion of the Pacific Rail Road, which has become a military, commercial and religious necessity to the Territory."[52] Kingsley's letter to Simpson was followed by a letter to the *Northwestern Christian Advocate* from Schuyler Colfax, which provided a similar assessment of the situation and specifically praised the Methodist Church for its fine new church and its seminary. He wrote, "I need scarcely tell you that your former fellow citizen, Gov. Evans, is foremost here in every good word and work ."[53]

June ended reasonably well for Evans. On June 21, his daughter, Josephine, was married to Samuel H. Elbert, Evans's secretary and confidant in Colorado, at the family home in Evanston. Bishop Simpson performed the wedding.[54] Harlan was finally in charge of the Department of the Interior and ready to go after the "pack of thieves" in the Indian Office, which Evans hoped would relieve the pressure to remove him.[55] Harlan had already made it clear to William P. Dole that he had to go, and on July 6, 1865, Dole resigned as Commissioner of Indian Affairs.[56] In July, the *Northwestern Christian Advocate* and the *Christian Advocate and Journal* of New York published articles from Bishop Kingsley, who was detained in Denver "by the depredations of the 'noble red man.'" They consisted mainly of praise for the economic potential of the West, emphasizing that "the great want of this country is the speedy completion of the Pacific Railroad."

Kingsley scarcely mentioned moral or spiritual concerns. In a lengthy discourse on the railroad, he called it a military necessity to speed the subjugation of the

Bishop Calvin Kingsley. Kingsley was unsympathetic to the Indians. He wrote about the West, but focused on its economic future and the importance of the railroads. (General Commission on Archives and History of The United Methodist Church, Drew University, Madison, New Jersey)

Indians. He wrote, "These Indians being yet in a state of childhood, so far as intellectual and educational development is concerned, need occasional chastising. Nothing else will do. To the questions, 'What shall be done with the Africans and the Indians?' I have short answers. *Make men of them.*" He added, "I have no fellowship with that sentimentalism which is ready to die of grief because the red man is not allowed to hold back civilization and Christianity just for the sake of being a savage. There is no reason why an ignorant savage should be allowed land enough for hunting ground to sustain a thousand civilized and Christianized persons living in accordance with the precepts of the Gospel."[57]

Secretary of State Seward Asks for Evans's Resignation

Evans could not be saved, however. The report of the Joint Committee on the Conduct of the War was published in mid-July, and on July 18, Secretary of State Seward formally requested Evans's resignation.[58] Bishop Simpson and Secretary Harlan made one final effort to save Evans, without success. Secretary Seward told Harlan that he was "satisfied" with Evans as governor but that the committee's report made it impossible to keep him as part of the administration. Simpson tried to see President Johnson, but was unable to meet with him. He then visited Seward at Cape May, New Jersey, for a final appeal.[59] It was a futile gesture. On August 1, 1865, Evans resigned under protest.[60]

With a touch of irony, Evans requested that the transfer of power be delayed until he had concluded a treaty with the Utes. Unaware that Evans had been removed, General John Slough, in Colorado with Delegate Bradford, wrote President Johnson concerning Evans, "He is not only unpopular, but is a constant subject of ridicule. He is rarely spoken of as Governor but is called, 'Granny,' 'Old Woman,' &c."[61] As a gesture to Simpson and the Methodists, Seward and Johnson approved Bishop Simpson's recommendation of Alexander W. Cummings, editor of the Philadelphia *Evening Bulletin* and another of Simpson's rich Methodist friends, as Evans's successor.[62]

The publication of the Joint Committee's report brought down a storm of criticism. The *Chicago Tribune* called Sand Creek "an act of hideous cruelty garnished with all the accessories of fraud, lying, treachery, bestiality" and proclaimed that Chivington should be tried by court martial "and shot like a wolf."[63] The *Nation* declared, "Comment cannot magnify the horror."[64] The *Boston Daily Evening Traveler* reported, "The testimony before the committee proved the most dreadful violation of honor, and the most wanton disregard of life on the part of Col. Chivington."[65] The *Washington Chronicle* denounced Sand Creek as a "bloody offense, which could hardly be surpassed in the warfare of the savage tribe with another."[66]

Evans Defends His Management of Indian Affairs

In September, Evans published his long awaited *Reply* to the report of the Joint Committee on the Conduct of the War. It was not a defense of Sand Creek. He was quite explicit on that point: "I do not propose to discuss the merits or demerits of the Sand Creek battle, but simply to meet the attempt to connect my name with it, and to throw discredit on my testimony." He blamed his problems on his political enemies who "conspired to connect my name with the Sand Creek battle, although they knew that I was in no way connected with it." He defended his management of Indian affairs. He denied having any part in sending the Cheyennes and Arapahos to Lyon after Camp Weld, although he had testified before the Joint Special Committee on the Condition of the Indian Tribes just weeks earlier that he had "suggested to Major Wynkoop through Colonel Shoop [*sic*] . . . that my judgment was that for the time being it was better to treat them as prisoners of war."[67]

The *Chicago Tribune,* which had said Chivington should be shot like a wolf just weeks before, now asserted that Evans "was in no manner responsible for what happened at Sand Creek."[68] The *Central Christian Advocate* concluded that "his defense is triumphant," and the *Northwestern Christian Advocate* declared "there has been no testimony which has involved Governor Evans in wrong."[69] The *Rocky Mountain News* and *Central City Miner's Register* added their endorsement as did other Western papers from Nebraska to Montana. On the other hand, the *Atchison Freedom's Champion* said that while Evans might have been guilty of acts that were hasty and ill-advised prior to the expedition and "yet not be responsible for the actual atrocities and cold-blooded barbarities that followed." It added:

> But his connection with Chivington is too clearly established to be denied without the very best evidence, and unless this is given in his defense, the public will neither overlook nor pardon him. The infamy of the Sand Creek Massacre is established beyond a question; three different Committees have thoroughly investigated the affair, and all agree in pronouncing it the most diabolical and atrocious villainy known in recorded history. The evidence is voluminous and given by some of the best men in Colorado; even the friends of Chivington could say nothing to

excuse or even palliate his crimes. If therefore, Gov. Evans does not succeed in establishing that he had no connection with this clerical monster, he is branded as Chivington is branded, with enduring calumny.[70]

Evans's defense was surprisingly weak. One editor noted that Evans took "the
utmost pains to show that he knew nothing of Chivington's movements and was not
privy to his plans or intentions."[71] Another observer said that "Gov. Evans is afraid
to look Sand Creek in the face, and either justify or condemn it."[72] Even the *Rocky
Mountain News* expressed regrets that Evans had not covered the "whole ground,"
with a full-scale defense of Sand Creek that would demonstrate that Sand Creek had
been fought according to the "usages of warfare, with no more attendants of barbarity than usually occur in such cases."[73] The *Black Hawk Mining Journal* said that Evans had chosen personal vindication over vindication of Sand Creek.[74] The *Atchison
Weekly Champion and Press* was "woefully disappointed." Evans's *Reply* was "only an
evidence of his repentance and shame that he was connected, even remotely, with
this fearful infamy, and not the established proof of his innocence as he had hoped.
And so Sand Creek yet remains unjustified and unexplained, in all its revolting and
sickening brutality."[75] The *Denver Gazette* raised so many questions about his failure
to defend Sand Creek that Evans wrote a letter to the *Rocky Mountain News* assuring the voters that he wanted to see Colorado's soldiers vindicated and favored an
aggressive Indian policy. Again, he stopped short of a public endorsement of Sand
Creek.[76]

Condemnation of the Sand Creek Massacre

The report of the Joint Special Committee on the Condition of the Indian Tribes
was not published until 1867, but interviews with the members of Congress who
visited Colorado and with General Alexander McD. McCook, their escort, made it
clear that they were all outraged by Sand Creek. General McCook wrote a separate
report that was never published that also condemned Sand Creek as a massacre.[77] It
was difficult to dismiss the response to Senator Doolittle's speech in Denver, when
he asked whether Indians should be placed on reservations and taught to support
themselves or be exterminated. The response was jolting as the crowd shouted, "Exterminate them! Exterminate them!"[78]

Judge Advocate General Joseph Holt wrote a particularly strong condemnation
of Sand Creek as a "cowardly and coldblooded slaughter," after reviewing the record
of the military commission, but it was not published. He condemned the "shocking

and demoniac barbarities" of the action, but concluded that Chivington could not be tried because he was no longer in service. He did recommend that the army express its "utter abhorrence of the savage crimes thus committed in its name."[79]

By the end of August 1865, Sand Creek had come to symbolize the worst instincts of humanity. "Under the rule of Christian nations," General McCook wrote, "I do not think this attack has ever been exceeded in barbarity."[80] Colorado leaders and the majority of its citizens were shocked by the characterization. The controversy did divide the territory further, and in due course its editors, who had so uniformly praised the Sand Creek action in the beginning, would splinter in their assessments in light of the evidence. The anti-Evans, anti-Chivington factions used the national condemnation to promote their local political agendas wrapped in moral outrage.

One Kansas editor described Chivington's actions as "disgusting." He predicted the truth would prevail, adding, "And when it is known, and all the enormity of this Sand Creek massacre is exposed, we are sure that nowhere will Chivington find a defender, or even an apologist."[81] He was wrong. Many Coloradans were not ready to abandon the fighting parson yet. The Sand Creek controversy had virtually shattered the old Union Administration Party (Colorado Republicans), but there was now surprising unity among politicians in the territory on the question of statehood and, ironically, for action against the renewed threat of Indian attacks. In June, a referendum for statehood and a new constitution was approved by a mere 155 votes, suggesting that the people were still divided on the territory's capacity for taking care of itself without the federal presence.[82]

Sand Creek, not statehood, was the central issue in the fall elections. News of a proposed peace council with the Cheyenne and Arapaho increased the fury. The effect was soon felt. The Union Administration Party was anxious to avoid controversy because they did not want to jeopardize statehood. A mixed slate of state officers was selected, including several critics of Sand Creek, but when the party platform was presented, a series of amendments endorsing Sand Creek and a policy of extermination against the Indians were introduced. These sweeping amendments sabotaged the new coalition, and Ned Byers of the *Rocky Mountain News* sought to make Sand Creek the test question in the upcoming election. He singled out Henry Leach and Amos Steck for particular abuse.[83]

Inevitably, the Sand Creek men bolted the party and presented their own slate of officers for the "Sand Creek Vindication Party." Of the Union Administration Party's nominees, only four survived the scrutiny of the Sand Creekers. They did not nominate Chivington for any office, however. Once more, many of the supporters were disappointed that Governor Evans did not take a stronger position. He made another statement, without explicitly endorsing Sand Creek. Late in October, Chivington, "Old Sand Creek himself," announced as an independent candidate for Congress, but he withdrew before the election.[84] On November 11, 1865, the *Atchison Weekly Champion and Press*, sarcastically compared Chivington to Captain Henry Wirz, the Confederate commandant at Andersonville Prison. The paper said, "If Colorado wants to get into the Union wouldn't it be better for Colorado people to keep quiet on affairs that shock the sentiment of the whole Nation?"

The latter thought had also occurred to some Coloradans who warned of the consequences of linking statehood and vindication of Sand Creek. On November 14, 1865, the Union Administration Party swept the election. Only George Shoup, former commander of the Third, was elected from the Vindication ticket. The new "state legislature" subsequently named John Evans and Jerome Chaffee as Colorado's United States senators.[85]

But the congressional response to the statehood proposal was lukewarm. To make matters worse, the new chairman of the Senate committee on the territories was Benjamin F. Wade, the former chairman of the Joint Committee on the Conduct of the War. While the debate focused on population and the failure of Colorado to include a plank for black suffrage, Sand Creek did produce a heated exchange on the Senate floor.[86]

In April, the *Rocky Mountain News* reported that Henry Leach was in Washington lobbying against statehood. Eventually, the enabling act passed, but Andrew Johnson vetoed it. Many Coloradans believed that Leach and Sand Creek were responsible for the veto.[87] Colorado statehood would not be achieved for another decade, and Sand Creek played a part in the delay. Alexander Cummings, who succeeded Evans as governor, had urged the legislature in January 1866 to present any evidence that would throw new light on the subject.[88] In exasperation, he later wrote William Seward, "there is no peace for any United State official here unless he will endorse all the horrible atrocities of Sand Creek."[89] Sand Creek was Colorado's albatross, but the territory wore it like a medal of honor, slowly sanitizing it more and more.

CHAPTER 10

METHODISTS, SAND CREEK, AND THE "INDIAN QUESTION"

TRUTHFULLY, THE SAND CREEK Massacre was more a distraction than a grand moral issue to the Methodist Episcopal Church in 1865. Compared to the great issues of the Union and slavery, an attack on Indians in the West was trivial to its members, especially in light of the great war still being fought in Georgia, Tennessee, and Virginia. William Tecumseh Sherman had taken Atlanta, and Abraham Lincoln had been reelected, but the Civil War was not over, and the future of freedmen and the South itself remained uncertain. Methodists were still debating their role in reconstruction and emancipation, the future of the Methodist Episcopal Church, South and the role of their own church in the post-war nation. Reports of Sand Creek were disturbing more because of its potential to taint the Church's reputation because of the roles of John Chivington and John Evans in it.

Except for the voices of various editions of the *Christian Advocate*, some reserved, some more vocal, the Church did not confront the Sand Creek Massacre directly. Not even Bishop Simpson confronted it directly, even though he was involved in the efforts to preserve Governor Evans's job. Methodists waited and watched and adapted their viewpoints according to the events that transpired over the years that followed. The Methodists emerged from the war as the largest and perhaps the most influential religious denomination in the country. Unfortunately, as Richard Carwardine has written, "There is a sad irony that Methodism, a major instrument in the process of American national integration in the early republic, became a principal channel of spiritual alienation during the middle years of the nineteenth century."[1]

For religious organizations such as the Methodist Church during the years immediately following the Civil War, attention was focused primarily on the South and its former slaves. The great challenge to churches was the completion of the promise of freedom to blacks. Missionary efforts accelerated among the former slaves, and

Methodists initiated a strong effort to reclaim white churches that had joined the Methodist Episcopal Church, South before the war. This took on the appearance of an extension of federal power over the churches to some and created a dispute within the church that would continue. The Methodist Episcopal Church, South, naturally enough, fought to hold on to its identity and organization.[2] Methodists were a fractious, divided denomination on many fronts and with a variety of answers that would determine who they were and what their relationship to government and national growth would be. Indians seemed foreign to those primary concerns.

Ramifications of the Massacre

While the Church contemplated its future, giving little thought to Sand Creek or to Native Americans, the immediate response of the majority of Cheyennes and Arapahos to the Sand Creek Massacre was to move north of the Platte to join their Lakota allies. Not only did they now share the Lakota hatred of whites, but also the combination of tribes established a new zone of control on the northern plains, pushing back other tribes, east and west, to secure dominance of the region ranging from below the Platte to the Canadian line, and from the Missouri River to the front range of the Rockies. It was an aggressive Native response that held the American army at bay for three years and more. Hidatsa, Mandan, Arikara, Pawnee, Omaha, Shoshoni, Crow, Gros Ventre, and others ventured into the Powder River country and Black Hills only with great caution, and most of them found few options beyond alliance with the white Americans. The combination of the Minnesota Uprising and the Sand Creek Massacre had succeeded in building an alliance of five thousand fighting men.[3]

At first, neither the settlers nor the government took the challenge seriously. Much of the public discourse was shallow and overconfident. More important, only a few whites understood the reasons that Sand Creek was so important. It was, first of all, a massacre, but more than that, a slaughter that taught even the most peacefully inclined that whites could not be trusted. Few officials, if any, understood that Sand Creek was a chiefs' village. It was an experiment that all of the Cheyennes and Arapahos were watching. Practically, it was a chance to prove the white man's intent. It was an experiment with the potential to have brought peace to the central plains. Instead, Chivington's attack eliminated virtually every voice for peace among the Cheyennes. Trust was broken. The white man had proven the value of his word.[4]

The numbers killed at Sand Creek were not great, but nearly one-fourth of the Council of Forty-Four was killed, devastating the political order and leading to a more militant leadership. A serious rift in the Cheyenne political order was a direct result, and 1864 became the last time that all of the Cheyennes gathered for the renewal of the council. The council was rendered impotent, and the soldier chiefs gained new power. Sand Creek pushed the Cheyennes and Arapahos toward a new system dominated by war, which replaced trade as the primary source of essential re-sources. The Southern Cheyennes, led by the Dog Soldiers, were more determined than ever to hold on to the Smoky Hill country, which guaranteed continued con-flict in eastern Colorado and western Kansas.

Sand Creek precipitated a winter war, the one thing that conventional wisdom said could not happen. The Cheyennes, Arapahos, Brule Lakota, and Oglalas struck the Platte River route with fury, destroying ranches, stage stations, bridges, and tele-graph lines. They attacked wagon trains and even towns. On January 7, 1865, they attacked and looted Julesburg on the Platte and besieged Camp Rankin. On January 28, the Cheyennes attacked American Ranch, ran off five hundred cattle, and burned a hundred tons of hay. They attacked other ranches, and on February 2, more than a thousand Cheyennes, Arapahos, and Lakotas again descended on Julesburg. This time they burned the town. They destroyed fifty miles of telegraph lines and burned the poles. They fought the soldiers at Mud Springs and Rush Creek. Afterward, most of the Cheyennes moved to join the northern bands in the Powder River country, while the Lakota moved farther east.

It was an unprecedented assault. "Indians have got hold of the Platte Route again killing & destroying in every direction," one Colorado businessman wrote. "NO coaches are running, no mails have left for some days. . . . These Indian troubles kil [sic] everything & paralyze all commerce." He favored a harsh policy, but he con-demned both Sand Creek and Chivington. He added:

> A Report is prevalent here that "Black Kettle" is in command of the In-dians on the Plains. It is quite possible I should think. What is more natural than that they should retaliate in every way possible. I believe it is good policy to exterminate the whole race or at any rate put them beyond the power of doing harm. Can you imagine anything more pu-erile or idiotic to say the least to attack a body of Indians once & then immediately to disband?[5]

Others, including military officers from the region shared this view that, at the very least, Chivington had made a single attack then marched his troops back to Denver where they were disbanded and the entire territory left with scarcely more than two hundred soldiers. Now, Colorado could do little more than observe the renewed fighting until Colonel Thomas Moonlight, the new commander of the District of Colorado, could complete the reenlistment of a Veteran Battalion of the First Colorado Cavalry. Chivington had stirred up the hornet's nest and left it to others to deal with the results.[6] One after another, expeditions were launched by American officers—General Connor, General Pope, and more—and they failed miserably to overawe the tribes. American campaigns were predictable—large commands with supply trains moving across the plains, creating extended lines of supply, exhausted men, and worn-out horses.[7] As Robert M. Utley writes, "only the most careless Indians failed to get out of the way."[8]

The combination of the knowledge that the Cheyennes and Arapahos had just cause, and the poor showing of the expeditions sent against them, persuaded the government that some offer of peace had to be made. At the negotiation on the Little Arkansas, again with the most tractable Cheyennes and Arapahos, it was plain that the commissioners had Sand Creek on their minds. Virtually every commissioner damned Sand Creek as an atrocity and agreed to the unheard-of provision of apologizing for Sand Creek and offering compensation to the families of those who had been present.[9] But the Dog Soldiers and others on the Platte and above were still furious. They remained quiet, for the most part, and occupied lands in western Kansas and eastern Colorado during an uneasy peace.[10] Ultimately, however, the Treaty of the Little Arkansas merely managed a truce. As Black Kettle himself warned at the negotiations, too few Cheyennes were parties to it, Congress fiddled with its provisions, and the proposed reservation was south of the Arkansas River on lands never a part of the Cheyenne and Arapaho domains. Its provisions were never implemented, and most of its promises were stillborn despite the good intentions of both the chiefs and the commissioners.

Other things changed after Sand Creek as well. The Sand Creek Massacre polarized debate on American Indian policy for at least twenty years. It became an issue in negotiations not only with the Cheyennes and Arapahos, but with other tribes as well. Sand Creek was emblematic of the untrustworthiness of white promises. "Why should we believe you?" Native leaders asked. "Remember Sand Creek?" Sand Creek affected direction. It bequeathed an image of the army as saber-wielding murderers, even though Sand Creek had been carried out by short-term volunteers, and with the end of the Civil War "Indian fighting" gradually returned to the regular army. Sand Creek also led to a debate on civilian versus military control, intensified by a growing movement for the reform of Indian policy. And turning history on its head, the ongoing conflict was used by Westerners to justify the "Chivington style."[11]

Five Recommendations and a New Indian Policy

The seriousness of the problem was the reason that the Joint Special Committee on the Condition of the Indian Tribes was established in 1865. Although it was created in the aftermath of Sand Creek (and because of it), the committee attempted a widespread review of conditions and options throughout the West. Three separate groups gathered evidence and traveled across the West considering a wide range of questions, the "deterioration" of the Indians, land tenure, schools and missions, annuities, and whether Indian affairs could best be handled by the Interior Department or the War Department. The report was not completed until January 26, 1867. It condemned the Sand Creek Massacre, but more important it also provided the framework for a new Indian policy.

It made five recommendations. First, it concluded that Indians, except for those in the Indian Territory, were dwindling in numbers because of disease, intemperance, war, and white emigration. Second, it blamed Indian wars largely on "lawless white men," with Sand Creek as a prime example. Third, the Indians were rapidly losing their essential resources and land base, noting especially the effects of railroads on the buffalo. Fourth, it recommended that Indian affairs remain under civilian control rather than transferred to military control as many had hoped would happen. The problem, the committee concluded, was not so much policy as abuses of the system. Fifth, based on this assumption it recommended the creation of boards of inspection designed to reduce violence and fraud. Five districts would be created, each served by a three-man board, including representatives from the Office of Indian Affairs, the regular army, and a member chosen by the president based on recommendations from church-related groups. This report would become the fulcrum of debate, and lead, ultimately, to Grant's "Peace Policy," which proposed to turn the management of Indian affairs over to religious denominations as a means of depoliticizing Indian affairs and preserving the tribes.[12]

The report was timely. The discovery of gold in Montana led to plans to build the Bozeman Trail from Fort Laramie north along the eastern side of the Big Horn Mountains in modern-day Wyoming, then west to the mining camps like Bozeman and Virginia City. This carried a new wave of settlers into the heart of the Sioux country and prompted more resistance. It led to a string of new forts, and on December 21, 1866, the disastrous slaughter of eighty troopers from Fort Phil Kearny.[13] The "Fetterman Massacre," as it was called, produced more investigations and a fresh campaign by General Winfield Scott Hancock on the central plains stirred up the Cheyenne Dog Soldiers who had remained quiet for a time. When Hancock approached one of the Cheyenne villages, the people fled, fearing another Sand Creek, while the general interpreted their action as a sign of hostility and burned the village. This opened "Hancock's War" in 1867.[14]

One of the important commissions reported in July 1867 that the majority of Indians on the plains favored peace. On July 20, 1867, Congress authorized the creation of a Peace Commission. The new Commissioner of Indian Affairs, Nathaniel G. Taylor, formerly a Methodist minister, was named as chairman. It was a distinguished group. In addition to Taylor, the commission included General William T. Sherman, General William S. Harney, General Alfred E. Terry, General John B. Sanborn, Senator J. B. Henderson, and Colonel Samuel F. Tappan, Chivington's old enemy and now a dedicated advocate of Indian reform.[15]

Not everyone was happy with the appointment of Taylor. He had little experience in Indian matters; his primary qualifications were a reputation for honesty and zeal for reform. But Orville Browning, Secretary of the Interior, lamented, "I now have a Methodist preacher at the head of the Bureau, and I will do the best I can with him."[16] Taylor faced a hard task. New treaties negotiated at Medicine Lodge and Fort Laramie by the commission had a familiar flaw to previous treaties. The traditional, less tractable groups either stayed away or expressed their dissatisfaction with the terms. It was Taylor's design to create large reserves from which whites would be excluded while beginning programs of acculturation that hopefully would make the tribes self-supporting and even eligible for citizenship.[17]

At one point Taylor and Tappan advocated a separate Department of Indian Affairs. The debate over control by the War Department or the Interior Department was clearly flawed, they argued, by the fact that both departments had interests other than the welfare of Indians. The Interior Department also had responsibility for the distribution of land, and the War Department was the military instrument of national power. The commission grew increasingly divided, however; and when it met in Chicago in the fall of 1868, the majority agreed that the treaty system was obsolete and that tribes were wards of the government and should no longer be treated with as independent nations. The military was given the authority to police tribal hunts north of the Arkansas, and, over the dissent of Taylor and Tappan, the majority voted to return the management of Indian affairs to the War Department.[18]

Preoccupied with other matters, Congress did not consider ratification of the Medicine Lodge and Fort Laramie treaties for ten months. Browning gave little support to Taylor, and Tappan hurt more than helped with his combative style. General Sherman then complicated matters further by reorganizing the western departments, creating northern and southern districts that conformed roughly to the proposed northern and southern reservations. This meant that whatever status the Indian Bureau found itself in, the military presence would be there.[19]

Division Among the Indians

During the warring times since Sand Creek, the division between Southern and Northern Cheyennes and Southern and Northern Arapahos had deepened. The Southerners struggled to hold on to their favored lands on the Smoky Hill and the Republican, but caught between the two main overland routes and pressed by settlement from the east and the west, they gradually gave ground. After Custer's attack against the Cheyenne village on the Washita River one day short of four years after the Sand Creek Massacre, and the Battle of Summit Springs in July 1869, Cheyenne and Arapaho occupation of the lands between the Platte and the Arkansas came to an end.[20]

The attack at the Washita renewed conversations about Sand Creek and invigorated the Indian reform movement. Commissioner Taylor deplored the death of Black Kettle and said of the Cheyennes, "Can they ever forget the insignia of those who shot down, by military orders, their old men, women, and children under the white flag and under our own banner at Sand Creek?" On the other hand, a Kansas editor hoped openly that Kansas's governor would "put himself at the head of our western men, follow the Indians to their homes, and do his work, *a la Chivington.*"[21] Peter Cooper, Lydia Maria Child, John Beeson, Alfred H. Love, and more of the leading advocates of Indian reform (many of whom had been leading abolitionists) demanded that Taylor's plan to give responsibility for managing Indian affairs to private organizations, including the Christian churches and missionary societies, be given a chance. Taylor left office with some satisfaction based upon the prospect of President Grant's new "Peace Policy," which would embrace the goals of concentration, Christianity, education, and private property under the direction of religious denominations, all initiatives that Taylor favored.[22]

Black Kettle died at the Washita still the advocate of peace, and the Dog Soldiers' power was broken at Summit Springs with the death of Tall Bull. The survivors of Summit Springs pushed north into Nebraska, and the rest of the Southerners eventually surrendered at Fort Supply. The fighting was clearly over in the south when Stone Forehead, the Keeper of the Sacred Arrows, came in.[23] Those who escaped north joined the continuing resistance as allies of the Oglala, Hunkpapa, and Minneconjou Lakota until the end of the wars in the north following the Battle of the Little Big Horn in 1876 and the campaign that followed.[24]

The Age of Exploitation

Yet while it had taken 240 years to push Native peoples beyond the Mississippi River, the Trans-Mississippi West was taken in 40 years. Some scholars liken what happened to a Western Reconstruction that accompanied the Reconstruction of the South, one equally important. With the end of the Civil War, the push west accelerated, driven by railroads, mining, and industrialization. Politicians no longer talked about the Union but preached the new concept of the Nation. Ruthless, freewheeling, capitalistic Americans pressed forward at an astonishing rate in astonishing numbers. Organization, money, and transportation drove the economy and the political system. The Age of Exploitation also reinforced old ideas with new "scientific" justifications of racism taught in universities and explored by scholars, although "scientific racism" and "Social Darwinism" appear to have had little direct impact on policy. Such "scientific" justifications were merely rationalizations of attitudes and beliefs already accepted. The treaty system would be abandoned, and the Cheyennes and Arapahos, along with other indigenous peoples, ultimately saw everything they had known subordinated to the great, hungry behemoth called America.[25]

The extraordinary expansion was also seen as proof positive of the superiority of the white man's way. That linear line of progress "proved" the point and made leaders even less likely to listen to Native voices or respect Native ways. Therein lay the well-intentioned but misguided answer to the problems that indigenous people faced. All Indians had to do to be "saved" was to accept and embrace the inevitability of progress. Despite the occasional diatribes of Western newspaper editors or the inflated rhetoric of soldiers in the field, there was no longer any need for a policy of extermination. For whites, the solution was self-evident, and they marveled at the Natives' resistance to the "obvious" benefits of salvation through civilization.

Methodist Indian missions had been disrupted by the war, and it took time to re-claim the initiative lost. The steady William H. Goode made a serious effort to reen-gage with the Indian missions in Missouri, Kansas, and Nebraska. The volumes of the *Missionary Advocate* regularly recorded the problems and occasional successes, but they were surprisingly free of any discussion of the debate over Indian policy or about extending missions to new groups. There was no groundswell of support for the pro-grams of fellow Methodist, Commissioner Taylor. At least part of the problem was that the Methodist Church chose to rely upon the various conferences to support Indian missions. The "itinerant style of ministry" never adapted well to Indian missions be-cause it lacked the long-term form needed for cross-cultural understanding. Without centralized organization and financial support most of the Indian missions dried up.

Perhaps most important, the marriage of Church and Union during the war—that reoccurring connection between God and country that Bishop Simpson and many others preached, that joining together of Christianity and civilization—was a unifying theme in the approach the Church took toward Native Americans. When Schuyler Colfax wrote the *Northwestern Christian Advocate* in the summer of 1865, he painted a bleak picture of the damage done by Indians along the overland routes. He wrote:

> There has been a good deal of sympathy lost over the "massacre" of the Indians who committed these deeds, and who had, after months of out-rage worse than death, sold a young maiden who they had captured, but whom at last their chiefs had tired of. But if presents such as the government has lavished on them, and annuities, will not keep them at peace, what can be done?

> Without attempting to settle this grave problem of what should be done with the Indians, and then what can be done with them, I have become convinced that these Plains should be kept open as a peaceful uninterrupted highway to the States, no matter how many soldiers are required, or what may be the expense.

> Every citizen of the United States, especially if he remains within its limits, and, even more, if he aids by his labor in developing the magnificent min-eral resources of this country of the far West, has a right to demand the protection of his life and property, and it is the duty of the government to punish or overthrow all the enemies of its citizens and the contemn-ers [sic] of its power whether they are rebels South, or savages West.[26]

Of course, Colfax was a politician, with interest in opening the West to settlement, but a more striking insight into the same sentiment was found in the letters of Bishop Calvin Kingsley, who wrote to the *Christian Advocate and Journal* in June 1865, "Our government is now at war with the Indians. The latter have destroyed and stolen millions' worth of property and taken many lives, and are still continuing their depredations in all parts of the West." He added, "Even the most friendly tribes are stealing continually; and they have been left alone so long that they have become emboldened, believing that they can do as they have done with impunity." He provided his solution:

> To make men of the Indians, in my opinion, requires that they should be collected together and put in one place, large enough and fertile enough to enable them to make a good living, and to grow rich even, by following the pursuits of civilized life. . . . It now costs millions of money to disburse the annuities to the Indians, scattered as they are all over the territories. It is time they were collected together and governed, and taught that they must now earn a livelihood by honest industry, and not by hunting, war, and plunder. This course, in my judgment is most humane to the Indian himself, and the only one that will preserve the race from utter extinction, if even this will do it. But at present there is a war on hand, and the Indian must be caught before he can be reduced to civilization.[27]

Kingsley concluded that the transcontinental railroad was the answer— a military necessity—and the key to the growth of a new order. Indeed, what is most striking about Kingsley's letters is their primary focus on the railroad and its economic benefits. In effect, Kingsley reduced Native people to an obstacle. The real mission work to be done, in his view, was the economic development of the West for the nation. Social reform was of limited concern.[28]

Methodist Efforts to Vindicate Chivington

Sand Creek was dealt with gingerly by the Church, but a certain tone remained dominant. On July 26, 1865, the *Central Christian Advocate* noted that "Bishop Kingsley returned to New York, not having been able to go overland to California on account of 'friendly Indians.'" The same journal reported on the same day that Chivington was in town, and that he was fully sustained by Colorado. It expressed "great pleasure" that the Colorado Conference had endorsed his actions, which was not true. Plainly, Methodists wanted the charges against Chivington to be false.

In August 1865, after the report of the Joint Committee on the Conduct of the War was released, the *Northwestern Christian Advocate* admitted that it was "perplexed" by the case of Colonel Chivington. The editor had known him personally and favorably, the paper said, "and have regarded him as a high-minded Christian gentleman, and a gallant soldier." He pointed out that Lincoln had nominated him for a brigadier's commission. So, the claim of a bloody massacre was inconsistent with what they knew of him. They reported contrary claims that the Cheyennes and Arapahos were hostile, and views of some that Chivington deserved promotion rather than censure, then added:

> We take it for granted that those who say so do not believe that women and children were slain, and that Colonel Chivington can show and will show that such was not the fact. For such an act there can be neither defence nor apology. We take it for granted that in endorsing his course the Colonel's friends are prepared to disprove these horrible reports.

The paper continued:

> It is true that even mild, humane men residing on the lines of Indian atrocity defend a stern decisive treatment of red men in war. They claim that mercy is construed as cowardice, and that only the most decisive policy can prevent another outbreak—that the death of every Indian found in war is the most merciful policy, as it prevents other tribes from rising; in short, that death is the only argument the red man understands.

> We hesitate to accept a theory so utterly at war with Christianity, and so repugnant to human instincts. We concede the ignorance, the brutality, the fiendishness of the Indian warfare, but Christians must not even in war, be brutal or fiendish.

The editor called upon Chivington and his friends to clear his name: "Give us the facts which will enable us to clear his record from charges of cruelty from either causing or permitting the slaughter of helpless women and children." He promised to be the instrument of "clearing away the evil reports" if Chivington's friends would supply the refutation.[29]

On August 24, R. M. Hatfield wrote a strong rejoinder to this editorial, objecting to the paper becoming the advocate of Colonel Chivington:

Will you allow me to suggest a doubt whether, as things now stand, Col. Chivington's case can be materially improved by anything his friends may say through the public press. As I understand the matter, more than one committee has been appointed by the government to investigate the Sand Creek massacre. If Col. Chivington's course in that affair admits of justification or excuse, let him be vindicated before these committees. They are the legally appointed and proper tribunals for collecting all the facts in the case. Unless it can be shown that the gentlemen composing these committees are incompetent, or prejudiced, no ex parte vindication of Col. C. by his friends will have the weight of a feather with the country. Reports and resolutions in his favor passed by a conference of Methodist Preachers may leave an indelible stigma upon the Church, without doing him the least good.

The country will insist on knowing whether women and children were butchered by men wearing the uniform of the United States, and led by Col. Chivington. If this atrocious crime has been committed they will demand the punishment of the guilty parties. The case is not one that calls for precipitate action. Speaking as a Methodist, I venture to express the hope that we shall do nothing that can be tortured into the semblance of an attempt to apologize for the murder of unoffending women and innocent children.[30]

Hatfield's warning was well placed. Subsequently, the letter of support from the Colorado ministers, written in April 1865, was released by Chivington as the pressure on him mounted. Several newspapers, including the *Central Christian Advocate*, claimed that the letter was officially endorsed by the Colorado Conference of the Methodist Episcopal Church. When the claim was published in the *Chicago Tribune*, the *Northwestern Christian Advocate* responded quickly, "We demand the proof." Pointing out that the paper cited was "signed by some members of that conference" before the congressional report was published, "We aver furthermore that the members of the Colorado Conference have never approved of what is reported to have occurred at Sand Creek."[31]

The *Northwestern* editor backed away from Chivington, but when Evans wrote his *Reply*, it exulted:

Hon. John Evans, late Governor of Colorado, has proven himself an able, statesman like and patriotic administrator of the trust reposed in his hands. He has made a thorough reply to the allegations of certain Reports, has made an ample vindication of his administration from charges affecting his treatment of the Indians, and this day no man [more] fully enjoys the confidence of the people of Colorado.

That much of the opposition was purely political there is, there can be no doubt. Time proves all things, and even the much chronicled "Sand Creek Massacre" has another side than the one so studiously turned to the public eye.[32]

Later, the paper announced that Evans and Chaffee had been chosen Senators-elect by the Colorado legislature, adding, "This election of Governor Evans is the answer of Colorado to the insinuations of the writing portion of a certain committee of examination. The Governor has published his own refutation, and its array of logic and facts was unanswerable. Now the State speaks for him." The editor proceeded with a laudatory biographical sketch of Evans, and concluded, "The NORTH-WESTERN has never endorsed what is called 'The Sand Creek Massacre.' It has said there are two sides to all questions; and time may show some facts not stated in published reports. It has said, however, that there has been no testimony which has involved Governor Evans in wrong. On the contrary there is evidence that while his care saved the population of the territory from massacre, he was also the protector of the lives and rights of friendly Indian[s]."[33]

The *Central Christian Advocate* took a different, yet consistent, view. "We profoundly regret that a shadow should rest for a moment on either name and hope that they will at the end be justified." Of Chivington, it said, "If Chivington was the author or agent of cruelties and atrocities contrary to the laws of war, we will submit, though with pain, to his condemnation." The *Central* found it harder to condemn Evans. "That he lied or equivocated is beyond credence by those who know him."[34]

Chivington's extended exchange with the Atchison, Kansas papers, continued through the fall of 1865 and into 1866. When Chivington preached at the Atchison Methodist Church, the paper(s) added some additional barbs that provoked Chivington into writing a three-column response. In it he asked if he were the monster he had been portrayed as being, "why do not the authorities of the M. E. Church cut me off? Or why do not the orders of Odd Fellows and Masons, of which I am a member, expel me?" In describing the circumstances of the Sand Creek affair, he wrote, "As to the charge that women and children were killed and their persons brutally mutilated, *it is utterly false.*" He claimed that he saw only one woman killed and said she was fighting with the men. "If any children were killed, I did not see them nor was any such occurrence reported to me by my officers or men."[35]

He attached to his letter, the statement of the six Colorado ministers, written in April 1865, and a lengthy set of resolutions from the Masonic Lodges and Chapters in Colorado in support of Chivington. Two days later, he added another lengthy letter promising to continue his fight with the editor, "I have one month set apart to be devoted to this especial business, when the time comes to perform it, and about election day he may ascertain the extent of 'Church condolence,' and 'Lodge sympathy,' for the person whom he ironically terms the 'Hero of Sand Creek.'" The editor responded by saying that rather than defending himself with arguments to disprove the charges, Chivington has chosen to offer "groveling, dirty insinuations against us."

Finding a Solution to the "Indian Question"

The public at large was less interested in Chivington's self-justification than in what to do about Indian affairs, more generally. What policy would correct the obvious evils and failures that had led to Sand Creek? In 1865, the *New York Times* had declared that conditions on the frontier were in crisis, but that "the history of the Chivington massacre is too fresh in the public mind, and will forever be too atrocious in history" to continue current policy.[36] *Frank Leslie's Illustrated Newspaper* blamed the situation on the government.[37] That was hardly a startling argument. Lincoln had recognized the need and had promised Bishop Henry Benjamin Whipple, the Episcopalian cleric and defender of Indian rights, "If we get through this war, and I live, this Indian system shall be reformed."[38] But, it was Secretary of War Stanton who offered Whipple the more telling advice, "the government never reforms an evil until the people demand it."[39] That was the biggest problem in the short term. The country's reform zeal was directed at completing the promise of freedom to former slaves and to reconstructing the South on a different economic model.

The problem was the conflict between a solution to the "Indian question" and the national mission. Lincoln's plan for the development of the West had been simple. Pass a Homestead Act to encourage settlement. Develop the West's mineral resources. And build a transcontinental railroad. This was the way of "progress." This vision, in all three of its aspects, guaranteed continuing conflict with indigenous people. Lincoln's views on what they must do were far from exceptional. They had to become farmers and live at peace. Senator Doolittle—the same Senator Doolittle who condemned Sand Creek so strongly—said that Indians were dying out as a race. He said the Indian's fate was determined by "natural causes" linked to contact with a "superior race."[40]

Roger Nichols, a leading authority on Indian policy during the Civil War, wrote of the dilemma of policy makers:

> Therefore, the reformers' major proposals contained unresolvable con-
> tradictions. They sought to find him a place in the face of an advancing
> civilization that envisioned only continuous removal and eventual ex-
> tinction. They wanted to advance the Indian to civilization while pre-
> suming a civilization that was in dynamic progress, symbolized by an
> accelerating locomotive that Indians could never catch.[41]

Nichols suggested, "The only solution would have been the acceptance of ideals or racial and cultural equality for which nineteenth-century white Americans were not prepared. Neither reformers nor non-reformers respected Indian culture. Indeed they did not even perceive the existence of a Native culture."[42] It was not hatred of Indians nor even racism in simple terms that stood in the way; it was a mind-set that could only comprehend civilization in terms of white understand-ings. Civilization was progress, Christian, agrarian, material, and set in their forms of government and economy. As a result, not even the best, most well-intentioned "friends of the Indians" could see any alternative except changing the Native ways of life. There was no sense of "multiculturalism" or concept of "ethnic cleansing." There were simply the "gifts" of civilization, which would save the man, and Chris-tianity, which would save the soul. The only real question was how best to bring about the intended result.

In 1865, Senator William Windom approached Bishop Whipple to ask for advice on policy solutions. Whipple had his own views, clearly well-intended, that went about as far as any representative of a major Christian denomination could go in his time, saying that "They are not idolators. They believe in a Great Spririt. They have home affections. They have strong national pride and love of country. They are generally chaste, truthful, honest, generous, and hospitable." He preached respect for them and blamed the degradation and poverty many of them experienced on "a curse given to them by a Christian people."[43]

Whipple had condemned Sand Creek strongly when it occurred and offered advice to the Joint Special Committee on the Condition of the Indian Tribes. It released its report in January 1867. Methodists participated in the debate only in limited ways. In March of 1866, when one of the several Indian commissions began its work, the *Northwestern Christian Advocate* opined that the only real question was "what is the true policy of a Christian Nation to its unfortunate wards?" The editor suggested that "a wise and humane Indian policy" should involve "gathering of as many as possible of the civilized Indians into the Indian Territory, and thus securing their rights under the government." The paper even suggested the possibility of territorial organization across tribal lines with the possibility of an Indian state down the road. The article concluded: "It is a cold, cruel, wicked policy, which abandons a whole people to death with no single effort for their rescue. It may be the descendants of the owners of this continent are to vanish like mist, but while they live we should not abandon them to rapacity and greed."[44]

In May of 1866, the same paper again claimed the vindication of Governor Evans in the form of a speech by Senator Lane of Indiana on Colorado statehood.[45] A strong Western point of view was offered in the fall by the Reverend Henry Bannister, of Evanston (and the father-in-law of Oliver Willard). He spoke of Colorado's promise, but added this:

> They are surrounded and infested by hostile Indians whose spirit of late years has been that of murder and plunder, and in respect to whom the feeling of the people there is that of insecurity and their attitude that of unfriendly defensiveness. They are, perhaps, not too acutely sensitive at what they deem unjust criticism in the East upon their feelings toward the Indians—incited as they think this criticism has been by insincere objections raised by disappointed, ambitious politicians from Colorado. Cut off by the Indians from the necessary supplies of life and business, bereft of their citizens by the tomahawk, or by a captivity more horrible to the women captured than a thousand deaths, relieved by no prospect of seeing these nomadic, untamable tribes, conciliated by presents and kind treatment and by ineffective government treaties— why should these Colorado people be a marvel to us if they do consider ours an impracticable sentimentalism that condemns them as barbarians and prescribes a withdrawal of sympathy from them?

He added that "Our ministry [sic] there have [sic] come in for a good share of the depressing influences of their criticism." The church was dealing with "A whole population given over to intense worldliness with no heart for religious things."[46] Little had changed in attitude within the church at large. Bannister's view of missions was support for the Western conferences. At the same time, he implied that, wrongfully, the Methodist Church in Colorado had suffered because of its connection to Sand Creek.

In 1867, while critical negotiations were developing on the plains, the *Northwestern Christian Advocate* revived an old issue, generated by some of the problems associated with the Gilded Age. In July 1867, the paper printed a lengthy editorial on "Barbarism." The piece noted that "the men who gather upon the frontiers of civilization often grow rude and set up the empire of force. Removed from society they neglect comeliness of person, become forgetful of the amenities of culture, and tend toward lawlessness. Violence rules until organized violence arrests it." Now, the editorial declared, this downward spiral had spread into the cities. It enumerated violent acts in New Orleans, Memphis, and New York. "Human life is cheap and held in little esteem," the paper proclaimed. The United States was descending into barbarism, and the church had to take a stand.[47]

The focus revealed a revival of classism in the post-war America set in motion by the breakdown of community that came with industrialization, growth, and immigration. Methodism was now clearly the voice of middle class virtue and increasingly distant from the freewheeling populism of earlier times. This was reflected in the social causes the Church championed. When the *Northwestern* did turn to Native people, its sentiments were not primarily concerned with winning souls. On July 27, 1867, it addressed Indian policy, proclaiming that "the most fearful atrocities are committed by the Indians—atrocities which are fiendish." It called policy "a shameful reproach to our statesmen." It advocated the transfer of policy to the War Department in order to "secure a wiser, more efficient and more humane administration." It took a hard line:

> At all events the present policy is weak, cruel, bloody, inefficient, arrests the growth of our western gold and silver-bearing plains, and costs thousands of lives. Let it be changed. It is imbecile and demoralizing.
>
> The country demands security. The lives of our fellow-citizens must no longer be sacrificed to a system both brainless and heartless. The com-

175

merce of the country demands protection. The way to the mineral treasures of the country must be opened and kept open.

Give us an Indian policy which we can look upon with respect, and
which will stay the horrid carnival of butchery.

Just four days later, the paper published a letter from Ft. Morgan, Colorado Territory, from the Reverend J. C. Hartzell. He was no reformer. He called for strong
action. He said of the Indians' methods of war:

> But numbers are comparatively unimportant, owing to the Indian mode
> of warfare. A few hundred Indians may foil and exhaust an army of thou-
> sands moving in the pomp of civilized warfare. Divided up into parties
> of from five to twenty-five, well mounted and armed, they can play on
> all sides of the best organized army, cutting off stragglers and scouts,
> stealing stock, poisoning springs, and yet by their native shrewdness
> and acquaintance with the country, elude capture. They have no ex-
> penses to meet and care nothing for time. So that with their squaws and
> pappooses hid away in some distant canon, and their animals growing
> fat on grass the same parties can carry on a continued fight for months.
> They never think of attacking only where they consider victory certain.
> What we consider our best means of warfare are for this reason of no
> use. It is the journeying "pilgrim," the lone stage coach, the unguarded
> corral, the poorly garrisoned and protected fort, or the unarmed settler,
> that they delight to find and attack.

He added:

> Savages can only be conquered but by meeting them in their own way.
> Every warrior killed thus far has cost the Government over a hundred
> thousand dollars. Let small bodies of troops well mounted and com-
> manded sweep through the country, sparing nothing, and if need be,
> not even saving women and children. This plan may seem cruel and un-
> christian, but is it not more humane than to permit the murdering of
> citizens and destruction of property along our highway year after year?
> One season of such warfare would make them content to remain upon
> their ample reservations peaceably, and learn the use of the plow and

hoe. . . . They have rights it is true, but those do not guarantee to them the privilege of scalping me and throwing my body to the wolves for amusement.[48]

In October, 1867, during the work of the Peace Commission, a party of reporters visited Cheyenne, Wyoming Territory. Cheyenne was still a railroad camp on the new Union Pacific at the time. One of the reporters, identified simply as "B," wrote the *Northwestern Christian Advocate* about the experience. At a dinner held in their honor, he said, events became tense when General Stevenson, their escort, "reflected on Col. Chivington of Sand Creek fame. This was at once resented not only in western but in true frontier style. Several present had a hand in the Sand Creek massacre, and loudly declared they gloried in it as the one grand deed of their lives." The mayor cooled the temper of the gathering by offering a toast: "Here's to the City of Cheyenne; may she ever prosper, and the tribe of Indians after whom she is named be completely exterminated." The reporter said, "I am satisfied of one thing—our boasted civilization has not taken the savage out of us yet."

The locals dismissed the Peace Commission as a humbug. One said, "Why don't the government hand over the job to us." When asked what he would do, he replied, "I'd give 'em Chivington to the last red d----l, woman and child. We'll have no peace while one of 'em lives to curse the ground." The reporter was shocked and closed his article with this observation: "No, Mr. Mayor, all the champagne in the world cannot wash down this sentiment with the writer. Such a sentiment for American citizens, drunk or sober, is a blot on our Christian civilization—it is atrocious—it is downright savage."

Methodism and Social Concerns

Despite such vigorous proclamations, Methodist itinerancy declined, and a higher, more middle class, educated ministry took charge of most conferences. The frontier point of view and the new educated ministerial approach combined to change the view of social activism if not evangelical zeal. The emphasis of missions became increasingly international. At home, Methodism was more community based and rooted in the new middle class system of the late nineteenth century. Enlightenment prevailed over enthusiasm. Supporting the causes of abolition and union opened the door for a wider range of social concerns within the church, including some that, like union, involved politics. The use of politics to promote temperance, prison reform, children's issues, and even women's suffrage reflected a combination of middle class values in response to social ills that accompanied urbanization and industrialization. Missing from the list was any significant initiative on behalf of American Indians.[49]

As one scholar notes about the mood of Methodists toward Indians, "The context was not propitious. Broken treaties, commercial exploitation, white violence, land confiscations, rampant white-borne disease, and immense cultural chauvinism all made it difficult for Methodism to establish a strong presence among Native Americans."[50] Worse, it blocked any meaningful dialogue among Methodists about what was right and wrong. The old "anti-Indian sublime" was as fundamental to Methodist thinking as grace or sanctification. The best that could be said of Methodist efforts among Indian people was that enough was done to make the annual reports of the Missionary Society respectable. But there was no aggressive or enthusiastic support for the effort beyond a few missionary spirits.[51] There was no heart for Indian missions because the soul of Methodism was bound up in American exceptionalism.

Wade Crawford Barclay, the standard authority on Methodist missions, found it difficult to laud the efforts. "It cannot be fairly claimed that the Church had an Indian mission program," he wrote. "Although the Missionary Society nominally sponsored the missions it exercised no real supervision over them." He did claim, however, that Methodists contributed "to the moral and religious progress of the race." He wrote, "Churches were founded, Christian leaders developed, hundreds of men and women brought into the Church as members, and the whole tone of Indian community life elevated. In addition to scores of Indian churches, many tribesmen who had achieved citizenship and learned the English language were welcomed without discrimination into membership in English language churches."[52] It was an overly generous assessment.

An Agreement to Do Nothing

The weak support for missions among the western tribes was demonstrated at the General Conference in 1868, when the Missions Committee, chaired by the venerable William H. Goode, offered a set of resolutions, arguing that as a denomination Methodists could not "be indifferent to the policy of our Government in the management of the Indian tribes within the limits of the United [S]tates involving as it does, the fate of the entire remnant of the race." The resolutions approved "the pacific policy inaugurated for the settlement of existing difficulties; and we do earnestly recommend that this policy be carried out so far as it can be consistently with the protection and safety of the frontier." The report endorsed previous Methodist efforts and deemed them a "signal success." The committee proposed a state organization, or at least a territorial organization, of the Indian Territory and promised to "direct increased effort to their [the Indians'] civilization and moral improvement, and will cooperate with the strong arm of the Government, in saving from extermination and oblivion the remnant of this race now remaining upon our soil."

The report was a testimonial to the work of William H. Goode over the years, but T. H. Pearne moved to amend the resolution to include the passage, "But in our judgment that policy can only be fully and permanently successful by our government, through its agents and officers, keeping strict faith with the Indians; by removing them from contact with corrupt and degraded white men; by teaching them the arts and industries of civilization, and by permitting and protecting unobstructed access to them of the influence of an active and earnest Christianity." At that point, Reverend A. N. Fisher from Utah delivered an impassioned address presenting the more aggressive Western point of view and closed by asking to indefinitely postpone the first resolution. His motion failed. Goode then called for a vote on the report, and it passed by a vote of eighty-one to twenty-four. There were other maneuvers, but, in the end Reverend B. N. Spahr moved that the entire consideration of the report be indefinitely postponed. The vote was then reconsidered on the motion of B. I. Ives, and the resolution was "laid on the table." The most courageous and forthright stance so far taken by the Church was squelched by an agreement to do nothing.[53]

President Grant and the "Peace Policy"

When Ulysses S. Grant became president in 1869, he announced in his inaugural address his plan to reform Indian policy. During 1869 and 1870 he took steps to implement what became known as the "Peace Policy." It would be controversial from the beginning, both derided and praised, and often misinterpreted both then and since. It was, in fact a bold effort to eliminate the worst elements of the failed policies of the past, both in terms of corruption and of connections between mismanagement of Indian affairs and the Indian wars. He believed that blaming the Indian wars on unscrupulous and corrupt Indian agents who exploited their charges for personal profit was a simplistic explanation of what had happened and that any effort to return the management of Indian affairs to the War Department would be opposed by reformers who viewed the army as the agents of extermination (using Sand Creek as their primary example).[54]

He began by appointing Ely S. Parker as Commissioner of Indian Affairs. Parker was a Seneca educated at a Baptist mission school, trained as a lawyer but denied admission to the New York Bar Association on grounds of his race. He studied civil engineering and served with Grant from Vicksburg to Appomattox. Parker had ideas of his own about how best to smooth the transition from traditional ways to new ways of life for the tribes through the creation of protected enclaves within which the tribes could adapt at a pace that would give them more control over their own lives. He appears to have been chosen, however, because he represented the transition from the old ways to the new as a living example of what could be done.[55]

Grant also created a Board of Indian Commissioners to consist of ten distinguished laymen representing various Christian denominations who would serve the cause of the Indians and advise the government at their own expense. Two of the original board—John V. Farwell, a Chicago businessman, and Henry S. Lane, former governor and U.S. Senator from Indiana—were Methodists. The president's plan also included greatly increased federal aid to Indian education and missions. The most radical part of his reform was to hand over the control of Indian agencies to religious organizations. He reasoned that this church-government partnership would eliminate corruption and be more humane. He did not concern himself with questions about constitutional issues that such a plan might raise. Given the mood of the times, questions about separation of church and state were unlikely to arise. The agencies would be divided among various Christian denominations. In practice, the churches would appoint agents subject to the approval of the president. The agents would then manage the reservations in order to "Christianize and civilize the Indian, and to train him in the arts of peace."[56]

At the time the policy was initiated, Methodists had few Indian missions left, and three-fourths of them were controlled by the Methodist Episcopal Church, South. The first denominations chosen under the policy were Hicksite and Orthodox Friends (Quakers), who were already working with Indian agencies. They were assigned sixteen agencies. Surprisingly, Methodists were assigned fourteen agencies (all of them to the Northern Church). Presbyterians were assigned nine agencies, Episcopalians eight, Roman Catholics seven, the American Missionary Association six, Dutch Reformers four, Baptists three, and Unitarians two.[57]

The majority of the agencies assigned to the Methodists were in the Pacific Northwest, Montana, and Michigan. This hardly reflected fresh enthusiasm for Native missions. In fact, as one authority put it, "The Peace Policy ... allowed Methodists to undertake efforts they did not choose to finance themselves."[58] The government underwrote all of the Methodist mission efforts on their new agencies. Nevertheless, with 20 percent of the agencies in their hands, charges quickly arose that the Methodists were improperly favored. Critics pointed out that Grant had been raised a Methodist and associated with Methodists (although he never joined the church). They listed a string of Methodists that Grant had nominated for various government posts. *The Nation* claimed that Reverend John P. Newman, pastor of the Metropolitan Memorial Methodist Church in Washington had undue influence over Grant, and that Methodist former U.S. Senator and Secretary of the Interior James Harlan controlled "the Indian Ring." When he retired from the Board of Indian Commissioners in 1881, A. C. Barstow claimed that the board was nothing but a "Methodist Kitchen Cabinet."[59]

Still active in all things related to Methodists and politics, Bishop Matthew Simpson was on hand as chief lobbyist. He delivered the invocation at the 1868 Republican Convention in Chicago. Grant also appointed him to the Santo Domingo Commission. By 1872, Methodists were overwhelming Simpson with requests for support of the Church and their requests for positions. Simpson tried, but Grant was not as cooperative with Simpson as Lincoln had been.[60]

The Catholic Church claimed that Grant had been duped by Methodist propaganda. Almost at once, a battle arose between the Catholics and Methodists over the assignment of agencies. In fact, Catholics had been active on many of the agencies before the Peace Policy. Methodists did not acquit themselves well in the fight, resorting to slander, anti-Catholic propaganda, and even violence. In 1873, a government inspector, Edward Kemble, himself an Episcopalian, wrote of the Methodists, "The denomination having charge here, are not, in one instance, carrying on a religious work separate from the Govt. The Methodists are not able to carry on the Agencies they have grasped here." In 1875, the Commissioner of Indian Affairs said that the Methodist Church was using its authority "for the promotion of Church interests rather than for . . . Indians."[61] Methodists invested more in the Yakima Agency than any other. James "Father" Wilbur was the agent there, and the Church lauded Yakima as the "Model Reservation." Wilbur was acclaimed for his promotion of white culture, although he used tyranny and even forced starvation to make the Indians work.[62]

The Methodist record was miserable elsewhere. Methodists were regarded as the least engaged and least successful of all of the denominations. In 1880, even the Methodist Missionary Society proclaimed its efforts as part of the Peace Policy generally a failure.[63] As one scholar notes, "It did little to improve the service or the condition of the Indian. It did much to perpetuate sectarianism and intolerance and bigotry in America."[64] Barclay was kinder in his assessment, although he noted "a pervasive sense of despondency concerning the possibility of Indian evangelization and civilization had developed." What was missing, he said, was any enthusiasm for Indian ministry, which led to a pervasive pessimism.[65]

And yet, the Methodist Episcopal Church was the last denomination to abandon the Peace Policy. In April 1882, one month before Congress relieved the Board of Indian Commissioners of all its duties and powers, Dr. John W. Reid, the secretary of the Methodist Missionary Society, complained to the Secretary of the Interior that he had not honored the Church's nominations for agents in Michigan and at Yakima. The secretary, Henry M. Teller, was himself a Methodist. He was also a former U.S. Senator from Colorado and an associate of John M. Chivington and John Evans in the early days. He took office as an admitted supporter of military control of Indian affairs and an opponent of allotment in severalty, which was growing in popularity as the preferred solution to the "Indian question."

Teller told Reid that the Methodists no longer controlled federal appointments and that he did not know what was meant by a "peace policy." He added that church selection of agents had failed to improve the Indian Service, but worse "had resulted in some of the greatest frauds in American history." Reid responded that the loss of the agencies would not pose a problem because "upon a moment's reflection, you will perceive that the peace policy has no relation to the spiritual and religious interests of the Indians. The Government could not, in any way, be cognizant of religious matters."[66]

William T. Sherman, the unrelenting advocate of harsh action against the Indians, wrote to Robert Clarke on February 29, 1880, with his assessment of the changes:

> No government on earth has expended as much money, so much charity, so much forbearance in this great problem as has the Govt of the U.S. and if the Christian policy has failed it has not been for want of effort but because the problem is insoluble—unless the Indian will change his nature & habits, select his spot on earth, and become as a white man he is doomed. It is not because the white man is cruel, inhuman, and grasping but because it is the Law of Natural Change & development—the wrong began at Plymouth Rock and will end in the Rocky Mountains.[67]

As one of his recent biographers notes, "Sherman had little compassion for the Indians and no guilt about the failure of the United States to live up to its treaty obligations."[68] That was by 1880 the most widely held view of white Americans.

Failure of the Peace Policy

The Peace Policy had not brought peace. Even before it was in place, on January 23, 1870, Colonel E. M. Baker attacked a camp of Piegans in Montana and killed 173 men, women and children.[69] *The New York Times* immediately condemned it as a "sickening slaughter" in "the Chivington style."[70] The Baker Massacre deepened the divide between reformers and the military.[71] In 1871, the treaty system was formally abandoned, although previous obligations could not be ignored.[72] There would be more wars across the West. The Southern Cheyennes and Arapahos would be involved in the Red River War of 1874, and the Northern Cheyennes would be a part of the Great Sioux War of 1876 in which George Custer would make his "Last Stand." Northern Cheyennes were sent south to the reservation in Oklahoma where they were very unhappy. In 1878, Dull Knife and Little Wolf left the reservation in a desperate effort to return to Montana. Dull Knife decided to surrender at Fort Robinson, Nebraska. Imprisoned in freezing weather, his people broke out and paid in blood in their drive to reach Montana. Little Wolf's group reached Montana before the remnant of Dull Knife's. They had fought their way back and their fate was still uncertain when the Peace Policy was abandoned.

So, with the end of the Peace Policy, Methodist efforts among the Indians reverted to the traditional emphasis on missions and education, but in the absence of government funding support for Indian missions dropped dramatically. Thereafter, Methodists played a limited role in Indian missions or in moral and ethical discourse on the fate of indigenous peoples. No aggressive reform element emerged within the Church. It was plainly an establishment church. A Methodist presence remained in policy circles, however.

Traditional Culture vs. Civilization

Hiram Price, who served as Commissioner of Indian Affairs between 1881 and 1885 was a devout Methodist. As an advocate of allotment in severalty, he had a hard-nosed point of view: "Let the laws that govern a white man, govern the Indian. The Indian must be made to understand that if he expects to live and prosper in this country, he must learn the English language and learn to work."[73] In December 1882, he was directed by Secretary Teller "to formulate certain rules . . . to abolish rites and customs so injurious to the Indians."[74] This led to a code of laws governing participation in certain ceremonies and dances, practices of medicine men, plural marriages, purchase of wives or concubines, opposition to the "civilization program," the destruction of property by mourners, and other traditional ways. A court composed of three Indians was formed to enforce the new code at each agency. In this manner, a Methodist Secretary of the Interior and a Methodist Commissioner of Indian Affairs instituted a program designed to eliminate traditional cultures as a means of promoting their view of civilization.

Curiously, though, Price and Teller differed on the basic policy issue of the 1880s. Price was a strong advocate of allotment in severalty, seeing it as the only way to end corruption and dependence on government annuities. On the other hand, Teller opposed allotment. In 1880, Teller, then a U.S. Senator from Colorado, told his colleagues in the Senate:

> If I stand alone in the Senate, I want to put upon the record my prophecy in this matter [of allotment], that when thirty or forty years shall have passed and these Indians shall have parted with their title, they will curse the hand that was raised professedly in their defense to secure this kind of legislation, and if all of the people who are clamoring for it understood Indian character, and Indian laws, and Indian morals, and Indian religion, they would not be here clamoring for this at all.[75]

The president of the Board of Indian Commissioners between 1881 and 1890 was Clinton B. Fisk, a Methodist, and Daniel Dorchester, a Methodist minister, was named Superintendent of Indian Education during the time that allotment of land began under the Dawes Act, passed in 1887. Methodists and their publications generally favored this policy. It would, as the *New York Advocate* suggested in 1886, allow the Indian to "take care of himself as a self-respecting individual."[76]

Oklahoma Indian Missionary Conference

The greatest success for Methodists came in mission areas where Native preachers were able to preach the gospel while showing respect for traditional ways and even incorporating tribal spiritualism and symbology into the services. The old Indian Mission Conference of the Methodist Episcopal Church, South, continued its work in the Indian Territory (Oklahoma after 1889) until it was absorbed into the

184

Oklahoma Conference in 1906.[77] With this change, the Oklahoma Conference shed its missionary emphasis and became more concerned with issues of membership, money, and buildings, typical of other conferences. In the process, the new conference lost about half of its Indian members. In 1910, the Oklahoma Conference was split into the East Oklahoma Conference and the West Oklahoma Conference. In this process, the new white-dominated conferences segregated Indian work from other congregations.

This was an era of major exploitation of Indian people in Oklahoma, and the Church was a conscious partner in the process and dismissed Indian churches as "unsightly relics of the past." The justifications were the familiar themes of progress, and assimilation. Methodist evangelism rested squarely on the need for individual repentance and the need to forsake old ways as sinful and accept a new birth. That meant, practically, abandoning Native ways altogether.[78]

Indian congregations dwindled, but their churches survived. Indian congregations, both those of long standing like the Cherokees and Creeks, and more recent ones such as John Jasper Methvin's Kiowa congregation in Anadarko, were able to maintain connections with their past and to accept what one scholar calls "selective adoption" of Christian beliefs and ways. In 1918, a new Indian Mission was created, which existed from 1918 until 1939, when the northern and southern branches of Methodism were merged. This new arrangement helped, but Native congregations continued to be marginalized. Nevertheless, with more autonomy, Indian congregations grew. With Christianity at the center, camp meetings, and quarterly singing conventions, church officials interfered less often. Even so, the Indian Mission continued to have issues. As part of the Native struggle, in 1972, The United Methodist Church established the Oklahoma Indian Missionary Conference.[79]

J. J. Methvin, who was traditional in his belief that Christ was the sole way to salvation, recognized the good in Native society and engaged individuals in respectful conversation about their beliefs. He never loosened his own Methodist beliefs, but he succeeded more than others because he involved the Kiowa (and other) members in understanding the process of believing. As Smith concludes, a few missionaries, like Methvin, understood their mission differently than the majority:

> For them, Indians could not only control Christianity among their communities, they were necessary for Christianity to take hold at all. Understanding how religious beliefs motivate groups, rather than judging these beliefs on more modern terms that stress their ethnocentric

or adversarial overtones, reveals a broader picture of the missionization process and the ways in which individuals exploited religion and church structures for their own needs.[80]

Bishop Whipple, the Episcopalian reformer, wrote of his service among the Ojibwes, "Nothing lingers longer in memory than the nights spent around the Indian campfire. There, in the heart of primeval nature, under the subtle influence of the ever-shining stars and the murmur of fragrant pines, we have been able to draw forth the legends and traditions of the Indians as we could have done no other way."[81] He was very close to understanding the missing link in missionary efforts—the need to know and understand the Native way of seeing. He was, after all, the man who had gone to Washington in 1862 to plead the cause of the Sioux in Minnesota and try to save the lives of those sentenced to death, when the white people of Minnesota were demanding extermination. Gustav Neibuhr has written of Whipple, "He recognized that moral authority, when kept sheathed like a sword in its scabbard, eventually loses its purpose."[82]

Yet, ultimately, Whipple saw no answer other than capitulation to civilization that ironically made him as much the instrument of conquest as the soldiers who hunted down the Minnesota Sioux he sought to understand and to protect. It was not a bad heart that made him so. He loved. But he could not get beyond the way of seeing that was his inheritance. He could not comprehend that the solution he saw would require Native people to give up the things dearest to them. Their disparate histories offered proof of their capacity to adapt, of their ability to change, but they also revealed the need, ever present, to adapt and to change within the context of their own culture and way of seeing. Given the velocity of change in the nineteenth century, time was too short for the transition that was needed, but it would have been helpful had the churches—which, after all, played such a great role in the shaping and implementation of policy—seen the need.

The Methodist Episcopal Church had no equivalent to Bishop Whipple as an advocate for Indian rights. William H. Goode had a "good heart" and a passion for mission work among the Indians, and there were others within the Church as ministers and laymen who expressed concern, but most of them found no calling to political activism on behalf of American Indians. They relied instead on the conviction that Christian faith itself was the only solution. The dilemma was inherent in Lincoln's vision of the West as expressed in his annual message in 1864—"to render it secure for the advancing settler, and to provide for the welfare of the Indian."[83] It was an inherently flawed conception given the shared view of both those who favored a harsh policy and those who wanted to "save" the Indians that Natives were "savages" who had to give way to the forces of "Civilization." As David Nichols has pointed out, "*Civilization*, not *culture*, was White America's key word-concept." "Savage" was, by definition, "anti-civilization." It was not a view unique to Methodists, by any means; but by the Civil War, the Methodist Episcopal Church in the North saw itself as the agent of civilization and committed to its advance. The only option was "change or die," whatever the solution to the "Indian question" was offered.[84]

In his review of the Church from 1860 to 1875, Bishop Simpson wrote of new missions to Italy, Japan, and Mexico but he did not mention any issues related to the United States' Native tribes. So far, no discourse has been found written by Bishop Simpson on Sand Creek or post-war Indian policy. In his 1877 treatise, *A Hundred Years of Methodism*, he mentioned the Wyandot Mission and the beginnings of missions in Oregon. His only commentary was far too familiar: "There is something sad connected with the condition of the Indian population. Gradually they are melting away. They imitate the vices of the whites, without cultivating their virtues. Tribe after tribe is disappearing, and only a poor remnant remains."[85] One recent study concludes that "as far as we know [Simpson] asked no questions about Sand Creek, and never mentioned the event throughout the rest of his public life, much less express any remorse."[86]

Dr. Charles Eastman, the Santee physician, told the story of a missionary who came to his people to preach. He told them of the Creation and the fall of humankind by the eating of the forbidden fruit. The Indians listened quietly and respectfully, and when he had finished, one of them told him an ancient story about the origin of maize.

The missionary then said to them, "What I have told to you are sacred truths, but this that you tell me is pure fable and falsehood!"

"My brother," the Indian replied quietly, "it seems that you have not been well grounded in the rules of civility. You saw that we, who practice these rules, believed your stories; why then do you refuse to credit ours?"[87]

Hoistah was a Cheyenne woman who lost her children and grandchildren at Sand Creek. As a member of Black Kettle's manhao, she was also present at the Washita as well. It was then that "her heart turned against the pale-faced people." Later, on the reservation in Oklahoma, she was encouraged to follow the missionaries' teachings and adopt white society's ways. Her response was plain: "When I die I hope that I shall be wrapped in a robe and hoisted on a scaffold. Perhaps whistling winds will soon blow me down to earth, and my bones will be rattled over the plains by wild beasts. But until my bones are separated one from the other I shall remain a Cheyenne and continue to despise the pale-faced people and all their ways."[88]

James West, a Southern Cheyenne and an ordained minister in the American Baptist Church, speaks of a conversation he had once had with Mutsiiuiv, Sweet Medicine, who told him of the long-ago time at Bear Butte when he gave the people the knowledge they needed to know, including the idea that the Medicine Wheel could only be broken by the decisions of the people. After the conversation, West said that he did not want to leave, "But, He sent me into the world to share the truth of Maheo's love."

This concept of seeing in Native spirituality elements consistent with the Christian gospel was surprisingly absent from the missionary rhetoric of nineteenth-century Methodism or from the theological discourse of the times because white Christians never learned or even looked for the spiritual ways of Native peoples. Rather, Church doctrine emphasized that God gave Christians the destiny of conquering the rest of creation in his name. "This has not been an expression of an inevitable fate," West writes, "but rather a purpose or justification of historical events." West says that when Sweet Medicine gave Mahuts, the Sacred Arrows, to the Tsistsistas, he told the people, "Do not forget me. This is my body I am giving you. Always think of me."[89]

CHAPTER 11

CHIVINGTON AND EVANS: THE LATER YEARS

On August 19, 1865, after the report of the Joint Committee on the Conduct of the War was released, the *Denver Gazette* published an editorial on John Evans and John Chivington, labeling them "the Damon and Pythias of Colorado." The *Gazette* gleefully declared that these "Siamese Twins of Indian notoriety have so inextricably got their feet into the jaws of the VIRGIN (which anglicized means mantrap) of Indian difficulties, that it is amusing to see them . . . wriggle and twist like impaled centipedes." The paper pointed out that Evans had told the editor of the *Northwestern Christian Advocate* that all of the Indians in Colorado were hostile except for one group of "friendlies" at Fort Lyon who were loyal to the government. "These facts were given to the public in the columns of the Advocate," the paper gloated, "and before a copy of the paper reached Denver, his partner had massacred his friendly Indians." The *Gazette* continued:

> This accounts for the shuffling and prevarication; either Pythias must fall or Damon must prevaricate, ERGO Damon prevaricated—Pythias was temporarily saved. But ere long Damon finding he cannot save his friend without endangering his own life, must and will throw him over. It may save his life, but the Senate is lost for ever. If he wept when he signed his abdication of the Senate last fall, what will he do, when throne and scepter, good name and character is gone. We forget, he will have a character which the highest tribunal of his country has given him, that of "gross shuffling and prevarication."

The paper recounted Chivington's circumstances and the seemingly universal condemnation of his course. "Can it be possible, that such a universal verdict is unjust or untrue?" editor F. J. Stanton asked. "These are no copperhead charges, these are no Democratic libels, the best Republican papers in the East all sing the same song, play the same tune, but all agree in the meter and the key—for all agree in adopting the popular march of the 'Bloodhound of Zion.'"

The *Gazette* was correct in pointing out the difficulty that Evans's statement put Chivington in, and it furthered the idea that Chivington and Evans had been partners in the grand design that led to Sand Creek. But there is no evidence that the friendship between John Chivington and John Evans survived the Sand Creek Massacre. John Chivington always insisted that the Sand Creek Massacre was just. John Evans distanced himself from Sand Creek while justifying his policies toward the Cheyennes and Arapahos and blaming the tribes for what happened.

The argument can be made that they were never as close as the literature has suggested, even before Sand Creek. Their positions and their common connection to the Methodist Church forced them together, and for a time they doubtlessly saw their futures linked. But while Chivington appreciated Evans's connections, Evans was not the kind of man a frontier-type like Chivington could respect. And by the summer of 1864, Evans had lost confidence in Chivington and begun to make his appeals directly to General Curtis and Secretary of War Stanton. By the time that Chivington declared martial law in Denver in August 1864, the governor's enemies (who had been fond of linking Chivington and Evans) were claiming that "Chivington and his friends kept up their reports of indians [*sic*] to throw the governor into contempt and become candidate for the Senate himself."[1]

Evans was blindsided by the Sand Creek Massacre, and while he took the public position of not saying anything about it until he knew the facts, he and Chivington never stood together again. In the heat of controversy during 1865, both men were defending themselves, so that it was difficult to sort things out; but although he never said so publicly, Evans distanced himself from Chivington. He felt betrayed, but he could not afford to admit it because of the public mood in Colorado. He hid instead in his defense of Colorado's soldiers and his own policies. The debacle of the 1865 election left both men reeling from the impact. Though defended in the press, they both felt the sting and imagined the consequences for their futures. Years later, Mrs. John Evans, in an interview made this cautious but telling remark: "Gov. Evans and Col. Chivington were in close sympathy, especially in the Methodist Church, and Gov. Evans got more credit than he liked for a good many of Chivington's acts which he did not countenance or approve of."[2]

Chivington: A Social Pariah

The river-town prize fighter reemerged in Chivington. He was an angry man in 1865 and 1866, uncertain of his future and striking out at his perceived enemies. His journalistic feud with the Atchison, Kansas, newspaper editor was a case in point. He did not build a clear argument against his editorial critic but assailed his character in a storm of angry rhetoric. Sand Creek had been a desperate gambler's throw that Chivington hoped would rescue his career, make him a hero in the mold of Harney and Connor, and move him to high office. Instead, it made him a social pariah.

On December 13, 1864, the *Rocky Mountain News* had called the Sand Creek campaign "the most effective expedition against the Indians ever carried out," claiming that "the chastisement given to the savages is more severe than the celebrated threshing Harney gave the Sioux at Ash Hollow a few years since." It had gravely predicted that Sand Creek would strike terror "into all of the Indian tribes of the Plains" and have a similar effect as Harney's victory. Alexander Safely, who had testified for Chivington at the military commission, reported that General Harney, the hero of Ash Hollow and one of the treaty commissioners at the Little Arkansas, had said that if he had had his way, he would have given the Indians "a little more of Sand Creek" and proclaimed that "he liked Colonel Chivington's style of treating with Indians."[3]

General Harney reacted angrily. Harney said that he had never "felt or expressed any approval or any sentiment but loathing and abhorrence, respecting the Sand Creek Massacre and its author Col. Chivington." He admitted that he had used "exemplary severity" in his own dealings with the Indians, but he continued, "There are things which I have never allowed myself to do, or to consider permissible, and foremost among these is the violation of plighted faith. I never granted to any man or any band of men, terms of capitulation which I permitted to be afterwards broken. I never made a treaty to lull my enemies into security, in order that I might abuse their trust for their ruin; still less in order to gain an opportunity of destroying men who were friendly to me."[4]

Although Chivington was applauded by Coloradans and Westerners in other territories who favored "Chivington's style of warfare," he still faced the charge that Sand Creek was "an act of hideous cruelty, garnished with all the accessories of fraud, lying, treachery and beastially [*sic*]."[5] More and more people distanced themselves from him, including soldiers from the Third Regiment as well as the First Regiment and an imposing list of line officers from Salt Lake City to Washington, D.C. General

Connor distanced himself from Chivington and reminded others of his warning that any attack that did not crush Indian resistance would only make things worse.

Frank Hall, one of the editors of the *Black Hawk Mining Journal* in the 1860s and a man who served as Secretary of Colorado under four governors, reflected on Chivington's dilemma in his massive *History of the State of Colorado*:

> No doubt the gigantic Colonel felt, as he surveyed the gory field strewn with dead savages, that he had won a brilliant victory which would cover his name with imperishable renown, and perhaps embellish his uniform with coveted stars of a Brigadier. He had in mind also, General Harney's famous achievement at Ash Hollow in September 1855, and felt that he had eclipsed the glory of that historic massacre, but forgot that Harney gave no orders to kill everything in sight, and hence saved himself the disgrace of an indiscriminate slaughter.[6]

Chivington never grasped the point. He rationalized and denied the charge, but he was still denounced as a "violator of treaties and mutilator of the dead" and compared to Henry Wirz, "starver of Yankee prisoners and patron-saint of Andersonville" rather than to officers like Harney and Connor. Even many of the Sand Creek "vindicators" in 1865 understood that sending him to Washington would be disastrous for Colorado's interests and doom statehood. Once he withdrew from the Colorado Senate race in November 1865, he was without a rudder.

The Colorado Conference of the Methodist Church could not afford to readmit him to the ministry given the controversy (though some would have voted to do it), and he could expect no fresh appointment from the military that was distancing itself from him as far as possible and blaming him for the renewed violence in the overland routes. For the first time in more than thirty years, he had to make his own way, apart from the Methodist Church or the government. He traveled between Denver and Nebraska City, Omaha, and Atchison, Kansas. He found support for his handling of Indian affairs in Nebraska, and he preached some as well, but he was drawn more and more toward freighting for his livelihood.

His son, Thomas Chivington, and his son-in-law, Thomas Pollock, were both successful freighters during the Civil War, hauling civilian goods and contracting to move government supplies. Colonel Chivington may have worked with them in the short run, but he soon decided to create his own freighting operation. In March 1866, with the backing of the Reverend Oliver A. Willard, who borrowed $10,000 from an Omaha bank, and the advice of Pollock, he purchased 114 four-yoke ox teams and wagons from Henry M. Porter, a Denver businessman, by promising to haul a million dollars in goods from Atchison, Kansas, to Denver, at the rate of ten cents a pound to pay off his debt. But instead of meeting the terms of his contract, Chivington proceeded to Atchison where he loaded half the wagons with goods for Porter, and took the rest to Nebraska.[7] Porter recalled that Chivington hoped, in this way, to make enough money to pay his men and expenses.[8]

Some of Porter's goods were shipped on other men's wagons, but when they arrived in Denver, Chivington had not paid those freighters, which forced Porter to recover his property through a writ of replevin. Porter contacted Willard's banker and

Colorado Conference, 1865. This photograph, misdated 1866, was taken at the end of the annual conference in Denver in 1865 at the suggestion of the Reverend John L. Dyer. Seated left to right are Oliver A. Willard, John L. Dyer, Bishop Calvin Kingsley (who presided over the 1865 Conference), and Charles King. Standing left to right are C. H. Kirkbride, George Richardson, William Ames, W. W. Baldwin, B. T. Vincent, John Gilliland, and O. P. McMains. (Archives of the Rocky Mountain Conference, The United Methodist Church, Iliff School of Theology, Denver, Colorado)

departed for North Platte, then for the end-of-track on the Union Pacific Railroad. He determined that Chivington had contracted to deliver government goods to military posts in the Dakota Territory for Wells, Fargo & Co.[9]

When Porter arrived, he learned that Chivington had "lit out" and sold the wagons and teams to his son-in-law without mentioning the mortgage to Porter or other debts. Furious, Porter headed to Omaha, where he sought an injunction to prevent the teams from moving until his contract with Chivington was fulfilled. Wells Fargo challenged the order, arguing that government freight had to move. Porter said, "Not in my wagons." Eventually, Wells Fargo arranged to buy the teams from Porter and his backers, and Pollock accepted a small sum for the train.

Reverend Willard lost his investment. The promising young preacher, who in 1863, at age 27, was the youngest presiding elder in the Church, had fallen on hard times. Drinking heavily and deeply depressed, on June 20 he requested of the Colorado Conference that he be located and left the ministry. By the time the Conference met, Willard was back in Evanston, Illinois, an alcoholic and a disappointment to those who had predicted his grand success as minister and orator. His sister, Frances, noted in her journal, "Our constant thought is *Oliver*—the noble, gifted boy who really is in great jeopardy, in many ways. That wild western country has wreaked its vengeance on him."[10] And Chivington was still hauling freight with a mule train he had acquired from his son-in-law when he sold the Porter teams and wagons to him.[11]

Chivington was still embroiled in controversy, however. He had wintered in the vicinity of Fort Laramie, where various contract manipulations angered General I. N. Palmer, the post commander. To make matters worse, Chivington was writing "abusive letters" about Fort Laramie and its officers to Denver and Omaha papers. The *Omaha Weekly Herald* refused to print them. It did publish an article that defended the officers at Fort Laramie, exposed Chivington as the author of the letters, and denounced him as a "rotten, clerical hypocrite."[12]

During all of this, Chivington was dividing his time between Denver and Nebraska City, where people still remembered him as a fire-and-brimstone preacher. He seemed to be accepted there, and although he was not readmitted to the Nebraska Conference at that point, he preached on a regular basis. In June 1866, Thomas W. Chivington, his son, drowned in the North Platte River while trying to rescue passengers from a stagecoach that had overturned.[13] In September 1866, John Chivington attended the Republican convention at Brownsville, Nebraska, where he gave a rousing speech against the Democrats. He said at one point, "If I am so fortunate as to go to Heaven, I will get a pair of copper-toed, square-toed boots, and standing on the battlements of paradise, will kick them to hell as fast as they appear; and if I go to hell, I will provide a red hot cauldron of boiling sulphur to chuck them in when they come there."[14]

The comments resulted in a flood of articles. The *Richmond* [Virginia] *Whig* called him "The Child Butcher" in its brief account, adding, "This from a minister and a colonel!"[15] The *Ebensville* [Pennsylvania] *Democrat and Sentinel*, said of his speech, "This language would sound strangely from the mouth of a true Christian soldier; but coming from Chivington, whose sole military exploit was the cold-blooded massacre of the Sand Creek Indian women and children, it is just what might be looked for."[16]

Chivington's Personal Tragedies

In March 1867, Chivington showed up in Omaha, "to assume command of religious interests," one paper quipped. "If Rev. Colonel Chivington can succeed as well in saving souls, as he did in slaughtering innocent Indians, once upon a time we shall expect to see a grand revival of the grace of God among our people and a great good accomplished."[17] Then, in May, personal tragedy struck again, when Chivington's two-year-old granddaughter accidentally fell from a riverboat on the Missouri and, like her father, Thomas, only the year before, drowned.[18] Later the same month, the *Des Moines Daily Iowa State Register* reported that Chivington's wagon train was attacked by Indians thirty miles above Fort Laramie, capturing thirty horses, fifteen of which were recovered. Five days later near Fort Mitchell the train was attacked again, but the Indians were repulsed.[19]

In June, 1867, Chivington spoke to the Nebraska legislature on the "Indian question." The *Rocky Mountain News* reported the story gleefully, saying that his sentiments were endorsed by the legislature "very unanimously." But the Nebraska papers were more divided. On June 14, the *Omaha Daily Herald* lambasted his comments "upon the congenial subject of Indian-murder as a pastime," with the opinion that "viewing him as a representative mocker of humanity, we arraign and denounce his teaching as a slander upon the Christian name and a hideous insult and disgrace to human nature."[20] In August 1867, while attending a camp meeting at Mount Pleasant in Cass County, Nebraska, Chivington's wife died unexpectedly.[21]

By then he had managed to find some acceptance in Nebraska City. He was active in Republican politics, the Odd Fellows, the Masons, and the Methodist Church.[22]

With the creation of the Peace Commission and a revival of debate over the "Indian question," his connection to Sand Creek was revived. In April 1867, under the title "The Child-Butcher," the *Petersburg* [Pennsylvania] *Index* excoriated Chivington, lamenting that "to the great disgrace of this rotten republic, the reverend scoundrel was not hung." The paper reviewed the story of Sand Creek and his commentary on Democrats the previous fall, concluding "This from a loyal minister and a colonel!"[23]

In June 1867, O. S. Glenn of La Porte, Colorado, wrote J. L. Boardman in Ohio that Coloradans were offering to pay twenty dollars apiece for *"Indian scalps with the ears on."* He said that "the Connor and Chivington policy is the one that suits the majority of the people here now, evidently not seeing that while the prosecution of a war with fiendish barbarism will be degrading to themselves, it will in no wise weaken the Indian or hasten a peace."[24] On the other hand, a correspondent of the *Montana Post* in Virginia City, opined that "a few more Col. Chivingtons would be a good thing."[25] Chivington was as controversial as ever.

Chivington Returns to Preaching

On December 6, the *New York Commercial Advertiser* announced that Chivington "has repented and gone to preaching again." The paper presented a confused account of his family and financial losses, followed by this commentary:

> Considering all these afflictions as a visitation of Providence, he has asked and has been restored to the Church with which he was formerly connected, and has assumed clerical duties. Many who condemn the Sand Creek affair think Chivington was not so much to blame for the attack and atrocities committed there, having been urged on by the public sentiment of Denver—by the very men who afterward went back on him, when they saw that it was unpopular.

The *Quincy* [Illinois] *Herald* reported his return to the ministry as the result of his many afflictions as the consequence of Sand Creek. The editor closed with the remark, "Verily, 'God judgeth in the earth.'"[26] It was a plausible hypothesis that Chivington's troubles had led him to repentance and back to the ministry. And on April 3, 1868, he submitted his "certificate of location" to the Nebraska Annual Conference and was "readmitted into a traveling connection." In other words, he was not assigned a local church, but could preach as needed. He was listed as "Agent of the Nebraska Conference Church Extension Society and member of Nebraska quarterly Conference" and named the Corresponding Secretary of the Church Extension Society.[27]

Chivington had returned to the Church, but controversy dogged him. At that point, his son's estate had not been settled, and Chivington believed that he was entitled to part of the property as a partner with his son. On July 6, 1866, he had been appointed special administrator of his son's estate. On April 6, 1867, he was named the regular administrator, but on September 10, he resigned and was replaced by J. J. Hochstetter, who was duly appointed on November 2, 1867.[28] All of this was by design. Following the death of his wife in August 1867, Chivington determined to claim his son's estate by marrying his son's widow. She had two children and was pregnant at the time of Thomas's death.

Chivington Marries His Daughter-in-law

On May 13, 1868, Chivington and his daughter-in-law, Sarah Lull Chivington, were married in Chicago by Bishop Ames. This news created a firestorm of reaction even among his supporters. Even the *Rocky Mountain News* declared, "What he will do next to outrage the moral sense and feeling of his day and generation, remains to be seen; but be sure it will be something, if there is anything left for him to do."[29] Sarah Chivington's parents called the marriage a vile outrage that they would have prevented had they known of it in advance—"even if violent measures were necessary."[30] They disowned their daughter, and even on her deathbed, her mother refused to see Sarah.[31]

With the marriage, most of the Nebraska press turned on Chivington.[32] On June 13, the *Nebraska City News* reported that Chivington had left for Omaha and that he would join the editorial staff of the *Omaha Republican*. Ironically, the editor of the *Republican* was Dr. I. C. Taylor, who had been appointed the Cheyenne and Arapaho agent after the Treaty of the Little Arkansas. Quipped the *Nebraska City* editor: "The Colonel is a writer of much vigor and will, undoubtably give a much better tone to the morals of the *Republican* than has characterized the efforts of ex-Indian Superintendent Taylor." The *News* also reported the rumor that "the Rev. Col. marry-your-daughter Chivington had his wife's life insured in his favor for five thousand dollars, before leaving this city." The editor added, "We should be pained to record the death of Mrs. C."[33]

The Chivingtons stayed in Omaha for nine months. Sarah would later claim that Chivington went to work for an insurance company that year but lost his job "by some crooked work."[34] In February, 1869, the couple moved back to Nebraska City.[35] They were living in a hotel when the home that she had shared with Thomas caught fire. It was not destroyed, but suffered serious damage. The *Rocky Mountain News* reported that the fire had been set. The insurance paid $175 to Sarah, and Chivington tried to make a claim for his uniform lost in the fire. It was denied, but his wife said that he took her $175.[36]

Chivington's conduct was already causing concern among his Methodist brethren. At the Nebraska Annual Conference on April 2, 1869, "Brother Giddings moved that the case of J. M. Chivington, with the papers therewith, be referred to the Presiding Elder of the Nebraska City District for investigation according to the discipline and that passage of his character be dependent upon the decision of the committee."[37] The conference records were vague, and the *Daily Nebraska Press* could only report on March 31, 1869, that "When the case of Rev. J. M. Chivington was called, Rev. Mr. Giddings said he had papers containing a statement bearing upon some business transactions of Mr. Chivington and that a committee of inquiry or investigation would probably have to be raised in the case."[38] At the annual conference in 1870, "J. M. Chivington's case was reported by the P. E., his character passed and he located at his own request."[39]

June 8, 1870, the *Daily Nebraska Press* reprinted a scathing article on Nebraska Methodism because of its involvement in politics. There was, according to the article, a movement to elevate the church to control the balance of power in Nebraska. It took to task several ministers but saved special remarks for John Chivington: "We know something of the incestuous Rev. Col. Gen. J. M. Chivington of Nebraska City, who no doubt will be a right bower in the deliberations of the coming convention or political caucus to be held in Plattsmouth. This pharisaical old snob wants the standard of his church elevated and politics purified too. He is the man who inaugurated this magnificent movement." It added, "Chivington is one of the progressive and reformatory party and has evidenced his fealty to those principles by marrying his own son's wife, she having three living children by that son."

Chivington Flees to Canada

Chivington's marriage to Sarah was not a happy union. Chivington managed to receive only $360 from his son's estate. He did file a claim against the government allegedly for property lost to Indians in 1864 when Thomas's wagons were pressed into government service. In May of 1870, he and his wife went to Washington to pursue the claim. While there, he found out that Henry Porter had received $410,000 for losses in 1865. He realized that he had the same lawyer as Porter and demanded a portion of the settlement. The lawyer agreed to pay him half the settlement, if Chivington could provide an indemnifying bond. Chivington gave him a bond signed by himself, George O'Brian, and Senator G. W. Tipton, of Nebraska. But Tipton advised authorities that he had not signed the bond. He also discovered that the notary seal used had been stolen, and the government moved to indict Chivington for forgery.[40] It also came to light that Chivington had been arrested and appeared in police court in Washington for having "grossly insulted a lady" named Mrs. M. A. Swetland.[41]

Chivington fled Washington on the run, abandoning Sarah. She managed to return to Nebraska City, leaving her bags behind at the National Hotel, which were confiscated because the hotel bill had not been paid. Chivington fled Washington and went to Canada. En route, he stopped in Troy, New York, where he preached at the First Baptist Church. This prompted a strong reaction from the *Albany Evening Journal*. The paper reviewed and denounced Sand Creek, and concluded, "if this preaching 'Colonel Chivington' is the same one who has gathered such a harvest of shameful notoriety, it seems to us that regard for the honor of the cause of religion, should make upright clergymen exceedingly careful about inviting him into their pulpits, unless he give ample evidence of 'change of heart.'"[42]

Back in Nebraska, Sarah secured a divorce on grounds of desertion and non-support. She spent the rest of her life in Nebraska City and assisted in several investigations into Chivington's past conduct. Chivington admitted that he stayed in Canada for three weeks after leaving Washington and that he had gone from there to Mexico. There were even reports that he spent time in California.[43]

The Return to Ohio

By 1873, however, he had moved back to his home state of Ohio. He claimed that he returned to take care of his mother "in her declining years."[44] He also married for a third time to Mrs. Isabella Arnzen of Cincinnati in November 1873. They settled in Warren County, but another mysterious fire left them without a home, and they moved to Blandchester in Clinton County. They had not been married long when Mrs. Chivington swore out a warrant against her husband for assault and battery. She alleged that he had forged her name on a note owed to her and secured payment for it. She then accused him of stealing her property, whereupon he struck her in the face "trying to make me promise to say nothing about it and take no legal action against him which I refused to do." She later dropped the charges. The grand jury did not indict, and the Chivingtons lived together for the rest of his life.[45]

Chivington worked for a time as the editor of the *Blandchester Press* and began a comeback. He remained active in the G. A. R., the Masons, and the Odd Fellows. He was sufficiently rehabilitated by 1883 that the Republicans nominated him to run for the state legislature. The *Lebanon Patriot* revived the Sand Creek story, and the Republican committee persuaded him to step aside. The *Patriot* claimed that Chivington campaigned with "the gospels in one hand and a flaming Indian scalping sword in the other."[46] This led the *Clinton County Democrat* to a scathing indictment of Chivington:

> Chivington is patronizing, oily-tongued, and understands to perfection the art of dissembling. Hypocrisy and deceit are distinguishing characteristics of his being. Virtue and honor are strangers to his moral character. Under the cloak of religion he seeks to hide the deformity of his moral nature. . . . While professing better things, and falsely claiming to be a laborer in the Master's vineyard, he has dishonored religion by committing deeds which, when brought under the searching influence of the moral horoscope, stand out, so conspicuously, as dark and damning blotches, that unfit him to represent a people celebrated for integrity, prosperity and honor.[47]

Chivington blamed the situation on a Quaker influence and threatened to sue the *Patriot*, but nothing came of it. In a particularly strong article, the *Cleveland Plain Dealer* reviewed his career:

> While pretending to be a preacher of the gospel this Chivington is a scamp deserving of the reformatory influence of the whipping post. He planned and executed what is known as the Chivington massacre, one of the bloodiest and most infamous deeds of cruelty recorded in modern history. He is also charged with marrying his son's widow, and after squandering his dead son's estate, leaving his wife to procure a divorce on the grounds of non-support. He married again and crowned his record of villainies by becoming a wife-beater. If one half of what Chivington is charged with be true, there is an institution located on the banks of the Scioto at Columbus that he is far more deserving of being an inmate of than in warming a seat in the State Capitol.[48]

An item appeared in the *Rocky Mountain News* three days later, curious in its tone about the man it had championed. Reporting that Chivington had "gradually passed from public notice and for some years nothing was heard of him unless when his name was mentioned in connection with the deed of blood in which he took so prominent a part," the paper reported that only the men he led speculated about him. The *News* recalled his role as presiding elder of the Methodist Episcopal Church, then mused, "The light air of Colorado appeared to imbue him with a desire to abandon the service of the meek and lowly peace-loving Saviour and to imbue his hands in gore. He accordingly ceased to be a clergyman and adopted the half civic, half military title of colonel as used in Colorado." After Sand Creek, "he was in bad odor with the authorities, if not the better class of citizens, and this was probably what prevented him from remaining and growing up with the place."[49]

The Move to Colorado

With his prospects shattered in Ohio, Chivington decided to accept an invitation to attend the first annual meeting of the Pioneer Society of Colorado.[50] On September 13, 1883, Chivington addressed the society on the subject of Sand Creek. He vigorously declared, "it is but justice to the pioneers of Colorado, as well as myself that I should give the true history of the Sand Creek fight." The crowd responded enthusiastically, and he concluded by declaring, "I say here, as I said in my home town in the Quaker county of Clinton, Ohio, in a speech one night last week: 'I stand by Sand Creek.'"[51]

As the crowd gathered around him that night, Chivington decided that he had come home. He quickly settled his affairs in Ohio and returned to Colorado. He was welcomed as a hero. He gave interviews. He wrote articles about the glory days of 1862 and the bitter times of 1864. He renewed his affiliations with the Masons, Odd Fellows, G. A. R., and the Methodist Episcopal Church. He wrote articles on the early days of Methodism in Colorado. He joined the Lawrence Street Methodist Episcopal Church (later Trinity). He preached, but he did not apply for admission to the Colorado Conference.[52]

Still, even the Colorado years were not without controversy. In the spring of 1884, Chivington filed a lawsuit against the Colorado Springs Company, the Manitou Mineral Water Bath and Park Company, and Thomas C. Green. Chivington argued that he was the original owner of most of the property on which the town of Manitou was located. Thomas Pollock, his son-in-law, had, in 1867, through power of attorney, transferred the property to the Colorado Springs Company. Chivington claimed that he never gave power of attorney to Pollock. He was not successful in making his case.[53]

Nevertheless, in 1884, the *Rocky Mountain News* announced that "a ground swell is beginning to come in for Colonel Chivington. The Republican opinion is that if he wants any office in Colorado he should have it, as long as he wants it."[54] The effort was stillborn. However, he did later become undersheriff of Arapahoe County. His reputation as a fighter was given as a reason for the appointment, and in 1887, he became something of a local hero when he flushed a hardcase named Newt Vorce from hiding with a simple threat to blow him to kingdom come if he did not surrender.[55] Later that year, he and Sheriff Fred Cramer were accused of perjury. Chivington was charged with lying when he submitted a bill for twenty-five days service as bailiff in the district court at the rate of $2.50 per day and for claiming mileage for 522 miles for the month of May. The county commissioners had investigated the charges, thinking that the records included "pretty good traveling" for a bailiff in one month. He was acquitted in a brief trial.[56]

Later, Chivington held the position of coroner in Denver. In 1892, he was accused of taking eight hundred dollars from the body of one Francesco Gallo and keeping it for himself. Charges were filed, and when a judge ordered him to surrender the money he had taken or face prosecution, he turned the money in to the judge.[57] Still, later, Chivington's house caught fire, and rumor was widespread that he set it in order to collect insurance.[58] On one memorable occasion, Chivington was introduced by a proper Denver lady to Amache Prowers, the wife of rancher John Prowers and the daughter of Lone Bear (One Eye) who was killed at Sand Creek. The socialite asked her if she knew Colonel Chivington. "Know him?" Amache responded. "He murdered my father."[59]

Chivington's health was failing by then. In 1891, he had filed for a military pension. It was denied. Then he brazenly filed a claim against the Oglala Sioux for $32,850 for the loss of horses near Fort Laramie in 1867, a substantial indemnity for fifteen horses. In denying the claim, Assistant Attorney General L. W. Colby filed a countersuit that argued that the losses of the Indians at Sand Creek far exceeded in value Chivington's losses. Colby hired a special investigator to review the case. In a supreme irony, the man he chose was Samuel Forster Tappan. Tappan went after Chivington with a vengeance, reviewing his entire life from the time he left Colorado in 1865 until his return there. At one point he wrote Colby, "We are driving from cover a monster. I thought I knew him, but was mistaken."[60]

Death of Chivington

Chivington did not live long enough to see his claim denied. His health deteriorated rapidly. He suffered from palsy. He exchanged a few letters with the Reverend Jacob Adriance from the early days, but in time he could no longer write legibly. His wife said that he had "spells" in which he was out of his head, and he eventually reached the point that she had to help him dress. During his last months, he was visited often by the Reverend Isaac Beardsley. He died on October 4, 1894, attended by his wife and Beardsley, who had grown close to him.[61]

John Milton Chivington was buried on October 7, 1894, with full Masonic honors. More than six hundred Masons marched in the funeral procession to Trinity Church, followed by members of the Colorado Pioneer Society and the Grand Army of the Republic. In his eulogy, the Reverend Robert McIntyre lavished him with praise. "I never in my life knew a man who so represented the soldierly element in Christianity as did the man whom we are here to honor . . ." he intoned. "As a pioneer, as a spiritual warrior, as a pathfinder and a patriot, he combined the elements of a Christian and a man." He opined, "When Colorado lifts aloft the scroll of honor, the name of Colonel John Chivington will be emblazoned near the top." McIntyre's only hint of the storm around the departed Colonel came with the remark, "The real battle ground of Chivington was the battle he fought with his own self." Even Beardsley found these words telling, but he too could not avoid lionizing Chivington.[62]

Charles Ferguson saw something insidious in the Church's response to Chivington. He wrote, "Chivington's warlike behavior was but an egregious instance of the collusion between conviction and violence that followed the standards of an age. . . . With only a small part of the populace involved in actual combat, violence then became vicarious and verbal, perhaps revealing all the more the ease with which the emotions of the day, at stark variance of the Christian idea, could be championed and promoted in a fervid religious order."[63]

Ambition, it is fair to say, consumed Chivington. He wore Sand Creek like a badge of honor, never seeming to comprehend why he had been condemned and determined to justify his actions. Reverend Beardsley opined that entering the army changed the "whole trend of his life." He recalled that Chivington "often wondered what it would have been had this not occurred." He admitted that "the colonel committed not a few mistakes" but insisted that he never lost interest in the Church and "got right with God" before he died.[64] That may all be true, but, tragically, John Chivington lost his way on the road to glory and squandered his gifts on the altar of ambition. Worse, Sand Creek loosed demons he was never able to control.

Effect of Sand Creek on Governor John Evans

If not for his tenure as governor of Colorado Territory, John Evans would be remembered as a physician, entrepreneur, philanthropist, and builder of universities, hospitals, and railroads. But, he did become governor, and the decision to seek and to accept the job changed both the direction of his life and how he is remembered. In December, 1864, when he first learned of the Sand Creek Massacre, he was in a familiar place, Washington, D.C., working with congressmen, government officials, and lobbyists mostly on goals that had little to do with Cheyennes and Arapahos or Utes or any other Indians within Colorado. He was still celebrating Abraham Lincoln's reelection and looking forward to Lincoln's second inauguration. He was concerned with railroads and economic development, with building a stronger Republican base in Colorado, and with statehood. He spent his time in board rooms, committee rooms, hotel dining rooms, cabinet offices, and the White House, working to make his dream of Denver as the great new Western city a reality, straddling the transcontinental railroad, passing across the plains of Kansas, through the Smoky Hill country to the Rockies, Berthoud Pass, and beyond.

But now, he found himself accused of complicity in an atrocity and condemned on the floor of Congress and in the public press. He had never been in such a place before. He had had failures before, of course, but those he understood. They were miscalculations in business and relationships. He knew how to rebound from them. This was different—an attack on his character—and he found trouble grasping what was happening or how to deal with it. No man had ever challenged his intentions or conduct in such a way. He reacted to it as a political problem and approached it as he had other political situations. It was not that he was afraid of a fight. He was in Washington in the first place not merely to urge a winter war against the Plains tribes, but more fundamentally to secure the removal of the territorial judges, U.S. Marshal Alexander Cameron Hunt, and U.S. District Attorney Samuel E. Browne, who had opposed statehood, and he was already enlisted in the movement to replace Secretary of the Interior John Palmer Usher with his friend, Senator James Harlan.[65]

Because he was in Washington in close proximity to many of his allies, friends, and mentors, few documents were created that provide insight to what he said to them or what they said to him. He had the advantage of allies who wanted to be-

204

lieve in him because he was one of them and important to their goals as well. Ashley served him well as a go-between with Lincoln and might have kept his position had Lincoln lived, but Evans aided in the removal of Usher while Usher was trying to save Evans's job for him. But Sand Creek was not a matter that could be easily brushed aside. In the months that followed, Evans watched as his advantages slipped away. Lincoln's assassination was a terrible blow to his hopes of surviving politically. Bishop Simpson had little leverage with Andrew Johnson, in fact had little but contempt for him. Simpson managed to rationalize support, especially after Harlan was quickly elevated to the post of Secretary of the Interior. Simpson tried to meet with Johnson three times on Evans's behalf, without success, and Simpson concluded that Johnson "had no heart." At the suggestion of Harlan, Simpson turned to Secretary of State Seward, but Simpson already knew the outcome by then. When he wrote Evans on June 28, 1865, he closed his letter with this curious and terse remark, "I hope you will fully realize your highest expectations of financial success."[66]

The report of the Joint Committee on the Conduct of the War sealed his fate with its stinging indictment of his management of Indian affairs in Colorado. The *Denver Gazette*, on September 16, 1865, wrote of him:

> With all due deference to Gov. Evans—who after all [is] said and done, makes a pretty fine old woman, if he had come out here with scarce a cent as Governor of Colorado, he might have stood a much better chance for the Senate than now. . . . He has been ruined by those that have pimped for him—fawned on him—puppy licked him—soft sawdered him—and in the dark—stabbed him. He was never made for politics or office hunting. We would advise him to go back to Chicago and Evanston, lay his politics on the shelf, endow a Methodist Church with his large fortune, and leave Sam [Elbert] his cast of clothing, and good name.[67]

He saw himself as a victim of Sand Creek. But, worse, he miscalculated how to respond. If Chivington's mantra was, "I stand by Sand Creek," Evans's was, "It wasn't my fault." From his first newspaper response to Sand Creek in Washington to his confused testimony before the Joint Committee on the Conduct of the War to his *Reply* to the committee's report to his letters to the *Rocky Mountain News* in 1865, he avoided the subject of Sand Creek almost entirely, saying at most that he supported the soldiers of Colorado and favored an aggressive Indian policy. The heart of his argument was self-justification. He avoided direct connections between his policies and the massacre. It was personal vindication that he sought. His approach found some traction, especially among those who had known him as businessman, politician, and layman, largely because they wanted to believe in him. Business associates and the hierarchy of the Church, mindful of his accomplishments, remained loyal to him, even if uncomfortably.

In 1865, when he was chosen to be a Senator for the new state of Colorado, he seemed justified. The *Northwestern Christian Advocate* claimed his vindication in May 1866, when Senator James H. Lane of Indiana forcefully defended Evans against remarks made by Senator Charles Sumner on the floor of the Senate and against the charges that Evans had lied before the Joint Committee on the Conduct of the War. He was prepared, Lane said, to show that the committee had done Evans an injustice by presenting "an abstract of all the documents bearing on the subject." In November, the *Northwestern* noted, "We had the pleasure of greeting Ex-Gov., and now Senator, Evans who has just returned from Colorado." On January 28, President Andrew Johnson vetoed the Colorado statehood bill, but Senators-Elect Evans and Chaffee remained in Washington until October 1868, before officially resigning to clear the way for another Colorado bid, "free of personal considerations."[68]

In August 1867, Evans was drawn back into the Sand Creek quarrel, as the result of harsh criticism from Samuel F. Tappan, who was serving on the Peace Commission at the time. Evans's commentary on the "Origin of the Indian War," which was published in the *New York Tribune* was perhaps his best-argued response. Therein, he said that the war did not start in Colorado, but in Minnesota. He reviewed his actions as governor, generously but selectively quoting from official documents. His response succeeded in countering some of Tappan's hyperbole. He argued that the Indians practiced only "guerilla war" consisting of theft, arson, and murder. He defended the settlers as being "remarkably kind and forbearing toward friendly Indians." He denied even the possibility that any whites had been in favor of Indian war on the Plains. In a private letter to the editor, Evans added, "This Indian war is an inevitable consequence of a rapid march of civilization in a region inhabited by wild and savage Indians." Yet the *Tribune* was not wholly convinced by Evans's defense: "Governor Evans may ignore the real causes of war and defend his own and the reputation of the people of the border; the country demands adequate forces for protection, and the response to that demand must come no longer in the shape of imbecility and child's-play."[69]

Evans had little to say about Sand Creek after that until he was interviewed by H. H. Bancroft in 1884 and 1888, and even then he said surprisingly little. He admitted that the Indians had been mistreated at times, but he added, "At the same time when we come to be butchered by them, it is right to defend ourselves and there my Quaker sentiments desert me." The closest he ever came to defending Sand Creek was in the Bancroft interviews, when he said, "So the benefit to Colorado, of that massacre, as they call it, was very great, for it ridded the plains of the Indians, for there was a sentiment that the Indians ought not to be left in the midst of the community. It relieved us very much of the roaming tribes of Indians." Unfortunately, the statement was not true. Sand Creek did not rid the plains or Colorado of Indians. Cheyennes and Arapahos would continue to fight in Colorado from 1865 until 1869. As late as 1871 and 1872, Cheyenne and Arapaho parties continued to attack railroad construction crews and ranches in the southern part of the territory.

Evans provided insight into his view of the "Indian question" reminiscent of Thomas Jefferson, John Quincy Adams, Bishop Kingsley, and more. The Cheyennes and Arapahos, he said, refused to deal with him, arguing that

> ... they did not want anything more to do with the government, that the whites had no business in this country anyhow. This was their country, and by the way, let me remark that the idea that this country belonged to them in fee gets its most ridiculous aspect from the proposition that a country a thousand miles long and five hundred miles wide, one of the most fertile in the world, should belong to a few bands of roving Indians, nomadic tribes in fee as their own property. It was taught by William Penn when he landed in this country, and that doctrine has been the cause of most of our Indian wars since then. I never saw the ridiculous nature of it until I got to see the consequence of teaching people that the country belonged to them and then robbing them of it. You teach a man that this is his property and then take it away by force and it is highway robbery. . . . I never before realized the effect of such a mistake in teaching the Indians that the country belonged to him, but nearly all the Indian wars have resulted from the fact that the Indians took in that doctrine, which was acknowledged by the U.S. Government that the country belonged to the Indians and that we had to buy it of [sic] them by treaty or purchase, instead of teaching them what was the proper doctrine as the British government did, that they had a right

to hunt on the land, but that that right must be subject to the higher occupation, for a larger population and for civilization. Their wildness should have been impressed upon them from the beginning.[70]

John Evans and the Railroad

After statehood failed in 1867, Evans did not run for public office again. Instead, he devoted himself full-time to business enterprises, especially railroads. He still had the dream of a transcontinental railroad on a Western route. Union Pacific fortunes were still uncertain. Two separate lines were competing to reach the 100th meridian (roughly the middle of Nebraska). One was moving slowly from Omaha. The other, the Union Pacific, Eastern Division, was building through Kansas from Kansas City (formerly Wyandotte). This line had already had a stormy history. Two competing groups claimed control of it, and in 1865, the quarrel pitted two acquaintances of Evans in a brawl. John Palmer Usher was involved with one faction, hoping to be president of the company. James Harlan, Usher's successor as Secretary of the Interior, was anxious to bring down Usher as corrupt. He slowed the progress, but eventually the two factions worked out a compromise. Usher was named Solicitor General of the Union Pacific, Eastern Division; Harlan monitored things closely from Washington; and the race west continued.[71]

By 1866, the Union Pacific out of Omaha had won the race to become the main line. The UPED was driving west along the Smoky Hill River beyond Russell and Fort Hays in 1867 and nearing the Colorado line west of Fort Wallace by 1869. On March 31, 1869, Congress granted permission to the line, now renamed the Kansas Pacific, to move across Colorado and join the Union Pacific at Cheyenne. As early as June 1866, while Evans was still in Washington as Senator-elect, the Kansas Pacific had been authorized to join the Union Pacific no more than fifty miles west of Denver. From that point on, Evans was in the fight to link Denver to the Union Pacific. However, he had competition from W. A. H. Loveland and Henry M. Teller who had organized the Colorado Central and Pacific Railroad. Loveland announced his intention to link his road with Cheyenne.[72]

Denver's fate was still far from certain. The Kansas Pacific was considering other options—following the Santa Fe Trail, moving along the Arkansas to the Huerfano, and into the Rio Grande Valley, then driving through the Royal Gorge to secure a position at the headwaters of the Arkansas and Colorado Rivers. This southerly route would miss Denver altogether.[73] On the other hand, Grenville M. Dodge, the chief engineer of the Union Pacific rejected the Berthoud Pass route as impractical. After the Berthoud Pass route was ruled out, Evans suggested another route through South Park, but Dodge was not interested in a Colorado line. He had already committed to a route across what is now Wyoming, with Julesburg the only point touched in Colorado.[74]

Once this became clear, Evans and other investors committed themselves to connect Denver to the Union Pacific in Wyoming. Evans and Loveland fought for control of the new line. Evans secured the support of Dodge and Thomas C. Durant of the Union Pacific, and in November 1867, Evans secured a charter for the Denver Pacific Railroad, which would connect Denver directly to the Union Pacific at Cheyenne. Evans was on the original board of directors, and in March 1868, he became the president of the company. The competition with Loveland continued, and the Union Pacific found itself in a tangle of confusion.

The Denver Pacific was largely a paper company, seriously in need of support and real financing, while William Jackson Palmer of the Kansas Pacific Railroad building into Colorado on a more southerly route was still considering his options. Evans eventually worked out a deal with Thomas Durant, Sidney Dillon, and the Ames brothers, Oakes and Oliver, principal investors in the Union Pacific. In exchange for a majority of stock in the Denver Pacific and a lease to the Union Pacific, Evans had to extend the road to the mining camps in Colorado and secure a land grant. He struck a deal with the Kansas Pacific to accomplish these goals—or so it seemed. But the agreement with the Kansas Pacific caused the Union Pacific to back out. At that point Evans was given complete control of the Denver Pacific's assets, and he managed to salvage his plan by striking another bargain that effectively made the Denver line a subsidiary of the Kansas Pacific. In March 1869, Evans secured from Congress an act that allowed the Denver Pacific to build a line from Kansas City to Cheyenne. That meant that a railroad would finally run across Kansas and Colorado to Denver and link to the Union Pacific at Cheyenne. The Union Pacific was not happy with this arrangement, which left Evans at the center of more controversy. To complicate matters, in the summer of 1870, the Kansas Pacific was harassed by Cheyennes, but the road went through.[75] The Kansas Pacific reached Denver in June of 1870, and in August, the Denver Pacific completed the road from Cheyenne to Denver.

Evans could now look with some pride upon the result. He had not secured the main line of the Union Pacific for Colorado, as he had hoped, but Denver was linked by railroad service to the main lines of traffic east and west. He had achieved one of the goals that had brought him to Colorado as governor eight years before. Evans was now more deeply involved in railroads than ever. In 1872, Evans sold his Kansas Pacific stock and created the Denver, South Park, and Pacific Railroad, which threw him into competition with his former partner William Jackson Palmer of the Kansas Pacific, who put together the Denver and Rio Grande Railroad. The struggles between Evans and Palmer would continue for years.[76] In 1874, R. G. Dun and Company investigated Evans. The company's agents reported him to be a man "of exclnt [excellent] char [acter], habs [habits] and bus [isness] ability." He was reported to have had $200,000 worth of property in Chicago and to have an estimated worth of "3/4 to 1 million dollars."[77]

In 1876, Evans saw a chance to make some progress with his road, but the Kansas Pacific, the Santa Fe, and the Rio Grande agreed to a pooling arrangement that blocked the South Park. Evans was forced to depend upon local resources that led to the creation of the Denver and San Juan Construction Company.[78] In 1878, Jay Gould became involved in the controversy. He envisioned a system of interconnected railroads that would extend the Union Pacific. He began with an attempt to buy a half interest in the South Park. When this effort failed, Gould, who was a master of such matters, tried other tactics. He tried to force the road into receivership and accused Evans of mismanagement. By virtue of controlling the Kansas Pacific and the Denver Pacific, Gould was able to offer an agreement between the Rio Grande and the South Park railroads to allow the completion of the South Park line to Buena Vista, along with the promise to assist in extending the line to Gunnison and Utah. For this, he wanted a quarter interest in the South Park. Evans's colleagues were not happy with this prospect, but agreed because Palmer saw value in the extension of the road to Leadville and feared that Gould would not support planned extension of the Rio Grande beyond Buena Vista and Alamosa.[79]

During this time, W. A. H. Loveland, who had purchased the *Rocky Mountain News,* mounted a campaign against Evans for mismanagement of the South Park. Eventually, though, the *News,* for financial reasons, reversed its position, writing, "The South Park road is an institution which Denver and Colorado, not less than Gove. Evans and his associates in the management may feel proud of."[80] Evans would face more charges, however. The *Denver Tribune* attacked Evans personally, which resulted in a lawsuit. His skirmishes with Gould and Palmer continued until Gould managed to negotiate what was called the "Boston Treaty." Still, Palmer managed to best Evans by driving from Leadville past Gunnison and west to link up with the Union Pacific at Ogden, Utah. Eventually, facing more criticism, the Denver, South Park, and Pacific was sold at foreclosure.[81]

The foreclosure was little more than a paper transaction, and Evans emerged from it without losses. He then initiated plans to build a railroad between Denver and the Gulf of Mexico. He had nurtured the idea for a long time, but in 1881, a group of Denver investors organized the Denver and New Orleans Railroad Company. Evans maneuvered through a series of challenges to formalize a contract between his line and the Fort Worth and Denver Railway Company that would also have connections with the Texas and Pacific, the Missouri Pacific, and the Missouri, Kansas, and Texas railroads. The major obstacle to the plan came from the Rio Grande, which owned controlling stock in the *Denver Tribune* and the *Denver Republican,* and used the papers as a platform to attack Evans and his railroad. In the fall of 1881, Evans filed a libel suit. More aggressively, he and other Republicans coalesced with prominent Democrats to support a common slate for city and county offices on a "People's Party" ticket. Evans won that round. His group was not successful in the 1882 Senatorial race.[82]

Evans's business acumen showed in other ways. Evans had purchased substantial blocks of property in downtown Denver, some of it designed to thwart the plans of railroad competitors, and more than eleven hundred acres east of Colorado Springs at the coal deposit at Franceville. Despite some manipulations, the construction assets were transferred by the trustee, the Mercantile Trust Company of New York, to the Denver and New Orleans. Eventually, the Denver and New Orleans and the Fort Worth and Denver were consolidated in a deal negotiated with Grenville M. Dodge. The maneuvering and manipulating continued, involving virtually every railroad with interests in the Southwest, including the Central Pacific. Evans would eventually become president of a successor line to the Denver and New Orleans, the Denver, Texas, and Gulf Railroad. In the long run, over Evans's hopes, the system was taken over by the Union Pacific and created as the Union Pacific, Denver, and Gulf Railway Company, but he was financially successful nonetheless.[83]

Evans never slowed down his railroad projects, including plans to build lines between Denver and El Paso, Denver and Duluth, Denver and the Black Hills, and Denver and Galveston. In 1887, the Denver Chamber of Commerce and Board of Trade recognized his contribution, "his indefatigable energy and skill . . . which have made the city of his adoption the commercial metropolis of the Rocky Mountain Region."[84]

In 1888, Evans began to retire from his railroad ventures. Beyond any doubt, he had contributed greatly to the Western railway system. In this more familiar field for his talents, he was capable, creative, and ruthless. Although he took the long way around, he achieved the goal he had first dreamed about before the Civil War of making Denver the center of railroad development in the West. He deserved a place among the railroad magnates. He knew their tactics, embraced them, and profited from them. Despite some difficult times, he became a wealthy man.

Evans also continued his investments in real estate and other properties, linked with a group of investors he had known since the 1850s. Bishop Simpson, James Harlan, Samuel Elbert, Samuel Pomeroy, and more sought his advice and shared schemes. Bishop Simpson had managed to help secure the appointment of Alexander Cummings to succeed Evans and Dennis Nelson Cooley to succeed William P. Dole, who was removed from office in the summer of 1865, another victim of Sand Creek. But he was soon involved in other matters.

On the other hand, Simpson did profit considerably from his association with John Evans. He had mining interests in Colorado, oil wells in Pennsylvania, a farm in Iowa, and other investments. In 1880, Evans sent him a direct monetary contribution. Simpson was also involved with James Harlan in a plan to purchase Native American lands at one-tenth their value. He was in the middle of a controversy in 1866, as a result of his association with Harlan and Senator Pomeroy of Kansas. The scheme was so egregious that the Leavenworth *Daily Times* wrote, "I cannot look upon this extraordinary affair in any other light than a most cold-blooded swindle, and a most flagrant violation of the obvious intention and spirit of a sacred trust."[85]

This added one more charge that the Indian Office was corrupt and undermined Harlan's claim that he was cleaning up Usher's mess. Harlan was condemned as "a pious swindler, and the Indian office was described as the seat of an enormous corruption, the fruitful source of Indian wars, the scandal of the government." Even after the deal was voided by Harlan's successor, Simpson held on to his shares until the summer of 1868 when he was persuaded to allow his investment to ride in a railroad scheme in anticipation of doubling his investment.[86]

His connections to Harlan and to Evans remained vital. Simpson continued to act as a character reference for Evans, and in October 1874, he wrote of the former governor, "He has acquired a handsome property, has been president of a Railroad Company. Thus a reputation [of] far more than ordinary skill. I would put the most implicit confidence in any statement he might make, in being his honest understanding and judgment in such cases." Evans returned the favor with generous gifts to the bishop and financial advice. Evans and Simpson remained close until Simpson's death in June 1884, following the meeting of the General Conference.[87]

John Evan's family life was important to him, but his movements hindered his attention to family. He also suffered personal losses. His grandchild, John Evans Elbert, died in his first year, 1868, and before the year was over, the child's mother, Josephine, died in Evanston. Bishop Simpson preached her funeral and wrote a lengthy article about her for the *Northwestern Christian Advocate.*[88] Evans's wife appears not to have been happy in Denver. Beginning in 1870, she spent less time there. She left for England with the children. She shared much of her time in London with Mary Todd Lincoln. When John joined them later in the year, Mrs. Lincoln asked his advice about Tad's education. Margaret had another child in England in January 1871, and she spent the rest of the year there. She visited Europe more than once in the years that followed. She was a dutiful wife, but she resented what she considered the unfair treatment of her husband.[89]

Evans and the Methodist Episcopal Church

John Evans also remained loyal to the Methodist Church. Colorado Seminary, created in 1863, floundered, and in 1867 it closed. The property was kept by Evans, Samuel Elbert, and a few others, but was eventually consolidated into Evans's sole ownership. In 1874, a plan was floated to make it a Union Evangelical University, but again the plan failed. In 1879, Evans returned the property to the Colorado Conference of the Methodist Episcopal Church, and began plans to develop Denver University. Evans was elected president of the board, and he continued to be associated with the University through the years as president and member of the board of trustees. The University struggled for a time, but sound management and effective public relations with both the Church and the community enabled it to become a successful and academically strong institution. Evans did become embroiled in a personality clash with Chancellor David Moore, which led to Moore's resignation in 1889.[90]

Evans also attended General Conferences of the Methodist Episcopal Church on a regular basis and advocated lay membership in its governance. In 1872, when laymen were added, he was elected and would be reelected every four years until 1892.[91] In 1880, he supported efforts to have four bishops elected to live in the West, with Denver as one of the posts. At the last minute, Des Moines, Iowa, received one of the new bishops rather than Denver, but Evans continued to work for recognition of the Western conferences. In 1884, Bishop Henry Wright Warren moved to Denver. Evans helped a number of smaller churches, from both Methodist and other denominations.[92] He also maintained his connection with Northwestern University.[93]

Evans continued to be interested in the city of Denver. In 1887, he worked to enlarge City Park. In 1894, he became involved in a public controversy when he suggested that the city buy land for parks in all sections of Denver with boulevards leading to the parks. The *Rocky Mountain News* opposed his plan and argued the main beneficiary of the plan would be the Denver Tramway Company, in which John Evans and his son Will were major stockholders. The plan failed, but did not affect his financial situation.[94]

John Evans was hit hard financially by the Panic of 1893. He faced foreclosure and increased mortgage liability. In 1895, his family concluded that he was no longer capable of managing his financial affairs. His sons Evan and Will found his records almost incomprehensible—incomplete, tangled, and confusing. His holdings were worth only a fraction of what they had been. As his sons worked to bring some order to his accounts, John Evans slowly retreated from reality. Dementia slowly robbed him of his former self until he was conscious of little around him. On November 18, 1896, Margaret Evans was appointed guardian of his estate.[95]

Death of John Evans

On July 3, 1897, John Evans died. On July 6, his body lay in state at the Capitol until 1:30 p.m. It was then removed to the Union Lodge of the Masons for ceremonies there. After another brief service at the Evans home, he was laid to rest at Riverside Cemetery. Evans died intestate, but the "Inventory of the Real and Personal Estate of John Evans," filed by Margaret Evans on August 15, 1897, estimated the estate at nearly a million dollars. But the estate was heavily mortgaged and his holdings "hypothecated." It would be several years before court proceedings determined clear title to the estate.[96]

Measured by a list of his accomplishments, John Evans was a success, worthy of recognition by universities, cities, political parties, and churches. He even had a mountain named for him. But that was not the full story of John Evans's life. In addition to his failed governorship, when H. H. Bancroft visited Denver in 1884 to interview Coloradans for one of his ambitious histories, he wrote in his notes about John Evans and Samuel Elbert, "About ex-Governor Evans and his son-in-law, Judge Elberts [sic] there is much humbug. They are cold-blooded mercenary men ready to praise themselves and each other profusely, but who have in reality little patriotism.

I have never met a railroad man who was not the quintessence of meanness in more particulars than one."[97]

Evans made his fortune and his reputation as a businessman as part of the new industrial order that gained control of the economy and of politics in the late nineteenth century. He shared the hard values of that time. He believed that business tactics could be ruthless and hard if matched by generous contributions from his earnings. Coloradans judged him by his record of public service, not his tactics. He epitomized the business mind-set of the late nineteenth century and believed his means were justified by the results. Even reviewing his papers against the backdrop of his accomplishments and dreams, it is difficult to determine his ethics or moral perspective beyond a rigid, rule-bound subscription to Methodism. More important, despite his accomplishments, he never escaped the shadow of the Sand Creek Massacre or the fact that he was responsible for the policies that led to it.

CHAPTER 12

THE BALANCE SHEET

THE SAND CREEK MASSACRE challenges Americans' perceptions of themselves as a fair and just people. As a result, it has been either characterized as a great aberration or dismissed as a myth created by romantics and social activists. But damned or denied, it remains a persistent thorn in the national consciousness and conscience. It has to be confronted as more than an aberration, and it cannot be brushed aside as the creation of politics or jealousy. The proof of its horror is found not only in the charges of its critics but also in the freely made statements of its defenders. It was not unique in the history of Indian-white relations, but it was exceptional in its impact upon national discourse and development. For that reason its history and the issues it raises still have far-ranging implications.

Sand Creek as a historical event quickly turns all who dare to study it inward to questions of meaning and conscience. It cannot be denied whether people find within it a cause or a rationalization. It demands a moral reckoning so powerfully that being dispassionate about it challenges even the most objective observers. And yet, even its power to raise passions and to promote "taking sides" underscores the need for understanding rather than judgment. What is involved is more than who was right and who was wrong. What is at stake is the nature of humanity itself, the raw, exposed reality of human existence and the capacity to deal with the evil that is part of the human condition.

The "Other"

The so-called Indian War of 1864 and the Sand Creek Massacre were not fought merely over the particular issues between Colorado settlers and the Cheyennes and Arapahos, but over a generalized "otherness" between whites and the dehumanized image of "the Indian." The image was embedded in the white mind by more than a hundred years of conflict; the settlers who went to Colorado carried with them something like a dormant virus that gained new life with the fear and dread that was born with first contact between gold miners and merchants on the one hand and Cheyennes and Arapahos on the other. The dehumanization of the enemy by way of image is "total enmity for the image of evil that possesses our imagination."[1] The consequences in Colorado were self-fulfilled expectations.

This is why it is so difficult to come to grips with specific historical trauma, such as Sand Creek. Humans on both sides of such conflicts, both aggressors and victims, are left with seemingly irreconcilable dilemmas. Aggressors must justify their excesses and assuage their guilt. Victims must find explanations that provide understanding and some sense of meaning. Frequently, for both, this means idealizing the past in ways that sustain the resentments. In that way, for all of the talk and reflection aimed toward doing right, the "savage other" is preserved. Yet, oddly, as Antonio Machado, the Spanish poet, wrote, "The other does not exist: this is rational faith, the incurable belief of human reason. Identity = reality, as if, in the end, everything must necessarily and absolutely be one and the same. But the other refuses to disappear; it subsists, it persists; it is the hard bone on which reason breaks its teeth."[2]

The theme of the "other" has been a persistent one in this report. It is ancient in origin and widely explored in works of history, political science, psychology, gender studies, and philosophy down to the present as a means of emphasizing the weaknesses of marginalized groups by those in power.[3] Its most obvious use in American history has been its consistent application to Native Americans as "savages." In turn, it has fostered the "victims" ideology of reformers and modern American Indian activists as an understandable reaction to the concept.[4]

The Cheyennes and Arapahos learned from the experience of Sand Creek that white men's words were meaningless and self-serving, even if there were some who meant to do right. Some of the people sought accommodation because they could see no other way to survive, but the majority embraced resistance as a just response to white perfidy and fought as hard as they could for as long as they could to sustain who they were as peoples. They were hardly naïve in their understanding of what the outcome would be, but they determined to live free even if it was at the point of a lance. One recent historian even argues that they bought time for themselves. "Late and limited conquest meant more cultural survival into the twentieth century," he writes. They were not so much "history's victims" as "riders of the whirlwind."[5] Their resistance allowed them to preserve their dignity while enabling them to cope better with the ordeal of the reservation that followed.

Settlers as Victims

Sometimes forgotten, especially in revisionist history, is the extent to which early settlers saw themselves as the victims—or why. The steady diet of rumors and provocations in 1864 created a growing distemper in Colorado. It created a sense of community among whites and a conviction that they had to stick together in defense of community. This is one of the leading causes of violence—the belief that the community is in imminent danger of attack. It does not matter whether the threat is real or imagined. It only matters that it is perceived. Reviewing the available contemporary sources, both pro-Evans and anti-Evans, it seems plain that white Coloradans, as a group, developed a siege mentality, even though the majority of them, safe in their mountain towns, were never in danger of Indian attack. Rightly or wrongly, they saw themselves as the victims. They blamed the Indians for their distress, and they fed off of the ancient images of Indian warfare that they brought with them to Colorado until they were suddenly made relevant by the Hungate killings.[6] The response was consistent with the historical role of the "savage other" since the time of the ancient Greeks.

Fear is often the mother of violence in times of trouble, but in this case the fear and sense of impending disaster were reinforced by expectations driven home by more than a century of westward expansion and the deeply embedded image of the "savage Indian." What they feared was what they believed an Indian to be—an Indian, not an Arapaho or a Cheyenne, not a Kiowa or a Ute, but an Indian. Real events were filtered through the image. The fear itself was real enough, but settlers enhanced their view of themselves as victims because of their belief that the white man had the right to take the land from "the Indian."[7]

J. Glenn Gray, in his classic work, *The Warriors: Reflections of Men in Battle*, argued that in the "encompassing environment of threat and fear" that is created by war, men find "delight in destruction."[8] He wrote that men can kill and be killed in conflict more easily "if they possess an image of the enemy sufficiently evil to inspire hatred and repugnance." He said:

> In a sense hatred is always abstract to some degree, since as a passion it
> is unable to view anyone or anything in entirety. The hatred that arises
> for the enemy in wartime . . . is peculiarly one-sided, for it is a fear-filled
> image. The enemy is not an individual man or woman, but a hostile
> power intent upon destroying our people and our lives. Our unreflec-

219

tive response is normally total enmity for the image of evil that possesses our reflection.[9]

Gray also suggested that warfare becomes more deeply noxious when the image
is of the enemy "as a creature who is not human at all." He wrote:

> This image of the enemy is fear-filled as no other is, since no one at-
> tributes calculable ways of behavior to the foe, but, on the contrary,
> expects any manner of enormity from him. Though he be animalic in
> being without human emotions and reason, he is thought to be capable
> of treachery, recklessness and bloodlust to superhuman extent. Based
> as it is on ignorance and primitive dread, this image prevents those who
> hold it from any reasonable calculation of the enemy's actual strength
> or weakness. . . .[10]

He observed that "the ugliness of war against an enemy conceived to be sub-
human can hardly be exaggerated. There is an unredeemed quality to battle experience under these conditions which blunts all senses and perceptions. Traditional
appeals of war are corroded by the demands of a war of extermination, where conventional rules no longer apply."[11] Gray was writing about the common experiences
of "men in battle" throughout history, but his view has a peculiar relevance in the
violent contact between whites and Indians. In this case, the image to be destroyed
was not something unique to the conflict in Colorado in 1864; it was an image fixed
in the pre-revolutionary past and sustained by westward expansion. By the time of
the settlement of Colorado it was deeply embedded in the psyche of whites by generations of conflict, and it had the effect of determining the expectations and the
response of settlers to the Cheyennes and Arapahos.

Loss of the Plains Culture

How long the Cheyennes, Arapahos, and Lakota could have resisted had circumstances remained the same as they were when the Treaty of the Little Arkansas was
signed in 1865 can only be imagined. They had shown already a capacity to adapt
to change. Before Sand Creek the Cheyennes and Arapahos were part of a Plains
culture that had coexisted with whites for a long time beginning even before they
actually met the "hairy-faced men" that Sweet Medicine had warned them about.
They were experienced "European-handlers" who held their own and managed to

sustain their life ways as they adopted and rejected potential changes that came from the interaction.[12]

After the California Gold Rush and the pressures it brought to bear upon their domain, they coped, but the Civil War, more than the Colorado gold rush changed that. The War Department was engaged in a war to save the Union and turned military matters in the West over to settler-soldiers whose sympathies favored whites. The Department of the Interior was more interested in land policy than Indian policy, putting in place the means of rapid settlement—the Homestead Act and the Pacific Railway Act. The War also created a new kind of national consciousness that permeated even religious denominations and validated the mission of spreading the nation from sea to sea.

Even those tribal leaders who understood the advantages that whites had over them, could hardly have imagined what was about to happen once the Civil War ended. Within a decade a spider-web of railroads brought settlers and businesses and towns and farms and ranches throughout Cheyenne and Arapaho lands. Miners and mining companies extracted gold and silver and more treasures from the mountains. The buffalo were slaughtered. Industry intruded into the new country. The regular army was able to move faster and farther than ever before. The post-war army was different from the pre-war army. Before, the military had acted as a barrier between settlers and Indians as a means of maintaining peace; after, the army was the government's primary instrument for resolving the "Indian question."[13]

Given their technological disadvantages and the size of their population, the Plains tribes were surprisingly effective as fighters and tacticians, and many officers repeatedly underestimated them. But the tribes could not prevail. Without doubt the professional army directed by Sherman and Sheridan tried to distance itself from Sand Creek while at the same time pursuing a policy of conquest.[14] In the 1880s, after the Plains conflict had ended, a reporter for the *Denver Times* asked General Sherman about the future of the Indians. "I do not see what is to prevent them from gradually becoming an extinct race," he replied, "but in any event I don't think they will ever again become a factor in the general policy of this country; the railroads have settled that."[15]

In an 1878 report comparing the United States' Indian policy with Canada's, General Philip Sheridan blamed greater violence in the U.S. on illegal white encroachments (a theme that went all the way back to President Washington). General Nelson Miles suggested that the Canadians had less violence by not forcing new customs on tribes and by holding individuals responsible for their actions rather than entire tribes. The report also pointed out that the number of whites moving west in Canada was significantly smaller.[16] This last point seems controlling. There was neither time nor space for the Canadian model. What subdued the tribes in the post-Civil War West was the sheer volume of settlers, the industrial growth of the country, the railroads, and the conviction of white Americans that taking the land was the right thing to do. These developments multiplied the power of the United States extravagantly. And when it was done, whites looked over what they had built and, like God at Creation, declared that it was good.

Historical Tragedies: Rationalizations and Condemnations

It is easy to condemn the racism and violence of earlier times in the service of modern causes. Racism, savagery, and the rhetoric of extermination are reprehensible and outrageous in retrospect, but they are mere symptoms of conditions that exist in the histories of all peoples. Understanding must take into account not merely the forces that feed the possibility of such inhumanity but also the power that enables it. To pass judgment from afar, whether spatially or over time, is to dismiss the human experience itself, to expect of humans in every time, place, and circumstance to have anticipated the same abstract conclusions of the present judge, who is removed from the visceral experiences judged and often is motivated by present feelings, attitudes, and understandings that are as emotional and irrational as the events judged.

That is why the best way to approach historical tragedies like the Sand Creek Massacre is to be taught by the past itself. It is critical to understand what motivated contemporaries to commit such crimes and to consider, contextually, the rationalizations and condemnations of those who were there. The more measured task of understanding what happened—as opposed to building a case for or against what happened—is far more revealing, not merely of what happened but also of the great principles for good and the great causes of evil that explain what happened. This approach not only creates a more balanced understanding but also a more powerful indictment of past wrongs.

The purpose of this study has been to determine the responsibility of John M. Chivington, John Evans, the Methodist Episcopal Church, and other leaders for a particular tragedy in the nineteenth century, the Sand Creek Massacre. In seeking answers, the report has become something more, an examination of the context of Sand Creek in order to be able to understand the actions and ideas that enable a

222

meaningful explanation. The results suggest the following conclusions about the roles of John Evans, John M. Chivington, and the Methodist Church in the Sand Creek Massacre, the massacre's causes and effects, and the greater forces that help to explain how and why it happened.

Conclusion No. 1: John Evans, more than any other person, was responsible for the conditions that made the Sand Creek Massacre possible. He failed in his responsibilities, panicked when his plans failed, and lacked the moral conviction to take responsibility for his actions or condemn Sand Creek after the facts became known.

John Evans, as Governor and Superintendent of Indian Affairs, seriously mismanaged Indian Affairs in Colorado Territory. He came to the territory with a clear agenda to secure a route for the transcontinental railroad through Colorado, to make Denver the great metropolis of the West, to encourage settlement and economic development, to promote the Republican Party, and to secure statehood for Colorado. His plan had little place or concern for Colorado's Indian population. The Indian was an obstacle to everything he promoted. He justified his economic and political interests with rhetorical appeals to patriotism and civilization. There was no place for the Cheyennes, Arapahos, or other tribes that dared to stand in the way of his agenda.

Evans was opposed to the treaty system, and he found no problem with unilaterally changing the interpretation of the Treaty of Fort Wise once he realized that treaty did not cede lands north of the South Platte, where most of the settlements were located. He found the Cheyennes and Arapahos recalcitrant, but made only feeble gestures to understand why. The non-signatories said that the Treaty of Fort Wise did not apply to them. Evans's aggressive approach intensified through 1863 and into 1864, especially after the spring skirmishes with Downing, Dunn, and Eayre. Evans grew increasingly frantic in his demands for troops and expressions of fear of an impending crisis. He bombarded both military commanders and the Office of Indian Affairs with pleas for help. In June 1864, following the Hungate murders, while he continued to pressure Curtis and Stanton for more troops, he introduced another element into his policy.

On June 27, Evans issued a proclamation "to the friendly Indians of the plains." His purpose, he said, was to prevent friendly Indians from being killed while war continued with hostiles until they were "subdued." The proclamation was too little, too late. In mid-July the incident occurred at Fort Larned that precipitated raids in western Kansas. Then on August 7, full-fledged attacks began on the Little Blue in Nebraska. On August 9, Evans renewed a request he had made to Secretary of War Stanton for authorization of a regiment of one-hundred-day volunteers for the purpose of fighting Indians. Two days later, he released a second proclamation authorizing citizens to pursue all hostile Indians, "kill and destroy" them, and seize their property. Evans advised citizens to avoid killing "friendlies," although he never explained how citizens were to determine the difference. In effect, he declared open season on the Cheyennes and Arapahos.

Evans wanted to prove to Coloradans that he could act decisively against the Indians and to salvage the statehood movement in the bargain. Unfortunately, the Cheyenne-Arapaho peace initiative that led to the Camp Weld Conference took him by surprise. He responded by passing off the management of Indian affairs to the military, in effect placing Indian affairs in the hands of Colonel Chivington. He did this in the face of Commissioner Dole's explicit instructions to be prepared to welcome all overtures for peace from his charges. It was a serious abrogation of his authority as Superintendent of Indian Affairs. He appears to have decided simply to let someone else make the hard decisions.

At the Camp Weld Conference on September 28, Evans passed the matter off to the military. And yet, by the time Evans departed for Washington in mid-October, the officials in charge of both civil and military affairs clear up the line to Commissioner Dole and General Curtis regarded the Arapahos and Cheyennes who had come in to Fort Lyon as de facto prisoners of the army. Even Evans admitted as much to Dole, to Curtis, and in his interview with the *Northwestern Christian Advocate*.

When news broke about the Sand Creek Massacre, however, Evans was not prepared. He initially refused to comment on Sand Creek. He decided to defend himself rather than Sand Creek. This would be the tactic he followed for the rest of his life. Essentially, he pleaded not guilty to any part in the massacre, swore to defend the honor of Colorado soldiers, and affirmed his belief in an aggressive Indian policy. The closest he came to actually defending Sand Creek would be his statement to Bancroft that the benefit of Sand Creek was very great. Never once did he publicly defend Colonel Chivington.

What may be more revealing with respect to his character and style were his tactics behind the scene while he was in Washington. He had gone to Washington in the first place to recoup the damages of the failed statehood campaign and to deal with his political enemies in Colorado, as well as to promote the winter campaign he had concocted with General Curtis. But he soon found himself under attack because of his Indian policies, and he was removed from office.

The evidence is strong that Evans did not know what Chivington planned to do. Even if he knew that Chivington planned an expedition, he certainly could not have anticipated the wholesale slaughter or the massacre of women and children. But he knew what kind of a man John Chivington was. More important, he, himself, had contributed more than any single individual to the atmosphere of fear and hate that dominated Colorado. He had given Chivington the Third Colorado Regiment, without which Chivington would have lacked a force sufficient to do anything more than protect lines of travel. He left the territory at a critical juncture, when his presence could have made a difference. Recent comparisons between Evans and other Civil War territorial governments in the management of Indian policy make his culpability even more obvious.[17]

His policies and actions were marked by a calculated design to remove the Cheyennes and Arapahos from Colorado. To achieve it, he failed to negotiate in good faith. Using the example of the Minnesota Uprising of 1862, he claimed an

Camp Weld Conference, 1864. This photo was taken at the Camp Weld Conference. The two men kneeling in front are Major Edward W. Wynkoop and Captain Silas S. Soule. The seated figures, left to right, are White Antelope, Bull Bear and Black Kettle (Cheyennes), Neva and Notanee (Arapahos). Standing, left to right, unidentified, unidentified, John Simpson Smith, Heaps of Buffalo and Bosse (Arapahos), Dexter Colley, unidentified. (History Colorado, Denver, Colorado)

imminent threat long before such a threat existed and helped to make the threat real by his own actions. Thus, he fed the fears of the white population to the point of creating public hysteria and then succumbed to it himself. He abrogated his responsibilities as ex officio Superintendent of Indian Affairs and eventually lost public confidence in his ability to lead. His response to the Sand Creek Massacre was self-serving and weak.

Even though he survived the scandal by turning his attention in new directions, he never confronted the moral or the political issues raised by the massacre. He had linked himself to Colorado, and he understood that denouncing the Sand Creek Massacre would cripple him politically and hamper his ability to attract investors for his railroad schemes. But despite his silence on the hard questions (or perhaps, in part, because of it), Evans emerged from the sorry story as a cold, manipulative capitalist, whose ineptitude and general attitudes toward Indians, provoked a war by his policies. He then fell prey to his own story, panicked, and passed off his responsibilities to the army. Afterward, he refused to face the reality of what had happened. He found consolation in business success and "doing good." In the end, after all, the Sand Creek Massacre was swept away by railroads, settlers, development, and growth of the new nation. He was culpable, however, for what happened—grievously so.

Therein lies a terrible irony. Although John Evans was removed as governor because of Sand Creek and his political ambitions crushed as a result, one part of his original design in moving to Colorado in the first place was achieved. John Evans made a fortune on railroad and land deals involving Cheyenne, Arapaho, and Ute lands. He was able to take advantage of the last struggles of the Plains tribes to amass personal wealth just as he had planned to do in 1862. Perhaps this explains why he never condemned the massacre, but, in fact, saw it as beneficial to the development of Colorado and the West. Thus, he directly profited from the Sand Creek Massacre. He was able to see in what happened proof of Manifest Destiny and the primacy of Anglo-American civilization. He was an unrepentant sinner because he saw no sin, only justification.

Conclusion No. 2: John Milton Chivington planned and carried out the Sand Creek Massacre to further his own ambitions. Afterward, he encouraged and defended the outrageous excesses that took place that day with no trace of regret.

The Sand Creek Massacre was Chivington's folly. By September of 1864 Chivington was a desperate man. His hopes to become a congressman were dashed at the polls during the statehood election. His commission as an officer in the army was due to expire on September 24, although he understood that he would hold the command indefinitely given General Curtis's preoccupation with the fight with Confederates in Kansas. His district had been stripped of veteran soldiers. The bulk of the First Colorado Cavalry was stationed in the District of the Upper Arkansas at Fort Lyon and Fort Larned and due to be mustered out. The rest were scattered from Fort Lupton on the Platte in the north to Fort Garland in the south. The only substantial force was the "rag, tag, and bobtail" Third Colorado Cavalry. With only one hundred days of service, he had too little time to mount a serious campaign against the center of Indian resistance, even had the Third been properly trained, armed, and mounted. He had no laurels to rest upon since the battle of Glorieta. His troops had fought no major engagements since New Mexico, not even against the Cheyennes and Arapahos. His was a failed command, torn apart by rivalries among officers (many of them of his own making) and with a general unrest among the troops. In October, circumstances grew worse with news that General Connor, a man who had won a reputation as an "Indian fighter" against the Shoshonis, was coming to Denver, with plans to launch a winter campaign against the Indians of the plains. Any such campaign would gain glory for Connor, not for him.

One problem was that Chivington had no record against the Indians. The few fights, or more properly, provocations of the spring of 1864, had all been the work of Chivington's most pugnacious and belligerent officers, Downing, Dunn, and Eayre. Other actions were directed by post commanders at Lupton, Lyon, and Larned. Chivington had wasted too much time stumping for Congress. Following the panic and martial law in August, one of his critics wrote, "During all this time[,] though Chivington had U.S. troops under him[,] he did not go himself or send a soldier to learn the truth of the reports."[18] Another wrote, on October 4, "You must already be aware of the fact that our late troubles are due chiefly to the perfidy & ambition of Gov Evans & Col Chivington[,] our military dictator urged on by the Washington Authorities."[19]

Chivington saw in General Connor both a threat to his own ambitions and an opportunity to rescue them. The Third Colorado Regiment provided the means. Even before Connor arrived in Denver, Chivington was moving troops south. He brusquely dismissed Connor's plans and chose a dangerous alternative to rescue his reputation and ambitions. He was on his own. Curtis was preoccupied with Price's Confederates. Evans was on his way to Washington. It would take weeks for Connor to muster an expedition. Chivington had time for one desperate gambler's throw before the Third's one hundred days were up. But it had to be a sure thing. He had no time to hunt for his target on the Smoky Hill or Republican. His only sure target was the Arapahos and Cheyennes at Fort Lyon, but he had to keep his movements secret to prevent them from fleeing. Once at Fort Lyon, he misrepresented his intent to Major Anthony by claiming that Sand Creek would be only the first encounter of an extended campaign against the center of Native resistance.

At Sand Creek he attacked a village promised protection by him. He incited his troops to kill men, women, and children, indiscriminately. He lost control of all but a few of his soldiers. He misrepresented the casualties. Afterward, he made no move against the centers of resistance on the Smoky Hill and Republican. Instead, he made a half-hearted feint after Little Raven's Arapahos down the Arkansas, before abruptly ending his campaign and hurrying back to Denver by stage to oversee news of his victory. At Fort Lyon, he strutted before other officers, comparing himself to Kit Carson, General Harney, and General Connor. He was on hand when his troops returned to Denver, their saddles festooned with scalps, body parts, and other grisly trophies of the "great victory."

In the short term, his plan worked. He rode a wave of renewed popularity among Coloradans anxious to believe that a blow had been struck rightly. They wanted to believe that the fighting parson had saved them from the Indians just as he had saved them from Sibley's Confederates. As the news leaked out, even from Thirdsters, that Sand Creek was not the battle royal that initial reports claimed, Chivington defended himself in letters and speeches. But it did not take two congressional hearings and a military commission to prove that Sand Creek was an atrocity. The proof was right there in the newspapers and writings of the time, confirming what the investigations revealed—and from the lips of those who endorsed the attack as well as from his critics. One of Chivington's defenders, writing to a Kansas newspaper, exulted that "... scalps are at a discount; every Thirdster has his pocket full." Newspapers and private correspondence were both filled with descriptions of the trophies, noting that "scalps were as thick as toads in Egypt," reporting the three small children who were paraded on the stage of a local theater, or the Arapaho boy who was given to one of the Thirdsters and used as an attraction to a traveling circus.

Private Jesse Haire, who admired Chivington as a minister in 1860 but detested him after Sand Creek, reflected on the changes he saw in the man. Even he was shocked to find Chivington in a Denver saloon in 1865, drinking and cursing "as eazey [sic] as any old Sport or boat captain . . . but to See him holding that glass up before his eyes, his elboe [sic] on the counter and that recless [sic] laugh and big

228

othes [oaths] and ha haws; my god I thought to myself what a change." He recalled how the miners had stopped everything and stood listening to him for hours in 1860, but noted "maney [sic] of them besides myself was astonished at his actions Since then." He mused, "I thought to myself you had better of Stayed Sadisfied [sic] as the [preacher] of Colorado."[20] Reverend Isaac Beardsley, who befriended Chivington late in his life, opined that entering the army changed the "whole trend of his life." He recalled that Chivington "often wondered what it would have been had this not occurred."[21]

Chivington was a man concerned about his reputation. He was surprised when the praise changed to outrage. When Senator James Harlan, a Methodist friend and associate of Evans, condemned him on the floor of the United States Senate, Chivington complained to Bishop Simpson less about Harlan's condemnation of Sand Creek than about his characterization of Chivington's "moral and religious character."[22] He struggled throughout his life with contradictions. Reverend Haynes, who knew him in Nebraska, provided the key to his battle: "His suavity and ambition secured for him a great influence over men, both strangers and friends, and if his life had with constancy been that of an exemplary man, his usefulness might have been unlimited."[23] David Marquette, another Nebraska Methodist, wrote of him: "John Milton Chivington was one of those strong, forceful characters who find it difficult to either control themselves or to subject themselves to the requirements of a Church, or to the rules of war, but who are a law unto themselves. But for these defects, he would have been a power for good, as he was a strong preacher and possessed many of the elements which constitute successful leadership."[24]

David H. Nichols, an officer in the Third Colorado Cavalry and a defender of Sand Creek, said of his former commander: "Chivington was justly unpopular with the soldiers. . . . The great trouble with Chivington was that he was ambitious to be promoted."[25] Thornton K. Tyson, another Thirdster, said of him, "Col. Chivington always impressed me as a man who was inclined to live beyond his means—who wanted to maintain the style of a Major General on the pay of a Colonel."[26] As C. S. S. Maberly, a Colorado businessman, observed afterward, "The time of the 3rd Regiment having nearly expired, Col. Chivington, the commander wanted to get renown for political purposes, before being mustered out."[27]

Tragically, John Chivington lost his way on the road to glory and squandered his gifts on the altar of ambition, never really understanding why. He was an unbending personality who never acknowledged his faults or the contradictory personality traits that were the faces of his demons. That is why the Sand Creek Massacre was Chivington's folly. He had watched his hopes unravel until they rested on an ill-trained, mixed-bag of Coloradans already derided as the "Bloodless Third." They had enlisted to kill Indians, but so far only a few of them had seen any action at all. Chivington's future was linked to theirs. If he could not get them into action quickly, he would take the blame with him into oblivion. Without that simple fact, the Sand Creek Massacre might not have happened at all.

Conclusion No. 3: The Methodist Episcopal Church embraced the prevailing mind-set of its time, avoided a strong stand against Sand Creek, defended both Chivington and Evans, and played a minimal role in the dialogue over Indian policy in the years that followed.

The Methodist Episcopal Church never confronted John M. Chivington's role in the Sand Creek Massacre in any formal way. In spite of the overwhelming condemnation of Sand Creek in 1865 in the public press and official reports, the Church hierarchy never directly addressed Chivington's actions or their impact upon the Church itself. Not only was he never "defrocked," but also he was never asked to defend what he had done in any Methodist forum, a fact that he himself pointed out in 1866, when he asked the editor of the *Atchison Daily Free Press*, "Or why do not the authorities of the M. E. Church cut me off?"[28] Methodist newspapers avoided that question. Even those papers that expressed concern or outrage filled out their columns with equivocations and "ifs."

In fact, he was accepted into the Nebraska Conference afterward. He was subsequently located by the conference for reasons not explained in the available records. Even then, when there were additional questions about his moral character, he served briefly as editor of the *Western Christian Advocate* at Cincinnati, wrote articles for the *Rocky Mountain Christian Advocate,* and continued to preach (without assignment) until he became too frail. He maintained his ministerial credentials (elder's orders) throughout his life in spite of the Sand Creek Massacre and the series of scandals that marked his later years. The Church's silence was truly remarkable in light of the charges made against Chivington.[29]

The Church's response to John Evans was more understandable. He was not a minister. He was not present at Sand Creek. Even though he was removed from office because of his role, Evans's defense in 1865 provided a rationale that the Church hierarchy could embrace. And he never suffered any direct rebuff from the Church he continued to serve. This is noteworthy, however, because the *Discipline* of the

Methodist Episcopal Church provided clear procedures for transgressions and for punishment. The procedures were different for the clergy and for the laity, but they provided means for reprimanding or excluding either. James Finley, who had worked with the Wyandots, wrote in *Sketches of Western Methodism*, published in 1854, that Methodists

> with Christian charity . . . bore each other's burdens, and with Christian zeal and fidelity, they watched over each other for good. Each one seemed to be the insurer of the other's reputation, and felt himself as responsible for this upright character as though he was his special guardian; hence, every thing that indicated, in the slightest degree a departure from the path of holy rectitude, would at once awaken the liveliest apprehensions and interest on the part of the rest.[30]

That there was never any forthright condemnation of the Sand Creek Massacre or its architects by the Church in the 1860s nor any apparent effect upon the Church's response to issues related to Indian affairs more broadly speaking in the rest of the nineteenth century underscores the Church's indifference to Indian affairs. There were individual voices against Sand Creek and the treatment of American Indians, but the Church itself never took a stance. This is the basis for asking what role the Methodist Episcopal Church played in the event that General Nelson A. Miles called "the most unjustifiable crime in American history."[31] The Church failed to condemn the act itself. It never demanded an accounting from either of the two primary actors in the tragedy—the Reverend John M. Chivington and Dr. John Evans. And it responded to the results of Sand Creek with rationalizations. The question that remains is why?

The Methodist Church in the nineteenth century reflected not just the theological perspectives of Wesley and Asbury. It also was part of the expanding Anglo world and inherited with other Europeans and Americans a set of values that defined "Christian civilization." It shared with other Protestant denominations a commitment to evangelization or spreading the gospel to all that have not heard. Inherent in that commitment was an assumption that the Christian way was superior to other ways. It bought into the idea of the "Right of Conquest" and into beliefs that Christians were "the chosen people" and, for Anglo-Americans, that the "New World," at least in North America was "the promised land." At its mildest, it embraced a benign paternalism toward all who were not Christians. At its extreme, it promoted a militant contempt and even violence against them. The association of the mind-set of "them" and "us" was not initially focused on "race" but on "savagery." When dealing with the "savage others," the Church was divided among those who saw conversion as necessary before civilization and those who saw civilization as necessary for conversion. Perhaps that is why by the nineteenth century, the Methodist Episcopal Church was largely a white church not only in membership but also in mission.

In its early years, American Methodism found its greatest successes among the yeoman classes in the colonies and states along the Eastern seaboard and among the settler colonists who pushed west into the interior. The latter, in particular, provided the points of contact and conflict with Native people. They were the very same people who developed the strongest antipathy toward American Indians. By the nineteenth century, there was a long and bloody history of "Indian wars," as they were invariably called, and a deep-seated mythology about who the indigenous people were, especially in relationship to their modes of warfare. This meant that Methodist itinerants preached their revivals and camp meetings among people who saw Indians as a threat to their lives and to their hopes for land. Not surprisingly, Methodist ministers frequently shared the values and attitudes of their constituencies.

Methodism shared both a populist base and an elite leadership, a division between those settler Christians, on the one hand, of which John Chivington was one, and leaders, theologians, educators, and laymen who sought to build a different kind of church in the wake of settlement as the purveyors of civilization, as did John Evans. They shared both a theological base and a social perspective based upon general agreement respecting the Anglophilic principles the Methodist Church began with. Long before the Civil War, those beliefs embraced the "anti-Indian sublime" that placed Native people in an inferior position. While this was not unique to Methodists, Methodist Episcopal missions to Native tribes were limited mostly to particular conferences and rested on the presumption that progress in the "civilized arts" was the measure of success.

The West, then, was dangerous not because of settlers, but because of "the Indian." One had to be overcome by the other. But there was also an evangelical concern that the westward movement led to a regression of settlers into a state of barbarism. This amounted to an establishment fear that white settlers left untutored in the faith would descend into anarchy and savagery. It was essential, then, that missions follow the patterns of settlement to minster to the fringe elements on the frontier in order that social order would be preserved. Moreover, this concern made it easy to connect love of country to the love of God.

232

The emblem of the cross with the flag beneath became standard during the Civil War. Bishop Simpson preached the link of one with the other with fervor until faith in the one demanded loyalty to the other. In the two decades before the Civil War, pietism was overwhelmed by political activism. By the end of the war, Methodists were also measuring faith in terms of restraint, sobriety, and self-control. A new middle class Methodism emerged that came to be linked with material success. The settler Methodism of open-air camp meetings and evangelization was displaced by more formal churches. These changes could not be set with precision upon a calendar but rather reflected trends over time.

What can be traced with certainty in Methodist publications and the recollections of ministers and circuit riders is a portrayal of American Indians consistent with those of the settlers they served. The churchmen saw Indians as a savage threat just as the settlers did. This remained true in accounts of the Sand Creek Massacre. "We saw these things in the light of self-defense," the Reverend J. L. Dyer wrote. "While our Eastern friends would say 'Poor Indian!' my own observations have been that many of the whites were killed, while the red man went free. . . . It is impossible to have a sinner converted unless he is first [spiritually] convicted; and it is just as impossible to tame and educate an Indian until he is subdued. My prayer is that all wars may cease, and that the red men of the forest may be civilized and Christianized."[32]

More specifically, politics in Colorado was dominated by Methodists. Not only were John Evans and John Chivington Methodists. So, too, were Samuel H. Elbert, Henry M. Teller, Jerome B. Chaffee, W. A. H. Loveland, David H. Moffat, Amos Steck, Major Jacob Downing, A. J. Gill, Hiram Burton, Richard Sopris, and others in the political and business leadership of the territory. William N. Byers, the editor of the *Rocky Mountain News,* who, while not officially a Methodist, was a member of the board of the Colorado Seminary. In November 1864, he wrote an editorial declaring that reports of a "Methodist Clique" were "baseless, groundless, unjust, ungenerous, and undeserved" rumors spread by "busybodys" [sic] motivated by "bigotry, jealousy, prejudice, or malice." At the very least, it can be said that Methodists played a significant role in the territory's politics because of Methodist support for the Union and the Republican Party as well as its preeminence as the largest religious denomination.

In the wake of the first reports of Sand Creek, Methodist newspapers were reluctant to believe that Chivington or Evans could be responsible for such actions as those reported. Both received the benefit of the doubt. This was perhaps understandable, even laudable, especially when the reports were about men who had standing within the Church. Bishop Simpson, the editor of the *Northwestern Christian Advocate*, and others came to Evans's support because they were friends and wanted to believe the best. Simpson worked to help him keep his position, but there is no letter or other evidence in which he directly defends Evans from the charges.

The statement of the six Colorado ministers in April 1865 was a strong endorsement of Colonel Chivington and of Sand Creek, and Bishop Kingsley's letters to Bishop Simpson and to the *Advocates* affirmed the support of Coloradans for Chivington and his action at Sand Creek. A review of Methodist papers during the remainder of the 1860s reveals a mixture of positions relating to Sand Creek and differences of opinion concerning Indian policy. What is missing is any Church resolution supporting or condemning Sand Creek, Chivington, or Evans. The closest thing to a stand taken by the Church was the resolution passed at the General Conference in 1868, supported by William H. Goode, which was tabled.

These facts are telling. The Methodist Episcopal Church became a reflection of society instead of a mirror for society. In the years after the Civil War, the Methodist Episcopal Church was not only a white man's church (with limited gestures toward missions, mostly foreign missions), but also it was a militant church that reflected upper middle class values, including the essential goodness of making money. Methodism had become an establishment church, which, as suggested by the Northwestern University study of Evans, took hard work and doing good through charitable giving to be evidence of spiritual development and God's grace. This goes far in explaining the nineteenth-century Church's choices in the social issues it supported, and its substitution of Victorian morality for Christian principles. This is not meant to imply that most Methodists were not devout, but rather to underscore the influence of American exceptionalism and destiny as tenets of Church policy and ministry.

During the 1860s, the primary positions on Indian policy related to military control or civilian control. Lesser known were those reformers who advocated a slower process, in which Native groups were allowed to assimilate on their own terms. They sought larger, protected reserves that would insure tribal ownership and sovereignty and change according to their own timelines. Hardline assimilationists predominated once it was determined that civilian authority would remain in control. Methodist participation in President Grant's Peace Policy was regarded as the worst by any denomination.

Assimilation, designed to bring "progress" and to get ahead of the rapid settlement of western lands, was believed to be the most humane approach in the long run. The object was to save the Indians, not to destroy them. Survival depended, the reformers believed, upon the willingness of Native peoples to change, and to change at the rate and under conditions dictated by whites. Only a few ever realized that the Christian program to "save" the American Indians had a lot in common with the program to eliminate them. Its violence was not the overt act of massacre, but the slower destruction of the spirit through the systematic undermining of nature, culture, religion, and personality. Methodist attitudes in these matters followed broader patterns of white response. What stands out most strikingly in the Methodist response to Sand Creek and the events that followed, however, is indifference. Sand Creek was simply not important enough to the Church to matter.

Final Thoughts and Reflections

Robert F. Berkhofer, Jr., who wrote perhaps the most important history of Protestant missions and Native responses, warned that "only an analysis of the contact situation [the circumstances of contact between different groups within the context of the times] in terms of the participants' beliefs will meet the canons of historical accuracy."[33] That, within itself, is a difficult task. It means, practically, not imposing modern standards on past generations or blaming them for all of the changes that have taken place since their time and place. George E. Tinker has pointed out that we cannot ask the "forebears in the faith to have done the impossible—namely, to have demonstrated an awareness beyond what was culturally possible at the time."[34] But he also warns that it is not enough to explain away what happened because of the "good intentions" of either individuals or of the Church. Past wrongs do have present consequences.

The question remains how best to approach them, especially when the terms of the present debate were unknown to those who were part of the events at the time. Concepts like "multiculturalism," "cross-culturalism," "cultural pluralism," even "culture" itself in the sense it is used today were unknown. The self-serving use of *presentism* for whatever cause or point of view is not the answer, but understanding what happened and why, in terms of itself, permits both a more balanced understanding of past generations and how they responded to events like Sand Creek and a means of acknowledging past error while discovering lingering evidence of the same kinds of attitudes and wrongs in the present.

235

In 1850, E. G. Meek, writing for the *Methodist Quarterly Review,* predicted:

> The fate of these great tribes may be easily foretold, the buffalo will rapidly decrease in numbers, being wantonly slaughtered both by the Indians and emigrants; hostile collisions of the tribes will become more frequent. . . . [A] conviction that the inroads of the whites are rapidly destroying the game on which they rely for support, will lead to heart burnings and bitterness, which will induce them to assume a permanently hostile attitude and render it incumbent on the government to establish among them military posts, in order to protect emigrating parties. After this, their progress toward extinction will be fearfully rapid; for, although the conclusion we have drawn is not inevitable, it has in its favor the greatest degree of probability.[35]

The Reverend Meek was not a prophet or a seer. He said the outcome he predicted was not inevitable, but there was something bittersweet, angry, and frustrated in what he and other ministers, reformers, and even soldiers wrote about what was to come, something amounting to a kind of helplessness that they could find no alter-

Sand Creek Massacre National Historic Site. (National Park Service). Reprinted by permission of Jeff C. Campbell, Kiowa County, Colorado (2002-2016).

native to General Sullivan's Revolutionary War dictum, "Civilization or death to all American savages!" For those who cared, for those who were ashamed, for those who wanted to help, alternatives eluded them because they were trapped in the same way of seeing that made Meek's outcome seem inevitable. Even now, when the issues seem clearer, solutions that would have been possible given the ways of seeing and the forces they unleashed hide from view and leave in question whether anything has truly changed beyond regrets about past wrongs.

The bloody ground at Sand Creek is a symbol of a terrible blindness in the American experiment that "fixed a stain" on the national honor, as Henry Knox predicted it would before the Constitution of the United States became the governing rule of law. It is a reminder that bigotry is not merely the illness of wicked and profligate people but a disease that can become an epidemic even among those who think of themselves as good and decent and God-fearing. It can hide itself within thickets of rationalizations and fields of good intentions. Sand Creek is also a reminder that humans should not be so quick to judge past generations while deluded into believing that they are inoculated against the effects of arrogance and prejudice themselves.

For those who may have lingering questions about the harsh judgment sometimes presented here—and perhaps for those who think the judgments not harsh enough—it is important to remember that Sand Creek was first condemned not by latter-day historians or modern activists. It was labeled an atrocity by contemporaries. This is evidenced by the outraged reaction of soldiers and settlers and officeholders who demanded an accounting for it, by the insistence of public officials that it be investigated, by vigorous debates on the floor of Congress that addressed the slaughter of women and children and violations of plighted faith directly, by the reports of the Joint Committee on the Conduct of the War, the Joint Special Committee on the Condition of the Indian Tribes, and the Judge Advocate General who called it a "cowardly and coldblooded slaughter."

It was that contemporary outrage that led to the removal of John Evans and William Palmer Dole from office. It was contemporary guilt that caused the government to publicly acknowledge the crime of Sand Creek in the Treaty of the Little Arkansas. Sand Creek was cited by both civilian and military officials as the cause of Indian troubles and in support of Indian reform. Ulysses S. Grant, William T. Sherman, Kit Carson, William S. Harney, Nelson A. Miles, William Bent, Lydia Maria Childs, Bishop Henry B. Whipple, Wendell Phillips, and Helen Hunt Jackson were only a few who damned Sand Creek as a crime. Those who tried to defend Sand Creek could only deny what happened there or rationalize it, and even in the defenses there was an awareness that something wrong had been done.

The damnation of Sand Creek was, then, a contemporary judgment that has been confirmed by history. Even Frank Hall, the early Colorado editor, who tried to understand Sand Creek, even defend it, was forced to conclude:

> Whether the battle of Sand Creek was right or wrong, these fiendish acts can never be palliated, nor can there ever be in this world or the next any pardon for men who were responsible for them. It was this more than any other stain attaching to this historic tragedy which brought the condemnation of mankind upon the leaders of that terrible day, and which, strive as we may to efface it, will remain as the deliberate judgment of history.[36]

The greater problem was that the horror of the crime obscured its underlying causes. Sand Creek was treated as an aberration rather than as evidence of systemic flaws not only in federal Indian policy which, at the very least, was mindful of problems, but also in the fundamental mind-set of the times. It was the latter that made resolving policy issues nearly impossible. White Americans could be outraged by the violation of plighted faith, the slaughter of women and children, and the mutilation of the dead, without seeing that their "humane" alternatives were also destructive in their effects. Paternalism survived both guilt and reform.

The Sand Creek Massacre was exceptional in its impact. The Plains Indian wars, military policy, the Indian reform movement, and the policy changes that did come in the months and years that followed, all occurred in the shadow of Sand Creek. No discussion of the fate of Native peoples or of Indian policy debate was free of the influence of Sand Creek. What Sand Creek did not do—could not do—was to puncture the white American mind-set, even among those who realized that a radical new perspective was needed. Instead, the nation barreled into the twentieth century and preeminice as a world power with surprisingly little control or even awareness of this crucial flaw.

On December 21, 1898, President William McKinley issued a proclamation concerning the policies to be pursued in the Philippine Islands. His remarks are instructive in what they reveal about what had been learned after more than a century of debate over federal Indian policy:

> Finally, it should be the earnest and paramount aim of the military administration to win the confidence, respect, and affection of the inhabi-

tants of the Philippines by assuring them in every possible way that full measure of individual rights and liberties which is the heritage of a free people, and by proving to them that the mission of the United States is one of benevolent assimilation, substituting the mild sway of justice and right for arbitrary rule.[37]

"Benevolent assimilation." Though perhaps well-intended, McKinley's naïve use of this term reveal how little the mind-set had changed. Good intentions never guarantee justice and right at any point in history. Humans are swept along not so much by the common principles they share as by the cultural values of their societies and their self-interest. The principles are surprisingly universal; values, by contrast, are often disparate and in contradiction to expressed principles. Reformers have been shackled by their traditions and perceptions and politics and economic interests like settlers and like policy makers, and when they have been fortunate enough to have their way, they have often discovered that their solutions are oppressive too.

Roger Nichols, in his *Lincoln and the Indians,* observed that the reformers were never able to break "the chain of ideas that bound the Indian and doomed him." He wrote:

What could have broken the chain? This is where the historian must view the situation as a historic tragedy rather than circumstances in which personal blame can be assigned. The only solution would have been the acceptance of ideals of racial and cultural equality for which nineteenth-century white Americans were not prepared. Neither reformers nor nonreformers respected Indian culture. Indeed, they did not even perceive the existence of a Native culture. Their recitals of Indian characteristics (imagined or real) occasionally approximated descriptions of cultural patterns but were not conceptualized as such. To them, those traits and behavior patterns were, if anything, an anticulture. *Civilization* not *culture,* was their key word-concept. "Savage" characteristics were anti-civilization, something heathen and evil to be stamped out rather than praised. There was only one civilization in the world and it was theirs—white, Christian, materialistic, agrarian, and on the march.[38]

Charles Alexander Eastman (Ohiyesa), the Santee Sioux medical doctor, who was for a time cited as "Exhibit A" of the value of forced assimilation, wrote in 1911 of the amazing inconsistency of Christianity's message to the Indian:

There was undoubtedly much in primitive Christianity to appeal to this man, and Jesus' hard sayings to the rich and about the rich would have been entirely comprehensible to him. Yet the religion that is preached in our churches and practiced by our congregations, with its elements of display and self-aggrandizement, its active proselytism, and its open contempt of all religions but its own, was for a long time extremely repellent. To his simple mind, the professionalism of the pulpit, the paid exhorter, the moneyed church, was an unspiritual and unedifying thing, and it was not until his spirit was broken and his moral and physical constitution undermined by trade, conquest, and strong drink, that Christian missionaries obtained any real hold upon him. Strange as it may seem, it is true that the proud pagan in his secret soul despised the good men who came to convert and enlighten him!

Eastman pointed out the inconsistencies in what was preached, the irreverence and sacrilege of whites who did not practice the faith that was being imposed upon Indian people, and the inconsistency of conduct even among those who professed to be Christians. Native people could understand the profligacy of white individuals, he said, but when church leaders came as treaty negotiators and pledged the national honor with prayer and mentioned God to gain support for treaties that were subsequently broken, the result was not only anger, but contempt as well. "It is my personal belief, after thirty-five years' experience of it, that there is no such thing as 'Christian civilization,'" he wrote. "I believe that Christianity and modern civilization are opposed and irreconcilable, and that the spirit of Christianity and of our ancient religion is essentially the same."[39]

Wooden Leg, a Northern Cheyenne who fought Custer at the Little Big Horn, had a similar view, less angry perhaps, but nevertheless pointing out the same problem:

> I think the white people pray to the same Great Medicine we do in our old Cheyenne way. I do not go often to the church, but I go sometimes. I think the white church people are good, but I do not believe all the stories they tell about what happened a long time ago. The way they tell us, all of the good people in the old times were white people. I am glad to have the white man churches among us, but I feel more satisfied when I make my prayers in the way I was taught to make them. My heart is

much more contented when I sit alone with my medicine pipe and talk
with the Great Medicine about whatever may be troubling me.[40]

Similar themes of an essential inconsistency between what has been preached
and lived by the emissaries of the Church among Native people and the essence
of the gospel appear over and over again in the historical record and in the writings of contemporary American Indian critics, historians, and advocates, including
Native Christians. John Beeson was one of those who recognized this failure. He
wrote President Lincoln on November 18, 1862, "The truth is, the Indians as a Race
have the common characteristics of humanity varied only by circumstances and sur-
roundings. They have as few vices and as many virtues, and as much capacity and as
great desire for improvement as is possessed by the average of mankind."[41]

Yet, even with this "radical" insight, he could not entirely escape the way of seeing
that limited his vision. His solutions were determined by the same world view that
produced John Evans and John Chivington. There was the rub. The failure was, as
Nichols wrote, that the best-hearted, best-intentioned "could not break the chain
of ideas that bound Native Americans." The reason they failed was not so much the
consequence of conscious design but of a way of seeing that limited vision. It made
the conflict "irrepressible" and generations of Indians victims.

Sand Creek had the impact that it did because it confronted white Americans
with "the savage within" and reminded them that the tether that restrains the worst
in human beings is fragile. At Sand Creek white men released "the worst passions
that ever cursed the heart of man," as the Joint Committee on the Condition of
the Indian Tribes put it. It put into question the very "civilization" that nineteenth-
century white Americans claimed for themselves. In the years that followed, both
those who rationalized Sand Creek away and those who remained haunted by its
indictment of their values could not step clear of it, but their intellectual and emotional efforts to come to grips with it did not alter the outcome for the Cheyennes
and Arapahos or for other Native tribes.[42]

Octavio Paz, the renowned Mexican writer, has written:

> What sets worlds in motion is the interplay of differences, their attrac-
> tions and repulsions. Life is plurality, death is uniformity. By suppress-
> ing differences and peculiarities, by eliminating different civilizations
> and cultures, progress weakens life and favors death. The ideal of a single
> civilization for everyone, implicit in the cult of progress and technique,

> impoverishes and mutilates us. Every view of the world that becomes
> extinct, every culture that disappears, diminishes a possibility of life.[43]

This is, of course, a conclusion based upon looking back on what happened and its effects. The past cannot be changed, but Paz points out the cost, hoping new generations may profit from understanding it. The need is still there, after all. Though institutions and groups and individuals may recognize the sins of the past, the linear way of seeing continues to dominate responses. The will is there to help, without realizing the implicit paternalism "help" contains. To "lift up" implies that the "helper" is in a superior position. It also allows those who help to take pride in their goodness as a primary reward. Native groups have never looked for help in this traditional "missionary" way; they seek involvement in the processes of change, recognition of their lifeways and spirituality as vital and life-sustaining.

Perhaps the greatest barrier to white Americans' ability to accomplish this was indifference. Especially for those people who were distant from contact with tribal peoples, indifference was a more insidious response than hatred. Hatred is visible, hot, identifiable. Sometimes hatred burns out, or smolders into an inexplicable prejudice, but its effects remain plain. Indifference—the absence of caring, the absence of feeling—allows and encourages mistreatment not by design but by lack of awareness or concern. Indifference endures. It survives wars. It survives neglect. It forgets. It allows even the appearance of past wrongs to slip from meaningful memory. It replaces human beings with caricatures that are sometimes not intentionally pejorative but merely thoughtless. In a sense, then, American Indians as people "vanished," if not in fact, then surely in consciousness.

Jacob Needleman has written that "conscience is the only sure guide to moral action," but he cautions that it "is often heard only in a whisper and only for a moment."[44] The flash-like moment of deep moral feeling can deviate "in quality and form, and even in aim, from the original impulse and does so without the actor's awareness." As a result, he argues, "While striving outwardly to eradicate injustice, it is imperative that humanity strive to feel the sorrow of its own capacity for evil." The ultimate irony is that a country founded upon principles of freedom, equality, and justice can also have a history of brutality and oppression. The deviations from founding American principles always proclaimed, Needleman suggests, most often have not been conscious or calculated. He argues that to understand this process:

242

one needs to try to enter into the position not only of the victim, *but of the oppressor*. It is not hard to imagine, up to a certain point, of course, the suffering of the slave or the brutalized Indian. What is in its way much harder, but absolutely essential, is to let oneself feel what it was like to murder and brutalize wrapped in a sure sense of self-justification. And if we have worked to understand the greatness of the humanity we have destroyed and the greatness of the culture we have annihilated, and if we then can imagine ourselves as the agents of these actions, we may catch a glimpse of this deep-rooted phenomenon of moral auto-hypnosis, the sleep of conscience, the sorrowful capacity of fallen man to hide from our profound betrayal of the good in our actual and potential actions.

It is imperative that the seeker confront this aspect of oneself in the midst of everyday life as well as in one's place as part of mankind's actions in the sweep of history. We need myths, symbols, and stories that make us both raise our heads in the vision of authentic human dignity and lower our heads in the vision of authentic remorse—and that then prepare us to live our lives with eyes and head straight forward, stepping into the future of the new America we may discover in ourselves and of the old Earth, which is yearning for all of us to become genuine men and women of the soul.[45]

The problem may be explored by reference to a story that has become vitally linked to the Sand Creek controversy in recent years. In 1893, the Reverend R. M. Barns presented a book to the Iliff School of Theology. The book, Johann Lorenz von Mosheim's *Institutionum Historiae Christianae Compendium (The History of Christianity)*, published in 1752, was bound in the skin of an American Indian reportedly killed in Virginia by General David Morgan. A 1934 article from the *Rocky Mountain News* described the book as "one of the most treasured relics in the library of the Iliff School of Theology of Denver University." The *News* added, "In spite of the age and wanderings of the book, it is remarkably well preserved. The skin is not broken or cracked; its smoothness and texture equal those of the finest parchments; its color has mellowed to deep ivory mottling into saffron, and by an ironic twist of fate, *it endures as a priceless vestment for the teachings of brotherly love* [italics added]."[46]

According to the story that accompanied the book, the Indian whose skin covered the book was killed in 1779 by Morgan in retaliation for the murder of members of his family. After it was given to Iliff, the book was placed in a glass cabinet at the entrance of the Iliff library where it remained on display until 1974. It was seen by literally hundreds of students and visitors during the near eighty years that it was on public display.

In 1974, a graduate student named Mike Hickcox, who was also president of the Iliff League, brought the matter of the book to the attention of the student body organization. As a result of student efforts, Vincent Harvier, a member of the Denver group of the American Indian Movement, met with the student representatives to discuss a proper way to dispose of the book's cover. Both the librarian and assistant librarian admitted that the book was an embarrassment, but, as Hickcox wrote later, "felt constrained by the book's connection with an influential supporting family," to bring the school president into the conversation. Eventually the cover was removed from the book and turned over to Harvier's group for proper burial.[47]

The story is relevant to this report for several reasons. That it was accepted in the first place indicates the insensitivity of Church leaders to the moral questions raised by the book. That it remained on display from 1893 to 1974 as a "treasured relic" without being questioned is even more astonishing in light of changing social values. That students rather than faculty, administration, or trustees initiated the effort to have the item removed is also revealing. Perhaps most interesting, however, is the letter of Jameson Jones, then the president of Iliff, to Vincent Harvier. Jones acknowledged that Harvier would "accept responsibility to see that the skin is handled with dignity and buried according to the religious beliefs of American Indians." He then added, "We understand that you will not give the matter any publicity, but will act with reverence according to your beliefs."[48]

The matter had been brought before the board of trustees, and "the Board acted out of respect for the Indian brother whose body was tragically mutilated many decades ago, and with genuine respect for the religious beliefs of Native American people." Yet, the governing board's insistence that the matter not be publicized is revealing. Rather than acknowledging a mistake, Iliff chose to avoid its moral implications. This story reflects the ongoing insensitivity of the Methodist Church toward American Indians. It is a classic example of the phenomenon of deviation of which Needleman wrote and the dilemma explored by Nichols. The United Methodist Church may not have been culpable for the sins of its fathers in the Methodist Episcopal Church a century and a half ago, but it was responsible for the way it handled the past and for the ways in which it related to an object clearly inconsistent with the teachings of the Church.

Although it was not his intent to address faith or even the problems of Indian-white relations, D. H. Lawrence, English novelist and critic, made provocative and challenging remarks on the subject. "I doubt if there is possible any real reconciliation, in the flesh between the white and the red," he wrote. "There is no mystic conjunction between the spirit of the two races." He concluded, "That leaves us only expiation, and then reconciliation in the soul. Some strange atonement; expiation and oneing." Lawrence explained, "The white man's spirit can never become as the red man's spirit. It doesn't want to. But it can cease to be the opposite and the negative of the red man's spirit. It can open out a new great area of consciousness, in which there is room for the red spirit too."[49]

Expiation involves a meaningful ritual of atonement, and atonement is essential for any true healing that will bring people together. This is what the Council of Bishops pledged itself to in 2012, not merely within the framework of The United Methodist Church itself but as an act of commitment to indigenous people more broadly. The great historical dilemma of the Church has been its efforts to dictate the terms of coming together by insisting that the Indian must be "elevated by means of a Christian civilization." John Pitezel, writing in 1883, presented a damning indictment of the ways that American Indians had been mistreated, but he added, "the only recompense we can make them is to give them the joy, the undying hope, imparted by the Gospel."[50]

This would be a good thing in the view of many Methodists, now as then, but it risks making the same mistakes that past generations made. Nichols suggested that for white Americans, Native people came to embody "the dark side of their own nature," which whites projected onto them.

Needleman added that this "dark side" is "screened from our awareness, and under the banner of the very moral ideals from which it is deviating. Our capacity to avert our awareness from the moral and metaphysical contradictions of our own nature is a fact that cannot be seen and studied without a serious commitment to truth and without help from companions and from the teachings of wisdom that call to us through the ages."[51]

Little profit is found in damning past actions or declaring great visions to be fraudulent if such responses do not yield clearer understanding and a keener sense of the present generation's own sense of moral superiority, including its own deviations from moral vision. Sanctimonious judgment of the past serves little purpose if it does not elevate the present's commitment to underlying principles of freedom, justice, and equality. The past cannot be changed, but it can be confronted and better understood without trying to rationalize its injustices or blaming past generations for not anticipating everything that the present generation now believes and knows. The "phenomenon of deviation" poses as great a threat to the present as it did to the past. When "fault" is determined in the study of the past, the question remains why individuals or a society acted as they did. The capacity to distort remains surprisingly vital not so much because individuals and groups wish to distort as because they have agendas—often selfish and sinister, but sometimes unconscious and even well-meaning—that trump the moral imperatives.

The failure to recognize the contradiction between the principles believed and actions taken serves the psychological purpose of distinguishing between civilization and savagery and justifies the exploitation of Indians for a "higher purpose." To break this rationalization of the past experience broadly conceived, and the historical trauma of Sand Creek in particular, the choice must involve, as Methodist historian Frederick A. Norwood has suggested, not merely the Indian's acceptance or rejection of Christianity, but also his right "to retain what is meaningful to him in his own unique spiritual heritage."[52] Acknowledging past error is but the first step. The harder part is demonstrating that the acknowledgment means something by using it to make a difference in the future.[53] Conscience must prevail. Ways of seeing or mind-sets should never be used as excuses for cruelty or evil. They are explanations, not justifications.

When Black Kettle spoke to the treaty commissioners at the Little Arkansas in October 1865, he brought his wife, Medicine Woman Later, into the council and showed them the nine scars on her body from bullets that struck her at Sand Creek, the ones that first toppled her into the sand and the ones that were fired into her body by soldiers after she fell. He let them touch the scars, so that they would understand what had happened to his people.[54] "My shame (mortification) is as big as the earth," he confessed. "I thought that I was the only man that persevered to be the friend of the white man, but since they have come and cleaned out (robbed) our lodges, horses, and everything else, it is hard for me to believe white men any more." He told the commissioners, "All my friends—the Indians that are holding back—they are afraid to come in; are afraid they will be betrayed as I have been."[55]

The commissioners understood. One of the secretaries at the negotiation was moved to prophesy, "Their fate ... will be that they died of too large views."[56] He was right. Although the treaty stated explicitly:

246

The United States being desirous to express its condemnation of, and, as far as may be, repudiate the gross and wanton outrages perpetrated against certain bands of Cheyenne and Arapaho Indians, on the twenty-ninth day of November, A. D. 1864, at Sand Creek in Colorado Territory, while the said Indians were at peace with the United States, and under its flag, whose protection they had by lawful authority been promised and induced to seek, and the Government being desirous to make some suitable reparation for the injustices then done . . .

offered "suitable reparations" for its action, the treaty would fail and its promises of reparations would go unfulfilled.[57] Black Kettle and Medicine Woman Later both would be killed on November 28, 1868, on the Washita River, one day short of four years after Sand Creek.[58] The tribes would be divided by the warring times and forgotten when they were confined finally to three separate reservations in the Indian Territory, Montana, and Wyoming.

Following the completion of the Treaty of the Little Arkansas, William Bent and Kit Carson, two of the treaty commissioners and both men of long experience with the Cheyennes and Arapahos, wrote to General John Pope, "by dispossessing them of their country we assume their stewardship, and the manner in which this duty is performed will add a glorious record to American history, or a damning blot and reproach for all future time."[59] They had touched the wounds of Medicine Woman Later and had seen the heart of Black Kettle, and they knew what needed to be done. It never was.

NOTES

Chapter 1

1. Francis Paul Prucha, "Doing Indian History," *Indian Policy in the United States: Historical Essays* (Lincoln: University of Nebraska Press, 1981), p. 11.

2. Ari Kelman, *The Misplaced Massacre: Struggling Over the Memory of Sand Creek* (Cambridge: Harvard University Press, 2013), provides a masterful explanation of the enduring presence of Sand Creek in relationships between the Cheyennes and Arapahos and the U.S. Government. Gary Leland Roberts, "Sand Creek: Tragedy and Symbol" (unpublished Ph.D. dissertation, University of Oklahoma, 1984), provides a more traditional review of the influence of Sand Creek on federal Indian policy.

3. Quoted in Raymond J. DeMallie, "'These Have No Ears': Narrative and the Ethnohistorical Method," *Ethnohistory*, 40 (Fall 1993): 535n. DeMallie, himself, p. 526, called Powell's book, "the most thoroughly consistent, culturally grounded interpretation of the history of an American Indian group ever written. To me, its publication serves as a watershed; it points the way to alternative narrative modes." Richard White, "Using the Past: History and Native American Studies," *Studying Native America: Problems and Prospects*, ed. by Russell Thornton (Madison: University of Wisconsin Press, 1998), pp. 225-226, offers a more critical review of Powell's methodology, insisting that, employing DeMallie's own proposition that the historian must replicate the world view of the participants without embracing it." He asks, "would we not expect him to disavow and critique it and deny him credibility?"— p. 226. DeMallie had argued in "These Have No Ears," pp. 516-525, that the challenge of ethnohistory is to bring two different types of historical data together "to construct a fuller picture of the past." White suggests that this would produce a third perspective of historical events—"that of the ethnohistorian." White, "Using the Past," p. 225.

4. Quoted in DeMallie, "These Have No Ears," p. 535.

5. Ibid., pp. 520-521.

6. Kate Bighead, a Cheyenne woman present at Custer's Last Stand, told Dr. Thomas B. Marquis that two Southern Cheyenne women present at the Little Big Horn who knew George Armstrong Custer from his days on the Southern Plains, punctured Custer's ear drums with sewing awls after his death because "he had not heard what our chiefs in the South said when he smoked the pipe with them. They told him then that if ever afterward he should break that peace promise and should fight the Cheyennes the Everywhere Spirit surely would cause him to be killed." Kate Bighead's account, originally published by Marquis as a pamphlet in 1933, is most accessible in Paul Andrew Hutton, *The Custer Reader* (Lincoln: University of Nebraska Press, 2004), pp. 366-374. Some historians consider this account to be apocryphal, but it is plausible considering the use of the metaphor by the Lakota and the Cheyennes.

7. Robert F. Berkhofer, Jr., *Salvation and the Savage: An Analysis of Protestant Missions and American Indian Response, 1787-1862* (New York: Atheneum, 1972), p. xvii.

8. John C. Ewers, "When Red and White Men Met," *Western Historical Quarterly*, 2 (1971): 150. Prucha, "Doing Indian History," p. 11, added that the goal of finding the truth cannot be set aside, "no matter how we all fall short of it." He cautioned against being "too much concerned

about making points for one side of a controversy or another." Expanding perspectives and considering other ways of seeing are ways to ensure a fairer analysis.

9. For an excellent, but somewhat dated, review of the historiography of Sand Creek see Michael Sievers, "The Sands of Sand Creek Historiography," *Colorado Magazine,* 49 (1972): 116-143. Efforts to justify Sand Creek and make Chivington and Evans into "good guys," began in the reminiscences of early Coloradans and in more general works such as J. P. Dunn, *Massacres of the Mountains* (New York: Harper & Brothers, 1886); Reginald S. Craig, *The Fighting Parson: The Biography of Colonel John M. Chivington* (Los Angeles: Westernlore Press, 1959); William R. Dunn, *"I Stand by Sand Creek": A Defense of Colonel John M. Chivington and the Third Colorado Cavalry* (Ft. Collins, CO: The Old Army Press, 1985); and Gregory F. Michno, *Battle at Sand Creek: The Military Perspective* (El Segundo, CA: Upton and Sons, 2004). This represents only a sampling of the Chivington-as-good-guy literature that portrays Sand Creek as a battle rather than as a massacre. By reason of its purposes, reform literature has provided the best examples of works written to "prove" the bad guys' approach to Sand Creek, beginning with Helen Hunt Jackson: *A Century of Dishonor* (Boston: Roberts Brothers, 1886); Dee Brown, *Bury My Heart at Wounded Knee* (New York: Holt, Rinehart and Winston, 1970); David E. Stannard, *American Holocaust: The Conquest of the New World* (New York: Oxford University Press, 1992); and Ward Churchill, *A Little Matter of Genocide: Holocaust and Denial in the Americas 1492 to the Present* (San Francisco, City Lights Books, 1997) reflect a similar approach. What these works share are predetermined agendas to make the case that Sand Creek was or was not a massacre. The list for both could be greatly enlarged, especially if popular works and periodical literature were included. Stan Hoig, *The Sand Creek Massacre* (Norman: University of Oklahoma Press, 1961) was a good-faith attempt to understand Sand Creek and remains a good place to start for readers who want a simple, straightforward introduction to the subject. Fortunately, a number of historians and writers have sought to "understand" Sand Creek rather than to "build a case" for or against Sand Creek as a massacre. Kelman, *Misplaced Massacre,* previously cited, represents a recent example of this effort. Others will be referenced within the notes of this report.

10. David Hackett Fischer, *Historians' Fallacies: Toward a Logic of Historical Thought* (New York: Harper Torchbooks, 1970). Lynn Hunt, "Against Presentism," https://www.historians.org/on-publications-and-directories/perspectives-on-history/may-2002/against-presentism, is a brief summary of the problem of presentism. She defines presentism as "interpreting the past in terms of present concerns." This, she argues, "usually leads us to find ourselves morally superior" to earlier generations. "Our forebears constantly fail to measure up to our present-day standards." What it involves is imposing present values on earlier times in order to demonstrate their failures, most often in moral and political terms. This practice should not be confused with the important function of revising history in light of new sources, changes in perspective, or the questions asked of history, which do, in fact, change over time. This report, for example, was mandated to answer particular questions about the responsibilities of John Chivington, John Evans, and the Methodist Church for the Sand Creek Massacre. It was not written to prove a particular view, one way or another. Rather, the object is to determine culpability. Particular conclusions were not mandated. This is an important distinction. The present may determine the questions asked; it should not determine the answers.

11. Frederick Jackson Turner's works are widely accessible. His essays "The Significance of History" (1891) and "The Significance of the Frontier in American History" are particularly important. These and other works may be found in Frederick Jackson Turner, *The Frontier in American History.* Edited by Wilbur R. Jacobs (Tucson: University of Arizona Press, 1986).

12. James Belich, *Replenishing the Earth: The Settler Revolution and the Rise of the Anglo World, 1783-1939* (New York: Oxford University Press, 2009), p. 552. See also Jurgen Osterhammel, *The Transformation of the World: A Global History of the Nineteenth Century*, trans. Patrick Camiller (Princeton: Princeton University Press, 2014), pp. 370-374.

13. Useful anthologies include, but are not limited to, such works as Thornton, *Studying Native America;* Calvin Martin, editor, *The American Indian and the Problem of History* (New York: Oxford University Press, 1987); M. Annette Jaimes, editor, *The State of Native America: Genocide, Colonization, and Resistance* (Boston: South End Press, 1992); Devon A. Mihesuah, editor, *Natives and Academics: Researching and Writing about American Indians* (Lincoln: University of Nebraska Press, 1998); Andrew Woolford, Jeff Benvenuto, and Alexander Laban Hinton, editors, *Colonial Genocide in Indigenous North America* (Durham, NC: Duke University Press, 2014). Churchill, Stannard, and Belich, and the many works of Vine DeLoria, Jr., are all important. Lisa Ford, *Settler Sovereignty: Jurisdiction and Indigenous People in America and Australia, 1788-1836* (Cambridge: Harvard University Press, 2010), also suggests the nature of new directions.

14. Lawrence H. Keeley, *War Before Civilization: The Myth of the Peaceful Savage* (New York: Oxford University Press, 1996), pp. 71-81, offers a particularly cogent argument for the effectiveness of indigenous warfare against Euro-American military forces.

15. Jared Diamond, *The World Until Yesterday: What Can We Learn from Traditional Societies?* (New York: Viking Press, 2012), pp. 153-154.

16. Belich, *Replenishing the Earth*, pp. 181-182.

17. Herman Melville's review of Francis Parkman's *The California and Oregon Trail*, appeared in *The Literary World*, IV (1849): 291. This quote is also found in Roy Harvey Pearce, *Savagism and Civilization: A Study of the Indian and the American Mind* (Baltimore: Johns Hopkins University Press, 1965), p. 251.

18. Among North American tribes who used some variation of "the people" as their original tribal identity (as opposed to the names they may be remembered by the historical names listed here) would be the Abenaki, the Chippewa, the Ojibwa, the Ingalik, the Cherokee, the Tanania, the Navajo, the Kiowa, the Illini, the Innui, the Inuit, the Delaware, the Menominee, the Klamath, the Apache, the Utes, the Mandan, the Comanche, the Hidatsa, the Yurok, the Arikara, the Cayuse, the Tonkawa, in addition to both the Cheyenne and the Arapaho. Similar usage is found in the etymological identifications of peoples around the world. Elliott West, *The Contested Plains: Indians, Goldseekers, and the Rush to Colorado* (Manhattan: University Press of Kansas, 1998), p. 76, writing about the Cheyennes; and Jeffrey Ostler, *The Plains Sioux and U.S. Colonialism from Lewis and Clark to Wounded Knee* (New York: Cambridge University Press, 2004), p. 27, writing about the Plains Sioux, illustrate the point.

19. These themes are explored in Donald L. Fixico, *The American Indian Mind in a Linear World: American Indian Studies and Traditional Knowledge* (New York: Routledge, 2003); Donald L. Fixico, *Call for Change: The Medicine Way of American Indian History, Ethos, and Reality* (Lincoln: University of Nebraska Press, 2013); and Joseph Campbell, *The Power of Myth* (New York: Doubleday & Co., 1988).

20. William G. McNeill, *The Rise of the West*. Second Edition (Chicago: University of Chicago Press, 1991) is a good place to start in understanding the development of the Western way of seeing. See also J. B. Bury, *The Idea of Progress: An Inquiry into Its Origin and Growth* (London: Macmillan and Company, 1920); Robert Nisbet, *History of the Idea of Progress* (New York: Basic Books, 1980); Christopher Lasch, *The True and Only Heaven: Progress and Its Critics* (New York:

W. W. Norton, 1991). Arthur O. Lovejoy, *The Great Chain of Being: A Study of the History of an Idea* (Cambridge, MA: Harvard University Press, 1964), remains the standard study of the concept. Robert A. Williams, Jr., *Savage Anxieties: The Invention of Western Civilization* (New York: Palgrave McMillan, 2012), offers an American Indian perspective on the topic. Also helpful is Robert F. Berkhofer, Jr., *The White Man's Indian: Images of the American Indian from Columbus to the Present* (New York: Alfred A. Knopf, 1978).

21. This presentation is a synthesis of ideas drawn from Robert A. Williams, Jr., *The American Indian in Western Legal Thought: The Discourses of Conquest* (New York: Oxford University Press, 1990); Lovejoy, *The Great Chain of Being*; Fixico, *American Indian Mind* and *Call for Change*; Martin, "The Metaphysics of Writing Indian-White History"; Vine DeLoria, Jr., *Spirit & Reason: The Vine DeLoria, Jr., Reader* (Golden, CO: Fulcrum Publishing, 1999) and *The Metaphysics of Modern Existence* (Golden, CO: Fulcrum Publishing, 2012); and Charles L. Woodard, *Ancestral Voices: Conversations with N. Scott Momaday* (Lincoln: University of Nebraska Press, 1989).

22. DeLoria, *Spirit and Reason,* pp. 290-353; Fixico, *American Indian Mind,* pp. 3-27.

23. Henrietta Whiteman (Mann), "White Buffalo Woman," in Martin, ed., *Problem of History,* p. 169.

24. Joseph Epes Brown, *The Spiritual Legacy of the American Indian: Commemorative Edition with Letters While Living with Black Elk,* ed. Marina Brown Weatherly, Elenita Brown, and Michael Drew Fitzgerald (Bloomington, IN: World Wisdom, Inc., 2007), p. 37.

25. Fixico, *Call for Change,* pp. 164-170.

26. Quoted in David E. Wilkins, "Afterword," De Loria, *Metaphysics,* pp. 288-289.

27. Fixico, *American Indian Mind,* p. 42.

28. Ibid., p. 44.

29. Quoted in ibid., p. 56.

30. Martin, "Epilogue: Time and the American Indian," *Problem of History,* p. 194.

31. Ibid., p. 206.

32. Prucha, "Doing Indian History," pp. 8-10.

33. *Northwestern Christian Advocate,* July 25, 1866.

34. James L. West, "Indian Spirituality: Another Vision," *Native and Christian: Indigenous Voices on Religious Identity in the United States and Canada,* ed. James Treat (New York: Routledge, 1996), pp. 30-31.

35. Edward W. Said, *Culture and Imperialism* (New York: Random House, 1993), pp. 288-289; Richard Slotkin, *Regeneration Through Violence: The Mythology of the American Frontier, 1600-1860* (Middletown, CT: Wesleyan University Press, 1973), pp. 538-561.

36. George Bird Grinnell, "The Indian on the Reservation," *Atlantic Monthly,* LXXIII (February 1899): 258-259.

37. Walt Whitman, *Leaves of Grass.* 150th Anniversary Edition, edited by David S. Reynolds. (New York: Oxford University Press, 2005), p. 32. Whitman used the word "savage" to equate the Indian with Nature (as had some earlier Enlightenment thinkers), rather than branding him untutored, ignorant, or cruel. See also, Calvin Luther Martin, *The Way of the Human Being* (New Haven: Yale University Press, 1999), especially his preface, where he proclaims his thoughtful reflections to be a response to "Perceptive people [who] have been asking the same questions and drawing the same conclusions since the sixteenth century" (p. ix).

38. Henry David Thoreau, *The Maine Woods, 1864* (New York: Harper & Row, 1982), pp. 247-249; Edward Fussell, *Frontier: American Literature and the American West* (Princeton: Princ-

eton University Press, 2015), p. 342. See also, Robert F. Sayre, *Thoreau and the American Indian* (Princeton: Princeton University Press, 1987), passim.

39. Ninth Annual Report, Southern Missionary Society, 1854, p. 123, quoted in Frederick A. Norwood, "Strangers in a Strange Land: Removal of the Wyandot Indians," *Methodist History,* 13 (April 1975): 59.

40. See Sayre, *Thoreau and the Indian;* Roy Harvey Pearce, *Savagism and Civilization: A Study of the Indian and the American Mind* (Baltimore, Johns Hopkins Press, 1965), pp. 147-150.

41. Quoted in DeLoria, Jr., *Spirit and Reason,* p. 43.

42. DeLoria, Jr., *Metaphysics,* p. 5.

43. Said, *Culture and Imperialism,* pp. 19-21.

44. Ibid., p. 20.

45. Ibid., p. 336.

Chapter 2

1. The literature is vast. For the purposes of this report, three works provided important insights: John McManners, editor, *The Oxford Illustrated History of Christianity* (New York: Oxford University Press, 1990), pp. 21-340; Jane Burbank and Frederick Cooper, *Empires in World History: Power and the Politics of Difference* (Princeton: Princeton University Press, 2010), pp. 61-92, and Karen Armstrong, *Fields of Blood: Religion and the History of Violence* (New York: Alfred A. Knopf, 2014), pp. 103-261. The latter two have the added benefit of comparative analysis between Western ideas, beliefs, and empires and other world religions and empires.

2. McManners, *History of Christianity,* pp. 21-232; Williams, *Savage Anxieties,* pp. 11-138; Williams, *American Indian in Western Legal Thought,* pp. 13-58.

3. Armstrong, *Fields of Blood,* pp. 131-261; Burbank and Cooper, *Empires,* pp. 23-116.

4. David Harry Miller and William W. Savage, Jr., "Ethnic Stereotypes and the Frontier: A Comparative Study of Roman and American Experience," *The Frontier: Comparative Studies,* ed. David Harry Miller and Jerome Steffen (Norman: University of Oklahoma Press, 1977), pp. 109-137. See also Williams, *Savage Anxieties,* pp. 33-180; and William Winthrop, *Military Law and Precedents,* 2nd ed. (Washington: Government Printing Office, 1920), pp. 903-1039.

5. Williams, *American Indian in Western Legal Thought,* pp. 15-18.

6. Ibid., pp. 32-47; Armstrong, *Fields of Blood,* pp. 210-216.

7. Williams, *American Indian in Western Legal Thought,* pp. 47-50.

8. Ibid., pp. 4-8.

9. Jason W. Moore, "The Crisis of Feudalism: An Environmental History," *Organization and Environment,* 15 (September 2002): 301-322.

10. Williams, *American Indian in Western Legal Thought,* pp. 71-81.

11. Ibid., pp. 59-108; Steven T. Newcomb, *Pagans in the Promised Land: Decoding the Doctrine of Christian Discovery* (Golden, CO: Fulcrum Publishing, 2008), pp. 23-50, 122-124; Lindsay G. Robertson, *Conquest by Law: How the Discovery of America Dispossessed Indigenous Peoples of Their Lands* (New York: Oxford University Press, 2005), pp. 98-100.

12. Reginald Horsman, *Race and Manifest Destiny: The Origins of American Racial Anglo-Saxonism* (Cambridge: Harvard University Press, 1981), pp. 7-24; Belich, *Replenishing the Earth* pp. 4-9.

13. David Beers Quinn, *The Elizabethans and the Irish* (New York: Cornell University Press, 1966); Nicholas P. Canny, "The Ideology of English Colonization: From Ireland to America,"

William and Mary Quarterly, Third Series, 30 (1973): 575-598; D. M. R. Essom, *The Curse of Cromwell: A History of the Ironside Conquest of Ireland, 1649-53* (Totowa, NJ: Rowman and Littlefield, 1971), pp. 102-114; Katie Kane, "Nits Make Lice: Drogheda, Sand Creek, and the Poetics of Colonial Extermination," *Cultural Critique,* 42 (Spring 1999): 81-103; William Edward Hartpole Lecky, *A History of Ireland in the Eighteenth Century.* 5 Volumes (London: Longmans, Green, 1892): I, 84-85.

14. Colin G. Calloway, *White People, Indians, and Highlanders: Tribal Peoples and Colonial Encounters in Scotland and America* (New York: Oxford University Press, 2008), p. xi.

15. Ibid., pp. 43-146, 257-272.

16. See Edmund S. Morgan, *Inventing the People: The Rise of Popular Sovereignty in England and America* (New York: W. W. Norton & Company, 1988). Belich, *Replenishing the Earth,* pp. 6-8.

17. Belich, *Replenishing the Earth,* pp. 153-169. See also, Walter L. Hixson, *American Settler Colonialism: A History* (New York: Palgrave Macmillan, 2013), pp. 45-85.

18. Michael L. Johnson, *Hunger for the Wild: America's Obsession with the Untamed West* (Manhattan: University Press of Kansas), pp. 17-109.

19. Slotkin, *Regeneration,* p. 557; Said, *Culture and Imperialism,* p. 288. See also Richard Slotkin, *The Fatal Environment: The Myth of the Frontier in the Age of Industrialization, 1800-1890* (Norman: University of Oklahoma Press, 1994), and *Gunfighter Nation: The Myth of the Frontier in Twentieth Century America* (Norman: University of Oklahoma Press, 1998).

20. Frederick Jackson Turner wrote in his essay, "The Significance of History," that "Each age writes the history of the past anew with reference to the conditions uppermost in its own times." He would not have been surprised, then, that with time, his more famous treatise on "The Significance of the Frontier in American History," would be challenged. His views on the nature of the frontier and its importance as a central feature of American development were increasingly criticized in the twentieth century, culminating perhaps with the publication of Patricia Nelson Limerick, Clyde A. Milner II, and Charles E. Rankin, editors, *Trails: Toward a New Western History* (Manhattan: University Press of Kansas, 1991). These essays challenged Turner's emphasis on the "frontier" as opposed to the "West" as a basis for studying the American West. But in dismissing Turner as "timeworn" and "quaint and mythical," the advocates of the "New Western History" misjudged Turner's importance to understanding the way in which the process of westward movement was conceived by earlier Americans. William Cronon, in his "Revisiting the Vanishing Frontier: The Legacy of Frederick Jackson Turner," *Western Historical Quarterly,* 18 (April 1987): 157-176, argued that Turner still is critical to understanding the process of settlement and contended that studying process is a different task than studying region. This was a vital insight that he enlarged upon in later essays. Also critical for understanding Turner's enduring legacy is Allan G. Bogue, *Frederick Jackson Turner: Strange Roads Going Down* (Norman: University of Oklahoma Press, 1998). See especially pp. 457-464.

21. Bernard W. Sheehan, *Seeds of Extinction: Jeffersonian Philanthropy and the American Indian* (W. W. Norton & Company, 1973), offers an in-depth look at the Enlightenment view of Thomas Jefferson and its origin in the writings of others. Anthony F. C. Wallace, *Jefferson and the Indians: The Tragic Fate of the First Americans* (Cambridge: Harvard University Press, 1999), is a thoughtful and more critical view of Jefferson. Berkhofer, *White Man's Indian,* pp. 12-49, provides a convenient summary. Williams, *Savage Anxieties,* pp. 197-217, is also critical.

22. Martin E. Marty, *Protestantism in the United States: Righteous Empire.* Second Edition (Charles Scribner's Sons, 1986), pp. 13-20. See also Berkhofer, *White Man's Indian,* pp. 113-152.

23. This assessment is based upon a review of a number of sources that have taken the time to explore the interactions of white and Native cultures beyond a mere recounting of events in search of a more balanced view of the processes involved. Some of the more important sources are James Axtell, *Beyond 1492: Encounters in Colonial North America* (New York: Oxford University Press, 1992); James Axtell, *The Invasion Within: The Contest of Cultures in Colonial North America* (New York: Oxford University Press, 1985); Michael Witgen, *An Infinity of Nations: How the Native New World Shaped Early North America* (Philadelphia: University of Pennsylvania Press, 2012); Gregory Evans Dowd, *A Spirited Resistance: The North American Indian Struggle for Unity* (Baltimore: Johns Hopkins University, 1992); Daniel K. Richter, *Facing East from Indian Country: A Native History of Early America* (Cambridge: Harvard University Press, 2001); Kathleen Du Val, *The Native Ground: Indians and Colonists in the Heart of the Continent* (Philadelphia: University of Pennsylvania Press, 2006); Richard White, *The Middle Ground: Indians, Empires, and Republics in the Great Lakes Region, 1650-1815*. Twentieth Anniversary Edition (New York: Cambridge University Press, 2011); Alan Taylor, *The Divided Ground: Indians, Settlers, and the Northern Borderland of the American Revolution* (New York: Alfred A. Knopf, 2006); Robert M. Owens, *Red Dreams, White Nightmares: Pan-Indian Alliances in the Anglo-American Mind, 1763-1815* (Norman: University of Oklahoma Press, 2015); Brady J. Crytzer, *Guyasuta and the Fall of Indian America* (Yardley, PA: Westholme Publishing, 2013). The list is not complete, and all of the books listed are recent efforts to bring greater balance to understanding the conflict between Native and Intruder cultures. They do not represent a seamless interpretation of the process, but they do reflect a shared awareness of the importance of understanding the multidimensional character of the conflict.

24. Belich, *Replenishing the Earth*, pp. 552-558, explores the issue from the perspective of "settler colonialism." All of the works cited in note 23 elaborate on this question. Burbank and Cooper, *Empires*, pp. 257-267, offers an interesting assessment, based upon comparisons with other colonial and imperial efforts internationally. Keeley, *War Before Civilization*, is perceptive as well.

25. Benjamin Church, *The History of King Philip's War*, ed. Samuel G. Drake, 2nd ed. (Exeter, NH: J. & B. Williams, 1840), pp. 41-46; Slotkin, *Regeneration*, pp. 162-178, 188. William Christie MacLeod, *The American Indian Frontier* (New York: Alfred A. Knopf, 1928), p. 239.

26. White, *Middle Ground*, passim.

27. Brooke Hindle, "The March of the Paxton Boys, *William and Mary Quarterly*. Third Series, III (October 1946): 461-486; Wilbur R. Jacobs, editor, *The Paxton Riots and the Frontier Theory* (Chicago: Rand McNally & Company, 1967); Winthrop D. Jordan, *White Over Black: American Attitudes Toward the Negro, 1550-1812* (New York: W. W. Norton Company, 1977), pp. 275-278. A more recent and important treatment is Peter Silver, *Our Savage Neighbors: How Indian War Transformed Early America* (New York: W. W. Norton Company, 2008), pp. 175-190, 202-208.

28. Wilcomb E. Washburn, *Red Man's Land—White Man's Law: A Study of the Past and Present Status of the American Indian* (New York: Charles Scribner's Sons, 1971), pp. 49-50.

29. John P. Brown, *Old Frontiers* (Kingsport, TN: Southern Publishers, 1938), p. 288n.

30. Quoted in Pearce, *Savagism and Civilization*, p. 55. A recent study of the new United States' conflict with American Indians during the American Revolution is Barbara Alice Mann, *George Washington's War on Native America* (Lincoln: University of Nebraska Press, 2008).

31. Silver, *Savage Neighbors*, pp. 265-276; Sheehan, *Seeds of Extinction*, pp. 187-188.

32. Silver, *Savage Neighbors*, p. 293.

33. How the image was crafted, and why, is detailed well in ibid., which makes Silver's book

especially important. See also Berkhofer, *White Man's Indian*, pp. 3-31, and Pearce, *Savagism and Civilization*, pp. 51-168. Pearce sums up the problem (p. 242) this way: "Civilization had created a savage, so as to kill him. Idea had begotten image, so as to kill it. The need was to go beyond image and idea to the man."

34. White, *Middle Ground*, pp. 315-517; Dowd, *Spirited Resistance*, pp. 90-190; Owens, *Red Dreams*, pp. 71-172.

35. Silver, *Savage Neighbors*, p. 291.

36. Quoted in ibid., p. 291.

37. The Northwest Ordinance of 1787 as quoted in Francis Paul Prucha, *The Great Father: The United States Government and the American Indian*. Two Volumes (Lincoln: University of Nebraska Press, 1984): I, 47.

38. Francis Paul Prucha, *American Indian Policy in the Formative Years: The Indian Trade and Intercourse Acts, 1790-1834* (Cambridge: Harvard University Press, 1962), p. 40.

39. Report of Henry Knox on White Outrages, July 18, 1788, and Report of Henry Knox on the Northwestern Indians, June 15, 1789, in Francis Paul Prucha, editor, *Documents of United States Indian Policy* (Lincoln: University of Nebraska Press, 1975), pp. 11-12, 12-13.

40. Prucha, *Policy in the Formative Years*, pp. 40-50. See also Sheehan, *Seeds of Extinction*, pp. 119-275, and Reginald Horsman, *Expansion and American Indian Policy, 1783-1812* (Norman: University of Oklahoma Press, 1992), pp. 95-96. Recent works are more critical of the policies of Washington and Jefferson. See, for example, Gary Clayton Anderson, *Ethnic Cleansing and the Indian: The Crime That Should Haunt America* (Norman: University of Oklahoma Press, 2015), pp. 87-127; Anthony F. C. Wallace, *Jefferson and the Indians: The Tragic Fate of the First Americans* (Cambridge: Belknap Press, 1999), pp. 206-240, 335-340. Finally, Colin G. Calloway, *The Victory with No Name: The Native American Defeat of the First American Army* (New York: Oxford University Press, 2015) is a fascinating account of the defeat of General Arthur St. Clair in 1791, possibly the worst defeat experienced by an American army at the hands of Native Americans.

41. Belich, *Replenishing the Earth*, p. 146.

42. Roger L. Nichols, *Warrior Nations: The United States and Indian Peoples* (Norman: University of Oklahoma Press, 2013), p. 35.

43. Prucha, *Policy in the Formative Years*, pp. 186-187.

44. Alan Taylor, *The Civil War of 1812: American Citizens, British Subjects, Irish Rebels & Indian Allies* (New York: Alfred A. Knopf, 2010) offers a good introduction to events related to the Indian-British-American conflict. Dowd, *Spirited Resistance*, pp. 123-190, is also valuable. For later conflicts, see Patrick J. Jung, *The Black Hawk War of 1832* (Norman: University of Oklahoma Press, 2007), and Kerry A. Trask, *Black Hawk: The Battle for the Heart of America* (New York: Henry Holt and Company, 2006).

45. Osterhammel, *Transformation of the World*, p. 340.

46. Williams, *American Indian in Western Legal Thought*, pp. 308-317; Newcomb, *Pagans*, pp. 73-136. The first book devoted entirely to *Johnson v. McIntosh* is Lindsay G. Robertson, *Conquest by Law: How the Discovery of America Dispossessed Indigenous Peoples of Their Lands* (New York: Oxford University Press, 2005). Stuart Banner, *How Indians Lost Their Land: Law and Power on the Frontier* (Cambridge: Belknap Press, 2005), also draws heavily on the case, as does Walter R. Echo-Hawk, *In the Light of Justice: The Rise of Human Rights in Native America and the UN Declaration on the Rights of Indigenous Peoples* (Golden, CO: Fulcrum Publishing, 2013) and Eric Kades, "History and Interpretation of the Great Case of *Johnson v. McIntosh*,"

Law and History Review, 19 (2001): 67-117. Also found as *Faculty Publications*. Paper 50. http://scholarship.law.wm.edu/facpubs/50. Curiously, earlier works on federal Indian policy put less emphasis on *Johnson*. Prucha, *Great Father*, for example, affords half a page to the case (I, 113), emphasizing Marshall's statement that the right of occupancy could bar forcible removal. Marshall said, "It has never been contended that the Indian title amounted to nothing. Their right of possession has never been questioned." Charles Warren, *The Supreme Court in United States History*. Two Volumes. Revised Edition (Boston: Little, Brown, and Company, 1926): I, 730, states that *McIntosh* "had settled the question of the nature of Indian title to the soil, and had held that the fee to lands in this country vested in the British government, by discovery, according to the acknowledged law of civilized nations; that it passed to the United States by the Revolution; and that the Indian tribe had a right of occupancy only."

47. Robertson, *Conquest by Law*, pp. 125-144. It should be noted that Marshall dissented in *Mitchel* and had left the court by the time of *Fernandez*. For a different perspective, see David E. Wilkins, "*Johnson v. M'Intosh* Revisited: Through the eyes of *Mitchel v. United States*," *American Indian Law Review*, 19 (1994): 159-181. See also, Williams, *American Indian in Western Legal Thought*, pp. 314-317; Prucha, *Great Father*, I, 208-213; Warren, *Supreme Court*, I, 729-779; and Report of the John Evans Study Committee, University of Denver, pp. 23-26.

48. Alexis de Toqueville, *Democracy in America*, trans. George Lawrence, ed. J. P. Mayer (New York: Doubleday & Company, 1969), p. 339.

Chapter 3

1. Quoted in Thomas F. Gossett, *Race: The History of an Idea in America* (New York: Schocken Books, 1965), p. 230. In his last speech to Congress, December 2, 1828, Adams observed, "We have been far more successful in the acquisition of their lands than in imparting to them the principles or inspiring them with the spirit of civilization." He lamented that they were forming communities as "rivals of sovereignty" apart from the Union. He said, "This state of things requires that a remedy should be provided—a remedy which, while it shall do justice to those unfortunate children of nature, may secure to the members of our confederation their rights of sovereignty and of soil." Quoted in Prucha, *Policy in the Formative Years*, p. 233.

2. *Johnson and Graham's Lessee v. William McIntosh* (1823), quoted in Prucha, *Documents of Indian Policy*, pp. 34-35.

3. Sheehan, *Seeds of Extinction*, pp. 245-250.

4. Toqueville, *Democracy in America*, pp. 338-339.

5. Michael Paul Rogin, *Fathers & Children: Andrew Jackson and the Subjugation of the American Indian* (New York: Vintage Books, 1975), pp. 113-248; Ronald N. Satz, *American Indian Policy in the Jacksonian Era* (Lincoln: University of Nebraska Press, 1975), passim; Robert A. Trennert, Jr., *Alternative to Extinction: Federal Indian Policy and the Beginnings of the Reservation System, 1846-51* (Philadelphia: Temple University Press, 1975), pp. 1-60; Brian W. Dippie, *The Vanishing American and U.S. Indian Policy* (Middletown, CT: Wesleyan University Press, 1982), pp. 3-55; and Horsman, *Race and Manifest Destiny*, pp. 81-138, 189-207, provide a good overview of the variety of thought.

6. Philip Borden, "Found Cumbering the Soil: Manifest Destiny and the Indian in the Nineteenth Century," *The Great Fear: Race in the Mind of America*, ed. Gary B. Nash and Richard Weiss (New York: Holt, Rinehart, and Winston, 1970), pp. 71-97; William Stanton, *The Leopard's Spots*,

Scientific Attitudes Toward Race in America, 1815-59 (Chicago: University of Chicago Press, 1960), passim. Prucha has argued that the influence of scientific racism was "practically nil" in the conscious shaping of Indian policy; likely, "scientific" ideas were imposed as a justification for views already held. See Francis Paul Prucha, "Scientific Racism and Indian Policy," in Prucha, *Indian Policy,* pp. 180-197. Craig Steven Wilder, *Ebony & Ivy: Race, Slavery, and the Troubled History of America's Universities* (New York: Bloomsbury Press, 2013), explores the ways in which academics fed the ideology of racism, although he mentions American Indians only in passing. See also, Horsman, *Race and Manifest Destiny,* pp. 139-157, and Gossett, *Race: The History of an Idea,* pp. 144-252.

7. Tom Dunlay, *Kit Carson & the Indians* (Lincoln: University of Nebraska Press, 2000), pp. 436-439. Robert Winston Mardock, *The Reformers and the American Indian* (Columbia: University of Missouri Press, 1971), while focused primarily on the post-Civil War period, is also particularly useful.

8. This is a critical point. Reformers and religious leaders thought of salvation and civilization as the greatest gifts that they could offer to indigenous peoples. The ideas were not malicious by design, and they found it difficult to see them as anything other than benefits.

9. Anderson, *Ethnic Cleansing,* is the most recent and extended explication of the concept. Tinker, *Missionary Conquest,* pp. 5-6, uses the term "cultural genocide" which he defines "as the effective destruction of a people by systematically or systemically (intentionally or unintentionally in order to achieve other goals) destroying, eroding, or undermining the integrity of the culture and system of values that defines a people and gives them life."

10. Silver, *Savage Neighbors,* explains the patterns as well as anyone, although it is narrowly focused on the second half of the eighteenth century.

11. Slotkin, *Fatal Environment,* p. 110.

12. Brenda Wineapple, *Ecstatic Nation: Confidence, Crisis, and Compromise, 1848-1877* (New York: Harper Collins, 2013), pp. 506-528; Slotkin, *Fatal Environment,* pp. 110-118; Belich, *Replenishing the Earth,* pp. 224-250.

13. Said, *Culture and Imperialism,* pp. xxv, 289; Osterhammel, *Transformation of the World,* pp. 105, 371-373; Belich, *Replenishing the Earth,* pp. 85-86, 166-168.

14. Elliott West, "Reconstructing Race," *The Essential West: Collected Essays* (Norman: University of Oklahoma Press, 2012), pp. 100-126; Prucha, "Racism and Policy," pp. 180-197; Horsman, *Race and Destiny,* pp. 116-157.

15. Elliott West, "Called-Out People: The Cheyennes and the Central Plains," *Essential West,* pp. 57-77, is critical as an introduction to the Cheyennes before plunging into the extensive ethnological and historical literature on the Cheyennes. The most important works include, George Bird Grinnell, *The Cheyenne Indians: Their History and Life Way.* Two Volumes (New York: Cooper Square Publishers, 1962), and *The Fighting Cheyennes* (Norman: University of Oklahoma Press, 1915); Peter John Powell, *Sweet Medicine: The Continuing Role of the Sacred Arrows, the Sun Dance, and the Sacred Buffalo Hat in Northern Cheyenne History.* Two Volumes (Norman: University of Oklahoma Press, 1969) and *People of the Sacred Mountain: A History of the Northern Cheyenne Chiefs and Warrior Societies, 1830-1879, with an Epilogue, 1969-1974.* Two Volumes (New York: Harper & Row, 1981); John H. Moore, *The Cheyenne Nation: A Social and Demographic History* (Lincoln: University of Nebraska Press, 1987); Karl N. Llewellyn and E. Adamson Hoebel, *The Cheyenne Way: Conflict and Case Law in Primitive Jurisprudence* (Norman: University of Oklahoma

Press, 1941); E. Adamson Hoebel, *The Cheyennes: Indians of the Great Plains*, 2nd ed. (New York: Holt, Rinehart and Winston, 1978); Donald J. Berthrong, *The Southern Cheyennes* (Norman: University of Oklahoma Press, 1963).

16. Grinnell, *Cheyenne Indians*, II, 345-381; Moore, *Cheyenne Nation*, pp. 313-317; Powell, *Sweet Medicine*, II, 433-471.

17. Roberts, "Sand Creek," pp. 44-45. See also Llewellyn and Hoebel, *Cheyenne Way*, pp. 67-98.

18. Karen D. Petersen, "Cheyenne Soldier Societies," *Plains Anthropologist*, 9 (1964): 146-172; Roberts, "Sand Creek," pp. 45-47.

19. Hoebel, *Cheyennes*, pp. 14-25.

20. Herein, the term "Lakota" is used to describe the division of the Plains Sioux with whom the Cheyennes were most closely involved. The use of the terms "Sioux," "Lakota," and "Dakota," can be confusing. The term "Sioux" derives from an Ottawa description, translated by the French as "Nadouessioux," which was simplified to Sioux, to describe the people of the Seven Council Fires, Oceti Sakowin. Within the Seven Fires, the people referred to themselves as "Lakota" or "Dakota," different dialects of a word indicating friendship. The Lakota-speaking Oglalas and Brules and the Dakota-speaking Yanktonai and Yanktons were the first to move west and embrace the horse and buffalo culture. Over time, other Lakota, including Minneconjou and Saones crossed the Missouri as well. The Sans Arc, the Hunkpapa, the Two Kettles, and the Blackfeet (not the Algonquian tribe of the same name), were all subgroups of the Saones. Together these groups comprised the Plains Sioux. This brief summary is drawn from a more extended account in Ostler, *The Plains Sioux and U.S. Colonialism*, pp. 21-26.

21. Powell, *People of the Sacred Mountain*, I, 70-73; Richard White, "The Winning of the West: The Expansion of the Western Sioux in the Eighteenth and Nineteenth Centuries," *Journal of American History*, LXV (1978): 319-331.

22. Berthrong, *Southern Cheyennes*, pp. 17-24.

23. David Lavendar, *Bent's Fort* (New York: Doubleday & Company, 1954), pp. 141-154; Anne F. Hyde, *Empires, Nations, and Families: A New History of the North American West, 1800-1860* (New York: Harper-Collins Books, 2011), pp. 151-170; David Fridtjof Halaas and Andrew E. Masich, *Halfbreed: The Remarkable True Story of George Bent—Caught Between the Worlds of the Indian and the White Man* (Cambridge, MA: Da Capo Press, 2004), pp. 1-66.

24. Elliott West, "Land," *The Way to the West: Essays on the Central Plains* (Albuquerque: University of New Mexico Press, 1995), pp. 13-50.

25. Roberts, "Sand Creek," pp. 62-66; Berthrong, *Southern Cheyennes*, pp. 118-123. Especially interesting are the reports prepared by A. B. Chambers and B. Gratz Brown for the *St. Louis Missouri Republican*, September 26, October 1, 2, 5, 29, November 2, 9, 30, 1851.

26. William Y. Chalfant, *Cheyennes and Horse Soldiers: The 1857 Expedition and the Battle of Solomon's Fork* (Norman: University of Oklahoma Press, 1989).

27. West, *Contested Plains*, pp. 115-235.

Chapter 4

1. David Hempton, *Methodism: Empire of the Spirit* (New Haven: Yale University Press, 2005), pp. 1-85.

2. December 2, 1737, Journal 1, W. Reginald Ward and Richard P. Heitzenrater, editors, *The Works of John Wesley* (Nashville: Abingdon Press, 1988): I: 201-204.

3. January 24, 1738, Journal 1, Ward and Heitzenrater, *Works of Wesley*, I, *210-211;* J. Ralph Randolph, *"John Wesley and the American Indian: A Study in Disillusionment,"* Methodist History, X (1972): 3-11.

4. "John Wesley's Big Impact on America," *Christianity.com.* http://www.christianity.com /church/church-history/timeline/1701-1800/john-big-impact-on-america-11630220.html. For a deeper analysis see Thomas S. Kidd, *George Whitefield: America's Spiritual Founding Father* (New Haven, CT: Yale University Press, 2014).

5. Thomas S. Kidd, *The Great Awakening: The Roots of Evangelical Christianity in Colonial America* (New Haven, CT: Yale University Press, 2009), pp. 38-83.

6. Hempton, *Methodism,* pp. 33-99.

7. Ibid.; Jeffrey Williams, *Religion and Violence in Early American Methodism: Taking the Kingdom by Force* (Bloomington: Indiana University Press, 2010), pp. 41-67; Russell E. Richey, Kenneth E. Rowe, and Jean Miller Schmidt, *American Methodism: A Compact History* (Nashville, TN: Abingdon Press, 2012), pp. 9-25.

8. Charles W. Ferguson, *Organizing to Beat the Devil: Methodists and the Making of America* (New York: Doubleday & Company, 1971), pp. 53-67; Hempton, *Methodism,* pp. 92-93, 100-101.

9. Richey, et al., *American Methodism,* pp. 18-34.

10. Hempton, *Methodism,* pp. 7, 101.

11. Ferguson, *Organizing to Beat the Devil,* pp. 69-77; Kevin M. Watson, *The Class Meeting* (Wilmore, KY: Seedbed Publishing, 2014), pp. 19-31, 35-51.

12. Ferguson, *Organizing to Beat the Devil,* pp. 95-117.

13. Quoted in Bruce David Forbes, "'And Obey God, ETC.': Methodism and American Indians," *Methodist History,* 23 (October 1984): 4.

14. Wade Crawford Barclay, *History of Methodist Missions.* Six Volumes (New York: The Board of Missions and Church Extension of the Methodist Church, 1949): I, 164-212.

15. Russell E. Richey, Kenneth E. Rowe, and Jean Miller Schmidt, editors, *The Methodist Experience in America: A Sourcebook.* Two Volumes (Nashville, TN: Abingdon Press, 2000): 82.

16. Ferguson, *Organizing to Beat the Devil,* pp. 69-137.

17. Richard Carwardine, "Methodists, Politics, and the Coming of the Civil War," *Church History,* 69 (September 2000): 579-580.

18. Richard Cameron, quoted in Ferguson, *Organizing to Beat the Devil,* p. 79.

19. Ibid.

20. See, as examples, Jacob Young, *Autobiography of a Pioneer* (Cincinnati: Cranston & Curtis, 1857), p. 246, and James B. Finley, *Life Among the Indians* (Cincinnati: Cranston & Curtis, 185?), p. 59. Even Bishop Asbury's journal was full of references that reflected settler fears and attitudes. Frederick A. Norwood, "The Invisible American—Methodism and the Indian," *Methodist History,* 8 (January 1970): 4-6.

21. Williams, *Religion and Violence,* pp. 110-114.

22. Ibid., p. 114.

23. Barclay, *Methodist Missions,* I, 164-258; Gary L. Roberts, "Violence and the Frontier Tradition," *Kansas and the West: Bicentennial Essays in Honor of Nyle H. Miller,* ed. Forrest R. Blackburn, et al. (Topeka: Kansas State Historical Society, 1976), pp. 96-111.

24. Horace Bushnell, *Barbarism, the First Danger: A Discourse for Home Missions* (New York: American Home Missionary Society, 1847), p. 4.

25. Ibid., pp. 16-17.

26. Ibid., p. 81.

27. Prucha, *Indian Policy,* p. 222.

28. Barclay, *Methodist Missions,* II, 112.

29. Ibid., I, 112-115.

30. Williams, *Religion and Violence,* p. 115. For a more detailed look at the missionary efforts of the Methodist Church, see Barclay, *Methodist Missions,* II, 112-169.

31. Barclay, *Methodist Missions,* II, 262-274.

32. Mary Stockwell, *The Other Trail of Tears: The Removal of the Ohio Indians* (Yardley, PA: Westholme Publishing, 2014), pp. 109-110.

33. T. Scott Miyakawa, *Protestants and Pioneers: Individualism and Conformity on the American Frontier* (Chicago: University of Chicago Press, 1964), p. 193.

34. Barclay, *Methodist Missions,* I, 203; Forbes, "And Obey God," pp. 6-7.

35. Frederick A. Norwood, "Strangers in a Strange Land: Removal of the Wyandot Indians," *Methodist History,* 13 (April 1975): 46-49; Norwood, "The Invisible Indian," pp. 7-9.

36. Quoted in, Forbes, "And Obey God," p. 18. Stockwell, *Other Trail of Tears,* pp. 120-123, that the majority of Wyandots found a new kind of peace and satisfaction in the new ways.

37. Miyakawa, *Protestants and Pioneers,* p. 193.

38. Stockwell, *Other Trail of Tears,* pp. 110-114.

39. Barclay, *Methodist Missions,* II, 201.

40. Ibid., II, 202-204.

41. Ibid., II, 200-262; Robert J. Loewenberg, *Equality on the Oregon Frontier: Jason Lee and the Methodist Mission, 1834-43* (Seattle: University of Washington Press, 1976). See also Forbes, "And Obey God," pp. 12-14.

42. Barclay, *Methodist Missions,* II, 223.

43. Ibid.

44. Ibid., II, 224-229.

45. Ibid., II, 254. Berkhofer, *Salvation and the Savage,* p. 177, said of Lee's Oregon Mission that it "was as dramatic as it was insignificant from the viewpoint of Indian missionary history."

46. Ibid., II, 262.

47. Alvin N. Josephy, *The Nez Perce Indians and the Opening of the Northwest* (New Haven, CT: Yale University Press, 1965), pp. 247-255; Ferguson, *Organizing to Beat the Devil,* pp. 155-173.

48. Hixson, *American Settler Colonialism,* pp. 133-134. See also Cameron Addis, "The Whitman Massacre: Religion and Manifest Destiny on the Columbia Plateau, 1809-1858," *Journal of the Early Republic,* 25 (2005), pp. 221-258, and Gray H. Whaley, *Oregon and the Collapse of Illahee: U.S. Empire and the Transformation of an Indigenous World, 1792-1859* (Chapel Hill: University of North Carolina Press, 2010).

49. Barclay, *Methodist Missions,* II, 171-200.

50. Ibid.

51. Ibid., II, 172-183.

52. Norwood, "Strangers in a Strange Land," pp. 46-55; Stockwell, *Other Trail of Tears,* pp. 308-320.

53. Perl W. Morgan, editor, *History of Wyandotte County Kansas and Its People* (Chicago: The Lewis Publishing Company, 1911), pp. 343-348; Barclay, *Methodist Missions,* III, 343-346.

54. William Elsey Connelley, editor, *The Provisional Government of Nebraska Territory and the Journals of William Walker, Provisional Governor of Nebraska Territory* (Lincoln: Nebraska State

Historical Society, 1899). See also three articles by Connelley, "Religious Conceptions of the Modern Hurons," "Wyandot and Shawnee Indian Lands in Wyandotte County, Kansas," and "Kansas City, Kansas: Its Place in the History of the State," *Kansas Historical Collections*. Seventeen Volumes (Topeka: Kansas State Historical Society, 1881-1928): XV, 92-191.

55. John P. Bowes, *Exiles and Pioneers: Eastern Indians in the Trans-Mississippi West* (New York: Cambridge University Press, 2007), pp. 201-218.

56. Stephen Dow Beckham, *Requiem for a People: The Rogue Indians and the Frontiersmen* (Norman: University of Oklahoma Press, 1978), pp. 147-167; E. A. Schwartz, *The Rogue River Indian War and Its Aftermath* (Norman: University of Oklahoma Press, 1997).

57. Robert M. Utley, *Frontiersmen in Blue: The United States Army and the Indian, 1848-1865* (New York: Macmillan Company, 1967), p. 183.

58. John Beeson, *A Plea for the Indians with Facts and Features of the Late War in Oregon* (New York: John Beeson, 1857), pp. 46-48; Beckham, *Requiem for a People*, p. 152.

59. Beeson, *Plea for the Indians*, pp. 76-98; Frederick A. Norwood, "Two Contrasting Views of the Indians: Methodist Involvement in the Indian Troubles in Oregon and Washington," *Church History*, 49 (1980): 178-187.

60. *Oregon City Argus*, June 28, 1856.

61. Beeson, *Plea for the Indians*, pp. 100-101.

62. Ibid., p. 101.

63. Ibid.

64. Bert Webber, *John Beeson's Plea for the Indians: His Lone Cry in the Wilderness for Indian Rights* (Medford, OR: Webb Research Group, 1994), pp. 35-36.

65. Beeson, *Plea for the Indians*, p. 113.

66. Williams, *Religion and Violence*, pp. 95-130.

67. Ibid., p. 121. See also Christopher Rein, "'Our First Duty Was to God and Our Next to Our Country:' Religion, Violence, and the Sand Creek Massacre," *Great Plains Quarterly*, 34 (2014).

68. Berkhofer, *Salvation and the Savage*, pp. 4-7, addresses this issue broadly. He cites articles from the *Christian Advocate* (New York), July 18, 1828, December 19, 1828, and the *Annual Report of the Missionary Society of the Methodist Episcopal Church*, 1839, p. 4, as examples of the conversion-first point of view, and the Missionary Society's annual reports for 1850, 1851, 1854, and 1856, advocating the civilization-first side. It appears that the Missionary Society's view became more cynical over time. Other sources cited herein provide additional evidence of the debate.

69. Ibid., pp. 121-130. See Norwood, "Contrasting Views," for the sharp contrast of views even within the Methodist Church. Beeson's writings made a special point of contrasting his own views with those of the Methodists in Oregon. He was amazed that the Church did not rally to support him. Eventually, his disappointment with Methodists led him to become a Quaker.

70. Williams, *Religion and Violence*, pp. 124-125.

71. William H. Goode, *Outposts of Zion: With Limnings of Mission Life* (Cincinnati: Poe and Hitchcock, 1863), p. 452.

72. Ibid., p. 453.

73. Ibid., pp. 453-464.

74. Barclay, *Methodist Missions*, III, 363.

75. Hempton, *Methodism*, pp. 187-209; Ferguson, *Organizing to Beat the Devil*, pp. 185-230; Williams, *Religion and Violence*, pp. 143-160; Richard Carwardine, "Methodist Ministers and the Second Party System," *Perspectives on American Methodism: Interpretive Essays*, eds. Russell

E. Richey, Kenneth Rowe, and Jean Miller Schmidt (Nashville, TN: Kingswood Books, 1993), pp. 159-177; Richard Carwardine, "Methodists, Politics, and the Coming of the Civil War," *Church History*, 69 (2000): 578-609; and Donald B. Marti, "Rich Methodists: The Rise and Consequences of Lay Philanthropy in the Mid-Nineteenth Century," Richey, et al, *Perspectives*, pp. 265-276.

Chapter 5

1. Reginald S. Craig, *The Fighting Parson: The Biography of Colonel John M. Chivington* (Los Angeles: Westernlore Press, 1959), p. 21; "Death of Brother J. M. Chivington, First M. W. Grand Master of Masons in Colorado," *The Square and Compass* (October 1894), p. 214; Gordon R. Merrick, "Chivington—Before Colorado," Paper presented at Research Lodge of Colorado, October 31, 1960; John Speer, "Sketch of John Milton Chivington: Report of an Interview with Mrs. John M. Chivington," Miscellaneous John M. Chivington Collection, Kansas State Historical Collection, Topeka, Kansas; Clarence A. Lyman, "The Truth About Colonel John M. Chivington," unpublished manuscript (Denver: Division of State Archives and Public Records, 1956); Roberts, "Sand Creek: Tragedy and Symbol," p. 116. Lyman was married to the granddaughter of John Chivington, and his manuscript is a mass of stories collected from family members and presented in a novelesque fashion. See Benjamin Draper, Interview with Clarence Augustus Lyman, July 30, 1957. Clarence A. Lyman Collection, Western History Collection, Denver Public Library, Denver, Colorado. Craig was a great-grandson of Chivington and an attorney. His biography is largely a brief defending Chivington. He relied heavily on Lyman. The best overview of Chivington's life is Lori Cox-Paul, "John M. Chivington, The 'Reverend Colonel' 'Marry-Your-Daughter' 'Sand Creek Massacre,'" *Nebraska History*, 88 (2007): 126-137, 142-147.

2. Josiah Morrow, *The History of Warren County* (Chicago: W. H. Beers & Company, 1882), p. 681.

3. Ibid. The marriage of Isaac Chivington and Jane Runyon is confirmed by License No. 451, Book 1, p. 57.

4. David R. Edmunds, *The Shawnee Prophet* (Lincoln: University of Nebraska Press, 1983); Adam Jortner, *The Gods of Prophetstown: The Battle of Prophetstown and the Holy War for the American Frontier* (New York: Oxford University Press, 2011).

5. Morrow, *Warren County*, p. 681; Merrick, "Chivington—Before Colorado." Runyon's service is better documented than Chivington's, but the consistency of the sources makes it probable that Chivington served as well.

6. John Sugden, *Tecumseh, a Life* (New York: Macmillan and Company, 1999); Robert M. Owens, *Mr. Jefferson's Hammer: William Henry Harrison and the Origins of American Indian Policy* (Norman: University of Oklahoma Press, 2007).

7. No birth records exist for Warren County before 1867. See Roberta Palmer, Deputy Clerk, Probate Court of Warren County to Raymond G. Carey, September 9, 1960, Raymond G. Carey Collection, University of Denver, Denver, Colorado. Date of birth is based upon obituaries at the time of Chivington's death and other sources. See also, Raymond E. Dale, "Otoe County Pioneers: A Biographical Dictionary," Nebraska State Historical Society, pp. 490-495. For a more detailed view of John's brother Isaac, see George E. Utterback, "Portrait of a Master Mason . . . Isaac Chivington, Mason and Man of God," *The Indiana Freemason*, 38 (1960): 4-5, 27-29, 32.

8. Cox-Paul, "Chivington," p. 127. At the time Isaac's estate was settled, it appears that an administrator or guardian was named. Docket of Estates, No. O, p. 308, includes an allowance for

Jane Chivington's first year's support and a copy of her receipt. More important, p. 316 includes a record of the guardianship for the Lewis Chivington estate, including the names of the four Chivington children. Apparently, James Hill, an early settler from Virginia, a justice of the peace, and a friend of the Runyon family acted as guardian. A document transferring property from Isaac and Jane Chivington to Benjamin Whitacre is found in the Deed Record, Volume 12, p. 109, Probate Court of Warren County, Ohio, Lebanon, Ohio. See also Morrow, *Warren County*, p. 681.

9. Raymond G. Carey, "The Tragic Trustee," *University of Denver Magazine*, 2 (1965): 9.

10. Lyman, "Truth About Chivington," pp. 19-30, provides an apocryphal account of his prize fighting career. Just when he moved to Indiana is unclear. Chivington was married in Milton, Indiana. Jordan Dodd, *Indiana Marriages to 1850* [data base on-line] (Provo, UT: Ancestry.com Operations, Inc., 1997).

11. Morrow, *Warren County*, p. 623.

12. Lyman, "Truth About Chivington," pp. 31-32.

13. Morrow, *Warren County*, p. 425.

14. *The History of Champaign County, Ohio* (Chicago: W. H. Bean & Company, 1881), p. 416.

15. Ibid., p. 418.

16. Most accounts have followed the lead of Nolie Mumey, "John Milton Chivington: The Misunderstood Man," *Denver Westerners Monthly Roundup*, XII (1956): 5-16, and Craig, *Fighting Parson*, p. 28, in launching his career as an elder at Zoar Church in the Goshen District. His guardian, James Hill, was one of the founders of Zoar Church, and it was the most vibrant Methodist church in the county. Kenneth E. Metcalf, "The Beginnings of Methodism in Colorado." Unpublished Ph.D. dissertation (Denver: Iliff School of Theology, 1958), p. 259, makes the connection to Marley. In April 1856, at his first Methodist Conference in Omaha, Nebraska, Chivington said that he was converted in 1842 and "had served eleven years in the ministry," which would place his length of service as a minister within half a year of the September 1844 date. See J. Sterling Morton and Albert Watkins, *Illustrated History of Nebraska*. Volume II (Lincoln, NB: Jacob North & Company, 1907): 196n.

17. Morrow, *Warren County*, p. 679. Merrick, "Chivington—Before Colorado," p. 1.

18. *Minutes of the Annual Conferences of the Methodist Episcopal Church for the Years 1846-1851* (New York: Carlton & Porter, 1856): IV, 279, 281, 389, 392, 398, 508, 510, 650, 652.

19. *Annual Conference Minutes*, V, 128, 130, 312.

20. Bowes, *Exiles and Pioneers*, pp. 201-218; Barclay, *Methodist Missions*, III, 344-345; Connelley, *Provisional Government of Nebraska and Walker Journals*, passim; Perl W. Morgan, *History of Wyandotte County, Kansas and Its People*. Two volumes (Chicago: Lewis Publishing Company, 1911); Martha Caldwell, *Annals of Shawnee Methodist Mission and Indian Manual Labor School* (Topeka: Kansas State Historical Society, 1939), pp. 75-84.

21. Caldwell, *Annals of Shawnee Mission*, pp. 76-77; Solomon Nunes Carvalho, *Incidents of Travel and Adventure in the Far West with Colonel Fremont's Last Expedition* (Lincoln: University of Nebraska Press, 1858), pp. 29-33.

22. Caldwell, *Annals of Shawnee Mission*, p. 77; Connelley, *Provisional Government of Nebraska and Walker Journals*, pp. 370-406. Walker had known Dofflemeyer earlier. He mentions attending services preached by several pastors, including Dofflemeyer, but no reference is made to Chivington.

23. Goode, *Outposts of Zion*, pp. 249-256, 307-310; Mrs. E. F. Hollibaugh, *Biographical History of Cloud County* (n. p. 1903), p. 22; Barclay, *Methodist Missions*, III, 344-345.

24. John T. Dormois, Francis M. Coleman, and Alan W. Farley, *Centennial Wyandotte Lodge No. 3, A. F. & A. M., Kansas City, Kansas* (Kansas City, KS: Wyandotte Lodge No.3, 1954), pp. 8-15.

25. Goode to *Western Christian Advocate,* reprinted in the *Missionary Advocate,* October 7, 1854, quoted in Barclay, *Methodist Missions,* III, 344-345. Goode, *Outposts of Zion,* pp. 249-256, recalled his visit, mentioning that Chivington was "in possession of the mission farm, then the property of our Church." He also recounts with Chivington and one or two others to the station on the Wakarusa. Dr. Abraham Still was the minister at the Wakarusa. Goode was very impressed with John H. Dennis, who replaced Chivington. Dennis was in bad health, but wrote regularly to the *Northwestern Christian Advocate* about conditions in Kansas. He died in August 1856. See *Northwestern Christian Advocate,* September 3, 1856.

26. *Annual Conference Minutes, 1854,* III, 478, 480.

27. *Annual Conference Minutes, 1855,* III, 661; James Haynes, *History of the Methodist Episcopal Church in Omaha and Suburbs* (Omaha, NE: Omaha Printing Company, 1895), p. 44.

28. Carwardine, "Methodists and Politics," p. 603.

29. Cox-Paul, "Chivington," p. 145n; Nichole Etcheson, *Bleeding Kansas: Contested Liberty in the Civil War Era* (Manhattan: University Press of Kansas, 2004), pp. 34-47.

30. William McClung Paxton, *Annals of Platte County, Missouri From its Exploration Down to June 1, 1897* (Kansas City, MO: n. p., 1897), pp. 198-200; *History of Clay and Platte County, Missouri* (St. Louis, MO: National Historical Company, 1885), pp. 642-644; Mary J. Klem, "Missouri in the Kansas Troubles," *Proceedings of the Mississippi Valley Historical Association,* XI (1919): 393-412; Etcheson, *Bleeding Kansas,* pp. 34-47; and Goode, *Outposts of Zion,* pp. 260-261. Goode had been warned about the possibility of "a gratuitous suit of tar and feathers, or some other lynching process" when he preached in Missouri in 1854. He conducted his service without incident, but he noted "the breaking out of violence in Platte county," the next year.

31. *New York Times,* April 23, July 19, 1855, quoted in Cox-Paul, "Chivington," p. 145n; Speer, "Sketch of Chivington," giving the account of J. H. Herzinger; entry for May, 1859, p. 12. Journals of Jesse Spurgeon Haire, 1859-1897, Five Volumes, Ohio Historical Society, excerpted by Jeff C. Campbell, 2010.

32. Speer, "Sketch of Chivington."

33. Haire Journal, p. 12.

34. "Death of Bro. Chivington," *Square and Compass,* p. 214; Morton and Watkins, *History of Nebraska,* II, 196n.

35. A. T. Andreas, *History of the State of Nebraska* (Chicago: Western Historical Company, 1882), p. 726.

36. *Annual Conference Minutes,* VI (1856), 169, 174; VII (1857) 282; *Minutes of the First Session of the Kansas & Nebraska Annual Conference of the Methodist Episcopal Church Held at Lawrence, Kansas Territory, October 23-25, A. D. 1856* (Omaha City: Nebraskian Book and Job Office, 1856), pp. 1-3; *Minutes of the Kansas & Nebraska Annual Conference of the Methodist Episcopal Church, Held at Nebraska City, N. T., April 16th, 1857* (Topeka, KS: Ross Brothers—Printers, 1857), p. 10.

37. Morton and Watkins, *History of Nebraska,* II, 196n; Cox-Paul, "Chivington," pp. 129, 146n; Raymond E. Dale, "Otoe County Pioneers: A Biographical Dictionary," Nebraska State Historical Society (typescript), p. 492; Dormois, et al., *Wyandotte Lodge No. 3,* p.13.

38. *1857 Kansas-Nebraska Annual Conference,* pp. 3-4.

39. David Marquette, *A History of Nebraska Methodism: First Half-Century, 1854-1904* (Cincinnati: Western Methodist Book Concern Press, 1904), pp. 57-58.

40. Lyman, "Truth About Chivington," pp. 64-65.

41. Dale, "Otoe County Pioneers," pp. 490-492; Cox-Paul, "Chivington," 129-130; W. B. Wetherell, "History of the Reverends John M. Chivington and Isaac Chivington in Their Relationship to the Early Methodist Episcopal Church in Kansas and Nebraska, 1856-1870," unpublished manuscript at Nebraska Methodist Historical Society, Nebraska Wesleyan University, Lincoln, NE.

42. Ibid., 492; Morton and Watkins, *History of Nebraska*, II, 197.

43. *Bellevue* (City) *Gazette,* March 25, 1858.

44. Ibid.

45. Ibid.

46. Ibid., April 1, 1858.

47. *Omaha Nebraskian,* quoted in ibid., April 8, 1858, with response from the *Gazette*'s editor.

48. *Brownville Nebraska Advertiser,* June 2, 1859.

49. Journals of the Kansas-Nebraska Conference, Fourth Session, April 14-18, 1859, insert after, p. 12, Methodist Historical Library, Baker University, Baldwin City, Kansas.

50. Chivington was compared to Peter Cartwright on more than one occasion. Cartwright was a no-nonsense revivalist of the old school with a simple message and a special affinity for the frontier settlers. Williams, *Religion and Violence,* pp. 140-143. See also Peter Cartwright, *The Autobiography of Peter Cartwright, the Backwoods Preacher,* ed. W. P. Strickland (New York: Carlton and Porter, 1857), reprinted by Abingdon Press, 1986.

51. *Minutes of the Kansas and Nebraska Annual Conference of the Methodist Episcopal Church, Fifth Session, Held in Leavenworth City, K. T. March 1860* (Leavenworth: The Herald Book and Job Office, 1860), p. 10.

52. *Nebraska City People's Press,* April 24, 1860.

53. West, *Contested Plains,* pp. 97-183; Isaac Haight Beardsley, *Echoes from Peak and Plain, or Tales of Life, War, Travel and Colorado Methodism* (Cincinnati: Curtis and Jennings, 1898), pp. 217-223; Howard Roberts Lamar, *The Far Southwest, 1846-1912: A Territorial History* (New Haven: Yale University Press, 1966), pp. 205-225.

54. John M. Chivington, "Footprints of Methodist Itinerants in Colorado," *Rocky Mountain Christian Advocate,* September 26, 1889; John M. Chivington "The Prospective (Retrospective)," 1884, Bancroft Library Collections, University of California, Berkeley, California; Goode, *Outposts of Zion,* pp. 391-404.

55. Goode, *Outposts of Zion,* pp. 399-451. This portion of Goode's book consists of a series of letters written on the 1859 visit to Colorado. Another important source on the beginnings of Methodism in Colorado is J. L. Dyer, *The Snow-Shoe Itinerant: An Autobiography of the Rev. John L. Dyer* (Cincinnati: Cranston & Stowe, 1890), pp. 117-147.

56. Jacob Adriance Diaries, 1860, Box 2/FF2 (See especially entries for May 8, June 16, 17, July 4, 15, September 1, 1860), Western History/Genealogy Department, Denver Public Library, Denver, Colorado.

57. Chivington, "Footprints," September 26, 1889; Chivington, "Prospective;" Metcalf, "Beginnings of Methodism," pp. 65-80.

58. Adriance, Diaries, June 16, 17, 1860.

59. Chivington, "Footprints," September 26, 1889; *Denver Weekly Rocky Mountain News,* June 27, 1860.

60. Haire Journal, November 10, 1860.

61. *Weekly Rocky Mountain News (WRMN)*, November 6, 1860.

62. *Central Christian Advocate*, April 10, 1861, quoted in Duane A. Smith, "Colorado's Joshua: John Chivington's Forgotten Years, 1860-1861," *Methodist History*. 29 (1991): 164-165.

63. Haire Journal, November 10, 1860.

64. *Weekly Rocky Mountain News*, May 1, 1861.

65. Chivington, "Footprints," October 24, 1889.

66. *Square and Compass*, October 1894, p. 215; Dormois, et al., *Wyandotte Lodge No. 3*, pp. 8-15.

67. Roberts, "Sand Creek," pp. 109-112.

68. Ibid., pp. 112-115.

69. John M. Chivington, "The Pet Lambs," *Denver Republican*, April 30, 1890. There are several other versions of this statement, but the essence is the same.

70. Irving Howbert, *Memories of a Lifetime in the Pike's Peak Region* (New York: G. P. Putnam's Sons, 1925), p. 136.

71. Susan M. Ashley, "Reminiscences of Colorado in the Early 'Sixties,'" *Colorado Magazine*, XIII (1936): 225.

72. *Denver Colorado Republican and Rocky Mountain Herald*, August 18, 1861.

73. Chivington, "Footprints," October 24, 1889.

74. Haire Journal, March 1862.

75. Roberts, "Sand Creek," pp. 120-121; Flint Whitlock, *Distant Bugles, Distant Drums: The Union Response to the Confederate Invasion of New Mexico* (Niwot: University Press of Colorado, 2006), pp. 62-70; Don E. Alberts, *The Battle of Glorieta: Union Victory in the West* (College Station: Texas A & M University Press, 1998), pp. 22-35; Ovando J. Hollister, *Boldly They Rode: A History of the First Colorado Regiment of Volunteers* (Lakewood, CO: The Golden Press, 1949), pp. 29-44. Hollister's book was originally published in 1863. After the New Mexico Campaign, Hollister and Frank Hall edited the *Black Hawk Daily Mining Journal* through 1865. It remains one of the critical sources on the First Colorado's expedition to New Mexico.

76. Whitlock, *Distant Bugles*, pp. 95-96. See also *WRMN*, February 7, 8, 1862.

77. Whitlock, *Distant Bugles*, p. 143; Alberts, *Glorieta*, pp. 29-30; William Clarke Whitford, *Colorado Volunteers in the Civil War: The New Mexico Campaign in 1862* (Denver: State Historical Society of Colorado, 1906), pp. 75-76.

78. Chivington, "Pet Lambs," April 30, 1890; Chivington, "Prospective." In the latter, Chivington places the date of this incident on February 27, 1862. It is also a shorter and less dramatic recounting, with Lt. Col. Samuel F. Tappan ordered to move the troops forward, whereas in the former, he was the officer Slough ordered to move the troops out. Chivington's accounts should be used with caution because of some discrepancies and exaggerations that appear in his recollections when compared to other accounts.

79. Nolie Mumey, "John Milton Chivington: The Misunderstood Man," *Denver Westerners Monthly Roundup*, XII (1956): 131.

80. Chivington, "Pet Lambs." Durias A. Philbrook was shot by firing squad, April 8, 1862, according to Regimental Order Book, First Colorado Volunteers, General Order 26, April 4, 1862, p. 27, Adjutant General's Office, National Archives and Record Administration, Record Group 94. Haire Journal, March 1862, provides a detailed account of the Philbrook matter. It is also covered in Hollister, *Boldly They Rode*, pp. 45-46. See also *Weekly Rocky Mountain News*, March 27, 1862. Philbrook was placed under arrest and tried later. Chivington presided over the court martial.

81. Hollister, *Boldly They Rode*, pp. 55-56.

82. For detailed accounts of the fight at Apache Canyon, see Whitlock, *Distant Bugles*, pp. 173-180, 184-185n; Alberts, *Glorieta*, pp. 44-68; Thomas S. Edrington and John Taylor, *The Battle of Glorieta Pass: A Gettysburg in the West, March 26-28, 1862* (Albuquerque: University of New Mexico Press, 1998), pp. 41-56; Whitford, *Colorado Volunteers*, pp. 85-97; Ray C. Colton, *The Civil War in the Western Territories: Arizona, Colorado, New Mexico, and Utah* (Norman: University of Oklahoma Press, 1959), pp. 50-56; Hollister, *Boldly They Rode*, pp. 62-67.

83. James C. Enochs, "A Clash of Ambition: The Tappan-Chivington Feud," *Montana, The Magazine of Western History*, 15 (1965): 59.

84. Roberts, "Sand Creek," pp. 127-129; Edrington and Taylor, *Battle of Glorieta*, pp. 89-100; Alberts, *Glorieta*, pp. 128-138. Chivington's reputation as a soldier rested largely on the actions at Apache Canyon and Johnson's Ranch. They assured his reputation as the "hero of Glorieta," but both would become the subject of public controversy in the months that followed.

85. Arthur Wright, "Colonel John P. Slough and the New Mexico Campaign," *Colorado Magazine*, XXXIX (1962): 89-105, reviews the relationship between Slough and the New Mexico commanders in depth. Also helpful is Enochs, "Clash of Ambition," pp. 63-64.

86. Letters and manuscript materials of J. M. Chivington, J. P. Slough, S. F. Tappan, E. W. Wynkoop, 1861-1869, Microfilm, History Colorado, Denver. See also Jeff C. Campbell, *The John Milton Chivington Record, June 2, 1813-October 4, 1894: Sand Creek Massacre, Background Booklet # 3* (Eads, CO: Kiowa County Pres, 2007), pp. 13-18, for other pertinent documents.

87. Chivington to John Evans, April 30, 1862, Regimental Letter Book, First Colorado Volunteers, pp. 35, 37.

88. Handwritten Minutes, Kansas Conference, 1862, Methodist Historical Library, Baker University, Baldwin Kansas.

89. *Leavenworth Daily Conserative*, May 2, 1862.

90. *Atchison (KS) Union*, quoted in *Denver Weekly Rocky Mountain News*, May 28, 1862.

91. Chivington to Fisher, June 25, 1862, John M. Chivington Collection, Western History/Genealogy Department, Denver Public Library, Denver, Colorado.

92. See copies in Commission Branch, Letters Received, C-737-CB, AGO, RG 94, NARA.

93. *Denver Weekly Rocky Mountain News*, August 6, 1862.

94. Chivington, "Pet Lambs." This has an apocryphal ring to it, as does much Chivington wrote in his recollections.

95. Evans to Lincoln, October 31, 1862, Commission Branch, Letters Received, C-1056-CB-1863, AGO, RG 94, NARA.

96. Chivington to Tappan, October 7, 23, 1862, Letters and Manuscripts written by Chivington, Tappan, et al.; Tappan to Jesse Henry Leavenworth, October 28, 1862, Samuel F. Tappan Compiled Military Service Records, AGO, RG 94, NARA.

97. *WRMN*, November 20, 1862.

98. Evans to Lincoln, December 24, 1862, Commission Branch, Letters Received, C-1056-CB-1863, AGO, RG 94, NARA.

99. *Daily National Intelligencer* (Washington, DC), January 26, 1863.

100. Gary L. Roberts, *Death Comes for the Chief Justice: The Slough-Rynerson Quarrel and Political Violence in New Mexico* (Boulder: University Press of Colorado, 1990), pp. 24-25.

101. Chivington to Simpson, December 30, 1863, File 2127-4:45, J. M. Chivington (1863), Matthew Simpson Papers, General Commission on Archives and History, United Methodist Church, Drew University, Madison, New Jersey.

102. *Frank Leslie's Illustrated Newspaper* (New York, NY), December 19, 1863.

103. Slough to Stanton, September 13, 1863, Commission Branch, Letters Received, S-700-CB-1863, AGO, RG 94, NARA. See also Tappan to Slough, December 28, 1862; Tappan to Chivington, January 23, 1863; Slough to Tappan, February 6, 1863, Chivington, Tappan, et al.

Chapter 6

1. Harry Kelsey, *Frontier Capitalist: The Life of John Evans* (Denver: State Historical Society of Colorado and Pruett Publishing Company, 1969), p. 2. The best brief account of the life of John Evans before he moved to Colorado appears in *Northwestern Evans Report*, pp. 11-18. It is brief, but insightful.

2. Ibid., pp. 1-4.

3. Ibid., pp. 6-7.

4. John Evans Dictations and Related Biographical Material, Bancroft MS, P-L 329, Fol. IV, 12, Bancroft Collection, Bancroft Library, University of California, Berkeley, California.

5. Kelsey, *John Evans*, pp. 9-14.

6. John Evans to Benjamin Evans, January 6, 1836, John Evans Collection, History Colorado, Denver, Colorado.

7. Kelsey, *John Evans*, pp. 14-16.

8. Ibid., pp. 20-29.

9. Ibid., p. 23.

10. Ibid., pp. 28, 246n.

11. Evans Dictations, P-L 329.

12. Ibid. Matthew Simpson was one of the most influential bishops of the nineteenth century. An Ohioan like Evans, he did not start his life with the expectation of writing and speaking. He was a frail child, but he did develop a strong interest in reading. With the encouragement of his mother, he also became absorbed in religious ideas. In 1830, still in delicate health, he decided to study medicine, completing his studies and acquiring his license as a physician in 1833, another reason that Evans would be attracted to him. Shortly thereafter, he was licensed as an "exhorter" in the Methodist Episcopal Church. Initially, his poor health proved to be an impediment to licensing as a minister, but, without ever having preached, he was recommended by the quarterly conference to the Pittsburg Annual Conference. George R. Crooks, *The Life of Bishop Matthew Simpson of the Methodist Episcopal Church* (New York: Harper & Brothers, 1891), pp. 11-30. Because of his health, he was disinclined to follow an itinerant ministry, but over time, his obvious strengths as a preacher and as a theologian served him well within the Church. Preaching, he believed, was for the common people, persuasion its goal, and extemporaneous discourse the most effective method. Ministers, he believed, were a "connecting link" between the rich and the poor. In 1839, he became president of Indiana Asbury University (now DePauw University). In 1848, he was named editor of the *Western Christian Advocate,* and in 1852, he was elected bishop. By then he was a tremendously influential leader in the Church, especially in the Midwest.

13. Robert Donald Clark, *The Life of Matthew Simpson* (New York: Macmilllan Company, 1956), p. 72.

14. Carwardine, "Methodists and Politics," pp. 579-580; Ferguson, *Organizing to Beat the Devil,* pp. 185-217.

15. An important work for understanding the impact of evangelical Christianity in the first half of the nineteenth century, see Nathan O. Hatch, *The Democratization of American Christianity* (New Haven: Yale University Press, 1989), pp. 17-189; and Martin E. Marty, *Protestantism in the United States: Righteous Empire*. Second Edition (New York: Charles Scribner's Sons, 1986), pp. 13-29, 39-96, 126-134.

16. Carwardine, "Methodists and Politics," pp. 580-581.

17. Ibid., pp. 583-584.

18. Ibid., pp. 585-586; Marty, *Righteous Empire*, pp. 86-95, 97-106; Ferguson, *Organizing to Beat the Devil*, pp. 185-200; Williams, *Religion and Violence*, pp. 131-160.

19. Kelsey, *John Evans*, p. 33.

20. Ibid. This concern about Methodists being affiliated with fraternal organizations is especially interesting in light of John Chivington's Masonic connections. Although there were anti-Masonic elements within the Methodist Church, the primary reason for its concern seems to have been less about animus against Masons than about worries that such connections would divide the attentions of members, and especially ministers, in ways that would negatively affect their service to the Church.

21. See Alfred Chandler, *The Visible Hand: The Managerial Revolution in American Business* (Cambridge, MA: Harvard University Press, 1977), and Charles Perrow, *Organizing America: Wealth, Power, and the Origins of Corporate Capitalism* (Princeton, NJ: Princeton University Press, 2002).

22. Kelsey, *John Evans*, pp. 35-36.

23. Robert D. Clark, *The Life of Matthew Simpson* (New York: The Macmillan Company, 1956), pp. 106-109.

24. Ibid., pp. 109-111.

25. Kelsey, *John Evans*, pp. 40-47, 49-55.

26. Ibid., p. 47.

27. Clark, *Life of Simpson*, pp. 110-118.

28. Ibid., pp. 146-160.

29. Ibid., pp. 189-193; Marti, "Rich Methodists," pp. 266-267.

30. Kelsey, *John Evans*, pp. 56-60.

31. Ibid., p. 68.

32. *Northwestern Evans Report*, pp. 13-14.

33. Kelsey, *John Evans*, pp. 72-74.

34. Helen Cannon, "First Ladies of Colorado—Margaret Gray Evans (Governor John Evans, 1862-1865)," *Colorado Magazine*, XXXIX (1962): 18-28.

35. A former student recalled that Simpson's motto was "Read and know. Think and be wise." Crooks, *Simpson*, p. 166. Crooks explored Simpson's view of education at length. Recalling Simpson's inaugural at Asbury of Indiana, Crooks noted, at p. 171, that he argued that "he proceeds to argue that individual character depends on the kind of education received, and that national character depends upon the same cause, and so gathers up a cumulative argument which must have made a great impression upon the assembly."

36. *Northwestern Evans Report*, pp. 14-16; Kelsey, *John Evans*, pp. 81-94; Darius Salter, "The Sand Creek Massacre: Matthew Simpson and the Broken Arrow of Patronage," *Methodist History*, 52 (2014): 209-211.

37. John Evans, *Oreapolis, Nebraska Territory: Its Institutions, Advantages in Site, etc., etc. Plan of the Co., for Building Up the Town, Inducements Offered to Emigrants to Settle There. Bonus for Manu-*

facturers, Tradesmen, etc. (Chicago: Press and Tribune, 1859); Kelsey, *John Evans,* pp. 104-108; Evans Dictations, P-L-329; John Evans to Margaret Evans, April 20, June 12, 1859, Evans Collection.

38. *Minutes, Kansas-Nebraska Annual Conference, 1859,* pp. 10-11, 14-17. As a member of the Education Committee, Chivington had apparently met with Evans prior to the annual conference. He, Professor George Loomis, and John Evans addressed the conference on the Oreapolis project. The conference passed the following resolution: "Resolved, That we will co-operate with the friends of Education in the establishment of said Seminary at Oreapolis, and that we will exercise control of said Institution provided for in its Charter in the appointment of Trustees." In the *Minutes* for 1860, a report was given on the status of the Oreapolis project (pp. 13-14). By then Chivington had left for Colorado, and William E. Goode replaced him as "Agent of Oreapolis University." *Minutes of Annual Conferences,* VIII, 87. In the copy of this volume in the Methodist Archives at Drew University, a list of appointments for the Kansas-Nebraska Conference is taped in, including this information.

39. John Evans to Margaret Evans, June 12, 1859, Evans Collection.

40. Kelsey, *John Evans,* pp. 108-109.

41. An Act to Incorporate the "People's Pacific Railroad Company" of the State of Maine, Thirty-Ninth Legislature, March 20, 1860, at http://cprr.org/Museum/Pacific_RR_Act_Maine_1860.html.

42. David Haward Bain, *Empire Express: Building the First Transcontinental Railroad* (New York: Penguin Books, 1999), p. 76. Curtis would become a critical player in John Evans's life story. He would resign his seat in Congress to resume a military career as a brigadier general, commanding the eleven thousand troops of the Army of the Southwest in operations in the Arkansas, Kansas, Missouri, Indian Territory quadrangle. See William L. Shea and Earl J. Hess, *Pea Ridge: Civil War Campaign in the West* (Chapel Hill: University of North Carolina Press, 1992), pp. 5-7. Curtis was a capable commander, but too proper to learn the art of self-promotion. He would later command the Department of Kansas, which included Colorado Territory. Chivington would be one of his district commanders.

43. Bain, *Empire Express,* pp. 90, 101.

44. Alexander Saxton, *The Rise and Fall of the White Republic: Class Politics and Mass Culture in Nineteenth Century America* (New York: Verso, 1990), p. 274.

45. Salter, "Sand Creek, Simpson, and Patronage," pp. 210-211; Kelsey, *Evans,* p. 106; Crooks, *Simpson,* p. 359.

46. Crooks, *Simpson,* p. 359.

47. Matthew Simpson, *A Hundred Years of Methodism* (New York: Nelson & Phillips, 1877) is a brief history and commentary on the Methodist Episcopal Church, its history, its doctrines, and its institutions. As such, it provides considerable insight into his conception of the Church and its mission. It does not have the fire or the eloquence of his sermons.

48. James Edmund Kirby, Jr., "The Ecclesiastical and Social Thought of Matthew Simpson." Unpublished Ph.D. dissertation (Madison, NJ: Drew University, 1963). Salter, "Sand Creek, Simpson, and Patronage," pp. 209-212, calls Simpson "the most influential patronage lobbyist among clergymen in all of America." See also Ferguson, *Organizing to Beat the Devil,* pp. 243-244. Even the most cursory review of the Matthew Simpson Papers at the Library of Congress in Washington, DC, confirms the claim.

49. Kelsey, *John Evans,* pp. 109-110.

50. Kirby, "Thought of Simpson," p. 245.

51. Salter, "Sand Creek, Simpson, and Patronage," pp. 211-212; Kelsey, *John Evans*, pp. 110-111.

52. Salter, "Sand Creek, Simpson, and Patronage," p. 211.

53. Victor B. Howard, *Religion and the Radical Republican Movement, 1860-1870* (Lexington: University of Kentucky Press, 2014), p. 19. See the Evans-Scates letters in the *Chicago Journal*, November 8, 15, 29, 1861. See also McMechen, *Governor Evans*, pp. 81-83.

54. Ibid., p. 212.

55. Williams, *Religion and Violence*, pp. 144-155; Hyde, *Empires, Nations, and Families*, pp. 419-421; Belich, *Replenishing the Earth*, pp. 331-345: Daniel Walker Howe, *What God Hath Wrought: The Transformation of America, 1815-1848* (New York: Oxford University Press, 2007), pp. 525-612, 837-855; Richard D. Brown, *Modernization: The Transformation of American Life, 1600-1865* (Prospect Heights, IL, Waveland Press, Inc., 1976), pp. 122-158.

56. Williams, *Religion and Violence*, p. 112.

57. Ibid., p.142. An especially insightful treatment of Methodists and politics within a broad context is found in William E. Gienapp, *The Origins of the Republican Party, 1852-1856* (New York: Oxford University Press, 1987).

58. *Northwestern Evans Report*, p. 13.

59. Richard Carwardine, "Methodists, Politics, and the Coming of the American Civil War," *Church History*, 69 (2000): 582.

60. Ibid., pp. 608-609.

61. Ferguson, *Organizing to Beat the Devil*, pp. 242-245.

62. Several noteworthy books have been published on the impact of the Civil War on religion in America, including Harry S. Stout, *Upon the Altar of the Nation: A Moral History of the Civil War* (New York: Viking, 2006); Mark A. Noll, *The Civil War as a Theological Crisis* (Chapel Hill: University of North Carolina Press, 2006); George C. Rable, *God's Almost Chosen Peoples: A Religious History of the American Civil War* (Chapel Hill: University of North Carolina Press, 2010). All consider the Methodist role in the conflict.

63. Ferguson, *Organizing to Beat the Devil*, p. 243.

64. Quoted in Hempton, *Methodism*, p. 151.

65. Saxton, *Rise and Fall of the White Republic*, p. 274.

66. *Denver Daily Rocky Mountain News*, May 17, 1862.

67. Bain, *Empire Express*, p. 116.

68. *WRMN*, June 27, 1862.

69. Ibid., July 25, 1862.

70. Kelsey, *John Evans*, pp. 126; Samuel D. Mock, "Colorado and the Surveys for a Pacific Railroad," *Colorado Magazine*, XVII (1940): 54-63.

Chapter 7

1. Lewis H. Garrard, *Wah-to-yah and the Taos Trail, or Prairie Travel and Scalp Dances, with a Look at Los Rancheros from Muleback and the Rocky Mountain Campfire* (Norman: University of Oklahoma Press, 1955), pp. 33-34.

2. West, *Way to the West*, pp. 13-50.

3. West, *Contested Plains*, pp. 97-194.

4. Horace Greeley, *An Overland Journey from New York to San Francisco in the Summer of 1859.* Edited by Charles T. Duncan (New York: Alfred A. Knopf, 1964), pp. 119-123; William Bent to

James W. Denver, October 5, 1859, in Leroy R. Hafen and Ann W. Hafen, editors, *Relations with the Indians of the Plains, 1857-1861* (Glendale: Arthur H. Clark Company, 1959), pp. 186-187. See also Roberts, "Sand Creek," pp. 85-88, and Margaret Coel, *Chief Left Hand, Southern Arapaho* (Norman: University of Oklahoma Press, 1981), pp. 82-109.

    5. William E. Unrau, "Prelude to War," *Colorado Magazine*, XLI (1964), 299-313; Roberts, "Sand Creek," pp. 90-102.

    6. Evans Interview, Banroft MSS, Folio II, p. 11.

    7. Kelsey, *John Evans*, pp. 120-124.

    8. Ibid., p. 124.

    9. Ibid.

    10. Chivington, "Footprints," *Rocky Mountain Christian Advocate*, November 6, 1889.

    11. Ruth Bordin, *Frances Willard: A Biography* (Chapel Hill: University of North Carolina Press, 1986), pp. 94-95, 255n, offers a brief sketch of O. A. Willard's short life. Details of his life are also presented in Carolyn De Swarte Gifford, editor, *Writing Out My Heart: Selections from the Journal of Frances E. Willard* (Urbana: University of Illinois Press, 1995). On March 3, 1860, Frances celebrated Oliver's decision to become a minister (p. 61). It is plain there, however, that the family was concerned about him. On July 3, 1862, he recorded that Oliver and his new bride, Mary Bannister (also Frances's best friend) had departed for Denver (p. 185). The reference to Mrs. Evans's evaluation of his preaching comes from Frances Willard's journal entry for October 27, 1893 (p. 386). She noted, "when he was 27 Mrs Gov. Evans of Denver Col. Said that she had heard the best speakers in England & America & her pastor Oliver Willard was equal to any one of them."

    12. *DRMN*, July 24, 1862.

    13. Evans to Dole, August 6, 1862, LR, Office of Indian Affairs, Upper Arkansas, NARA, RG 75.

    14. Evans Interview, Bancroft MSS P-L329, Folio II, p. 11.

    15. Evans to Dole, October 30, 1862, *Annual Report of the Commissioner of Indian Affairs for 1862* (Washington, DC: Government Printing Office, 1863), p. 376.

    16. Evans Interview, Bancroft MSS P-L329, Folio II, p. 11.

    17. Doreen Chaky, *Terrible Justice: Sioux Chiefs and U. S. Soldiers on the Upper Missouri, 1854-1868* (Norman: University of Oklahoma Press, 2012), pp. 131-142; Micheal Clodfelter, *The Dakota War: The United States Army Versus the Sioux, 1862-1865* (Jefferson, NC: McFarland & Company, Inc., 1998), pp. 35-67; Gary Clayton Anderson, *Little Crow: Spokesman for the Sioux* (St. Paul: Minnesota Historical Society Press, 1986); Gary Clayton Anderson and Alan R. Woolworth, eds. *Through Dakota Eyes: Narrative Accounts of the Minnesota Indian War of 1862* (St. Paul: Minnesota Historical Society Press, 1988); David A. Nichols, *Lincoln and the Indians: Civil War Policy & Politics* (Urbana: University of Illinois Press, 1978), pp. 65-118; Kenneth Carley, *The Sioux Uprisings of 1862* (St. Paul: Minnesota Historical Society Press, 1976); Jerry Keenan, *The Great Sioux Uprising: Rebellion on the Plains, August-September, 1862* (New York: DaCapo Press, 2003); Gustav Niebuhr, *Lincoln's Bishop: A President, a Priest, and the Fate of 300 Dakota Sioux Warriors* (New York: Harper One, 2014).

    18. Charles S. Bryant and Abel B. Murch, *A History of the Great Massacre by the Sioux Indians in Minnesota* (Cincinnati: 1863), pp. 46-49.

    19. Evans to Dole, February 26, 1863, LR, OIA, Colorado Superintendency, NARA, RG 75.

    20. Roberts, "Sand Creek," pp. 145-149; Unrau, "Prelude," pp. 309-310; Harry Kelsey, "Abraham Lincoln and American Indian Policy," *Lincoln Herald*, 77 (1975): 139-148. Ned Blackhawk,

Violence Over the Land: Indians and Empires in the Early American West (Cambridge, MA: Harvard University Press, 2006), pp. 215-219, gives Evans a generally favorable review in his dealings with the Utes.

21. Browne to John Palmer Usher, December 9, 1862, LR, OIA, CS, NARA, RG 75; Browne to Dole, February 4, 1863, LR, OIA, UA, NARA, RG 75; Dole to Browne, February 27, 1863; Browne to the editor of the *Rocky Mountain News*, March 31, 1863, quoting letters from the Interior Department, May 9, 1861, and from J. M. Edmunds, Commissioner of the General Land Office, May 13, 1861.

22. Evans to Dole, April 10, 1863, LR, OIA, UA, NARA, RG 75.

23. Hiram Pitt Bennet to Usher, April 14, 1863, LR, OIA, UA, NARA, RG 75; Benjamin F. Hall to Dole, May 24, 1863, LR, OIA, CS, NARA, RG 75; Case to Edmunds, March 13, 1863, LS, Bureau of Land Management, NARA, Denver, CO, RG 49.

24. Dole to Evans, May 18, 1863, LS, OIA, NARA, RG 75; Unrau, "Prelude," pp. 310-312.

25. Browne to Dole, June 6, 1863, LR, OIA, CS, NARA, RG 75.

26. Paul N. Beck, *Columns of Vengeance: Soldiers, Sioux, and the Punitive Expeditions, 1863-1864* (Norman: University of Oklahoma Press, 2008), pp. 50-152. A useful summary of the Sully and Sibley campaigns is found in Thom Hatch, *The Blue, the Gray & the Red: Indian Campaigns of the Civil War* (Mechanicsburg, PA: Stackpole Books, 2003), pp. 95-116. See also Utley, *Frontiersmen in Blue*, pp. 261-274.

27. Roberts, "Sand Creek," pp. 163-166.

28. Evans to Dole, June 24, 1863, LR, OIA, UA, NARA, RG 75.

29. Beck, *Columns of Vengeance*, pp. 153-173; Clodfelter, *Dakota War*, pp. 118-154.

30. Evans to Dole, December 22, 1863, Indian Letter Book.

31. Roberts, "Sand Creek," pp. 166-172.

32. Evans to Edwin M. Stanton, September 22, 1863; Evans to William H. Seward, September 22, 1863; Evans to Alexander W. Robb, September 22, 1863; Evans to Albert G. Boone and others, September 22, 1863; and Evans to Chivington, September 22, 1863, Indian Letter Book. See also Evans to Dole, October 14, 1863, *AR, CIA, 1863*, p. 240.

33. Evans to Colley, November 2, 1863, Indian Letter Book.

34. Kelsey, *John Evans*, pp. 132-134; Blackhawk, *Violence Over the Land*, pp. 215-216; *Evans Report*, University of Denver, pp. 28-29; Michael Burlingame, *With Lincoln in the White House: Letters, Memoranda, and Other Writings of John G. Nicolay, 1860-1865* (Carbondale: Southern Illinois University Press, 2006), p. 119. Harry Kelsey, "Background to Sand Creek," *Colorado Magazine* XLV (1968): 294-298, provides the best summary of Whiteley in Colorado.

35. Evans to Chivington, November 9, 1863, LR, OIA, CS, NARA, RG 75.

36. Evans to Dole, November 9, 11, 1863, Indian Letter Book; Statement of Robert North, November 10, 1863, *AR, CIA, 1863*, pp. 224-225. See Colin G. Calloway, "Arapaho Renegade: Robert North and the Plains Indians Wars," *Essays and Monographs in Colorado History* (Denver: Colorado Historical Society, 1985), pp. 1-20; "J. K." "Regretful Renegade: Robert North," *Wild West Magazine*, 24 (December 2011): 60.

37. *Denver Daily Commonwealth*, January 23, January 26, 1864. See also, Kelsey, *John Evans*, pp. 172-173. A fresh urgency was given to the railroad question in October 1863, when the Union Pacific launched a major effort to gain an advantage when it reorganized and set up operations in Omaha, Nebraska, with *intentions to move up the Platte River valley to the West*. There remained some issues, including a few that would require reforms in the Railway Act of 1862. See Maury

Klein, *Union Pacific: The Birth of a Railroad, 1862-1893* (Garden City, NY: Doubleday & Company, 1987), pp. 24-30, and Richardson and Farley, *Usher,* pp. 53-57. Secretary of the Interior John Palmer Usher and Commissioner of Indian Affairs William Palmer Dole, both had interests in the road.

38. Evans to Stanton, December 14, 1863, Indian Letter Book; also printed in *AR, CIA, 1864,* pp. 225-226.

39. Evans to Dole, December 20, 1863, LR, OIA, CS, NARA, RG 75.

40. *Santa Fe Weekly Gazette,* April 26, 1862; Rio Abajo Press, March 8, 1864. See John D. Miller to his father, April 3, 1862, "Fort Union, 1862," File 2, pp. 68-72, James West Arrott Collection, New Mexico Highlands University, Las Vegas, New Mexico. Miller gave the credit for the victory at Apache Canyon to Captain Samuel Cook of the First, who commanded one of the few mounted units in the fight. Colton, *Civil War,* pp. 77-78, reviews the contemporary criticism of Chivington's handling of the fight at Johnson's Ranch in favor of the leadership of Captain William H. Lewis and Captain Asa B. Carey, regulars who were attached to Chivington's command.

41. *Santa Fe Gazette* quoted in the *WRMN,* April 16, 1863.

42. Ibid.

43. Leavenworth to General E. V. Sumner, March 22, 1863, R. N. Scott, and others, editors, *War of the Rebellion, A Compilation of the Official Records of the Union and Confederate Armies.* 128 Volumes (Washington, DC: Government Printing Office, 1880-1901): Series I, XII, Pt. 2, pp. 172-173. For a careful review of Leavenworth's war experiences, see William E. Unrau, "The Civil War Career of Jesse Henry Leavenworth, *Montana, the Magazine of Western History,* 12 (Spring 1962): 74-83.

44. Not all Cheyennes were as understanding. See John Smith to Colley, November 9, 1863, LR, OIA, CS, NARA, RG 75.

45. C. W. Marsh to Chivington, August 29, 1863, Register of Letters Received, Department of Missouri, p. 23, USAC, NARA RG 393. For a summary of related events, see Roberts, "Sand Creek," pp. 173-183.

46. Enochs, "Clash of Ambition," pp. 60-65; Roberts, "Sand Creek," pp. 181-187.

47. Henry W. Halleck to John Schofield, September 5, 1863, *OR,* Series I, XXII, Pt. 2, 521-523. Halleck told Schofield that the delegate from Colorado Territory [Bennet] had advised him that "a Colorado regiment can very well be spared to re-enforce General Connor in Utah." Halleck added, "If so, it should be sent immediately."

48. Hervey Johnson to his sister, Sibyl, February 23, 1864, in William E. Unrau, editor, *Tending the Talking Wire: A Buck Soldier's View of Indian Country, 1863-1866* (Provo: University of Utah Press, 1979), p. 95. Johnson believed that Colonel William O. Collins, commander of the Eleventh Ohio Cavalry, would take command at Denver.

49. Curtis to Chivington, April 8, 1864; Mitchell to Colonel William O. Collins, April 7, 1864, Mitchell to Curtis, April 7, 1864, Chivington to AAG, Department of Kansas, April 9, 1864, Eayre to Chivington, April 18, 23, 1864, Chivington to Curtis, April 27, 1864, *OR,* Series I, Pt. 1, 880-882, Pt. 2, 85, 98, Pt. 3, 113, 218-219, 291. Curtis to Mitchell, April 7, 1864, Curtis Papers, IX, 188.

50. Roberts, "Sand Creek," pp. 218-225; Berthrong, *Southern Cheyennes,* pp. 174-185; Powell, *People of the Sacred Mountain,* I, 257-263.

51. Evans to Curtis, April 11, 1864, *AR, CIA, 1864,* p. 370.

52. Curtis to Mitchell, April 18, 1864, Curtis Papers, 205.

53. Eayre to Chivington, April 23, 1864, *OR,* Series I, XXXVI, Pt. 1, 880-882.

54. Downing to Chivington, April 20, 1864, *OR*, Series I, XXXIV, Pt. 3, 242.

55. Gerry to Sanborn, April 14, 1864, Colley to Evans, April 19, 1864, *OR*, Series I, XXXIV, Pt. 3, 167-168, 234.

56. Cook to George H. Stilwell, April 22, 1864, *OR*, Series I, XXXIV, Pt. 3, 262. See also Berthrong, *Southern Cheyennes*, pp. 181-182.

57. Curtis to Chivington, April 28, 1864, Curtis to Mitchell, April 28, 1864, Curtis Papers, IX, 222, 225.

58. Chivington to Mitchell (two letters), April 29, 1864, Curtis Papers, IX, 229.

59. *WRMN*, May 4, 1864.

60. Jacob Downing was an ambitious man who hated Indians and wanted Samuel Tappan's shoulder straps as lieutenant colonel. He was perhaps Chivington's most aggressive commander. Downing to Chivington, April 20, 21, 26, 27, May 2, 1864, *OR*, Series I, XXXIV, Pt. 3, 242, 250-252, 304, 314, 407. Downing relished telling the story of his torture of the Cheyenne chief. See *Denver Post*, December 31, 1903, *Denver Field and Farm*, December 19, 1891, "Chronicles of Frontier Days," *Inter-Ocean*, 5 (April 29, 1882): 276-277.

61. Chivington to Curtis, April 25, 27, 29, May 4, 13, 1864, Curtis to Chivington, April 27, 28, May 2, 16, 30, June 10, 1864, Curtis Papers, IX, 215, 220, 223, 225, 229, 240, 247, 251, 274, 282, 292, 348.

62. Eayre to Chivington, May 1, 1864, Parmetar to Curtis, May 17, 1864, Mitchell to Curtis, May 26, 1864, OR, Series I, XXXIV, Pt. 4, 101, 294, 334.

63. Evans to Curtis, May 28, 1864, *OR*, Series I, XXXIV, Pt. 3, 315.

64. Eayre to Chivington, May 19, 1864, *OR*, Series I, XXXIV, Pt. 1, 935.

65. Wolf Chief, quoted in Hyde, *Life of Bent*, p. 132. See also Bent to Hyde, March 26, April 12, 1906, George Bent-George Hyde Correspondence, Beinecke Library, Yale University, New Haven Connecticut; Bent to Hyde, George Bent Papers, Denver Public Library, Denver, Colorado; Alfred Gay and John W. Smith to George O'Brian, *OR*, Series I, XXXIV, Pt. 4, 460-462; Halaas and Masich, *Halfbreed*, pp. 118-119.

66. Most accounts, including Roberts, "Sand Creek," p. 238, have suggested that the Cheyennes attacked in force along the road between Fort Riley and Fort Larned, destroying property, stealing stock, and killing settlers. This was the view heard in much of the contemporary correspondence and newspaper accounts. Cheyennes did descend on Walnut Creek Ranch and order the ranch keeper to leave at once. They told Rath, who was married to a Cheyenne woman, that they intended "to kill all the whites they could find." When the Cheyennes left, they took his wife with them. Documents from Rath's later depredation claim are published in Ida Ellen Rath, *The Rath Trail* (Wichita: McCormick Armstrong Company, 1961), pp. 22-25, 44-54.

67. Larry C. Skogen, *Indian Depredation Claims, 1796-1920* (Norman: University of Oklahoma Press, 1996), pp. 156-178, offers a convincing analysis of both contemporary rumors and later depredation claims, and provides the quoted newspaper account cited here. For a list of contemporary reports, see Roberts, "Sand Creek," p. 798n. A more recent book that places more faith in the depredation claims is Jeff Broome, *Cheyenne War: Indian Raids on the Roads to Denver, 1864-1869* (Sheridan, CO: Aberdeen Books, 2013).

68. Chivington to Curtis, June 11, 1864, *OR*, Series I, XXXIV, Pt. 4, 318-319.

69. Evans to Curtis, May 28, 1864, Indian Letter Book.

70. Roberts, "Sand Creek," pp. 242-243. By this time, Governor Evans was firing letters to Curtis and to Dole on an almost daily basis.

71. Evans to Dole, June 8, 1864, Indian Letter Book.

72. Testimony of William Bent, *Senate Report No. 156, 39th Congress, 2nd Session, Report of the Joint Special Committee to Investigate the Condition of the Indian Tribes, With Appendix* (Washington: Government Printing Office, 1867), p. 73.

73. Evans to Stanton, June 14, 1864, Evans to Dole, June 14, 1864, Evans to Curtis, June 14, 1864, Indian Letter Book; Evans to Curtis, June 11, 1864, Curtis Papers, IX, 367; Maynard to Captain Joseph C. Davidson, June 11, 1864; J. S. Brown and Thomas Darrah to Evans, June 11, 1864, Chivington to Davidson, June 12, 1864, Brown, Darrah, and D. C. Corbin to Maynard, June 13, 1864, Maynard to Charlot, June 13, 1864, Reynolds to Chivington, June 15, 1864, Davidson to Maynard, June 19, 1864, *OR,* Series I, XXXIV, Pt. 4, 319-321, 330, 354-355, 462.

74. The extent of the panic the report caused is clear from both recollections and contemporary sources. See Mollie Dorsey Sanford, *Mollie: The Journal of Mollie Dorsey Sanford in Nebraska and Colorado Territories.* Edited by Donald F. Danker (Lincoln: University of Nebraska Press, 1959), pp. 187-188; Alice Polk Hill, *Tales of the Colorado Pioneers* (Denver: Pierson and Gardner, 1884), pp. 79-80. Hill wrote, "So great was the confusion incident to the fright, it is believed that one hundred Indians could have taken the town."

75. The Hungate Massacre remains a controversial topic in Colorado history, and it was certainly a rallying point for those who favored a major campaign against the Cheyennes and Arapahos. Although the killings were attributed to Arapahos by most—and as the result of a personal dispute with Isaac P. Van Wormer by some—the coroner's Inquest could only say that the Hungate family "came to their death by being feloniously killed by some person or persons unknown, but supposed to be Indians." See contemporary opinions in *Denver Commonwealth,* June 15, 22, 1864; Sarah Hively Journal, M356, Western History Collection, Denver Public Library; Henry Littleton Pitzer, *Three Frontiers: Memories and a Portrait of Henry Littleton Pitzer as Recorded by His Son, Robert Claibourne Pitzer* (Muscatine, IA: The Prairie Press, 1938), pp. 162-163; Ashley, "Reminiscences," pp. 74-75; Hill, "Letters," p. 246; Statement of Robert North, *AR, CIA,1864,* p. 228; Statement of Neva at the Camp Weld Conference, September 28, 1864, *Senate Report No. 26, 39th Congress, 2nd Session, Report of the Secretary of War, Communicating . . . a Copy of the Evidence Taken at Denver and Fort Lyon, Colorado Territory, by a Military Commission Ordered to Inquire into the Sand Creek Massacre, November, 1864* (Washington: Government Printing Office, 1867), p. 216.

76. Evans to Dole, June 15, 1864, Indian Letter Book.

77. McKenny to Charlot, June 15, 1864, *OR,* Series I, XXXIV, Pt. 4, 402-404.

78. Hill to his wife, June 19, 1864, Hill, "Letters," p. 249.

79. Evans to Curtis, June 22, 1864, Indian Letter Book; Curtis to Evans, July 5, 1864, Curtis Papers, X, 25.

80. Wallen to AG, Department of Missouri, June 20, 1864, *OR,* Series I, XXXIV, Pt. 4, 476.

81. Roberts, "Sand Creek," pp. 315-342, contains a detailed review of the statehood campaign and the parts played by Governor Evans and Colonel Chivington.

82. Carleton to Evans, June 26, 1864, *Condition of Indian Tribes, Appendix,* p. 186.

83. Proclamation to the Friendly Indians of the Plains, June 27, 1864, AR, CIA, 1864, p. 218; Colley to Evans, June 21, 1864, LR, OIA, CS, NARA, RG 75.

84. Testimony of William Bent, *Condition of Indian Tribes,* p. 98.

85. Kelsey, *John Evans,* pp. 140-171; Saxton, *Rise and Fall of the White Republic,* pp. 275, 283-285.

86. Chivington to Curtis, July 5, 1864, Curtis Papers, X, 14.

87. Ketcham to Evans, July 1, 1864, LR, OIA, CS, NARA, RG 75.

88. Ibid.

89. McKenny to Charlot, June 15, 1864, *OR*, Series I, XXXIV, Pt. 4, 402-404; Hardy to Wynkoop, June 29, 1864, Curtis to Chivington, July 7, 1864, Curtis Papers, X, 62, 29.

90. Evans to Curtis, July 16, Indian Letter Book.

91. "Charges and Specifications against Capt. James W. Parmetar, 12th Regt. Kan. Vols.," James W. Parmetar, Compiled Military Service Record, Adjutant General's Office, NARA, RG 94; Hyde, *Life of Bent*, pp. 134. A Kiowa account is found in James Mooney, *Calendar History of the Kiowa Indians, 17th Annual Report of the Bureau of American Ethnology* (Washington: Smithsonian Institution, 1898), pp. 313-314. See Coel, *Chief Left Hand*, pp. 192-194, for the Arapaho perspective. Roberts, "Sand Creek," pp. 265-269; 802-803n, provides a more detailed summary with documentation.

92. General Field Order No. 1, July 27, 1864, General Field Order No. 2, 1864, "Massacre of the Cheyenne Indians," *Senate Report No. 142, 38th Congress, 2nd Session, Report of the Joint Committee on the Conduct of the War.* Three Volumes (Washington: Government Printing Office, 1865): III, 75-76.

93. Curtis to Chivington, July 30, 1864, *OR*, Series I, XLI, Pt. 2, 483.

94. Curtis to Charlot, July 23, 1864, Curtis to Chivington July 30, 1864, Curtis to Evans, July 30, 1864, Special Field Order No 3, Department of Kansas, July 31, 1864, General Order No. 1, Headquarters, District of the Upper Arkansas, James H. Ford to Curtis, July 31, 1864, *OR*, Series I, XLI, Pt. 2, 379, 483-485, 491, 529.

95. Chivington to Curtis, August 8, 1864, *OR*, Series I, XLI, Pt. 2, 613-614.

96. Roberts, "Sand Creek," pp. 326-334.

97. Powell, *People of the Sacred Mountain*, I, 270-271.

98. Roberts, "Sand Creek," pp. 271-274.

Chapter 8

1. Ronald Becher, *Massacre Along the Medicine Road: A Social History of the Indian War of 1864 in Nebraska Territory* (Caldwell, ID: Caxton Press, 1999) is a detailed accounting of the August war in Nebraska. See also Leroy W. Hagerty, "Indian Raids Along the Platte and Little Blue Rivers, 1864-1865," *Nebraska History*, XXVIII (1947): 176-186, 239-260.

2. Chivington to Curtis, August 8, 1864, Curtis Papers, X, 128.

3. Evans to Curtis, August 8, 1864, Indian Letter Book.

4. Bent, *Life of Bent*, p. 140. Halaas and Masich, *Halfbreed*, pp. 126-127, underscore Bent's conviction that the conflict had entered a new phase with the August assaults on the Platte. For the first time, Cheyennes had joined their allies, the Lakota and Arapahos in an "indiscriminate war against whites," rather than retaliatory attacks for past wrongs or for plunder.

5. Joseph Kenyon to Samuel L. Barlow, August 8, 1864, Samuel Barlow Collection, Huntington Library, San Marino, California.

6. Kenyon to Barlow, August 12, 1864, Barlow Collection.

7. *Black Hawk Mining Journal*, August 15, 1864.

8. The Reverend Charles King was a charter member of the conference. He would later be removed because of rumors "which seriously affect his moral & ministerial standing & character."

In 1870, the conference accepted his withdrawal from the church. Graveley, "The Early Colorado Conference," p. 62.

9. Ibid., July 29, 1864, quoting a letter from Fort Lyon, dated July 19, 1864.

10. Ibid., August 8, 1864.

11. Evans to Stanton, August 10, 1864, *OR*, Series I, XLI, Pt. 2, 644.

12. *DRMN*, August 10, 1864.

13. *AR, CIA, 1864*, pp. 230-231.

14. Evans to Curtis, August 11, 1864, with endorsement of George K. Otis, *OR*, Series I, XLI, Pt. 2, 661.

15. Curtis to Evans, August 11, 1864, Curtis Papers, X, 139.

16. Curtis to Charlot, August 20, 1864, Curtis Papers, X, 165.

17. Raymond G. Carey, "The 'Bloodless Third' Regiment, Colorado Volunteer Cavalry," *Colorado Magazine*, XLI (1964): 279-298; Lonnie J. White, "From Bloodless to Bloody: The Third Colorado Cavalry and the Sand Creek Massacre, *Journal of the West*, VI (1967): 535-581.

18. Evans to Stanton, August 22, 1864, *OR*, Series I, XLI, Pt. 2, 809.

19. On August 23, 1864, the *Rocky Mountain News* launched its defense of Evans. It also indicated the extent of local fears when it observed, "We believe the Utes are friendly disposed *just now*. So were the Arapahoes and Cheyennes a little while ago. None of them are to be trusted."

20. Lincoln to Curtis, September 1, 1864, Roy P. Basler, editor, *The Collected Works of Abraham Lincoln*, 9 vols. (New Brunswick, NJ: Rutgers University Press, 1953): VII, 530.

21. *DRMN*, August 23, 24, 1864; Fitzjohn Porter to Barlow, August 27, 1864, Barlow Papers.

22. Tappan Diary, pp. 61, 68.

23. Dyer, *Snow-Shoe Itinerant*, p. 182.

24. Special Order No. 71, August 22, 1864, Special Order No. 76, August 29, 1864, District of Colorado, United States Army Commands, NARA, RG 393; Chivington to Curtis, August 23, 1864, Curtis Papers, X, 185; Curtis to Chivington August 24, 1864, Browne to Curtis, October 3, 1864, *OR*, Series I, XLI, Pt. 2, 843, Pt. 3, 596-597. On August 25, Curtis informed Chivington that in such cases "the final determination should be according to law which requires a review by [the] Department Commander," Curtis Papers, X, 198. See also Kenneth E. Englert, "Raids by Reynolds," *1956 Brand Book of the Denver Westerners*, ed. Charles S. Ryland (Boulder, CO: Johnson Publishing Company, 1957), pp. 151-168; Hoig, *Sand Creek*, pp. 70-72; Shaw, *True History*, pp. 39-47; Frank Hall, *History of the State of Colorado*, 4 vols. (Chicago: Blakeley Printing Company, 1889-1895): I, 313-316; Journal of John L. Dailey, 1864, September 5, 1864, p. 9, Western History Collection, Denver Public Library, Denver, Colorado; testimony of Joseph A. Cramer and T. G. Cree, *Sand Creek Massacre*, pp. 51, 191.

25. Porter to Barlow, August 27, 1864, Barlow Papers.

26. Testimony of Samuel E. Browne, *Condition of Indian Tribes*, p. 71.

27. *DRMN*, August 25, 26, 1864.

28. Kelsey, *John Evans*, pp. 158-159.

29. Evans to John Palmer Usher, September 23, 1864, Abraham Lincoln Papers, Manuscript Division, Library of Congress, Washington, DC, Microfilm Reel No. 82.

30. *DWMN*, August 31, 1864; Janet LeCompte, "The Indian War in Colorado—1864," Unpublished list in the papers of Gary L. Roberts.

31. Wynkoop to Evans, September 18, 1864, *AR, CIA, 1864*, pp. 233-235. Wynkoop's mission was a bold effort, perhaps even foolhardy and questionable by military standards. His own

account, written in 1876, is vital. See Edward W. Wynkoop, *The Tall Chief: The Autobiography of Edward W. Wynkoop*, ed. Christopher B. Gerboth (Denver: Colorado Historical Society, 1993), pp. 86-100. His account of his conference with the chiefs on the Smoky Hill is especially important for its insights.

32. Wynkoop to Chivington, September 19, 1864, LR, DK, USAC, NARA, RG 393. At the time of the Weld Conference Wynkoop was regarded as one of Chivington's favorites; after Sand Creek Wynkoop would become one of his harshest critics.

33. Chivington to Curtis, September 19, 1864, *OR*, Series I, XLI, Pt. 3, 261.

34. Chivington to Curtis, September 26, 1864, *OR*, Series I, XLI, Pt. 3, 399.

35. *DRMN*, September 28, 1864.

36. Testimony of Wynkoop, *Condition of the Indian Tribes*, p. 77.

37. *DRMN*, September 28, 1864.

38. *Black Hawk Mining Journal*, October 1, 1864.

39. *DRMN*, September 29, 1864.

40. Evans to Colley, September 29, 1864, *AR, CIA, 1864*, pp. 220-221.

41. Report of Evans, in ibid., p. 222.

42. Curtis to Chivington, September 28, 1864, *OR*, Series I, XLI, Pt. 2, 462.

43. Wynkoop to Curtis, October 8, 1864, LR, DK, AGO, NARA, RG 94.

44. Ibid.; Soule to Chivington, October 10, 1864, LR, DC, USAC, NARA, RG 393.

45. Bent to Hyde, September 26, 1905, April 2, 1906 (quoting Wolf Robe), January 29, 1913, Bent-Hyde Correspondence, Yale; Bent to Hyde, October 15, 1904, Bent Letters, HC; Hyde, *Life of Bent*, pp. 143-144; Blunt to Charlot, September 29, 1864, OR, Series I, XLI, Pt. 1, 818.

46. Evans to Curtis, September 29, 1864, Curtis to Evans, September 29, 1864, Curtis to O'Brian, September 29, 1864, Curtis to Mitchell, October 2, 1864, Curtis to Chivington, October 2, 1864, Curtis to Livingston, October 2, 1864, Curtis to Chivington, October 3, 1864, Curtis Papers, XI, 73, 74, 75, 79, 87, 89, 90. Volume XIII of the Curtis Papers is devoted entirely to the Price Campaign. See also Powell, *People of the Sacred Mountain*, I, 288-289.

47. Morse H. Coffin, *The Battle of Sand Creek*. Edited by Alan W. Farley (Waco, TX: W. M. Morrison, Publisher, 1965), pp. 5-9; Entry for October 10, 1864, Diary of Sergeant Henry Blake, 1864, A. A. Paddock Collection, Boulder, Colorado. See also, a photocopy of Blake's diary in the Raymond G. Carey Collection, University of Denver, Denver, Colorado. Blake's diary was also published in the *Boulder Daily Camera*, August 2, 1941. Nichols to Shoup, October 10, 1864, *DRMN*, October 10, 1864; Nichols to Chivington, October 11, 1864, Chivington to Nichols, October 14, 1864, Chivington to Curtis, October 15, 1864, *OR*, Series I, XLI, Pt. 3, 798-799, 876, 883.

48. Testimony of Wynkoop, Cramer, et al to Wynkoop, November 25, 1864, *Sand Creek Massacre*, pp. 91-92, 95; testimony of Wynkoop, *Condition of Indian Tribes*, pp. 75-77; Henny to Anthony, October 17, 1864, SO No. 4, DUA, *OR*, Series I, XLI, Pt. 4, 62; Anthony to AAG, DUA, November 6, 1864, "Massacre of Cheyenne Indians," pp. 70-71; J. E. Anthony, AAG, to Anthony, Henning to Anthony, November 4, 6, 20, 1864, Tappan to Anthony, November 22, 1864, FF2, No. 1, No. 2, No. 3, No. 4, No. 5, Scott J. Anthony Papers, History Colorado, Denver, Colorado. Anthony to AAG, DUA, November 25, 1864; RLR, DUA, DM, Vol. 359, pp. 62-63, USAC, NARA, RG, 393.

49. *Camp Douglas* (Utah) *Daily Union Vedette*, August 31, September 27, 1864. Captain Charles Hempstead of Connor's staff was the editor. Raymond G. Carey, "Colonel Chivington, Brigadier General Connor, and Sand Creek," *1960 Brand Book of the Denver Westerners*. Edited by Guy M.

Herstrom (Boulder: The Johnson Publishing Company, 1961), pp. 105-136, deserves credit for recognizing the importance of the Chivington-Connor connection.

50. Holladay to Stanton, October 15, 1864, *OR*, Series I, XLI, Pt. 3, 768.

51. Halleck to Connor, October 15, 1864, Connor to Halleck, October 17, 1864, Halleck to Connor, October 18, 1864, *OR*, L, Pt. 2, 1013-1015.

52. Connor to Chivington, October 22, 1864, *OR*, XLI, Pt. 3, 259.

53. Chivington to Curtis, October 26, *OR*, Series I, XLI, Pt. 4, 259.

54. Shoup to Chivington, October 24, 1864, LR, DK, USAC, NARA, RG 393.

55. Carey, "Bloodless Third," pp. 295-297.

56. Evans to Connor, October 24, 1864, *OR*, Series I, L, Pt. 2, 1036.

57. *DRMN*, November 16, 1864; Kelsey, *John Evans*, pp. 151-152, 303n.

58. John Evans, *Reply of John Evans of the Territory of Colorado to that Part Referring to Him, of the Report of "the Committee on the Conduct of the War," Headed "Massacre of Cheyenne Indians"* (Denver: n. p. 1865). The *Reply* was published in the *Denver Daily Rocky Mountain News*, September 12, 1865, *Black Hawk Mining Journal*, September 11, 1865, *Central City Miners' Register*, September 12, 1865. It was also published in *Condition of the Indian Tribes*, from which the quote is taken at p. 83. Evans made the same point at least three times in his *Reply*. He was anxious to distance himself from Chivington and Sand Creek.

59. Carey, "Chivington, Connor, and Sand Creek," pp. 125-132; Carey, "Bloodless Third," pp. 295-297. Chivington would later claim in "The Pet Lambs," May 18, 1890, that Connor pressed him about the location of the Indians he was after, but that he refused to tell him. "But I won't tell anybody," Connor supposedly protested, to which Chivington replied, "I will bet you don't."

60. Connor to Halleck, November 21, 1864, *OR*, Series I, XLI, Pt. 1, 908-910.

61. *Daily Union Vedette*, November 21, 1864. The *Rocky Mountain News*, November 19, 1864, expressed the view that if a winter campaign was found to be feasible, Connor would organize an expedition and "at the proper time" return to command it himself.

62. Evans to Curtis, November 23, 1864, Curtis to Evans, November 23, 1864, Curtis to Evans, November 24, 1864, Curtis Papers, XII, 242, 253, 258; Evans to Stanton, November 24, Curtis to Evans, November 24, 1864, LR, DM, 1865, C115 (Box 17), USAC, NARA, RG 393; Report of Evans, *AR, CIA, 1864*, p. 220; Lincoln to Curtis, September 1, 1864, *Collected Works, Lincoln*, VII, 530.

63. Chivington to Curtis, November 23, 1864, Curtis Papers, XII, 238.

64. Evans to Stanton, November 24, 1864, RLR, DUA, DM, Vol. 359 (October 1864-September 1865), pp. 62-63, USAC, NARA, RG 393.

65. *Northwestern Christian Advocate*, December 7, 1864.

66. Anthony to Curtis, November 16, 1864, *OR*, Series I, XLI, Pt. 1, 914.

67. Anthony to AAG, DUA, November 25, 1864, RLR, DUA, DM, Vol. 359, pp. 62-63, USAC, NARA, RG 393.

68. Report of Evans, *AR, CIA, 1864*, p. 220.

69. Henning to Anthony, November 20, 1864, Scott J. Anthony Papers, FF-2, No. 3, History Colorado.

70. Curtis to Henning, December 2, 1864, *OR*, Series I, XLI, Pt. 4, 751.

71. Curtis to Carleton, November 28, 1864, ibid., p. 709.

72. Curtis to Evans, December 5, 1864, ibid., pp. 771-772.

73. Lynn L. Perrigo, editor, "Major Hal Sayr's Diary of the Sand Creek Campaign," *Colorado Magazine*, XV (1938): 54. David H. Nichols interview, Box 2, Bancroft Collection, Historical Collections, University of Colorado, Boulder. Nichols said that Chivington was "justly unpopular with the soldiers."

74. A good summary of the march of the Third Colorado Regiment from Bijou Basin to Sand Creek is found in the letters of "W," published in the *Central City Miners' Register*, November 23, 26, 28, 1864. See also the testimony of John Prowers, *Sand Creek Massacre*, p. 107; Amy (Amache) Prowers interview, July 19, 1886, MSS P-L 198, Bancroft Collection; and Coffin, *Battle of Sand Creek*, pp. 15-17.

75. Testimony of J. M. Combs, *Sand Creek Massacre*, p. 115.

76. Testimony of Soule, ibid., p. 10.

77. Testimony of Soule, Cramer, Anthony, Lt. James D. Cannon, Lt. C. M. Cossitt, Lt. W. P. Minton, *Sand Creek Massacre*, pp. 13, 21, 46-48, 110, 147-153.

78. Samuel F. Tappan, unpublished autobiography. Kansas State Historical Society. Topeka, Kansas, p. 14.

79. Portions of five battalions were involved; none of them were at full strength.

80. Testimony of Cramer, *Sand Creek Massacre*, p. 41. Anthony would confirm that he was misled by Chivington.

81. Coffin, *Battle of Sand Creek*, pp. 18-19; "W" to editor, *Central City Miners' Register*, January 4, 1864.

82. Bent to Hyde, March 9, March 15, 1905, April 2, 14, 25, 30, 1906, August 2, 1913, October 23, November 7, 1914, January 20, 1915, Bent-Hyde Correspondence, Yale.

83. Statement of Little Bear, Hyde, *Life of Bent*, pp. 153-154.

84. Testimony of Lt. James Cannon, James Beckwourth, A. J. Gill, *Sand Creek Massacre*, pp. 68, 112, 179; testimony of Robert Bent, *Condition of Indian Tribes*, p. 96; *DRMN*, December 25, 1864; Coffin, *Battle of Sand Creek*, p. 19.

85. Testimony of Cramer, *Sand Creek Massacre*, p. 48.

86. Testimony of Luther Wilson, *Condition of Indian Tribes*, p. 67.

87. Testimony of Soule and Cramer, *Sand Creek Massacre*, pp. 13-14, 48-49.

88. Hyde, *Life of Bent*, p. 152.

89. Testimony of Beckwourth and David Louderback, *Sand Creek Massacre*, pp. 70, 137, 140.

90. Testimony of Louderback, *Sand Creek Massacre*, p. 135; Watt Clark, *Denver Times*, April 7, 1916.

91. Hyde, *Life of Bent*, pp. 152-154.

92. Andrew J. Templeton, "Life and Reminiscences of Andrew J. Templeton," unpublished manuscript, Pioneers Museum, Colorado Springs, Colorado.

93. Hyde, *Life of Bent*, pp. 152-153.

94. Powell, *People of the Sacred Mountain*, I, 301-305.

95. Howbert, *Memories of a Lifetime*, p. 125.

96. Testimony of Robert Bent, *Condition of Indian Tribes*, p. 96.

97. Testimony of Anthony, "Massacre of the Cheyenne Indians," p. 26.

98. Scott Anthony to Webb Anthony, December 1, 1864, *Condition of Indian Tribes*, p. 92.

99. Coffin, *Battle of Sand Creek*, p. 29.

100. Affidavit of Lt. Joseph Olney, *Condition of Indian Tribes*, p. 61; Private George M. Roan, Sergeant Lucian Palmer, and Corporal James J. Adams, *Sand Creek Massacre*, pp. 143, 145, 150, 151.

101. Hyde, *Life of Bent,* pp. 156-158.

102. Ibid., pp. 157-159.

103. Chivington to Curtis, November 29, 1864, *OR,* Series I, XLI, Pt. 1, 948-950.

104. Testimony of Roan, Palmer, Adams, and James, *Sand Creek Massacre,* pp. 142-146, 150-152; testimony of Miksch, *Condition of Indian Tribes,* pp. 74-75; Perrigo, "Sayr's Diary," p. 55.

105. Testimony of Smith and Anthony, "Massacre of Cheyenne Indians," pp. 10, 22-23; testimony of Beckwourth and Louderback, *Sand Creek Massacre,* pp. 71, 136; Coffin, *Battle of Sand Creek,* p. 28.

106. Testimony of Soule, *Sand Creek Massacre,* p. 28.

107. James E. DuBois in ibid., pp. 37-38.

108. Isaac Clarke, "Life of Isaac Clarke," pp. 40-43, Special Collections, Colorado College, Colorado Springs.

109. Chet and Kim Brackett, *Chet's Reflections: Into the Sagebrush Sea* (Privately Printed, 2014), pp. 19-20.

110. Anthony to Lt. A. Hallowell, AAAG, District of Upper Arkansas, December 2, 1864, Curtis Papers, XII, 282; Dailey Diary, pp. 71-72.

111. Dailey Diary, pp. 72-74; Shoup to Maynard, December 6, 1864, Shoup to Chivington, December 7, 1864, "Massacre of Cheyenne Indians," pp. 50-51; Anthony to his brother, December 28, 1864, Anthony Papers, FF-2, No 6, HC.

112. These figures are based upon an analysis in progress, taking into account, the reports of George Bent, Edmond Guerrier, the records of killed and wounded from military sources, and Cheyenne and Arapaho genealogies from multiple sources.

Chapter 9

1. *DRMN,* December 17, 1864.

2. *CCMR,* December 9, 1864.

3. *Black Hawk Mining Journal [BHMJ],* December 9, 1864.

4. *DRMN,* December 9, 1864.

5. Report of Captain Theodore Cree, December 6, 1864, *OR,* Series I, XLI, Pt. 1, 959.

6. Stephen S. Harding to John W. Wright, December 9, 1864, published anonymously in the *New York Herald,* December 26, 1864.

7. Roberts, "Sand Creek," pp. 163-166, 334-338.

8. Chivington to Curtis, December 16, 1864, *OR,* Series I, SLI, Pt. 1, 948-950; Chivington to Curtis, December 20, 1864, Chivington, CMSR, VA, NARA, RG 15.

9. Extract of a private letter from an officer of the first Colorado Cavalry, dated December 16, 1864, with Slough to Stanton, December 31, LR, General File, AGO, 2694-S-1864, NARA, RG 94.

10. Tappan to Anthony, December 10, 1864, Anthony to Cramer, December 11, 1864, Letters Received of 1st Lieutenant Joseph Cramer, 1st Colorado Volunteer Cavalry, 1864-1866, Gordon S. Chappell Collection, Oakland, CA; testimony of Captain Theodore S. Cree, *Sand Creek Massacre,* pp. 190-191.

11. Captain Henry Booth to J. E. Tappan, December 14, 1864, RLR, DUA, DM, USAC, Vol 359, p. 107, NARA, RG 393.

12. Soule to Wynkoop, December 14, 1864, presented in full in Gary L. Roberts and David Fridtjof Halaas, "Written in Blood: The Soule-Cramer Sand Creek Massacre Letters," *Colorado Heritage* (Winter 2001), pp. 25-27.

13. Tappan Diary, pp. 16-18, 69.

14. Cramer to Wynkoop, December 19, 1864, Roberts and Halaas, "Written in Blood," pp. 27-29.

15. *DRMN,* December 1, 12, 13, 22, 28, 29, 1864, January 4, 11, 1865.

16. *Auburn* (New York) *Advertiser and Union,* December 28, 29, 1864.

17. Edward Estill Wynkoop, "Edward Wanshear Wynkoop," unpublished manuscript, p. 77, File nos. 2-3, Edward W. Wynkoop Collection, Fray Angelico Chavez History Library, Palace of the Governors, Santa Fe, NM. See also Kraft, *Ned Wynkoop,* pp. 136-138.

18. Testimony of Wynkoop, *Sand Creek Massacre,* p. 92; Hiram Pitt Bennet, *Hiram Pitt Bennet: Pioneer, Frontier Lawyer, Politician.* Edited by Liston E. Leyendecker (Denver: Colorado Historical Society, 1988), pp. 99-101.

19. Chaffee to Bennet, January 10, 1865, James A. Hardie to Halleck, December 11, 1865, Halleck to Curtis, January 11, 1865, "Massacre of Cheyenne Indians," p. 74.

20. Bennet, *Pioneer, Lawyer, Politician,* pp. 101-102.

21. Bennet to Slough, January 30, 1865, Western Americana Collection, Yale University Library, New Haven, CN.

22. Chaffee to McLain, January 8, 1865, *DRMN,* March 29, 1865.

23. *Congressional Globe,* 38th Congress, 2nd Session, Pt. 1, 158.

24. Ibid., p. 173.

25. Ibid., pp. 250-256.

26. Ibid.

27. Bennet to Slough, January 30, 1865, Western Americana Collection, Yale; *Congressional Globe,* 38th Congress, 2nd Session, Pt. 1, 1336.

28. Richardson and Farley, *Usher,* pp. 74-79; Kelsey, *John Evans,* pp. 162-163; Evans to Simpson, December 13, 1864, Simpson Papers, Library of Congress.

29. *Congressional Globe,* 38th Congress, 2nd Session, Pt. 1, 250-254.

30. J. W. Wright, *Chivington Massacre of Cheyenne Indians* (Washington: Gideon & Pearson, 1865), pp. 5-6.

31. The Evans letters to Lincoln, dated March 6, 1865, and to Ashley, dated March 14, 1865, are found in the Lincoln Papers, LC, Reel 93. See also Lincoln to Evans, March 16, 1865, Basler, *Collected Works of Lincoln,* VIII, 356.

32. Richardson and Farley, *Usher,* pp. 80-81.

33. The Joint Committee on the Conduct of the War was a powerful congressional committee chaired by Benjamin Franklin Wade. For a review of its activities see Bruce Tap, *Over Lincoln's Shoulder: The Committee on the Conduct of the War* (Lawrence: University Press of Kansas, 1998). Sand Creek receives short shrift in this book, less than a paragraph on p. 232. Roberts, "Sand Creek," pp. 498-513, provides a more detailed look at the committee's investigation of Sand Creek and of the consequences of its conclusions.

34. Testimony of Evans, "Massacre of Cheyenne Indians," pp. 42-43.

35. "Massacre of Cheyenne Indians," pp. iii-iv.

36. Ibid.

37. Usher to Johnson, May 15, 1865, LS, OSI, ID, M-21, Roll 5, NARA, RG 48.

38. Ashley to Seward, May 22, 1865, Applications and Recommendations for Office, Department of State, NARA, RG 59.

39. Bradford to Andrew Johnson, May 22, 1865, in ibid.

40. *DRMN*, June 12, 13, 1865; Evans to Slough, June 14, 1865, William Gilpin Papers, Chicago Historical Society.

41. Wynkoop's report and supporting affidavits were published in "Massacre of Cheyenne Indians," pp. 81-93; *Sand Creek Massacre*, pp. 122-132; and *Condition of Indian Tribes*, pp. 57-64.

42. Anthony to Moonlight, January 21, 1865, published in *DRMN*, February 1, 1865; Anthony to his brother December 30, 1864, Scott J. Anthony Papers (FF-2, No. 6), History Colorado.

43. Curtis to Moonlight, January 11, 1865, Moonlight to Curtis, January 12, 1865, Curtis Papers, XIV, 102, 107; Moonlight to General Grenville Mellon Dodge, February 13, 1865, "Massacre of Cheyenne Indians," p. 95; Moonlight to Tappan, February 12, 1865, *Sand Creek Massacre*, pp. 3-4.

44. *DRMN*, February 19, 1865.

45. Tom Bensing, *Silas Soule: A Short Eventful Life of Moral Courage* (Indianapolis, IN: Dog Ear Publishing, 2012) is the most detailed accounting of Silas Soule's life and adds new information about the events of early 1865. He was placed in a very difficult position, with responsibilities to supervise martial law as declared by Colonel Moonlight, to locate and seize government properties in local businesses, and to investigate stock, buffalo robes, and other items taken at Sand Creek. Denver was full of disgruntled Third Regiment veterans whose pay had been suspended by Congress, and they frequently were troublesome. Cramer's story is less well known. See Roberts and Halaas, "Written in Blood," pp. 30-32, and Roberts, "Sand Creek," pp. 486-497.

46. Wynkoop to Cramer, April 9, 1865, Cramer Letters.

47. See, especially, the Deposition of Lipman Meyer, *Sand Creek Massacre*, pp. 184-187, which Chivington introduced into evidence after Soule's death. It accused Soule of cowardice, theft, and drunkenness. The maneuver was seen as a shoddy attempt to blacken the character of Captain Soule and did not help Chivington's case.

48. This committee had a broader commission than simply investigating Sand Creek. Its object was to review the condition of the Indian tribes and to make recommendations concerning policy changes. It not only visited Sand Creek and Denver, but it also traveled to other locations in the West and Southwest. The committee's travels are covered in Clarissa P. Fuller, editor, "Letter of Senator Doolittle to Mrs. L. F. S. Foster, March 7, 1881," *New Mexico Historical Review*, XXVI (1951): 148-158; Gary L. Roberts, editor, "Condition of the Tribes, 1865: The McCook Report—A Military View," *Montana, The Magazine of Western History*, XXIV (January 1974): 14-25; Lonnie J. White, editor, *Chronicle of a Congressional Journal: The Doolittle Committee in the Southwest, 1865* (Boulder, CO: Pruett Publishing Company, 1975); and Donald Chaput, "Generals, Indian Agents, Politicians: The Doolittle Survey of 1865," *Western Historical Quarterly*, 3 (1972): 269-282.

49. Leach to Cramer, June 20, 1865, Cramer Letters.

50. John M. Chivington, *To the People of Colorado: Synopsis of the Sand Creek Investigation* (Denver: Byers and Dailey, 1865).

51. Testimony of Willard, *Condition of Indian Tribes*, p. 70; *Atchison Daily Free Press*, June 26, 1866. The "Statement of the Preachers of Colorado," April 7, 1865, was published in the *Central Christian Advocate* (St. Louis), July 26, 1865. It was erroneously reported as an official document of the Colorado Conference, which led the paper to "take great pleasure" in publishing a vindication of Chivington. The *Northwestern Christian Advocate*, September 27, 1865, challenged the statement as a product of the conference and described it as "a private paper signed by some members of the conference." The statement was also printed in the *Atchison Daily Free Press*, June 26,

1866, as part of a letter written to the paper by Chivington. The ministers signing the document included O. A. Willard, presiding elder of the Denver District, Colorado Conference; George Richardson, pastor, First M. E. Church, Denver; John Cree, agent of the American Bible Society, Colorado Territory; B. T. Vincent, pastor, St. Paul's M. E. Church, Central City; O. P. McMains, pastor, M. E. Church, Black Hawk; Charles H. Kirkbride, preacher in charge, Nevada Circuit, Colorado Conference. The *Colorado Weekly Chieftain* (Pueblo), June 11, 1868, was still saying that Chivington was "endorsed by the entire Methodist conference of Colorado."

52. Kingsley to Simpson, June 20, 1865, Simpson Papers, LC.

53. *Northwestern Christian Advocate*, June 2, 1865. Henry Leach wrote Joe Cramer that while the Congressional Committee on the Condition of the Indian Tribes was in Denver, "Colfax and Ashley while here were under the Control of Evans and that Clique & Collier came down from Central with medicated paper for Colfax & kept close to him all the time so as to be handy. [Simeon] Whiteley nominated Colfax for President & took the occasion to say 'that Sand Creek was a good thing,' & that perjury of the blackest Kind had been committed to forestate [*sic*] opinion in Washington." Leach to Cramer, June 20, 1865, Cramer Letters.

54. Colfax to the editor, June 2, 1865, *Northwestern Christian Advocate*, June 28, 1865.

55. Gary L. Roberts, "Dennis Nelson Cooley, 1865-66," Kvasnicka and Viola, *Commissioners of Indian Affairs*, p. 99. Cooley replaced Dole. He was a close friend and associate of Harlan's. Dr. Anson Henry had been promised the post by Lincoln, but Lincoln's death meant choosing Dole's successor passed to Johnson and Seward. See Elbert F. Floyd, "Insights into the Personal Friendship and Patronage of Abraham Lincoln and Anson Gordon Henry, M. D.," *Journal of the Illinois Historical Society*, 98 (Winter, 2005-2006): 218-253. As late as July 19, 1865, Henry was claiming that Johnson had approved Lincoln's appointment of Henry five days earlier, which was after Cooley assumed the office. He was furious with Harlan. Mrs. Lincoln called Harlan's actions "contemptible." He was appointed governor of Washington Territory, but died in a shipwreck on the way to assume his post.

56. Harlan to Dole, June 22, July 5, 1865, Harlan to Stanton, July 6, 1865, Letters Sent, Indian Division, Vol. 5, pp. 262-263, 275, 278, NARA, RG 48.

57. *Central Christian Advocate*, July 12, 19, 1865; *Christian Advocate and Journal* (New York), July 20, 1865; *Northwestern Christian Advocate*, July 12, 19, 1865.

58. Seward to Evans, July 18, 1865, Evans Collection, HC.

59. Evans to Johnson, August 1, 1865, Evans to Seward, August 1, 1865, Simpson to Evans, August 4, 1865, Harlan to Evans, August 4, 1865, Evans Collection, HC; Salter, "Simpson and Patronage," pp. 222-223.

60. Evans to Harlan, August 1, 1865, August 14, 1865, State Department Territorial Papers, Colorado, No. 67, Folio No. 125, No. 69, Folio No. 128, M-3, NARA, RG 59; Evans to Washburne, Elihu Washburne Papers, Library of Congress; Evans to Simpson, June 28, 1865, Simpson Papers, LC. See also Clark, *Life of Simpson*, pp. 249-250, *Northwestern Evans Report*, pp. 82-83; Kelsey, *John Evans*, pp. 152-153; Kirby, "Thought of Simpson," pp. 243-248.

61. Slough to Andrew Johnson, August 7, 1865, Letters of Appointment and Recommendations of Abraham Lincoln and Andrew Johnson, 1861-1868, M-650, Roll 55, NARA, RG 59.

62. Clark, *Life of Simpson*, p. 250.

63. *Chicago Tribune*, July 26, 1865.

64. Quoted in Frederic Logan Paxson, *The Last American Frontier* (New York: Macmillan Company, 1924), p. 262.

65. *Daily Evening Traveler*, August 10, 1865.

66. *Washington Chronicle*, July 21, 1865.

67. John Evans, *Reply of Governor Evans of the Territory of Colorado to That Part Referring to Him, of the Report of the Committee on the Conduct of the War, Headed "Massacre of Cheyenne Indians"* (Denver: n. p., 1865). The three leading newspapers in Colorado printed his reply, and it was also published in *Condition of Indian Tribes*, pp. 78-93.

68. *Chicago Tribune*, quoted in *BHMJ*, October 14, 1864.

69. *Central Christian Advocate*, quoted in ibid.; *Northwestern Christian Advocate*, December 27, 1865.

70. *Atchison Freedom's Champion*, August 24, 1865.

71. Ibid., October 5, 1865.

72. *BHMJ*, September 19, 1865, quoted in *Atchison Freedom's Champion*, October 5, 1865.

73. *WRMN*, September 13, 20, 1865.

74. *BHMJ*, September 19, 1865.

75. *Atchison Freedom's Champion*, October 5, 1865.

76. Evans to Stephen Decatur, November 4, 1865, *DRMN*, November 5, 1865.

77. Roberts, "McCook Report," pp. 14-25. McCook also provided an interview for the *Atchison Freedom's Champion*, August 17, 1865.

78. Fuller, "Doolittle Letter," pp. 156-157.

79. Report of the Judge Advocate General in the Case of John M. Chivington, First Colorado Cavalry, Record Book, Vol. 17, pp. 424-434, JAG Office, NARA, RG 153.

80. Roberts, "McCook Report," p. 21.

81. *Atchison Weekly Champion*, August 17, 1865.

82. Roberts, "Sand Creek," pp. 619-634; Kelsey, *John Evans*, pp. 155-165.

83. Amos Steck was the first president of the Board of Trustees for the Colorado Seminary, created in March 1864. Henry C. Leach, a Baptist, was one of the first men to report the Sand Creek affair. He ran for the Territorial Council, Second District, on the Union Administration Ticket. Even the *DRMN*, September 9, 1865, wrote of him, "Henry C. Leach is a gentleman well known by our citizens and his sterling qualities as an honorable, upright man, induced the Convention to nominate him for the office of Councilman. All men are liable to err, but we do not think that Mr. Leach's errors will detract from his worthily filling the position for which he has been chosen." On October 31, the same paper listed him as one of the "defectors" from the regular Union Administration ticket. By November 14, 1865, he was grouped with Tappan, Wynkoop, Bennet, Bradford, General Slough, and others as "Indian lovers." In fact, as early as June, Leach was already working against Chivington and Evans. He was also in contact with Lieutenant Cramer. In the winter of 1866-1867, he was named the first president of the Young Men's Christian Association in Colorado.

84. Elmer Ellis, "Colorado's First Fight for Statehood, 1865-1868," *Colorado Magazine*, VIII (January 1931): 23-30; Leroy R. Hafen, "Steps to Statehood in Colorado," *Colorado Magazine*, III (1926): 97-110.

85. Roberts, "Sand Creek," pp. 632-635.

86. *Congressional Globe*, 39th Congress, 1st Session, Pt. 3, 2135-2136.

87. *DRMN*, April 6, 1866. Leach eventually left Colorado. He died in Boston in 1906. At the time of his death, the *Castle Rock Journal*, April 20, 1906, reported that Leach had been president of the Colorado Territorial Council, "to whose efforts was largely due the vetoing by President Andrew Johnson of the first bill admitting Colorado as a state."

88. *Governor's Message Delivered to the Territorial Legislature of Colorado in Joint Convention, Friday, Jan. 5th, 1866* (Denver: Byers & Dailey, 1866), pp. 6-7.

89. Cummings to Seward, quoted in Lamar, *Far Southwest*, p. 226. See also Eugene Berwanger, *The Rise of the Centennial State: Colorado Territory, 1861-76* (Urbana: University of Illinois Press, 2007), pp. 41-55.

Chapter 10

1. Carwardine, "Methodist Politics and the Coming of the Civil War," p. 598. See also Gienapp, *Origins of the Republican Party,* passim, which traces the role of Methodists in the political maneuverings that led to the war. Methodists had become a divisive force in the impending crisis from the 1844 split over slavery.

2. Clark, *Life of Simpson*, pp. 248-258; Ferguson, *Organizing to Beat the Devil*, pp. 244-295.

3. John D. McDermott, *Circle of Fire: The Indian War of 1865* (Mechanicsville, PA: Stackpole Books, 2003), pp. 1-14; Jeffrey Ostler, *The Lakotas and the Black Hills: The Struggle for Sacred Ground* (New York: Viking, 2010), pp. 49-53; Bob Drury and Tom Clavin, *The Heart of Everything That Is: The Untold Story of Red Cloud, An American Legend* (New York: Simon & Schuster, 2013), pp. 190-199; Doreen Chaky, *Terrible Justice: Sioux Chiefs and U.S. Soldiers on the Upper Missouri, 1854-1868* (Norman: University of Oklahoma Press, 2012), pp. 241-258; Utley, *Frontiersmen in Blue,* pp. 300-301.

4. Bent, *Life of Bent*, pp. 164-168; Halaas and Masich, *Halfbreed*, pp. 155-180; Powell, *People of the Sacred Mountain*, I, 311-322. An essential work for understanding the role of the Dog Soldiers is Jean Afton, David Fridtjof Halaas, and Andrew E. Masich, with Richard N. Ellis, *Cheyenne Dog Soldiers: A Ledgerbook History of Coups and Combat* (Niwot, CO: Colorado Historical Society and the University Press of Colorado, 1997).

5. Porter to Barlow, January 11, 1864 [Content indicates that this should be 1865], C. S. S. Maberley to Barlow, January 12, 1865, Barlow Collection.

6. Paul A. Malkoski, editor, *This Soldier Life: The Diaries of Romine H. Ostrander, 1863 and 1865, in Colorado Territory* (Denver: Colorado Historical Society, 2006), pp. 71, 76, 80, 82-83, 88. On January 19, 1865, Ostrander wrote of Moonlight that he was ferreting out individuals who had had "a good thing" for the past two or three years, "making money out of our dear old Uncle, when his back was turned." He wrote that Moonlight "has found out more . . . since he has been here than Chivington would have done for a year to come."

7. McDermott, *Circle of Fire,* pp. 158-169; David E. Wagner, *Patrick Connor's War: The 1865 Powder River Indian Expedition* (Norman, OK: Arthur H. Clark Company, 2010), pp. 261-268; Richard N. Ellis, *General Pope and U.S. Indian Policy* (Albuquerque: University of New Mexico Press, 1970), pp. 87-115; Micheal Clodfelter, *The Dakota War: The United States Army Versus the Sioux, 1862-1865* (Jefferson, NC: McFarland & Company, 1998), pp. 214-215.

8. Utley, *The Indian Frontier,* p. 95.

9. Samuel A. Kingman, "Diary of Samuel A. Kingman at Indian Treaty of 1865," *Kansas Historical Quarterly*, I (1932): 442-450; Powell, *People of the Sacred Mountain*, I, 396-403; Halaas and Masich, *Halfbreed*, pp. 204-213; Roberts, "Sand Creek," pp. 562-566.

10. Berthrong, *Southern Cheyennes*, pp. 245-265.

11. Critical sources for following the place of Sand Creek in the public policy debate include Mardock, *Reformers*; Prucha, *Policy in Crisis*; Robert H. Keller, Jr., *American Protestantism and*

United States Indian Policy, 1869-82 (Lincoln: University of Nebraska Press, 1983); and C. Joseph Genetin-Pilawa, *Crooked Paths to Allotment: The Fight over Federal Indian Policy after the Civil War* (Chapel Hill: University of North Carolina Press, 2012); Linda K. Kerber, "The Abolitionist Perception of the Indian," *Journal of American History,* LXII (1975): 271-295. Important contemporary examples of various approaches by reformers and critics of reform include Henry Benjamin Whipple, *Lights and Shadows of a Long Episcopate: Being Reminiscences and Recollections of the Right Reverend Henry Benjamin Whipple, D.D., LL.D., Bishop of Minnesota* (New York Macmillan Company, 1899), pp. 535-538 (written originally as part of a report in 1868); Francis A. Walker, *The Indian Question* (Boston: James R. Osgood and Company, 1874); George W. Manypenny, *Our Indian Wards* (Cincinnati: Robert Clark and Company, 1880); Helen Hunt Jackson, *A Century of Dishonor* (Boston: Roberts Brothers, 1886); Nelson Miles, *Personal Recollections* (Chicago: Werner Company, 1896); Lydia Maria Child, "The Indians," *The Standard,* I (May 1870): 1-6; Elliot Coues, "The Western Sphynx: An Analysis of Indian Traits and Tendencies," *The Penn Monthly,* 10 (March 1879): 180-193. There is also a substantial literature of recollections by Coloradans, both pro-Sand Creek and anti-Sand Creek.

12. Prucha, *Great Father,* I, 485-488; Chaput, "Doolittle Survey," pp. 269-282; Harry Kelsey, "The Doolittle Report of 1867: Its Preparations and Shortcomings," *Arizona and the West,* 17 (1975): pp. 107-120.

13. John H. Monnett, *Where a Hundred Soldiers Were Killed: The Struggle for the Powder River Country in 1866 and the Making of the Fetterman Myth* (Albuquerque: University of New Mexico Press, 2008); Robert M. Utley, *Frontier Regulars: The United States Army and the Indian, 1866-1890* (New York: Macmillan Company, 1963); pp. 93-110; J. W. Vaughn, *Indian Fights: New Facts of Seven Encounters* (Norman: University of Oklahoma Press, 1966), pp. 14-90.

14. William Y. Chalfant, *Hancock's War: Conflict on the Southern Plains* (Norman: Arthur H. Clark Company, 2010).

15. Prucha, *Great Father,* I, 488-496; Douglas C. Jones, *The Treaty of Medicine Lodge: The Story of the Great Treaty Council as Told by Eyewitnesses* (Norman: University of Oklahoma Press, 1966); Henry M. Stanley, "A British Journalist Reports the Medicine Lodge Peace Councils of 1867," *Kansas Historical Quarterly,* XXXIII (1967): 249-320; Chaky, *Terrible Justice,* pp. 341-359.

16. William E. Unrau, "Nathaniel Green Taylor, 1867-1869," Kvasnicka and Viola, *Commissioners of Indian Affairs,* pp. 116-117.

17. Ibid., pp. 117-120; Genetin-Pilawa, *Crooked Paths,* pp. 67-72.

18. Genetin-Pilawa, *Crooked Paths,* pp. 71-72.

19. Prucha, *Great Father,* pp. 494-496.

20. Powell, *People of the Sacred Mountain,* I, 507-619; Berthrong, *Southern Cheyennes,* pp. 318-371. See also Stan Hoig, *The Battle of the Washita* (Garden City, NY: Doubleday & Company, 1976), and Jerome A. Greene, *Washita: The U.S. Army and the Southern Cheyennes, 1867-1869* (Norman: University of Oklahoma Press, 2004).

21. *AR, CIA, 1868,* p. 12; *Kansas State Record* (Topeka), August 21, 1868.

22. See Cora Daniels Tappan and Wendell Phillips in *National Anti-Slavery Standard,* May 29, 1869, and June 12, 1869. See also Kerber, "Abolitionist Perception," pp. 288-295; Lydia Maria Childs, *Appeal for the Indian* (New York: William P. Tomlinson, 1868); and Mardock, *Reformers,* pp. 47-128. During this period General Sherman mounted a strong defense of the military and made every effort to distance the regular army from Sand Creek. He insisted, "We don't want to exterminate or even fight them. At best it is an inglorious war, not apt to add much to our fame or

personal comfort.... To accuse us of inaugurating or wishing such a war, is to accuse us of a want of common sense." Quoted in *Letter of the Secretary of War Communicating... Information in Relation to the Late Indian Battle on the Washita River*. Senate Executive Document No. 18, 40th Congress, 3rd Session (Washington: Government Printing Office, 1869), pp. 4-5.

23. Powell, *People of the Sacred Mountain*, I, 532-619; Hyde, *Life of Bent*, pp. 328-340.

24. Utley, *Frontier Regulars*, pp. 236-295.

25. Belich, *Replenishing the Earth*, pp. 336-349; Osterhammel, *Transformation of the World*, pp. 331-346, 368-374, 826-836; Heather Cox Richardson, *West from Appomattox: The Reconstruction of America after the Civil War* (New Haven: Yale University Press, 2007), pp. 160-178; Bain, *Empire Express*, pp. 341-390; Saxton, *Rise and Fall of the White Republic*, pp. 284-288; Wineapple, *Ecstatic Nation*, pp. 506-593; White, *Fatal Environment*, pp. 209-532; Elliott West, "Conclusion," Robert K. Sutton and John A. Latschar, editors, *American Indians and the Civil War: Official National Park Service Handbook* (Washington, DC: National Park Service, 2014), pp. 180-193.

26. *Northwestern Christian Advocate*, June 21, 1865.

27. *Christian Advocate and Journal*, July 20, 1865.

28. *Northwestern Christian Advocate*, July 12, July 19, 1865.

29. Ibid., August 16, 1865.

30. Ibid., August 30, 1865.

31. Ibid., July 20, 1865.

32. Ibid., December 6, 1865.

33. Ibid., December 27, 1865.

34. *Central Christian Advocate*, July 26, 1865.

35. *Atchison Weekly Freedom's Champion*, June 26, 1866.

36. *New York Times*, July 29, 1865.

37. *Frank Leslie's Illustrated Newspaper*, February 1, 1868.

38. Whipple, *Lights and Shadows*, p. 137. Lincoln also told John Beeson essentially the same thing. See Mardock, *Reformers*, p. 13.

39. Ibid., p. 144.

40. *Congressional Globe*, 38th Congress. 2nd Session, January 13, 1865, Pt 1, 254.

41. Nichols, *Lincoln and Indians*, p. 197.

42. Ibid., pp. 196-206. In light of these attitudes, Nichols asked the question, "What could have broken the chain?" He concluded, "This is where the historian must view the situation as a historic tragedy rather than circumstances in which personal blame can be assigned."

43. Whipple to the Secretary of the Interior, February 23, 1861, Whipple to Thomas Galbraith, April 15, 1861, Henry Benjamin Whipple Papers, Minnesota Historical Society, Box 40, Letterbook 3. Yet Whipple always conceded that Indians were "savages" in his efforts at reform.

44. *Northwestern Christian Advocate*, March 2, 1866.

45. Ibid., May 9, 1866.

46. Ibid., October 31, 1866.

47. Ibid., July 3, 1867.

48. Ibid., July 31, 1867.

49. Ferguson, *Organizing to Beat the Devil*, pp. 287-390; Hempton, *Methodism*, pp. 178-201; Marty, *Righteous Empire*, pp. 137-196.

50. Hempton, *Methodism*, p. 155.

51. Robert H. Keller, Jr., *American Protestantism and United States Indian Policy, 1869-82* (Lincoln: University of Nebraska Press, 1983), pp. 54-58.

52. Barclay, *Methodist Missions*, III, 363-364.

53. *Journal of the General Conference of the Methodist Episcopal Church Held in Chicago, Ill., 1868* (New York: Carlton & Lanahan, 1868), pp. 236-237; and *Daily Christian Advocate*, May 26, 27, 1868.

54. Prucha, *Great Father*, I, 501-527; Genetin-Pilawa, *Crooked Paths*, pp. 73-111; Keller, *Protestantism and Indian Policy*, pp. 17-45; Mardock, *Reformers*, pp. 47-66; Fritz, *Assimilation*, pp. 56-86.

55. Genetin-Pilawa, *Crooked Paths*, pp. 56-93, offers a fresh and challenging view of Parker's career as well as insights into Grant's reasons for choosing him as Commissioner of Indian Affairs in 1869. See also Henry G. Waltmann, "Ely Samuel Parker, 1869-1871," Kvasnicka and Viola, *Commissioners of Indian Affairs*, pp. 123-133.

56. Keller, *Protestantism and Indian Policy*, pp. 32-35; Forbes, "Methodism and Policy," pp. 21-23.

57. Keller, *Protestantism and Indian Policy*, pp. 35-36. Forbes, "Methodism and Policy," p. 22, says that Keller "exaggerates" the inactivity of Methodist Episcopal activity in 1870, although "in comparative terms he is close to the truth." He says that Robert Lee Witner, in his "The Methodist Episcopal Church and Grant's Peace Policy: A Study of the Methodist Agencies, 1870-1882," unpublished Ph.D. dissertation (Minneapolis: University of Minnesota, 1959), p. 280, was more careful when he said, "During the period in which the peace policy was in effect, the Methodist Episcopal Church had long since lost the great interest it once had in Indian mission work, and it made little effort and spent little money to implement it or extend them."

58. Forbes, "Methodism and Policy," p. 22.

59. Keller, *Protestantism and Indian Policy*, pp. 36-38.

60. Ibid., p. 38.

61. Ibid., p. 55.

62. Ibid., pp. 55-56; Barclay, *Methodist Missions*, III, 355-356.

63. Keller, *Protestantism and Indian Policy*, pp. 70-71.

64. Witner, "Methodist Episcopal Church and Peace Policy," p. 181, quoted in Forbes, "Methodism and Policy," p. 23.

65. Barclay, *Methodist Missions*, III, 364.

66. Keller, *Protestantism and Indian Policy*, p. 173.

67. Quoted in Marzsalek, *Passion for Order*, pp. 399-400.

68. Ibid., p. 391.

69. Roger J. Ege, *Tell Baker to Strike Them Hard! Incident on the Marias, 23 Jan. 1870* (Bellevue, NB: Old Army Press, 1970).

70. *New York Times*, February 24, 1870.

71. An excellent summary of reform reaction to the incident is found in Mardock, *Reformers*, pp. 67-72. Lydia Maria Child, Samuel Tappan, and even William Lloyd Garrison joined reform newspapers in denouncing the incident, which, in turn, drew strong reactions from the military, which saw comparisons to Sand Creek misplaced. See Utley, *Frontier Regulars*, pp. 188-214.

72. Prucha, *Great Father*, I, 527-533.

73. Extract from the Report of Hiram Price, October 24, 1881, *AR, CIA, 1881*, in Prucha, *Documents of United States Indian Policy*, p. 155. See also Floyd A. O'Neil, "Hiram Price, 1881-85," Kvasnicka and Viola, *Commissioners of Indian Affairs*, pp. 173-178, and Prucha, *Great Father*, II, 721.

74. O'Neil, "Price," pp. 175-176; Prucha, *Great Father*, II, 246-252.

75. Quoted in Prucha, *Great Father*, II, 666.

76. Prucha, *Policy in Crisis*, pp. 222, 255-256, 305-309.

77. Tash Smith, *Capture These Indians for the Lord: Indians, Methodists, and Oklahomans, 1844-1939* (Tucson: University of Arizona Press, 2014), pp. 131-133; Noley, *First White Frost*, p. 204.

78. Smith, *Capture These Indians for the Lord*, pp. 133-153, provides a cogent and disturbing view of the marginalization of Indian Methodists between 1906 and 1918.

79. Ibid., pp. 154-186; Noley, *First White Frost*, pp. 213-230.

80. Smith, *Capture These Indians for the Lord*, p. 194. Smith's book is a model for future research on the history of Church relations with indigenous people.

81. Whipple, *Lights and Shadows*, p. 149.

82. Neibuhr, *Lincoln's Bishop*, p. xiv.

83. Quoted in Nichols, *Lincoln and Indians*, p. 199.

84. *Ibid.*, pp. 199-201.

85. Simpson, *Hundred Years of Methodism*, p. 281.

86. Salter, "Simpson and Patronage," p. 223.

87. Eastman, *Soul of the Indian*, p. 31.

88. Stephen Melvil Barrett, *Hoistah, An Indian Girl* (New York: Duffield and Company 1913), pp. 116-117. Hoistah was apparently Masikota (the manhao largely wiped out by cholera in 1849). Afterward she lived with Black Kettle's people.

89. West, "Another Vision," pp. 30-37. See also John Stands in Timber and Margot Liberty, *A Cheyenne Voice: The Complete John Stands In Timber Interviews* (Norman: University of Oklahoma Press, 2013), pp. 32-33, 158.

Chapter 11

1. Porter to Barlow, August 27, 1864, Barlow Collection.

2. "Notes concerning Gov. John Evans, given by Mrs. Evans and Mrs. Dickinson," Bancroft Collection, Western Historical Collection, University of Colorado Library, Boulder, Colorado.

3. *DRMN*, November 27, 1865.

4. Harney to Thomas Murphy, Superintendent of Indian Affairs, Atchison, Kansas, December 5, 1865, *Atchison Weekly Champion*, December 14, 1865.

5. *Chicago Tribune*, July 26, 1865.

6. Frank Hall, *History of the State of Colorado*, 4 vols. (Chicago: Blakeley Printing Company, 1889-1895): I, 356.

7. *DRMN*, March 16, 20, April 18, August 4 1866, January 9, 1867; *Nebraska City News*, August 25, 1866.

8. Henry M. Porter, *Autobiography of Henry M. Porter* (Denver: World Publishing Company, 1932), pp. 34-35.

9. Chivington explained his version of events most completely in a deposition taken in 1892 in support of a depredation claim for the loss of livestock to the Sioux Indians in 1867. Other depositions were offered in support of his version. David Street, an agent for Wells Fargo, was deposed on May 17, 1892, and gave a very different view of what happened. See *John M. Chivington v. The United States and the Sioux Tribe, Band, or Nation of Indians*, Indian Depredation Case File No. 3473, United States Court of Claims, NARA, RG 123.

10. *Annual Conference Minutes,* XVI (1866): 121. Bordin, *Frances Willard,* p. 255n, reports a story that the Reverend Willard accidentally shot a man during a skeet shoot and was so emotionally overwhelmed by it that he began drinking heavily. See also Gifford, editor, *Writing Out of the Heart,* pp. 229-231.

11. This account is drawn from P. Heffley to (?), February 25, 1869, Affidavit of William Fulton, April 18, 1892, Tappan to L. W. Colby, Assistant Attorney General, May 14, 1892, Tappan to W. H. H. Miller, May 21, 22, 26, 28, 1892 (all relating to the testimony of Porter, Street, and others), James R. Porter to Miller, June 22, 1892, Mary B. Willard (widow of Reverend Willard) to Tappan, July 2, 1892, David Street to Tappan, July 7, 1892. Undated statements regarding the testimony of Street and Porter, memoranda regarding the testimony of John A. Martin, a Denver merchant who had dealings with Chivington and Willard, and an undated report that presents Chivington's case and points of contradiction with Porter and Street are also available. All are found in the case file of *Chivington v. U.S.,* Court of Claims Section, Department of Justice, NARA, RG 205.

12. Palmer to Major H. G. Litchfield AAAG, DP (P110-1867), Department of the Platte, USAC, NARA, RG 393. Palmer called Chivington "the notorious Colonel Chivington of the Sand Creek massacre memory." See also Palmer to Miller, July 18, 1892 (two letters), *Chivington v. U.S.,* USCC, NARA, RG 123, and the *Omaha Daily Herald,* April 5, 1867.

13. *Nebraska City News,* July 7, 1866.

14. *Nebraska Statesman* (Lincoln), September 8, 1866.

15. *Richmond Whig,* November 13, 1866.

16. *Ebensburg* (Pennsylvania) *Democrat and Sentinel,* November 8, 1866.

17. *Omaha Daily Herald,* March 29, 1867.

18. *Nebraska Herald,* May 8, 1867; *DRMN,* May 10, 1867. See also, Cox-Paul, "Chivington," pp. 135-136.

19. *Des Moines Daily Iowa State Register,* May 16, 1867; *Omaha Republican,* May 17, 1867.

20. *DRMN,* June 20, 1867; Cox-Paul, "Chivington," p. 135.

21. Cox-Paul, "Chivington," p. 136.

22. Ibid., p. 135.

23. *Clearfield Republican* (Pennsylvania), May 2, 1867.

24. *Highland Weekly News,* July 11, 1867.

25. *Montana Post,* July 13, 1867.

26. *Harrisburg* (Pennsylvania) *Patriot,* January 20, 1868.

27. *Minutes of the Nebraska Conference of the Methodist Episcopal Church. Eighth Session. Held in Peru, Neb., April 2d—4th 1868* (Nebraska City: Nebraska Press, 1868), pp. 5, 10.

28. Probate Record A, pp. 384-302, Otoe County, Nebraska City, Nebraska. See Chivington to Hochstetter, February 4, 1869, Tappan to Colby, April 14, 1892 (in which he quotes a conversation between P. A. Snyder and Chivington wherein Chivington cited the estate as his reason for marrying his son's widow. Tappan to Colby, April 18, 19 (two letters), 20, 1892, CCS, DJ, NARA, RG 205.

29. *DRMN,* June 10, 1868.

30. *Nebraska City News,* May 29, 1868. The news spread widely, with the statement of Sarah's parents published in several papers. See, as examples, *Washington Evening Star,* June 8, 1868, *New York Times,* June 11, 1868, *Daily Eastern Argus* (Portland, Maine), June 12, 1868, *New Hampshire Patriot and State Gazette* (Concord), *Atchison Weekly Champion and Press,* June 18, 1868 (which questioned why he should still be "permitted to defile a pulpit with his contaminating presence").

31. *Nebraska City Daily Tribune,* November 12, 1903; Deposition of Almira Lull, September 20, 1895, Pension File, 31647, NARA, RG 15; Cox-Paul, "Chivington," p. 142.

32. *Nebraska City News,* May 28, 1868, *Omaha Herald,* quoted in the *Nebraska City News,* May 29, 1868.

33. Cox-Paul, "Chivington," p. 136.

34. Ibid., pp. 136-137.

35. *Nebraska City Daily Nebraska Press,* February 1, 1869.

36. Sarah Chivington to Sherman Williams, February 4, 1895, Widow's Pension File 41647, Department of Veterans Affairs, NARA, RG 15, Tappan to Colby, April 20, 1892, Case No. 3473, CCS, DJ, RG 205; Cox-Paul, "Chivington," pp. 136-137.

37. *Minutes of the Ninth Session of the Nebraska Annual Conference of the Methodist Episcopal Church Held in the First M. E. Church, Nebraska City, Beginning March 31, 1869* (Nebraska City: Price, Miller & Co., 1869), p. 8. Each year clergypersons are examined to determine if they are "blameless in their life and official administration." This is called "passing of character."

38. *Daily Nebraska Press,* March 31, 1869.

39. *Minutes of the Nebraska Conference of the Methodist Episcopal Church, Tenth Session, Held at Fremont, March 31, to April 2, 1870* (Omaha: Republican Stream Printing House and Book Bindery, 1870), p. 4.

40. Tappan to Colby, April 2, 5, 6, 8, 1892, citing documents from the grand jury and from the case file in Thomas Chivington's claim. CCS, DJ, NARA, RG 205.

41. Tappan to Colby, April 20, 1892, quoting from a letter from Mrs. Swetland to Sarah Chivington, ibid.

42. *Albany Evening Journal,* June 8, 1870.

43. Two sworn statements by Sarah Chivington, April 18, 1892, and statement by J. B. Lull, Sarah's father, April 18, 1892, *Chivington v. U.S.,* USCC, NARA, RG 123; Sarah Chivington to Colby, July 8, 1892, Chivington Collection, Denver Public Library; *Sarah A. Chivington v. John M. Chivington,* Case File, Records of the District Court, Otoe County, Nebraska; Dale, "Otoe County Pioneers," pp. 1561-1563; State of P. A. Snyder in Tappan to Colby, April 14, 1892, CCS, DJ, NARA, RG 205.

44. Statement of P. A. Snyder in Tappan to Colby, April 14, 1892, CSS, DJ, NARA, RG 205.

45. Deposition of William Clevenger, Justice of the Peace, April 14, 1892, quoting from the testimony of Isabella Chivington, Tappan to Colby, April 13 (two letters), 14, 16, 1892, ibid. See also the *Clinton County Democrat,* August 17, 1883, which reported that when Mrs. Chivington appeared in court, she had a black eye and bruised face. "For this brutal act, Chivington was arrested and bound over to court on charge of assault," the *Democrat* reported. "The forgiving nature of this woman he had so brutally wronged saved him from incarceration in prison, and before the sitting of a grand jury the case was dropped, on promise by him to pay what costs had accrued, but which costs to this day remain unpaid." Quoted in Cox-Paul, "Chivington," pp. 142-143.

46. *Lebanon Patriot,* August 24, 1883, quoted in Cox-Paul, "Chivington," p. 143.

47. *Clinton County Democrat,* August 17, 1883, quoted in ibid.

48. *Cleveland Plain Dealer,* August 24, 1883. Other details about the campaign are included in letters from Tappan to Colby, April 1, 13, 14, 16, 1892, ibid. One of the witnesses Tappan deposed said that Chivington approached him with the promise of helping a suitable candidate be nominated if he would put up the money. A candidate was found, and the informant provided the

money. When the delegates gathered, however, they nominated Chivington. See also *Denver Daily Times,* October 6, 1883.

49. *DRMN,* August 27, 1883.

50. Chivington had been contacted by Thomas F. Dawson, the secretary of the Colorado State Historical Society and editor of the *Denver Times,* in the spring. Dawson had sent him an article from the *Times* concerning Sand Creek. He had written Dawson on May 24, 1883. He reported himself in ill health, but promised to write an account of Sand Creek for Dawson at an early date. He mentioned his campaign, but also expressed an interest in attending the meeting of the G. A. R. and the reunion of Colorado soldiers at Denver, "if I can make arrangements to do so." He did not attend this gathering, which met in July.

51. *Denver Daily Times,* September 13, 1883.

52. Ibid., October 6, 8, 1883, August 25, 1886, January 27, 30, 1892, *Fort Collins Courier,* October 4, 1883, *Denver Tribune,* May 30, 1883, *DRMN,* August 20, June 30, 1884, January 1, October 7, 23, 1885, February 13, 1889, *Denver Republican,* September 14, 1883, October 5, 1894; John M. Chivington, "Battle of Sand Creek," MSS-28, History Colorado; Chivington, "The First Colorado Regiment," October 18, 1884, Bancroft Library; Chivington, "The Pet Lambs," *Denver Republican,* April 20-May 18, 1890; Chivington, "Footprints of Methodist Itinerants in Colorado," *Rocky Mountain Christian Advocate,* September 26, October 24, 31, November 7, 1889.

53. *Denver Daily Times,* January 22, March 17, 1884; *Chivington v. Colorado Springs, Co., IX Colorado Reports,* 597 (1886); Tappan to Aldrich, April 21, 30, 1892, CCS, DJ, NARA, RG 205; *DRMN,* March 24, 1884, *Salt Lake Herald,* February 12, 1884.

54. *DRMN,* August 20, 1884.

55. *DRMN,* July 3, September 13, 15, 1887; *Denver Republican,* July 3, 1887.

56. *Denver Republican,* July 3, September 13, 1887; *DRMN,* July 3, September 13, 15, 1887.

57. Papers in the matter of the estate of Francesco Gallo, deceased, March 8, 1892, Tappan to Aldrich, April 27, 1892, filed with *Chivington v. U.S.,* USCC, NARA, RG, 123.

58. Statement of E. L. Gallatin, January 8, 1900, Thomas F. Dawson Scrapbooks, History Colorado. The court papers from Arapahoe County are in Case No. 3473, CSS, DJ, NARA, RG 123.

59. Statement of Amy (Amache) Prowers, P-L 198, Bancroft Papers, Bancroft Library, University of California, Berkeley, California; Agnes Wright Spring, "Cheyenne Girl and White Man's Way," *Frontier Times,* 44 (August-September, 1970): pp. 32-33, 46.

60. Tappan to Colby, April 14, 1892, CCS, DJ, NARA, RG 205.

61. John M. Chivington, Widow's Pension File, Pension File No. 41647, Veterans Administration, NARA, RG 15; Adriance Collection, Box 1, FF8, DPL; Beardsley, *Echoes,* pp. 252-253; Campbell, *Chivington Record,* p. 282. The attending physician gave as cause of death, diarrhea, injury to the rectum, and indigestion. Craig, *Fighting Parson,* pp. 236-237, said that he died of cancer.

62. *DRMN,* October 8, 1894; Beardsley, *Echoes,* pp. 252-253: "Death of Brother Chivington," pp. 214-217.

63. Ferguson, *Organizing to Beat the Devil,* p. 332. This analysis is consistent with the arguments of Williams in *Religion and Violence,* and Rein, "Our First Duty."

64. Beardsley, *Echoes,* pp. 252-253. Beardsley, who met Chivington after the colonel returned to Colorado, became close to him and wrote of him, "he had a noble heart, and was generous to a fault."

65. Evans to Usher, September 23, 1864, letters to Lincoln, March 6, 1865, Evans to Ashley, March 14, 1865, Abraham Lincoln Papers, Microfilm reels No. 82 and No. 93, Library of

Congress; Evans to Seward, October 18, 1864, Indian Letter Book, Evans Collection; Evans to Seward, December 14, State Department, Territorial Papers, Colorado, CXVI, 61, NARA; Lincoln to Evans, March 16, 1865, Basler, *Collected Works of Lincoln*, VIII, 356; Kelsey, *John Evans*, pp. 151-152; Richardson and Farley, *John Palmer Usher*, pp. 79-80.

66. Clark, *Life of Simpson*, pp. 242-250. He recorded in his diary on the evening of Lincoln's inauguration that Johnson was drunk at the ceremony. Salter, "Simpson and Patronage," pp. 222-223.

67. Quoted in Barbara Edwards Sternberg, Jennifer Boone, and Evelyn Waldron, *Anne Evans—A Pioneer in Colorado's Cultural History: The Things That Last When Gold Is Gone* (Denver: Buffalo Park Press, 2011), p. 79.

68. *Northwestern Christian Advocate*, November 21, 1866, October 7, 1868.

69. *New York Tribune*, September 5, 1867.

70. Evans interview, Bancroft Collection, MSS PL329, Folio V, pp. 35-36.

71. Richardson and Farley, *Usher*, pp. 86-96.

72. Kelsey, *John Evans*, pp. 172-173.

73. Wallter R. Borneman, *Rival Rails: The Race to Build America's Greatest Transcontinental Railroad* (New York: Random House, 2010), pp. 52-55.

74. Ibid., pp. 76-77. Borneman notes that "the governor's railroad enthusiasm knew no bounds." See also Maury Klein, *Union Pacific: The Birth of a Railroad, 1862-1893* (Garden City: Doubleday & Company, 1987), pp. 77-78; Kelsey, *John Evans*, pp. 173-174; S. D. Mock, "Colorado and Surveys for a Pacific Railroad, *Colorado Magazine*, 17 (March 1940): 56-61; Evans to John Pierce, February 24, 1866, Pierce to Evans, February 25, 1866, Evans Collection, Box 7, FF-78, History Colorado.

75. Klein, *Union Pacific*, p. 344; Borneman, *Rival Rails*, pp. 77-90. See also Elmer O. Davis, *The First Five Years of the Railroad Era in Colorado* (Golden, CO: Sage Books, 1948), pp. 38, 72, 90-91.

76. Borneman, *Rival Rails*, p. 86.

77. Report quoted in Lyle W. Dorsett, *The Queen City: A History of Denver* (Boulder: Pruett Press, 1977), p. 67. R. G. Dun & Company, founded originally in 1841 as the Mercantile Agency by Lewis Tappan, was the first successful credit reporting company. In 1933, it merged with J. M. Bradstreet & Company, its chief competitor, to form Dun & Bradstreet Corporation.

78. Kelsey, *John Evans*, p. 183; Borneman, *Rival Rails*, p. 86.

79. Kelsey, *John Evans*, pp. 184-197.

80. Quoted in ibid., p. 187.

81. Ibid., pp. 196-202.

82. Ibid.

83. Ibid., pp. 205-207.

84. Evans Interview, Bancroft Collection, PL-329, Folder 1, Bancroft Library.

85. Quoted in Salter, "Simpson and Patronage," p. 227.

86. Ibid., pp. 226-228.

87. Clark, *Life of Simpson*, pp. 305-306; Crooks, *Simpson*, pp. 469-471.

88. Kelsey, *John Evans*, p. 210; Sternberg, Boone, and Waldron, *Things That Last*, pp. 62-63; *Northwestern Christian Advocate*, December 12, 1868.

89. Sternberg, Boone, and Waldron, *Things That Last*, pp. 79-95; Kelsey, *John Evans*, pp. 209-218; Notes concerning Gov. John Evans, given by Mrs. Evans and Mr. Dickinson, Bancroft Collection, University of Colorado, Boulder.

90. William B. Graveley, "The Early Colorado Conference," *The Methodist, Evangelical, and United Brethren Churches in the Rockies, 1850-1976*, eds. J. Alton Templin, Allen D. Breck, and Martin Rist (Denver: Rocky Mountain Conference of The United Methodist Church, 1977), pp. 80-83; Kelsey, *John Evans*, pp. 219-225; Sternberg, Boone, and Waldron, *Things That Last*, pp. 385-395.

91. *Northwestern Evans Study Report*, p. 21.

92. J. Alton Templin, "Bishop Henry White Warren," *Churches in the Rockies*, pp. 90-95; Clark, *Life of Simpson*, p. 255.

93. *Northwestern Evans Study Report*, pp. 26-31.

94. Kelsey, *John Evans*, p. 226.

95. Ibid., pp. 227-228.

96. Ibid., pp. 228-229; Sternberg, Boone, and Waldron, *Things That Last*, pp. 161-163.

97. H. H. Bancroft, Colorado Notes (1884), Bancroft Collection, University of Colorado, Boulder. Charles Francis Adams, *Charles Francis Adams, 1835-1915* (Boston: Houghton, Mifflin Co., 1916), p. 190, took a similar view of railroad entrepreneurs in general.

Chapter 12

1. J. Glenn Gray, *The Warriors: Reflections of Men in Battle* (Lincoln: University of Nebraska Press, 1998), p. 135.

2. Quoted in Octavio Paz, *The Labyrinth of Solitude and Other Writings* (New York: Grove Press, 1985), p. 5.

3. See Derek Gregory, *The Colonial Present: Afghanistan, Palestine, Iraq* (Wiley-Blackwell, 2004); Edward Said, *Orientalism* (New York: Vintage Books, 1979); and G. F. W. Hegel, *The Phenomenology of Spirit (The Phenomenology of Mind)* (New York: Oxford University Press, 1977). See also the works of Jacques Lacan, Emmanuel Levinus, Michael Foucault, Simone de Beauvoir, and Patrick Jimmer.

4. Three articles that address this approach from different angles are M. Annette Jaimes, "Sand Creek: The Morning After," *The State of Native America*, pp. 1-12; Brendan Rensink, "The Sand Creek Phenomenon: The Complexity and Difficulty of Undertaking a Comparative Study of Genocide vis-à-vis the Northern American West," *Dissertations, Theses & Student Research, Department of History, Paper 26*, University of Nebraska, http://digitalcommons.unl.edu/historydiss/26; and Joseph P. Gone, "Colonial Genocide and Historical Trauma in Native North America: Complicating Contemporary Attributions," *Colonial Genocide in Indigenous North America*, eds. Andrew Woolford, Jeff Benvenuto, and Alexander Laban Hinton (Durham, NC: Duke University Press, 2014), pp. 273-291.

5. Belich, *Replenishing the Earth*, pp. 554-556.

6. Roberts, "Violence and the Frontier Tradition," pp. 96-111; Roberts, *Slough-Rynerson Quarrel*, pp. xi-xii. Raymond G. Carey, "Another View of the Sand Creek Massacre," *Denver Westerners Monthly Roundup*, 16 (February, 1960): 7. Raymond G. Carey explained the settler viewpoint this way, "Fear and insecurity are seldom the parents of temperate judgment, and Denver citizens, who had been thrown into a state of mass hysteria earlier in the summer [of 1864] were not inclined to be temperate and reasonable and to recognize that the simple enlistment of a regiment would not work immediate miracles."

7. Raymond G. Carey, "The Puzzle of Sand Creek," *Colorado Magazine*, XLI (1964): 289.

8. Gray, *Warriors*, pp. 27, 51-552.

9. Ibid., p. 135.

10. Ibid., p. 148.

11. Ibid., p. 152.

12. Belich, *Replenishing the Earth*, p. 552.

13. Osterhammel, *Transformation of the World*, p. 344.

14. Roberts, "Sand Creek," pp. 567-615, focuses on Sand Creek's impact on the military. In light of more recent scholarship, it is incomplete if not dated. It relies heavily on Utley, *Frontier Regulars*; Robert G. Athearn, *William Tecumseh Sherman & the Settlement of the West* (Norman: University of Oklahoma Press, 1956); and Russell F. Weigley, *The American Way of War: A History of United States Military Strategy and Policy* (New York: Macmillan Company, 1973). These are still critical sources, but other works, such as Robert Wooster, *The Military and United States Indian Policy, 1865-1903* (New Haven: Yale University Press, 1988); Neely, *Limits of Destruction*; Marsalek, *Sherman*; James M. McPherson, *Drawn with the Sword: Reflections on the American Civil War* (New York: Oxford University Press, 1996); and John Fabian Witt, *Lincoln's Code: The Laws of War in American History* (New York: Free Press, 2012) are but a few of the books that demand a reevaluation.

15. Quoted in Matthew Carr, *Sherman's Ghosts: Soldiers, Civilians, and the American Way of War* (New York: The New Press, 2015), p. 144. Osterhammel, *Transformation of the World*, p. 327, says that "the coming of the railroad—not only in the American West—destroyed the precarious balances already in existence."

16. Wooster, *The Military and Indian Policy*, p. 59.

17. *DU Evans Study Committee Report*, pp. 48-50.

18. Porter to Barlow, August 27, 1864, Barlow Collection.

19. Kenyon to Barlow, October 6, 1864, ibid.

20. Haire, "Diary."

21. Beardsley, *Echoes from Peak and Plain*, p. 262.

22. Chivington to Simpson, March 9, 1865, Simpson Papers, LC.

23. Haynes, *History of the Methodist Episcopal Church in Omaha*, p. 44.

24. Marquette, *Nebraska Methodism*, pp. 57-58.

25. Dictation of Capt. D. H. Nichols, Bancroft Collection, University of Colorado, Boulder.

26. Reverend Thornton K. Tyson to Sarah M. Chivington, September 12, 1892, quoted in Cox-Paul, "Chivington," p. 134.

27. Maberley to Barlow, January 12, 1865, Barlow Collection.

28. *Atchison Daily Free Press*, June 26, 1866.

29. The Reverend Dr. Darius Salter, author of a forthcoming biography of Bishop Matthew Simpson, offered thoughtful advice on this evaluation.

30. Miyakawa, *Protestants and Pioneers*, pp. 52-58, contains an excellent summary of the procedures provided in the *Discipline* for both minor and major offenses. The weekly class meetings were the primary vehicle for discipline of laymen. James B. Finley, *Sketches of Western Methodism: Biographical, Historical and Miscellaneous*, ed. W. P. Strickland (Cincinnati: Methodist Book Concern for the Author, 1854), p. 178.

31. Nelson A. Miles, *Personal Recollections* (Chicago: Werner Co., 1896), p. 139.

32. Dyer, *Snow-Shoe Itinerant*, pp. 182-183, 238.

33. Berkhofer, *Salvation and the Savage*, p. xviii.

34. Tinker, *Missionary Conquest*, pp. 15-19.

35. *Methodist Quarterly Review*, 32 (1850): 49, quoted in Norwood, "Strangers in a Strange Land," p. 60.

36. Hall, *History of Colorado*, I, 350-351.

37. William McKinley, December 21, 1898, quoted in Stuart Creighton Miller, *"Benevolent Assimilation:" The American Conquest of the Philippines 1899-1903* (New Haven: Yale University Press, 1982), p. ii.

38. Nichols, *Lincoln and the Indians*, pp. 199-200.

39. Eastman, *Soul of the Indian*, pp. 5-6.

40. Thomas B. Marquis, ed., *Wooden Leg: A Warrior Who Fought Custer* (Lincoln: University of Nebraska Press, 1957), pp. 364-365.

41. Quoted in Nichols, *Lincoln and the Indians*, p. 200.

42. Roberts, "Sand Creek," pp. 720-733; Nichols, *Lincoln and the Indians*, pp. 201-209; Tinker, *Missionary Conquest*, pp. 15-18.

43. Octavio Paz (1967) quoted in Anthony J. Marsella, "Cultural Aspects of Depressive Experience and Disorders," *Online Readings in Psychology and Culture*, 10 (2). http://dx.doi.org/10.9707/2307-0919.1081.

44. Jacob Needleman, *The American Soul: Rediscovering the Wisdom of the Founders* (New York: Tarcher, Putnam, 2003), p. 352.

45. Ibid., pp. 353-354.

46. *DRMN*, February 12, 1934.

47. George E. Tinker, "Redskin, Tanned Hide: A Book of Christian History Bound in the Flayed Skin of an American Indian: The Colonial Romance, Christian Denial, and the Cleansing of a Christian School of Theology," *Journal of Race, Ethnicity, and Religion*, 5 (October 2014): 1-43.

48. Jones to Harvier, July 1, 1974, Iliff Library Archives, Iliff School of Theology, Denver, CO. The letter is part of a complete file of correspondence among the various parties to the discussion of what to do with the book cover.

49. D. H. Lawrence, *Studies in Classic American Literature* (New York: Penguin Books, 1923), pp. 42-43.

50. Quoted in Norwood, "The Invisible American," p. 17.

51. Needleman, *American Soul*, p. 353.

52. Norwood, "The Invisible American," p. 24.

53. An interesting multi-disciplinary literature has emerged to explore ways to deal with historical trauma. A sample includes, Maria Yellow Horse Brave Heart, "The Return to the Sacred Path: Healing the Historical Trauma and Historical Unresolved Grief Response Among the Lakota Through a Psychoeducational Group Intervention," *Smith College Studies in Social Work*, 68 (1998): 287-305; Maria Yellow Horse Brave Heart and Lemyra M. DeBruym, "The American Indian Holocaust: Healing Historical Unresolved Grief," *American Indian and Alaska Native Mental Health Research*, 8 (1998): 56-78; Bridger Conley Zilkic and Samuel Totten, "Easier Said Than Done: The Challenges of Preventing and Responding to Genocide," *Century of Genocide: Critical Essays and Eyewitness Accounts*, eds. Samuel Totten and William S. Parsons, 3rd ed. (New York: Routledge, 2009), pp. 609-636; Eduardo Duran, Bonnie Duran, Maria Yellow Horse Brave Heart, and Susan Yellow Horse-Davis, "Healing the American Indian Soul Wound," *International Handbook of Multigenerational Legacies of Trauma*, ed. Yael Danieli (New York: Plenum, 1998), pp. 341-354; J. H. Elliott, "The Rediscovery of America," *New York Review of Books*, June 24, 1993, pp. 36-41; Joseph P. Gone, "Redressing First Nations Historical Trauma:

Theorizing Mechanisms for Indigenous Culture as Mental Health Treatment," *Transcultural Psychiatry*, 50 (2013): 683-706; Joseph P. Gone, "Reconsidering American Indian Historical Trauma: Lessons from an Early Gros Ventre War Narrative," *Transcultural Psychiatry*, 51 (2014): 387-406; Les B. Whitbeck, Gary W. Adams, Dan R. Hoyt, and Xiaojin Chen, "Conceptualizing and Measuring Historical Trauma Among American Indian People," *American Journal of Community Psychology*, 33 (2004): 119-130; Richard White, "Morality and Mortality," *New Republic*, January 18, 1993, pp. 33-36; Michalinos Zimbylas, "Reclaiming Nostalgia in Educational Politics and Practice: Counter-Memory, Aporetic Mourning, and Critical Pedagogy," *Discourse: Studies in the Cultural Politics of Education*, 32 (2011), 641-655.

54. Hyde, *Life of Bent*, p. 248.

55. *Annual Report of the Commissioner of Indian Affairs, 1865*, pp. 218-223. See also Hatch, *Black Kettle*, pp. 197-204, and Powell, *People of the Sacred Mountain*, I, 396-403.

56. Samuel A. Kingman, "Diary of Samuel A. Kingman at Indian Treaty of 1865," *Kansas Historical Quarterly*, I (1932), 450.

57. Charles J. Kappler, *Indian Affairs: Laws and Treaties*, 2 vols. (Washington: Government Printing Office, 1904): II, 889-890.

58. See especially, Greene, *Washita*, pp. 166-167, concerning Black Kettle. Albert G. Boone, formerly the agent for the Cheyennes and Arapahos and long-time resident of the Arkansas Valley in Colorado Territory, wrote of Black Kettle's death. He said simply that Black Kettle "was a good man; he was my friend; he was murdered." General William S. Harney, one of the commissioners at the Little Arkansas, said of him, that he "was as good a friend of the United States as I am." Greene, at pp. 186-187, presents a convincing case that Black Kettle was not involved in the conflict that preceded the attack on the Cheyenne peacemaker's camp.

59. Carson and Bent to Pope, October 27, 1865, LR, DM, USAC, C-185 (Box 17), NARA, RG 393.

69047234R00192

Made in the USA
Lexington, KY
24 October 2017